D0318618

Explorer
Boston
& New England

Tim Locke
and
Sue Gordon

 Publishing

Cover (front a): autumn colours
Cover (front b): The Old State House in Boston
Cover (front c): New England's lakes offer a variety of water sports
Page 3: the meeting house at Old Sturbridge
Page 4: mist over Mystic Seaport, Connecticut
Page 5 (top): York's Nubble Lighthouse, Maine
Page 5 (bottom): Longfellow Bridge and the city of Boston
Page 6 (top): Boothbay Harbor, Maine
Page 6 (bottom): Waits River, Vermont
Page 7 (top): weathervane, Vermont
Page 8: Faneuil Hall, Boston
Page 9: East Orange, in Vermont's Northeast Kingdom
Page 27: a 19th-century engraving showing the landing of the Pilgrim Fathers
Page 247: Trinity Church and the John Hancock Tower, Boston
Page 267: Mount Washington Hotel, New Hampshire
Cover (back): harbour scences at Rockport
Cover (spine): Enjoy yourself at Freyburg Fair

Written by Tim Locke and Sue Gordon
Revision verifier: Tim Locke
Original photography by Molly Lynch
Reprinted 1999, 2000
Revised third edition 1999
First published 1995

Edited, designed and produced by AA Publishing 1995, 1997, 1999

Distributed in the United Kingdom by AA Publishing, Norfolk House, Priestley Road, Basingstoke, Hampshire, RG24 4NY.

The contents of this publication are believed correct at the time of printing. Nevertheless, the publishers cannot be held responsible for any errors or omissions, or for changes in details given in this guide or for the consequences for any reliance on the information provided by the same. Assessments of attractions, hotels, restaurants and so forth are based upon the authors' own personal experiences and, therefore, descriptions given in this guide necessarily contain an element of subjective opinion which may not reflect the publisher's opinion or dictate a reader's own experiences on another occasion. Every effort has been made to ensure accuracy in this guide, but things do change, and we would be grateful if readers would advise us of any inaccuracies they may encounter.

Published by AA Publishing (a trading name of Automobile Association Developments Limited, whose registered office is Norfolk House, Priestley Road, Basingstoke, Hampshire RG24 4NY. Registered number 1878835).

Colour separation by Fotographics
Printed and bound in Italy by Printer Trento srl

Titles in the Explorer series...
Australia • Boston & New England • Britain • Brittany California • Caribbean • China • Costa Rica • Crete • Cuba Cyprus • Egypt • Florence & Tuscany • Florida • France Germany • Greek Islands • Hawaii • India • Ireland • Israel Italy • Japan • London • Mallorca • Mexico • New York • New Zealand • Paris • Portugal • Provence • Rome • San Francisco Scotland • South Africa • Spain • Tenerife • Thailand • Tunisia Turkey • Turkish Coast • Vietnam

AA World Travel Guides publish nearly 300 guidebooks to a full range of cities, countries and regions across the world. Find out more about AA Publishing and the wide range of services the AA provides by visiting our Web site at www.theaa.co.uk.

How to use this book

ORGANISATION

New England Is, New England Was
Discusses aspects of life and culture in contemporary New England and explores significant periods in its history.

A to Z
An alphabetical listing of places to visit. The book begins with a section on Boston, and is subsequently divided into states. Places of interest are listed alphabetically within each section. Suggested walks, drives and Focus On articles, which provide an insight into aspects of life in New England, are included in each section.

Travel Facts
Contains the strictly practical information that is vital for a successful trip.

Hotels and Restaurants
An alphabetical listing of places to stay and places to eat. Entries are graded budget, moderate or expensive.

ABOUT THE STAR RATINGS
Most places described in this book have been given a separate rating. These are as follows:

▶▶▶   Do not miss

▶▶   Highly recommended

▶   Worth seeing

MAP REFERENCES
To make the location of a particular place easier to find, every main entry in this book is given a map reference, such as 176B3. The first number (176) indicates the page on which the map can be found, the letter (B) and the second number (3) pinpoint the square in which the main entry is located. The maps on the inside front cover and inside back cover are referred to as IFC and IBC respectively.

Contents

Tim Locke's love of the great outdoors and interest in landscape, architecture and places has encouraged him to travel widely in Europe, the USA and the Far East. In his native Britain he has written several books on walking, including *The Good Walks Guide* (Which Books), as well as guidebooks to scenic regions of England. He is the author of *AA Explorer Britain* and contributed to Germany and Thailand in the same series.

Sue Gordon first got to know New England as an au pair in the 1960s. She now returns whenever she has the chance and has also written *AA CityPack Boston*. Closer to home, she is the author of *Explore Britain's Villages* (AA), and has contributed to several walks books, including *Walking Britain's Rivers and Canals* (HarperCollins) and *Country Walks and Scenic Drives* (Reader's Digest). Tim Locke and Sue Gordon are also guidebook editors.

My Boston by Tim Locke

Those six little states that are crammed into the north-eastern corner of the map of the USA must be one of the most written up and talked about areas of the world. They represent much of a great nation's historical and cultural emergence, the roots of modern America.

To me they are a never-ending source of discovery. The quintessential aspects of New England's character – its village greens, its delightful architectural variety, its covered bridges, its wooded hills to name but few – stay in the memory of all visitors.

But the more I see of the region, the more I realise how much there is yet to explore. Boston is a great city of many facets: follow the red line of the Freedom Trail and in a few hours you have a remarkable cross-section of its history. Yet the city harbours many lesser-known gems too – my favourites include the Athenaeum (which Sue Gordon urged me to visit), with its bookish tranquillity, the surreal stained-glass Mapparium, with its extraordinary echo, and the gas-lit backstreets of Beacon Hill.

History and heritage are celebrated with flair at the great museums at Mystic, Plymouth, Sturbridge, Shelburne, Strawbery Banke and elsewhere. Yet equally memorable are some of the more modest parcels of a well-preserved past: among those that spring immediately to mind are the idiosyncratic Paper House near Rockport and the little steam train that somehow manages to puff its way up to the summit of Mount Washington.

The natural scene is blessed with delightfully distinct seasons. The autumn foliage presents a truly spectacular show, while the winter snows again transform the scene magically. I savour impressions of the view on a summer dawn from Mount Cadillac in Acadia National Park, looking along the indented coast of Maine and across the vast inland forests and folded hills. And of basking in a hot outdoor tub in an inn in Stowe, Vermont, with snowflakes falling gently on me in the dark, after a day's cross-country skiing in the birchwoods. Meanwhile the events calendar is busy with country fairs, bean cookouts, maple sugaring, historical re-enactments and more – encouraging a return visit at any time of year.

I find New England gives a warm welcome second to none. It is a friend for life.

New England Is

The states of Massachusetts, Connecticut, Rhode Island, New Hampshire, Vermont and Maine constitute New England. Although relatively small in area, this is the cultural and historic cradle of the nation. There are qualities that characterise the region as a whole, but there are also subtle differences within it.

THE ELEMENTS The clichés have their own element of truth: against a blue sky the wooden steeple of a church stands high over a village green fringed with neat, white clapboard houses. Back roads wind over covered bridges and through seemingly endless forests which in autumn burst into brilliant hues of russet, gold and crimson. Bright orange pumpkins lie stacked in mounds by wooden barns and on farm stands. Lighthouses look out over the ocean from shores of rock and sand. Fishing boats unload the daily catch, and lobster and clam chowder appear on virtually every restaurant's menu.

New England is a region of firsts, in industrialisation and historical events. It has been the seed-bed of intellectual and political thought for three centuries. It has magnificent art collections in museums, colleges and universities. New England has produced – and continues to produce – many great names in music, art and literature.

New England has a small-scale quality that is an integral part of its charm, and not without reason has been described as 'America with the volume turned down'. Many of the

Point Judith Light, Rhode Island

A white steeple framed by autumn foliage: quintessential New England at Sugar Hill, NH

region's inhabitants greatly value their lifestyle and are fiercely proud of their history and roots. The Yankee mentality – formed by a keen work ethic, frugality, shrewdness and a serious, conservative outlook – is deeply ingrained.

EARLY DAYS The great ice masses that once covered this land have left their mark. Glaciers sculpted the mountains and valleys, and created a deeply indented coastline. The landscape was scoured, and the bedrock and boulder-strewn earth proved infertile for the first farmers. On this soil the first European settlers established themselves, primarily along the coast and the rivers. The Pilgrim Fathers arrived from England aboard the *Mayflower* in 1620. More than a

10

century later, in 1775, the first shots of the American Revolution at Lexington and Concord signalled the end of British colonial rule.

As settlers moved westwards over the continent, New England's farmlands were abandoned, and the trees, once cleared by the farmers, re-established themselves. Today 80 per cent of New England is forested, and much of Vermont, New Hampshire and inland Maine is also hilly or mountainous and sparsely settled.

VISITING THE REGION Boston is by far the largest city, and one that every visitor to the region should see. The Freedom Trail wends an intricate route past the city's historic sites. This is a city of superb museums, excitingly contrasting neighbourhoods and striking architecture. Visitors without a car can find plenty of rewarding excursions using public transport.

New England's thick tree cover can mean that sweeping panoramic views are hard to come by, at least from a car. For the most spectacular views, however, you can take high-level walks in the White Mountains or Acadia National Park, or explore the coast by boat. Outdoor pursuits in the hills and mountains of northern New England are well developed and include winter sports, watersports, hiking and fishing. The southern states of Massachusetts, Rhode Island and Connecticut are more densely populated and have historic sights.

The long and complex seaboard has a lasting appeal, with the sandy beaches of Cape Cod, the islands and southern Maine among the most popular. There are many opportunities for cruises and sailing, and a number of museums commemorate New England's maritime heritage, including the vanished whaling industry. Today, whale-watching cruises are big business, and no visitor should miss the chance to join an exhilarating tour to the feeding grounds of the humpback whales.

New England's many charms change with the seasons. Spring brings freshness and greenery. In summer, delicious Atlantic breezes make the coast a pleasant retreat from the heat, while autumn's foliage is deservedly famous. Winters are harsh but bring photogenic snowfalls and a Christmas-card look as sports enthusiasts put on their skis.

With so much of the area heavily forested, clapboard is universal

11

Explore New England and you experience a range of building styles from early colonial through to post-modernism. White clapboard is an integral feature of New England's charm, and is a dominant theme outside the major cities; observe closely and you should be able to identify stylistic variations.

EARLY COLONIAL The early English colonists brought with them a tradition of building in wood and, as hardwoods were plentiful in New England, the timber-framed house became – and remains – universal. The frames were covered with cedar shingles or clapboards (which originally were painted in a variety of colours). Built with steep roofs, as they had been back home to help the rain run off, the earliest colonial houses had an overhanging upper storey, central chimney and small, irregular casement windows. The steeper the roof, the older the house. Quite commonly a lean-to was added at the back under one sloping roof, the outline giving rise to the term 'saltbox'. Few of the very earliest houses survive, but Paul Revere's House in Boston and the House of Seven Gables in Salem, MA, both date from the late 1600s.

Colonial: the Mission House (1739) at Stockbridge, MA

GEORGIAN The classical Palladian style that was introduced to Britain from Italy reached eastern New England in the 18th century. The handsome houses in this style, many built by wealthy maritime traders, are recognisable by their strict symmetry. Still clapboarded, they typically have a hipped roof, a central door which is sometimes pilastered, and equally spaced sash windows; Portsmouth, New Hampshire, has a good collection (see pages 202–3). Many modern clapboard houses are still built in this style.

FEDERAL After Independence, Charles Bulfinch (see panel, page 72) introduced the neo-classical Adamesque style, known as Federal, with public buildings such as the State House in Boston and, notably, his Beacon Hill development of genteel, red-brick homes for the élite (see page 64). Built by merchants and often constructed of brick, these buildings – public and domestic – stand proudly four-square, lightly detailed, with a shallow, sometimes balustraded, hipped roof, an imposing porch and a fanshaped window over the door. Inside, rooms may be oval, circular or polygonal, with cornices and fireplaces decorated with garlands and urns of flowers. Salem, Massachusetts, and Providence, Rhode Island, have some of the finest examples of the Federal style.

VICTORIAN After the mid-1820s the design of public, academic and domestic building becomes more diversified, reflecting European influences. Boston's Quincy Market is an example of the Greek Revival style, featuring the columns and pediments of ancient Greek temples. The Gothic Revival

Above: a Second Empire house in Kennebunk, ME Right: the Federal-style Goodwin Mansion, Strawbery Banke, NH

style is easily recognised by its steeply pitched gables, turrets and intricately carved bargeboards. Italianate buildings (from 1840) include Victoria mansion in Portland (see page 134). A variety of historical and decorative elements such as mansard roofs and ironwork balconies characterise the Second Empire style (from 1860) – Parisian buildings were a major source of inspiration. The Queen Anne style owes little to the English Queen Anne period but is characterised by contrasts of texture – often shingle and clapboard laid out decoratively – as well as of colour and form; tall chimneys and round verandahs are typical hallmarks. The Renaissance Revival style of the 1880s and 1890s, and used for some public buildings such as Boston Public Library, is also termed 'Beaux Arts'. The architect of Boston's Trinity Church gave his name to the uniquely American Richardson Romanesque style, notable for its heavy stonework with chunky columns and arches. Many Victorian styles are represented in Newport's fabulously over-the-top mansions. Boston's Back Bay, one of history's most splendid pieces of urban planning, also makes a wonderful sampler of Victorian architecture, with bow-fronted '-rowhouses' of various styles.

A Cape Cod vignette: painted clapboard, screen door and wreath

MODERN By far the most exciting contemporary architecture in New England is to be found in Boston and Cambridge. The leading architects are international: IM Pei, responsible for the city's 1970s rejuvenation scheme, and the Bauhaus architect and Harvard professor, Walter Gropius.

Two houses by great 20th-century architects and open to visitors are the Gropius House, Lincoln MA (see page 170), and Frank Lloyd Wright's Zimmerman House, Manchester NH (see page 198).

13

After the demise of its maritime trade and then its textile industry, the region is now one the country's main centres of technology. Tourism is of major importance, and while agriculture and fishing are of somewhat diminishing significance, the pulp and paper trade is a major growth area.

14

Farming meets tourism: orchards and cider mills welcome visitors

INSURANCE, INDUSTRY, EDUCATION AND RESEARCH

Hartford, Connecticut, is the 'Insurance City'. The business started in the 19th century, in the heyday of New England's shipping trade, and today some of the largest US insurance companies have their headquarters here.

The academic institutions of New England make a significant contribution to the economy, partly by generating business locally, but chiefly through the research and development work on which the electronics and communications industries of the region depend. Connecticut has acquired the nickname of the

I Have Visited
OLD HOLLOW
CIDER MILL
erbury Center
mont 05677

'Gadget State', but the manufacture of electronic components and machinery is also the economic mainstay of Rhode Island, Massachusetts (particularly along Route 128) and the southern part of New Hampshire.

TOURISM The wealthy of the Northeast recognised New England's potential as a summer playground at the end of the 19th century. Today, with the spawning of snow sports, the region attracts as many visitors in winter as in summer to its mountain and coastal areas. In addition to these natural assets (and not forgetting the glory of the region's autumn foliage), the tourist industry can draw on a particularly fine maritime heritage. Tourism is New England's second largest industry, after health care.

❑ Pulp and paper mills at Rumford and Jay in Maine manufacture 1,500 tons of paper daily for books, magazines, catalogues and business stationery, with those at Bucksport and Madawaska following not far behind. ❑

THE TIMBER TRADE A visitor to the northern areas of New England cannot fail to be impressed by the extent of the tree cover – some 80 per cent in New Hampshire and Vermont, and 90 per cent in Maine. It should come as no surprise that these forests make a substantial impact on the region's economy, to the tune of some $6 billion a year, although in Maine, for instance, less than 3 per cent of the total forested area is actually harvested. Maine is the second largest paper-producing state (after Wisconsin) in the US, making around 4 million tons of paper per annum. The building trade and furniture-makers also make significant use of what is a relatively new natural resource, for only a century ago most of the region's timber had been cleared for farmland. Today both environmentalists and the trade are anxious to ensure that this rapidly expanding industry is managed well.

FARMING, FISHING AND QUARRYING Vermont is traditionally associated with dairy farming and this is still an important part of the state economy, albeit a declining one. Vermont too specialises in turkeys while Rhode Island is known for the breed of hen named Rhode Island Red. Immense quantities of potatoes are grown in

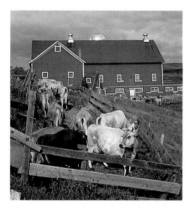

There are now about 2,400 dairy farms in Vermont, each with an average of 70 milking cows

15

northern Maine, the third largest crop in the country after Idaho and Washington. Other crops include tobacco in the Connecticut river valley, blueberries in Maine and cranberries near Plymouth, Massachusetts, and on Cape Cod and the nearby islands.

The fishing industry is now in decline. There is foreign competition in the Atlantic fishing grounds, and stocks of cod and haddock have been depleted, but fishing is still vital in ports such as Gloucester and Cape Ann in Massachusetts, and in the many lobstering ports along the coast of Maine.

New Hampshire, the 'Granite State', has many granite quarries. Vermont's Green Mountains are also quarried for granite (see Barre, page 226) and for marble at Proctor (see page 235).

Lobstering in Maine alone brings in over $70 million a year

New England Is   Shopping

For anyone who considers shopping one of life's greatest pleasures, New England has to be paradise. It is particularly famed for crafts and antiques, local produce sold at farm stands and in country stores, and factory outlets.

For a taste of everything New England has to offer, shopaholics need to visit a factory outlet, an antique shop or fair, a crafts gallery or show, a village store, a farm shop, and some of the one-of-a-kind shops that proliferate throughout the region. Museum shops often make good browsing territory; for example Mystic Seaport's bookshop has a huge range of maritime titles as well as the museum's own CDs of sea shanties. Then there is the shopping mall: in Boston try the Prudential

The outlet store (above, one of dozens in Freeport, ME) and the village store (right) offer two very different shopping experiences. Every visitor should try them both at least once

Center and Copley Place or, for a really grand one, Chestnut Hill. (For more on shopping in Boston, see pages 82–3.)

FACTORY OUTLETS Love it or loathe it, outlet shopping is one of New England's big draws. People come from as far afield as New York, over the Canadian border – and even Europe. All manner of merchandise – clothing, household goods and gifts – is offered at these manufacturers' and distributors' outlets, either at

wholesale prices or at discounts varying from 25 to 80 per cent. Some bargains are older lines being sold off while others are items made specifically for the outlets; many places have quarterly sales for which it is worth timing a visit precisely.

Well-known brand names to be found include LL Bean (the famous mail-order clothing company), Liz Claiborne, Calvin Klein, Benetton, Black & Decker, Van Heusen, Polo/Ralph Lauren, Levi, Nautica, Sansomite – the list is endless.

The outlet capitals of New England are Kittery and Freeport (also the home of LL Bean) in Maine (see also page 128); Fall River in southern Massachusetts; and North Conway – also known as Mount Washington Valley – in New Hampshire (particularly popular because New Hampshire has no sales tax). Worcester Common, Massachusetts, has 90 stores, all together and under cover at the heart of the city, with direct Peter

Bargain-hunters in Boston's downtown area make for Filene's Basement, where goods are reduced according to how long they have been on display

Pan buses (see page 258) from Boston, including a free service on Saturday. There are also smaller complexes in many other towns.

ANTIQUES While some visitors come to New England simply for the outlets, others come purely for the antique-hunting. Cape Cod, the Berkshires, much of Vermont, and Newport, Rhode Island, have particular concentrations of antique shops, but it is hard to go anywhere without coming across an emporium of some sort, whether it trades in rusty farm tools or exquisite European furniture. The best bargains may be in flea markets and antique shows (listed

❏ New England's most famous country store is in Weston, Vermont, where artefacts from the past jostle for space with Vermont Common Crackers, penny candy and much more. For a mail-order catalogue, tel: 802/824 3184. ❏

❏ For a full list of crafts outlets, including shows, see official state guides and local listings. The League of New Hampshire Craftsmen (205 North Main Street, Concord, NH 03301), the Maine Crafts Association (15 Walton Street, Portland, ME 04103) and the Vermont Crafts Council (PO Box 938, Montpelier, VT 05601) publish touring guides to studios, shops, fairs and galleries. ❏

locally), but you need to know what you are about. The biggest show is held in May, July and September in Brimfield, Massachusetts.

CRAFTS Visitors to New England can buy examples of traditional and contemporary crafts at a broad range of prices in shops and galleries. At any time, in any area, they will also be able to find a craft fair within easy distance. The Annual Craftsmen's Fair, the oldest in the nation, is held in the second week of August at the base of Mount Sunapee in New Hampshire. Some fairs are restricted to 'juried' designers who have been judged to meet, or exceed, the highest of standards. These standards are reflected in the prices, but the quality really is outstanding. While excellent crafts can be found all over New England, it is in Vermont that the arts and crafts are particularly important. The Vermont State Craft Center at Frog Hollow has retail galleries in Burlington, Middlebury and Manchester, and there are dozens of other outlets throughout the state.

17

In the northeast states of America the weather conditions and the wide variety of broad-leaved trees combine perfectly to produce a sensational display of autumn colour. During September and October virtually the whole of New England is given over to 'the fall'.

The red maple brings the first hint of colour to the hillsides

Vast areas of New England are forested and where, over the years, loggers have felled the evergreen softwoods, hardwoods have grown in their place, creating a full palette of autumn colours. Like the richest of oriental carpets, the vivid reds of the red maple, sugar maple, sweetgum, blackgum, sassafras, red oak and scarlet oak interweave with the deep reddish-purples of the sumacs and dogwoods, the golden-yellows of the hickories, trembling aspen and birches, and the rich bronzes and browns of beech and the other oaks.

❏ In September and October, call Fall Foliage Hotlines for a free calendar of events, a foliage guide (giving suggested leaf-peeping tours) and regularly updated reports. Connecticut: 806/270 8080. Maine: 1-800/932-3419. Massachusetts: 1-800/227 6277. New Hampshire: 603/271 2666. Rhode Island: 401/ 277 2601. Vermont: 802/828 3239. ❏

THE CAUSE OF THE COLOUR When the Great Bear was hunted down in the heavens, so goes the Native American legend, his blood dripped on to the forests, turning some of the leaves red, while the fat that spattered out of the hunters' cooking pot turned others yellow. A more scientific explanation has to do with the food-making process that goes on in leaves. The cells in which this takes place contain pigments, notably chlorophyll, which makes leaves green. Leaves also contain caroten-oids which give them a yellow colour, masked during spring and summer by the larger amount of green. When the days get shorter and the nights cooler, food-making slows down, the green goes as the chlorophyll breaks up, and yellows come to the fore. Similarly, when temperatures at night drop below 45°F, sugar made during the day is trapped, forming the pig-ment anthocyanin, responsible, for example, for the 'fire engine' red of the swamp or red maple.

No one can predict exactly when the leaf change will come, how long the season will be or how bright the colour. The most brilliant foliage occurs when warm, sunny days are followed by cool nights. The season (about three weeks) starts in the northwest of New England around mid-September and progresses in a southeasterly direction.

SEEING THE SHOW Every state has its comprehensive list of fall foliage attractions for enthusiasts, known locally as 'leaf-peepers', with suggested car and cycle tours (see box). Roads such as the Kancamagus Highway in New Hampshire's White Mountains (see Drive on pages 206–7) and the Mohawk Trail in

❏ 'No pen can describe the turning of the leaves – the insurrection of the tree people against the waning year. A little maple began it, flaming blood-red of a sudden where he stood against the dark green of a pine-belt. Next morning there was an answering signal from the swamp where the sumacs grow. Three days later, the hill-sides as far as the eye could range were afire, and the roads paved, with crimson and gold.'
– Rudyard Kipling, *Leaves from a Winter Notebook*, 1900. ❏

western Massachusetts can get extremely busy, and you may be better off on the back roads (see Drives on pages 98–9 and 240–1).

In Vermont you can combine leaf-peeping with craft shows, antiques fairs and apple festivals, taking in some covered bridges on the way. In Maine family outings can include visits to lighthouses and fishing villages, craft festivals and antiques fairs, farm stands and bean suppers. In New Hampshire, the Isle of Shoals Ferry runs cruises out of Portsmouth for a view from the sea, while the Lakes region offers a choice of cruises where the reflections of the trees in the water provide a double dose of colour. The Massachusetts fall foliage guide suggests hot-air balloon trips and areas that are particularly good for excursions by boat or canoe. In Connecticut, cruises go down the prettiest part of the Connecticut river.

The gold of sugar maple, most prominent around mid-October

Lobster may be undisputed king but seafood does not end there. And while New England is the home of maple syrup, there are many more treats for the sweet-toothed to enjoy. Orchard fruits and farm produce are of the very best.

Traditionally, New England farmers were set up for the day with a hearty breakfast of omelette with ham. Nowadays many inns and bed and breakfast establishments conjure up similar fare – typically cornmeal pancakes with maple syrup, fish cakes and semi-sweet cornbread – as well as other concoctions such as fruits puréed and served on waffles with sausages or omelettes with poached scallops and tarragon. In season, edible flowers sometimes put in an appearance. Depending on the season, there may be an outdoor cookout, an ice-cream social, a clam bake (see box) or a bean supper.

Baked beans, a favourite at church suppers, were invented by thrifty early colonists. Prepared in molasses, Boston baked beans, however, may be less easy to find in a restaurant than Boston cream pie, which is actually a custard-filled sponge cake covered in chocolate. Desserts tend to be sweet and wicked. Indian pudding is a traditional recipe, a light, spicy dessert made with cornmeal and molasses. Pumpkin pie, also learned from the Native Americans, is traditional fare at Thanksgiving celebrations. A more recent New England speciality is Ben & Jerry's ice-cream (see page 234).

SEAFOOD
Imagine a lobster 5 feet

A blue lobster, a rare sight

❑ The clam bake is a New England tradition, an outdoor event for at least 30 or 40 people. Traditionally, a deep hole is dug in wet sand, and clams, lobsters, potatoes, corn, sausages and chicken are steamed in it over hot rocks and covered with seaweed (or, nowadays, canvas). ❑

long, as they were reported to be back in colonial times, and you can understand why the Pilgrim Fathers, setting eyes on *Homarus americanus* for the first time, thought it had been sent by the Devil. Seeing the Native Americans catching the beasts, however, and feeling pangs of hunger as they waited for their first crops to take root, the early colonists soon recognised the lobster as an important food source. Before long it was regarded as poor-man's fodder, a far cry from the gourmet food of today. Lobster appears on menus throughout New England, but the best place to try it is from the boiling cauldrons of one of the many lobster 'pounds' or 'shacks' along the coast roads of Maine.

A mainstay of the New Englander's diet is the chowders, notably clam, fish or corn. Menus rarely exclude one or

Sweetcorn should be eaten as fresh as fresh as can be: peel back the end of each cob to check it is succulent

other of these delicious, thick creamy soups. Other seafoods which may not be familiar to Europeans include scrod (a flaky, tender white fish) and the strangely named large clam, the quahog (pronounced 'ko-hog'), native to southeast New England.

FRUITS IN SEASON The sweetcorn season (lasting from mid-July to early September) is short, but to be relished. Ideally you should eat the corn within three hours of its being picked – a sweet, moist, tender treat. A favourite is the yellow and white variety called 'butter and sugar'. In September, just before the first frost, the orange pumpkins are harvested. Stacked against a traditional red barn, they make a sight as colourful as the autumn foliage itself.

Fall also sees the start of the Pick Your Own apple season, while farm stands sell apple cider as well as ready-picked apples. Try Paula Reds, one of the earliest, and McIntosh, Cortland, Empire or Northern Spy.

Blueberries are a speciality of Maine, and turn up baked into anything from muffins and pancakes at breakfast to pie for dinner. Cranberries, traditionally eaten as a sauce with roast turkey, are exported all over the world from the bogs of the southeast corner of Massachusetts.

Above: Bean Suppers, often held in church halls, are a New England tradition. Visitors are welcome

SATURDAY, NO
5·00–7·00 PM
BAKED BEAN SUPPER
ADULTS $5 CHILDREN $2
CHRIST CHURCH, UNITED METHODIST

Education is a way of life in New England. With a number of well-regarded preparatory schools and over 250 universities and colleges, it courses through the veins of social and cultural life. As a spin-off, New England leads the field in technological and medical research.

❑ In October 1958 MIT student Oliver Smoot was carried prostrate by his classmates across what to MIT's chagrin is called Harvard Bridge. They marked off each head-to-toe length with paint and chalk. Thus the official length of the bridge is 364.4 Smoots plus one ear. The Smootmarks are regularly repainted – look out for them. ❑

intercollegiate football and other sports, it is for their high academic and social standing that these élitist Ivy League colleges are so revered.

The origin of the name Ivy League is uncertain: traditional ivy-covered buildings? From 'IV', standing for Inter Varsity? Or perhaps because initially there were just four, in Roman figures IV, members?

❑ 'You can tell a Harvard man, but you can't tell him anything.' ❑

Eliot House, typical of Harvard's elegant Georgian buildings

THE IVY LEAGUE Four of New England's universities, Harvard, Yale, Brown and Dartmouth, together with four other eastern universities, Pennsylvania, Princeton, Columbia and Cornell, make up that prestigious group known as the Ivy League. In the 1870s the colleges used to meet for football matches and in those early years they were a major force in American football. In the 1920s, however, their prowess faded somewhat and, although they still compete in

Harvard, the nation's oldest university, was founded in 1636 by the early colonists primarily as a training ground for Puritan clergymen. Many of Harvard's first graduates in fact went on to set up other educational institutions. By 1647, towns with 50 householders had to provide primary schooling and those with 100 or more to provide secondary schools. Today many of America's oldest and most highly regarded colleges and universities are in Massachusetts, notably the Massachusetts Institute of Technology (MIT), which was founded in 1861.

Yale, Harvard's traditional arch rival, is in New Haven, Connecticut. New England's second oldest university was founded in 1702 at Saybrook by Harvard graduates and renamed after its benefactor. It has a collegiate system modelled on that of Oxford and Cambridge universities in England, and its fine buildings recall their architecture (see pages 102–5).

Dartmouth College in Hanover, New Hampshire, the only Ivy League college in the northern part of New England, also has a beautiful campus. Founded in 1769 as a Native American charity school, Dartmouth by tradition waives tuition fees (so exorbitant as to eliminate most locals) for any resident of New Hampshire or Vermont with Native American ancestry. Consequently, the percentage of such undergraduates, although still tiny, is greater here than in other Ivy League universities. Brown University, in Providence, Rhode Island, was founded in 1764 as a

Below and opposite, top: Yale's Gothic Revival architecture

Fees at the Ivy League universities are around $30,000 per year (tuition $23,000, board and lodging $7,000); at Harvard, fees are nearer $40,000 a year. Compare this with a state, or public, university where fees for a state resident range from around $2,500 to about $4,500.

Baptist college by one of the leaders in the China trade, John Brown.

THE FIELD OF MEDICINE If the state of Massachusetts is pre-eminent in education, it is also one of the world's major medical centres and Boston has an illustrious tradition of leading the field in medical research. It was in Boston in 1846 that ether was first used as an anaesthetic during an operation, the first kidney transplant was performed there in 1954, and open heart surgery was first performed at the Boston's Children's Hospital in 1967.

23

One of the rich and diverse strands that make up the fabric of New England is its cultural life. Classical music, jazz and dance are a tradition in Boston's concert halls and churches but also in the region's universities and colleges, at festivals and, not least, on the village-green bandstand.

24

GREAT COMPOSERS One of America's first great modern composers was Charles Ives, who was born in Danbury, Connecticut, in 1874 and who graduated from Yale to become a successful insurance executive. In summer, outdoor concerts of classical music and jazz are held in Danbury at the Charles Ives Center for the Arts. The third movement of Ives's *Three Places in New England*, 'The Housatonic at Stockbridge', was suggested by a misty Sunday morning walk with his wife along the riverbank.

The New England scenery has been inspirational to many works, including Edward MacDowell's *New England Idyls* (1902) and William Schuman's *New England Triptych*. Another important New England

Seiji Ozawa conducts the Boston Symphony Orchestra at Symphony Hall

composer (although the number of his works is small, because he destroyed his early compositions) was Karl Ruggles, a close friend of Charles Ives. Walter Piston, whose works include the orchestral suite *Three New England Sketches*, was born in Rockland, Maine, in 1894 and was an influential teacher at Harvard, one of his most distinguished pupils being Leonard Bernstein.

❏ For more on the BSO see page 79. For more on venues for jazz, classical and light music in Boston see page 85. ❏

THE HIGHLIGHTS For more than a century, the Boston Symphony Orchestra's concerts in Symphony Hall have been a vital element in Boston life during the winter months (see page 79). The orchestra's founding spirit was Henry Lee Higginson, and it was he who started, in July 1885, the 'Popular Concerts', or 'Pops', summertime concerts of light music that were to become a national tradition. The social élite flocked to Music Hall to sit at tables arranged between potted plants, partaking of refreshments and listening to 'light music of the best class'. Little changed in form or content, the

One of Colonel Higginson's friends was Isabella Stewart Gardner, a patron of aspiring musicians, conductors and composers, as well as painters, sculptors, actors and writers. Her creation, Fenway Court, now the Isabella Stewart Gardner Museum, a fragrant oasis of beauty in Boston (see page 69), was a meeting-place for musicians and the venue for wide-ranging programmes of music, song and dance. Following in this tradition, the museum today puts on about 130 public concerts each year.

Tanglewood, in western Massachusetts, is the Boston Symphony Orchestra's summer home, and the Tanglewood Music Festival is one of the cultural highlights of the Berkshires region, drawing hundreds of thousands of visitors annually to the open-sided Music Shed and the balmy lawns that surround it (see page 146). Jacob's Pillow Dance Festival, held near by at Becket from late June to August, offers 10 highly acclaimed weeks of dance programmes.

The jazz scene is traditionally a strong one, with the Charles Hotel in Cambridge a long-established

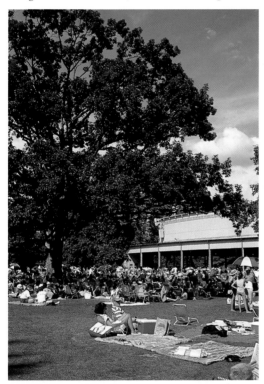

Summer music on the lawns of Tanglewood

concerts (held in May and June) remain a highlight of the year and the Boston Pops is the most recorded orchestra in the world.

In 1929 outdoor concerts were introduced on the Esplanade along the Charles river in Boston. Every summer, thousands of young and old flock to the Hatch Shell with their rugs and picnic baskets for a summer evening's music in the open air.

haunt of afficionados. Look out too for festivals; indoor and outdoor, and see page 85 for more suggestions for jazz venues in Boston and Cambridge.

Of the numerous regional festivals of music and dance advertised locally, the recitals held in the opulent salons of some of Newport, Rhode Island's mansions have become a summer tradition. And all over the region the village bandstand provides many a delightful hour of informal entertainment.

Hollywood, past and present, has not failed to tap the rich vein of New England's diversity. In the field of drama, theatre is as alive in small towns and villages as it is in the metropolis of Boston.

FILMS Among the galaxy of films with New England associations is *On Golden Pond*, based on Ernest Thompson's 1978 play. Set on Great Pond, near Augusta, Maine, the film was actually shot at Squam Lake, New Hampshire. *The Whales of August* is another delightful film set in New England. *Mystic Pizza* (1988) was filmed in Connecticut, not in Mystic, but nearby Stonington, on a specially built pizzeria set. Steven Spielberg's *Amistad* (1997), telling the story of Africans captured by slave traders and their fight for freedom (see pages 101 and 105), was partly shot at Mystic, Providence and Massachusetts State House in Boston.

Herman Melville's *Moby Dick*, with its settings on Nantucket, Henry James's *The Bostonians* and John Updike's *The Witches of Eastwick*, set in Wickford, Rhode Island, are but three New England novels to have been made into films.

PLAYS AND PLAYERS One of America's great playwrights, Eugene O'Neill (see page 47),

Madeleine Potter and Christopher Reeve in The Bostonians

set his final masterpiece, *Long Day's Journey into Night* (1957) in his boyhood summer home, Monte Cristo Cottage in New London, Connecticut. Today, the Eugene O'Neill Theater Center, in Waterford, champions new work by American playwrights.

World-class performers are regularly brought in for pre-New York shows in small town theatres. In Vermont in particular many village communities enjoy theatre on an intimate scale in revitalised 19th-century theatres and opera houses. From 1938 to 1976 the Shubert Theater in New Haven, Connecticut, hosted the premières of many famous Broadway shows (see panel, page 103), and today the Goodspeed Opera House, a resplendent Victorian concoction on the banks of the Connecticut river at East Haddam, hosts musicals old and new. Festivals proliferate, offering strong local summertime theatre programmes. Those held in the Berkshires (see pages 143–7) make it a particularly popular area for theatre-lovers.

Veterans Katherine Hepburn and Henry Fonda in On Golden Pond

New England Was

When the Pilgrim Fathers crossed the Atlantic in 1620 and founded the first permanent European colony in New England, they did so in the wake of many earlier explorers and merchant adventurers who had been probing a land that had been home to the Algonquin peoples since time immemorial.

❏ In 1492 Native Americans in New England are estimated to have numbered about 100,000; by 1620 most were dead. ❏

John Cabot, an Italian navigator and explorer based in London

It seems the ancestors of the Algonquin peoples of New England arrived in North America after the end of the last Ice Age, in a series of eastward migrations from Asia. By the time the first Europeans settled in the New World, Native Americans (the so-called American Indians) had been inhabiting these northeastern woodlands for well over 10,000 years.

EUROPEAN EXPLORATION To the Native American way of thinking, land – a source of food, like water – is not something that belongs to people; it is people who belong to the land. The 'People of the Dawnland', the Abenaki, once inhabited an area that extended from the Maine coast westwards to Lake Champlain, and from the St Lawrence south to the Merrimack river and northern Massachusetts. This was a forested land laced with lakes and waterways along which they travelled in their birchbark canoes to fish and hunt. These Abenaki would have been the first natives to meet with intruders, when, possibly about AD 1000, it is believed, Leif Eriksson arrived from Scandinavia with his dreaded Vikings. Over the following centuries a number of further forays were made across the Atlantic, many seeking the Northwest Passage round Canada. By the 1400s fishermen from Scandinavia, Portugal, Spain, France and Britain were coming regularly to enjoy rich pickings in the continent's then teeming offshore waters.

The excitement aroused by Christopher Columbus's voyages to the Caribbean between 1492 and 1504 tempted more and more Europeans. In 1497 King Henry VII of England authorised John Cabot to set sail from Bristol; exactly where he landed is uncertain, but Nova Scotia seems likely. Cabot staked an English claim to North America by hoisting the flag and returned home with promising reports, but little else. In 1524 France sent the Florentine, Giovanni da Verrazano (who reported a frosty welcome from the Abenaki), then, in the 1530s and 1540s, Jacques Cartier, who explored the St Lawrence river. In 1568 David Ingram captured the imagination of all with tales of 'a magic city of Norumbega', glittering with 'pillars of crystal and silver'.

> ❏ The term 'New England' was coined by John Smith, English founder of the Jamestown colony in Virginia, when he wrote *A Description of New England* (1616). ❏

ATTEMPTS TO SETTLE The Spanish, British and French continued to look for potential sites for settlement and began to trade with the Native Americans for furs. By the turn of the 17th century, fisheries had been established and rival trading posts were in operation. Beaver hats were by now all the rage in Europe and fur trading was serious business. In 1605 the area was mapped by Frenchman Samuel de Champlain, who gave his name to the lake that is situated on Vermont's western boundary.

Attempts to establish settlements in the region, however, failed, and relationships between Europeans and Indians became increasingly prickly. George Popham

established a colony at Sagadahoc but it did not survive the harsh New England winter of 1607–8. A French Jesuit colony was set up on Mount Desert Island but in 1613 it was burnt down by the English.

TRADING IN DISEASE The concept of hunting animals not for food and clothing but in order to sell their fur was an alien one to the Native Americans, but they were tempted by the Europeans' metal, which would improve their fish-hooks, snowshoes and canoe paddles, and welcomed their kettles and guns. However, traders also brought with them European viruses, to which the natives had no immunity, and which would in places wipe out practically the entire population. By the time the Pilgrims landed in 1620, the Indians were devastatingly weakened.

Pilgrims John Alden and Mary Chilton are the first ashore

29

The successful establishment of the English colony at Plymouth in 1620 encouraged a flood of settlers. They came with the hopes and ideals of 17th-century England, but their vision of a new world was not easily realised.

After a bad first winter, the Plymouth colony was soon settled and expanding, though closely dependent on contact with England and relying heavily on the advice of Native Americans for fishing, hunting and growing crops (see pages 180–1 for more on the Pilgrims). In 1630 another group of Puritans under the leadership of John Winthrop founded the Massachusetts Bay Colony on a spot they named Boston, after their home town in Lincolnshire, England. Quickly successful, it soon completely overshadowed Plymouth.

The meeting of Puritan and Native American was a meeting of two utterly different philosophies of life, yet at first, at least, they got on all right. Peace treaties made between the colonists and most of the neighbouring Native Americans held firm. Gradually, however, relations began to deteriorate. Not only had the Europeans brought diseases by which, catastrophically, the native people had been crippled, they had also introduced guns and alcohol which seriously disrupted their communities. Inter-tribal warfare broke out over trading, English missionaries tried to impose a foreign culture and, as colonists needed more land, the Native Americans were increasingly confronted by that totally alien, European desire to stake a claim on territory.

WARS OF CONQUEST By the mid-17th century the Puritans found themselves caught up in an unending round of skirmishes and shifting alliances between invader and native. In the Pequot War the settlers, aided by the Narragansett, annihilated the Pequots around the Connecticut river. In what is called King Philip's War (1675–6), however, the Puritans massacred the Narragansett, taking their land in Connecticut and Rhode Island. In the process hundreds of

Metacom or 'King Philip', sachem of the Wampanoags, who was finally driven to leading his people into vicious war in 1675

KING PHILIP

settlers were killed and many towns raided. During the French and Indian War (a part of Britain's Seven Years' War with France that basically was about beaver fur), which sputtered on from the late-17th century until the final flare-up that led to French defeat in 1763, the colonists were to fight countless battles along-side British troops against the French and their Native American allies.

A STAND FOR FREEDOM Even in their own communities, life was not all plain sailing for the settlers. The Massachusetts Bay Puritans were not, like some of the Plymouth colonists, Separ-atists who had broken with the Anglican Church. These were Puritans who were themselves dissenters in that they hoped to reform the Church, yet

John Winthrop: by 1670 his Boston colony had grown to 1,200

condemned any who showed signs of deviating from the (very) straight and narrow path of strict Puritanism. Men and women such as Thomas Hooker, William Coddington and Anne Hutchinson left to found new settlements. In 1636 a minister, Roger Williams, was banished for advocating freedom of religious thought. He went on to found Rhode Island, where church and state were always separate and religious freedom paramount. The Puritans were equally assertive in their public administration. Even when others joined them, power remained firmly in their hands and, with England absorbed in the Civil War, they were left to their own devices. When Charles II acceded to the throne in 1660, however, he found he did not like the extent to which the colony was running its own affairs. He therefore introduced the Navigation Acts, aimed at making New England merchants trade only with Britain, and ended the Puritans' monopoly of the vote. With suffrage, the merchants (who ignored the Acts) rapidly grew both wealthy and powerful. They no longer needed, or wanted, the close contact with England; soon they would want to be their own masters.

❑ When history is told by the victor, language is easily tainted by prejudice. Thus Native Americans had warriors, Europeans soldiers; Native American victories were massacres, European victories were battles; Native Americans had chiefs, Europeans generals and kings. ❑

During the early 1700s New England was growing fat on its burgeoning international trade. Resentment mounted at Britain's attempts to muscle in on this wealth, with events escalating in the 1760s to the inevitable shot famously 'heard round the world'.

'NO TAXATION WITHOUT REPRESEN-TATION' Britain emerged supreme from the French and Indian War in 1763, but it also emerged practically bankrupt. King George III decided the wealthy American colonies should pay for their own defence and also help recoup financial losses.

A series of tax-levying acts followed, but were met with protests from a core of colonists who argued that no one should have to give financial support to a government in which he had no representation.

❏ While the Sons of Liberty were hailed as heroes, the Daughters of Liberty enforced boycotts of British goods by serving herbal teas, using maple syrup instead of sugar and wearing homespun cloth instead of imported silks. ❏

The Sugar Act of 1764 reinforced the 1733 Molasses Act which aimed to end trade with the West Indies (in fact it was so lax that smuggling, bribery and therefore the rum industry continued to prosper). The Stamp Act of 1765 taxed printed matter, but met with riots and was repealed the following year. The colonists also responded to the 1767 Townshend Acts, which taxed tea, glass, paint, paper and lead, by boycotting British goods. In 1770 all except the tax on tea were repealed, ironically on the same day as five colonists were killed in the Boston Massacre. The colonists continued to smuggle tea in from Dutch traders.

The 'Boston Massacre', as portrayed by Paul Revere. The British resemble an execution squad firing on innocents at short range. Note the Custom House is labelled 'Butcher's Hall'

Disguised as Mohawks to escape detection, the Sons of Liberty tip East India Company tea into the harbour

THE BOSTON TEA PARTY The Tea Act of December 1773 was seen as giving the British East India Company a monopoly on tea sales to the colonies. It so fuelled resentment at the British government's power to legislate and levy taxes, that when three East India ships docked in Boston loaded with 342 chests of tea, the 'Sons of Liberty', a group of patriots led by Samuel Adams, John Hancock, Joseph Warren and Paul Revere, agreed to take decisive action. Disguised as Mohawks, they boarded the ships and threw the tea into the water. Britain retorted in 1774 with the Intolerable, or Coercive, Acts. Boston Harbor was closed.

THE OPENING SHOTS The American colonies united in response to these further threats to their liberty, and at the First Continental Congress plans were laid for the organisation of an army (later to be led by George Washington). On 19 April 1775 the War of Independence, or Revolutionary War, began.

The British knew about a cache of arms in Concord (see pages 168–70) and sent troops to seize it. As they left Boston, Paul Revere (see page 55) made his famous ride to Lexington, on the road to Concord, to warn the Sons of Liberty there that the British were coming. There were minor scuffles in Lexington, but when the British reached Concord they met with organised resistance from the colonial Minutemen, and the 'shot heard round the world', as described by Emerson in his *Concord Hymn*, was fired.

In May, Ethan Allen and his Green Mountain Boys captured Fort Ticonderoga on Lake Champlain from the British. In June, around Boston, the British won the Battle of Bunker Hill in Charlestown, but only with heavy losses, and when George Washington fortified Dorchester Heights (with arms captured from Fort Tic) they decided to quit. The British left Boston in March 1776, never to return.

33

❏　The battle of Bunker Hill actually took place on what in 1775 was known as Breeds Hill; Bunker Hill was near by. In spite of the mix-up of names, the battle's name stuck and Breeds Hill was subsequently renamed Bunker Hill. ❏

The Battle of Bunker Hill, one of a series of paintings by John Trumbull (1756–1843) recording events in the War of Independence

The history of New England is inextricably bound up with the sea. Whether it be through fishing, whaling, trading or ship-building, it is the sea that has shaped the region's economy, its society and its traditions.

FISHING Even before the Europeans first established colonies on New England's shores, they were coming to fish the region's coastal waters, greedy for cod, haddock and pollack. For 200 years fishing was to be the mainstay of New England's trade with Europe. It declined during World War II, but there is still activity in harbours such as Gloucester, Provincetown, New Bedford and Boston, and in the lobstering ports of Maine.

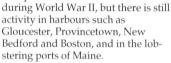

Marine art is a proud tradition

WHALING Today we look on whaling activities with revulsion, but in the mid-19th century it was a brave, romantic enterprise – and also very prosperous. Right whales had long been caught by Native Americans and colonists in the in-

shore waters, but in 1712 Captain Christopher Hussey caught a sperm whale which, with its oil, spermaceti and ambergris, proved a much more valuable species. So began the Yankee enterprise that every year sent hundreds of whaling ships across the oceans of the world, to return with the oil that would light the lamps of America and Europe until the discovery of kerosene in the mid-1800s. Other exported whale products were spermaceti for candles, bones for corset stays and ambergris for perfume. Today, this legendary era is vividly recalled in whaling museums in New Bedford, Nantucket and Mystic.

FOREIGN TRADE If whaling brought wealth in the 18th century, so too did the infamous Triangle Trade involving slaves from Africa, molasses from the West Indies and rum from the colonies' distilleries, a trade that thrived on smuggling and bribery. After Independence in 1776, trade

Ship's figurehead: the wood-carver's skill on show at Mystic Seaport, Connecticut

❏ Maine supplied the timber for the masts of 80 per cent of British Admiral Nelson's fleet. ❏

34

❏ In seaboard towns notice the 'widow's walk', a balustrade along the top of some of the sea captains' houses. From here wives would watch ships coming and going. ❏

A shipowners' advertisement for their 'first class clipper ship'

was opened up with China, and New England entered a golden age of commercial enterprise.

The capital of maritime New England during this 'Federalist Era', was not so much Boston as Salem, Massachusetts, and the elegant houses built here by the captains, ship-owners and merchants who amassed such vast fortunes are splendid monuments to their prowess. The Peabody Museum displays the trinkets they brought home, along with their cargoes of tea and silks. Boston's Back Bay and Beacon Hill neighbourhoods, Portsmouth (New Hampshire) and Newburyport (Massachusetts) also have their share of grand houses built on the China trade wealth.

SHIP-BUILDING Seafaring activity supported a wide range of other businesses – rope-makers (a 1,000-ton vessel needed 12,000 feet of rope), sail-makers, caulkers, chandlers and, of course, ship-builders. Northern New England's plentiful forests supplied scores of shipyards, mostly along the Maine coast. The Merrimack river was also busy, and here was invented the little work-boat, the dory, which fishermen would stack in nests of five or six on their sea-going boats.

In the 19th century Boston Wharf was a bustling area set against a forest of masts

This was the era in which insurance agents first began to make a killing. With premiums based on the dimensions and type of wood used for the different parts of the ship, the wise ship-owner would follow their recommendations – hard (yellow) pine for the keel, Douglas fir for the deck planking, and so on. The Maine Maritime Museum in Bath (see page 118) is excellent for a study of boat-building.

The era of the clipper was brief, eclipsed by the steam-powered ship. New England's maritime trade began to decline, and rich merchants put their capital into manufacturing.

❏ Plaques on many houses in Marblehead, a delightful small town on the North Shore of Massachusetts, indicate the range of maritime trades. 'Built for Benjamin Pritchard, Tailor, 1753', reads one; others are 'Blacksmith', 'Housewright', 'Scribe', 'Shoreman', as well as 'Mariner' and 'Merchant'. ❏

35

During the golden years of the China trade, it was the coastal areas of New England that generated the wealth. As maritime commerce declined and new industrial technology developed towards the end of the 18th century, the water-power of the inland river valleys became the basis for a new wave of prosperity.

'Tuck' is the Algonquin word for 'river with waves', and Pawtucket is 'a divided river with waves' – ideal for powering mills. It was in Pawtucket, at the mouth of the Blackstone River Valley, which runs southeast from Worcester, Massachusetts, to Providence, Rhode Island, that the American Industrial Revolution was born. Craftsmen in metal, leather and wood, as well as handloom weavers and fullers, had worked in Massachusetts since the days of the early settlers, but in 1793 the first water-powered cotton mill in America, Slater Mill, opened in a clapboard building beside the river in Pawtucket.

Samuel Slater had worked in Richard Arkwright's revolutionary spinning mills in Britain. With financial backing from Rhode Island's prosperous shipping merchants, including one of the Brown brothers, he was able to reproduce the machine designs he had learned there and made use of the local craftsmen's skills to harness water-power to drive the carders, spinning machines and looms that launched New England's textile industry and transformed daily life across the country. The mill and other buildings have been restored at the Slater Mill Historic Site in Pawtucket (see page 220).

Thomson, on the Thames river in Connecticut, one of dozens of factory towns that sprang up during the 19th century to meet the growing demand for manufactured goods

❑ Some mill towns – notably Lowell – are being turned into Heritage Parks. Immaculately restored, they barely resemble the noisy, grimy towns of the 19th century, but they do offer an excellent insight into a turning point in the region's history. ❑

❏ The exploitation of women and the use of child and slave labour were issues of great concern to 19th-century social activists such as feminist Margaret Fuller, anti-slavery campaigner William Lloyd Garrison (see panel, page 72) and the Concord circle of thinkers and writers (see pages 46–7). ❏

RISE... Other merchants were quick to seize the opportunity for diversification. Alongside rivers such as the Blackstone and the Merrimack, the landscape of rolling farmland changed rapidly into a quite different scene of mills, warehouses and workers' housing, smoke stacks, dams, canals and, in time, railways. Millbury, for instance, a town positioned to benefit from both the Blackstone river and the Blackstone canal, had six woollen mills in the 1830s. The most remarkable of these mill villages was Lowell, developed by the wealthy Boston merchant Francis Cabot Lowell on the Merrimack river northwest of Boston (see page 171). Lowell had seen the appalling conditions of some of the factory workers in Britain and planned decent company-owned housing, schools, places of worship and recreational facilities for his workers. Women as well as men were employed, daughters of New England farmers. Letters home describe good conditions, fair treatment and a lively social life. Lowell village became a showpiece. By 1850 it was producing 2 million yards of cloth a week and had one of the world's largest canal systems.

...AND FALL As mills grew larger and more numerous, more labour was needed. Workers were attracted off the land and immigrants flooded in from Europe. Some of the earliest were the Irish who constructed the Blackstone Canal in 1828 to transport goods from Worcester to Providence, though 20 years later this was replaced by the railway. The mills (most of which had never operated on such caring principles as Lowell's) became overcrowded and, even in Lowell, families of Irish, Portuguese, Greeks and others were crammed into squalid tenements. No-one visiting Lowell today can fail to be moved seeing the conditions in which people lived and worked. Child labour was introduced and all workers were desperately exploited. Wages were cut, and protests, petitions and strikes ensued, culminating in a major strike in 1912.

Gradually industrialists were lured by cheaper labour to the South, and by the 1920s 50 per cent of American cotton was being woven there. The Depression followed and most of New England's textile mills closed down. Industrial prosperity would only be regained with the development of the electronics industry in southern New England after World War II.

A re-creation of the long-gone days of sweat and toil at Lowell Mill

The 18th century saw a steady trickle of immigrants, but by the mid-1800s foreigners began to pour into New England in numbers significant enough to have a permanent effect on society, politics and the economy.

38

BOSTON'S IRISH AND ITALIANS The Potato Famine in Ireland of 1845–50 resulted in a flood of families seeking better prospects. Thousands went no further than Boston; there, hungry and poor, they crowded into the North End district. Initially, the Roman Catholic Irish met with prejudice from Bostonians, whose blood was basically still Puritan, and their place remained at the lower end of social ladder. Gradually they improved their image and proved they could hold their own in public office alongside the blue-blooded Bostonian aristocrats (with the result that the Democrats began to break the Republican hold on power).

In 1884 Hugh O'Brien became the first of many Irish mayors of Boston. In 1905 came 'Honey-Fitz', as John F Fitzgerald (grandfather of John F Kennedy) was known, and then the colourful James Michael Curley. What Curley lacked in education he made up for in charm, and between 1920 and 1950 he was not only mayor four times, but also governor and congressman – even though he was jailed twice, once while in office. Boston Irish politicians have become legendary, and today they make up half the city council.

Master of blarney, 'Honey-Fitz', JFK's grandfather

The Irish of the North End were joined by Jews from eastern Europe in the 1870s, who were in turn followed in the 1890s by the Italians. To this day the area has remained an Italian quarter. In 1993 Boston elected its first Italian–American mayor, who ran unopposed for re-election in 1997.

❑ St Stephen's, Rose Kennedy's childhood church, has changed its stance several times. In 1714 the New North Meeting House was founded on the site as a Congregationalist institution. In 1804 Charles Bulfinch designed the present building, and in 1813 it became a Unitarian church. In 1862, by which time the population of the North End was mostly Irish, the church, renamed St Stephen's, became Roman Catholic. ❑

Hugh O'Brien, first in a long line of Boston's Irish mayors

A COSMOPOLITAN MIX Many Irish immigrants found employment in the building of the railways. In Vermont, for instance, descendants of labourers on the Rutland and Central Vermont lines today make up the Irish population in towns such as Burlington and Rutland (their railway long since gone). Some of the Italian immigrants, from marble-producing areas of Italy, went to work in the marble quarries in Barre, Vermont, bringing skills with them in the same way as the Welshmen who went to the slate mines. The work-force for southern New England's textile and shoe factories was also largely formed by European immigrants. At the turn of this century, eastern Europeans formed a significant group in Providence, Rhode Island, and Connecticut's Naugatuck Valley.

Today, the influence of all these immigrants on their adopted home-town often goes beyond just ethnic food shops. Middletown, Connecticut, for instance, has recently had a number of Sicilian-American mayors. Many fishing fleets were manned by Portuguese from the Azores, and those that remain – at Stonington, Connecticut, and Gloucester, Massachusetts, for example – still

> ❏ The Sicilians of Middletown, Connecticut, have for several generations come from just one village in southeast Sicily called Melilli. ❏

hold the two-day Blessing of the Fleet. Festivities include a parade of ships and the blessing of wreaths which are thrown into the sea.

Immigrants also came into New England from other directions. After the Civil War French-Canadians came from Quebec, particularly to industrial cities of New Hampshire such as Manchester, but also to Connecticut and the mill villages of Rhode Island and Massachusetts. After World War II Jamaicans and West Indians came from the South and New York, chiefly to Boston and Massachusetts, Rhode Island and Connecticut. So too did Hispanics, many from Puerto Rico. In Hartford, Connecticut, 20 per cent of the population is Hispanic (public notices are printed in English and Spanish).

Top, opposite: the Blessing of the Fleet, Gloucester. Below: an Italian pizzeria in Boston's North End

As cities sweltered under a cloud of mid-19th-century industrial grime, New England's unsullied coast and mountains, easily reached by steamship or train, began to appeal to the wealthy of the Northeast as summer homes.

40

Some of the hotels had their own railways: the Profile and Franconia Notch ran from Bethlehem, NH, to the Profile House

From the 1830s the painter Thomas Cole and other artists (see page 44) had visited the then little-known White Mountains region, soon to be joined by the notable writers of the day, such as Hawthorne, Emerson and Thoreau (see pages 46–7). These early 'tourists' did much to publicise areas like this and, once steamships and railways had arrived, the stage was set for the development of New England as a playground for the wealthy new industrialists. Spas proliferated, and the rich built summer 'cottages', particularly in Bar Harbor and Acadia on the Maine coast, on the islands of Martha's Vineyard and Nantucket, and, notably, in Newport, Rhode Island (see pages 216–18). It is the 'grand hotel', however, that best evokes these days of early tourism.

THE FIRST RESORTS A pioneer of the summer vacation in America was Appledore House, which opened its doors in 1848 as a resort hotel on the Isles of Shoals, off Portsmouth, New Hampshire. Boston's socialites, including literary and artistic celebrities, flocked here in the new coastal steamers to spend idyllic summer months away from the stresses of urban life. Appledore's success spawned many more grand-style summer resorts on the coast and in the mountains, and by about 1880, with the benefit of a good railway network, the tradition of summer holidaying was firmly established.

Each year, wealthy families from the eastern seaboard would arrive at the hotels on magnificent trains such as the White Mountain Express, bringing young and old, servants and governesses – and the lifestyle enjoyed by the top echelons of urbane society.

THE GRAND HOTEL In the early 1900s there were 19 of these 'grand hotels' in the White Mountains alone. Many were self-sufficient, running their own farms, stables and ice-cooling barns. Some even had post offices (envelopes franked by a grand hotel post office are nowadays collectors' items). Each had its resident orchestra, often made up of musicians who in the winter season played for the Boston Symphony Orchestra. Artists in residence were kept busy painting souvenirs of the landscape.

Instruction was given in dancing (the tea

❏ In the White Mountains, a daily newspaper, Among the Clouds, used to keep local hotel guests up to date with exactly who was staying where. ❏

dance being a favourite) and sporting facilities were offered, from croquet to boating, bathing and fishing. The more adventurous guests would go hiking or horse-riding into the mountains; some, however, would get no further than the hotel's veranda. The veranda was an important feature of the grand hotel, built wide and long (indeed, hotels were rated by its length), with cane rocking-chairs pushed well back so guests had room to promenade. Summer romances flourished, and it was important to see and be seen.

The cuisine of the grand hotel chef was legendary, and menus listed up to 70 items per meal. Guests would sit at the same table, with the same waiter, for the whole season. It was important, therefore, in order to see and be seen, not to be stuck in a corner, and for this reason the dining room in the Mount Washington Hotel was octagonal.

By the 1930s the automobile was bringing a different sort of person to the resorts, someone with less money and only a week or two to spare, looking for cheaper accommodation. It was the automobile that sounded the death knell of the grand hotel. Some were torn down, while others were gutted by fire and never rebuilt. Today, only a few remain, such as the Mount Washington in Bretton Woods and the Balsams in Dixville Notch, testaments to a gloriously romantic, sadly bygone era.

Above: wish you were here – an early postcard, of the Cannon Mountain Aerial Passenger Tramway
Left: the Mount Washington Hotel (1902) at Bretton Woods, NH, is one of the few grand hotels still operating today

41

The political scene in Boston has always been active, and some of America's most influential politicians and diplomats, including five presidents, have cut their teeth in New England.

THE ADAMS FAMILY The first member of the Adams family to come to prominence was Boston-born Samuel Adams (1722–1803). A complete failure as a businessman and tax collector, he emerged as a terrier-like political agitator, a patriot whose orchestrated propaganda stirred up anti-British feeling in the run-up to Independence.

Sam Adams's second cousin, John Adams (1735–1826), was also a patriot. A more moderate man, he helped negotiate the Treaty of Versailles which ended the Revolution and was appointed the first US minister to Britain. On his return, he became George Washington's vice-president and a leading Federalist. When Washington retired in 1796, John Adams became America's second

President John Quincy Adams

president, with his wife Abigail, one of the intellectual women of the day, playing a strongly supportive role. Defeated by Thomas Jefferson in 1800, John Adams spent an active retirement in Quincy, Massachusetts (see page 182).

John Adams's eldest son, John Quincy Adams (1767–1848), had accompanied his father on various diplomatic missions and, after graduating from Harvard, pursued a distinguished career as a diplomat in Europe. Returning home, he became secretary of state and in 1824, when there was no clear majority in the presidential election, he found himself chosen in preference to Andrew Jackson. John Quincy's term of office was sullied by hostility from Jackson's supporters, and in the 1828 elections he was defeated. As a member of the House of Representatives, however, he put his energies into the anti-slavery campaign. During an impassioned speech on the subject he had a stroke and collapsed on the floor of the House, dying two days later.

Samuel Adams: an engraving of the portrait by Copley (1773)

'KEEP COOL WITH COOLIDGE' The life and death of Calvin Coolidge (1872–1933), America's 30th president, was not so colourful. Born in Plymouth Notch, Vermont (see page 233), Coolidge was a quiet and cautious man of few words who worked his way up the political ladder to become governor of Massachusetts. Elected Republican vice-president, he became president

42

The Kennedy era: Robert Rauschenburg's Retroactive (1964)

by the time he announced his presidential candidacy in 1960 an aura of charisma surrounded the couple.

Kennedy was the youngest man, and the first Roman Catholic, ever elected president. At home his main concern was for social welfare, while in foreign affairs he won admiration for his handling of the Cuban missile crisis in 1962. Shortly afterwards he secured the Nuclear Test-Ban Treaty with Soviet leader Nikita Khrushchev and British Prime Minister Harold Macmillan. Seen by many as a symbol of hope, for America and the world, Kennedy was shot dead in Dallas on 22 November 1963.

GEORGE BUSH President from 1989 to 1993, George Bush grew up in Greenwich, Connecticut, and graduated from Yale. He served under presidents Nixon and Ford before becoming loyal vice-president to Ronald Reagan. His presidency was marked by his involvement of American troops in the Gulf War. His holiday home is in Kennebunkport, Maine.

43

in 1923 when Warren Harding died unexpectedly. Coolidge's two terms of office were distinguished by such government inaction that when the writer Dorothy Parker was told he had died, she is reputed to have asked 'How can they tell?'.

THE KENNEDY STYLE President John F Kennedy (1917–63) was the great-grandson of an Irish immigrant. JFK's father, Joseph P Kennedy (1888–1969), a Harvard graduate, married Rose Fitzgerald, the daughter of mayor 'Honey-Fitz' (see page 38). While Joseph made a successful career in politics and business – he was a millionaire at the age of 30 – Rose bore him nine children. Four would die a premature death: Kathleen, Joe, John and Robert.

John first ran as a Democrat for Congress in 1946. In 1953 the handsome young senator married the beautiful Jacqueline Lee Bouvier (in Newport, Rhode Island; see page 218), and

George Bush, US president 1989–1993

The Museum of Fine Arts, the Isabella Stewart Gardner Museum, the Clark Institute and many college museums have good collections of European art, but the work of New England's own painters is also well worth seeking out.

44

COLONIAL PAINTING Colonial America produced three artists of note. John Singleton Copley (1738–1815) painted portraits of Boston's élite. His *Watson and the Shark*, in Boston's Museum of Fine Arts, is a famous depiction of mankind's struggle with nature, but it is Benjamin West (1738–1820) who stands out as a historical painter during this period. Gilbert Stuart (1755–1828) was another eminent portrait painter (his depiction of George Washington appears on the dollar bill).

THE WHITE MOUNTAIN SCHOOL Throughout the 19th century, New England artists continued to be influenced by Europe. Thomas Cole (1801–48) was a Romantic landscape painter and a founder of the Hudson River School. He frequently travelled about the Northeast making sketches, and in 1828 visited New Hampshire's White Mountains, instantly to be captivated by the scenery. Albert Bierstadt (1830–1902), another prominent member of the school, created grandiose views of the White

Top: from Boy in a Boatyard *by Winslow Homer (1836–1910)*

Mountains and the Connecticut River Valley.

COASTAL ART COLONIES The Maine coast has been inspirational to many artists, notably Winslow Homer (1836–1910), who spent the latter part of his life at Prout's Neck. Here he painted a prodigious number of powerful seascapes. Look out too for the seascapes of Fitz Hugh Lane (1804–65). John Marin (1870–1953) was a more recent abstract landscape artist obsessive about the Maine coast. Edward Hopper (1882–1967), one of a group known as the Painters of the American Scene, also worked here, his static, silent figures set in humdrum surroundings. The area around Cushing, Maine, where Andrew Wyeth (born 1917) has his summer home, is the subject of many of his tempera and watercolour paintings. Another American Scene painter, Wyeth is best known for

Shipping in Down East Waters *by Fitz Hugh Lane (1804–65)*

Boston Common at Twilight *by Frederick Childe Hassam (1859–1935)*

Christina's World, depicting a lonely figure in an open field.

Appledore, an idyllic summer artists' colony on the Isles of Shoals, was immortalised by the leading American Impressionist, F Childe Hassam (1859–1935). His Boston Common at Twilight is a favourite in Boston's Museum of Fine Arts. Childe Hassam also worked in Old Lyme, at the mouth of the Connecticut river, where Florence Griswold opened her house (now a museum) to an influential colony which became known as the Old Lyme Impressionists.

AMERICANS ABROAD No study of the art of 19th-century New England is complete without mention of two notable American artists whose work and influence straddled the Atlantic. These are James McNeill Whistler (1834–1903), who was born in Lowell, Massachusetts, and is perhaps best known for his paintings of London, and John Singer Sargent (1856–1925),

born in Florence, Italy, who painted portraits of Boston's prominent men and women.

THE 20TH CENTURY The two New England artists who have won the most widespread popularity in recent times must be the illustrator Norman Rockwell (see page 150) and Anna 'Grandma' Moses (1860–1961), a primitive painter who created brightly coloured scenes of everyday New England life (see page 226).

SCULPTORS One of America's foremost sculptors, Augustus Saint-Gaudens (1848–1907), worked, after training in Europe, in Cornish, New Hampshire (see page 195). His work includes the 1897 Shaw Monument on Boston Common.

Chesterwood in Stockbridge, Massachusetts (see page 147), was the home of another notable sculptor, Daniel Chester French (1850–1931). Best known for his seated *Abraham Lincoln* in Washington DC, French first won acclaim with his *Minute Man* statue in Concord, Massachusetts.

Writers in colonial times worked mostly on religious tracts and journals, but after the Revolution, American literature established a new identity, and for two centuries New England has nurtured writers of prominence.

❏ 'As the New England summer flamed into autumn, I piled cut spruce boughs all round the draughty cottage sill, and helped to put up a tiny roofless verandah along one side of it for future needs.'
– From *Something of Myself* by Rudyard Kipling (1865–1936). ❏

46

THE CONCORD CIRCLE Early in the 19th century there emerged a group of thinkers and writers, centred on Concord, Massachusetts (see pages 169–70), spiritual idealists known as the New England Transcendentalists. The leading figures were essayist and poet Ralph Waldo Emerson (1803–82), and Henry David Thoreau (1817–62), whose classic, *Walden* (1854), is a record of two solitary, transcendentalist years spent communing with nature in a log cabin in the woods around Walden Pond. Novelist Nathaniel Hawthorne (1804–64) also lived in Concord for a time, in the same house in which Louisa May Alcott

(1832–88) spent some of her teenage years, a period she was to draw on in *Little Women*.

THE BERKSHIRES Nathaniel Hawthorne also lived in Lenox, western Massachusetts, where he wrote *The Scarlet Letter* (1850) and *The House of the Seven Gables* (1851), inspired by the house of that name in his birthplace, Salem. In Lenox he became good friends with Herman Melville, who was living in nearby Arrowhead completing the whaling adventure story *Moby Dick* (1851) before fading into melancholia and virtual oblivion – it was not until the 1920s that his talent was recognised. In 1902 Edith Wharton, society hostess turned novelist, built The Mount, in Lenox, where she wrote her stories of trenchant social observation (such as *Ethan Frome* and *The Age of Innocence*) in between entertaining her high-flying circle of friends, including Henry James.

❏ 'There are three kinds of lies: lies, damned lies, and statistics.'
– Mark Twain, *Autobiography* (1871). ❏

THE HARTFORD COLONY In the Nook Farm area of Hartford, Connecticut (see page 96), Samuel Clemens, alias Mark Twain, and his wife built the exuberantly Victorian house where he wrote *The Adventures of Tom Sawyer* (1876) and his masterpiece of wit and insight, *The Adventures of Huckleberry Finn* (1884). Harriet Beecher Stowe was his neighbour, a minister's wife whose *Uncle*

Top: Tom Sawyer's band of robbers
Left: Mrs Keeley as Topsy, Uncle Tom's Cabin

"SLAVE LIFE, OR 'UNCLE TOM'S CABIN.'"
(Mr Keeley as Topsy) 'Is drefful wicked.')

Tom's Cabin of 1852 was a touch-paper that lit popular anti-slavery feeling to the extent that it is counted by some as one of the causes of the American Civil War.

❏ Kipling and his American wife, Caroline, lived for a few years in Brattleboro, Vermont, and this is where he wrote some of his best-known works, including the Jungle Books. Their house, Naulakha, has been restored and is available for rent (tel: 01628 825925 in the UK for bookings, or 802/254 6868 for a brochure in the US). ❏

Longfellow, one of a circle of writers associated with Harvard

POETRY AND DRAMA Born in 1807 in Portland, Maine, Henry Wadsworth Longfellow wrote many of his narrative poems, including *The Song of Hiawatha* (1855), while teaching at Harvard. Longfellow was part of an aristocratic group of New England writers closely linked with Harvard. Others were the poets Oliver

Wendell Holmes and James Russell Lowell. The sensitive recluse Emily Dickinson (1830–86) is also linked with Massachusetts (see page 176), while the poems of Robert Frost (1874–1963) are so steeped in the New England countryside he is often referred to as 'The Voice of New England' (see page 209).

The only American playwright to receive the Nobel Prize for Literature, Eugene O'Neill died in Boston in 1953. From a modest start with a one-act play performed in a wharfside playhouse in the Cape Cod fishing village of Provincetown, O'Neill's troubled career – much of his material was drawn from the torments of his family life – was to bring him to a position of pre-eminence among 20th-century dramatists. He is commemorated at his boyhood summer home, Monte Cristo Cottage, in New London, Connecticut.

Louisa May Alcott

47

Boston

49

Boston

-9223372036854775808## BOSTON A TO Z
CONTENTS

50

Boston seen from the Charles River: between Boston Common, the brownstone terraces of Back Bay and the tower blocks of the financial district rises the gilded dome of the Massachusetts State House

BOSTON The cradle of American history is a city of church spires, parks, statues and a remarkably thriving culture. To this, within the last 30 years, has been added an uncompromisingly American-looking high-rise skyline. To Americans and Europeans alike, the city's elements are partly familiar, partly refreshingly different. Boston also divides into strikingly contrasting neighbourhoods, from the trendy elegance of the Back Bay and the old-world charm of the North End to the striking modern sky-line of the financial district and Waterfront.

Boston looks smart and pleased with life nowadays, with its elegant shops, gleaming office towers, refurbished wharves and historic buildings, lively eateries and bars. Although it is by far New England's largest city – with a population of around 575,000 – 'the Hub' (referring to its position in the universe) often presents a pleasant surprise to visitors who find it liveable and manageable.

FINDING YOUR FEET Most Bostonians would tend to think of **Boston Common▶** and the neighbouring **Public Garden▶▶** as the true heart of the city. The Common is the oldest public park in the US, and is overlooked by the State House with its dazzling gold dome. A visitor information booth near by marks the start of the **Freedom Trail ▶▶▶** (see pages 58–61). To the east lies the main downtown district, with government buildings ranged around the huge piazza of **Government Center**. Here, too, is the renovated and ever-popular **Faneuil Hall Marketplace▶▶▶** (pronounced Fan'el), which comprises historic Faneuil Hall, Quincy Market and the adjacent North and South markets. Street performers entertain the shoppers and visitors, portrait artists sketch them and food stalls feed them: the atmosphere is conducive to lingering. The historic **North End▶▶**, the Italian quarter north of here, hosts lively street festivals at weekends in July and August, has excellent bakeries and restaurants, and has sites on the Freedom Trail.

Post Office Square is at the heart of the high-rise downtown Financial District. Near by rises Boston's first

The State House, designed by Charles Bulfinch. The dome was originally covered in copper, the work of Paul Revere

CITY CHEAPIES
(see also panel on page 78 for freebies)
● The Museum of Fine Arts has a 'pay as you wish' entry 4–10pm Wednesdays.
● The Children's Museum offers all tickets for $1 Fridays 5–9pm.
● The Computer Museum offers half-price entry on Sundays after 3pm.

'skyscraper', the Custom House, a slender Gothic-style clocktower that graces the downtown skyline. **The Waterfront** is no longer commercial, condominiums and offices having sprouted on the old wharves. It has some fine restaurants and the **New England Aquarium►►►**. Work is well under way on a project which will put the highway that crosses the Waterfront into a tunnel and transform the area into a 73-acre park. A waterside walk from the Aquarium, past Rowes Wharf and the Boston Harbour Hotel, makes the most of the Waterfront views. South of the Financial District, **Chinatown►** is a colourful neighbourhood with shops selling all manner of items and restaurants serving excellent food at bargain prices.

North and west of Boston Common are, respectively, the fashionable and delightful residential neighbourhoods of **Beacon Hill►►** and the **Back Bay►►►**. South of **Copley Square►►** is the main hotel district, a convenient area in which to stay; eastward lies the Theatre District. The **South End** is a trendy up-and-coming area of bow-fronted Victorian townhouses, where Union Park is one of the most attractive streets. The district is full of excellent eateries, and is ethnically and socially mixed.

Southwest of the Back Bay, the Fenway occupies the area around Back Bay Fens, a lakeside park. It has the pick of the city's art museums – the huge **Museum of Fine Arts►►►** and the intensely personal **Isabella Stewart Gardner Museum►►►**. Fenway Park, the home of the Boston Red Sox, is one of the smallest and oldest baseball parks in the major leagues.

Cambridge►►, on the north side of the Charles river, is actually a separate city, although it is close enough to walk to from the Back Bay over the Harvard Bridge. Harvard University (the oldest university in the US), and the street activity and nightlife in and around Harvard Square are among Cambridge's prime attractions. Cambridge is also home to Massachusetts Institute of Technology (MIT) and boasts some of the finest restaurants in the Boston area.

Close-up on the bow-fronted houses of the South End

Boston: Getting around

Getting around

WALKING Everyone will tell you that Boston is a walking city. Distances downtown are small, and there is so much to see. New visitors will often find that they have walked non-stop for days on end before noticing their tired feet.

During the day it is quite safe to wander around the central streets, although crossing them is another matter. Here, in what some people call the jay-walking capital of America, the tendency is to dodge the notoriously slow traffic lights and risk the traffic.

Compared to many US cities Boston is safe for visitors, but some areas, such as the Common and the back streets of Chinatown, should be avoided at night.

DRIVING Don't drive in Boston unless you absolutely must. Anyone unacquainted with America's most bewildering one-way system will need good nerves to cope with the traffic, to navigate through the city's confusing maze of streets, to understand the priority systems where no lines are painted on the road surface, and to try to find one of those elusive parking spaces. The construction of three road tunnels may help the traffic problem after 2006, but the building work in the mean time has exacerbated it. If you are planning a self-drive trip around New England, consider seriously picking the car up from somewhere out of the city and easily reached by train or subway.

PUBLIC TRANSPORT Fortunately, public transport in Boston is excellent, running from around 5am to 12.30am. The subway train network, known as the 'T', spreads across the city. You can buy tokens which you insert into a slot at the barrier; you do not get a receipt, and so travel without a ticket. Currently the cost is 85¢ for each journey on the 'T' (a little more for some journeys from the outer suburbs) irrespective of how many times you change lines.

The T's Visitor Passport gives unlimited travel on the T (plus discounts for certain attractions) for one, three or seven days. However, this is unlikely to save you money on fares if you are only making a few journeys each day; a better bet is to buy a stack of tokens first time round, thus saving time queueing at stations. Buses are slightly cheaper, but require a little more local knowledge.

From central Boston, journeys to Cambridge, the Museum of Fine Arts, the Isabella Stewart Gardner Museum and Logan Airport are best made by the 'T'. The colour-coded lines are reasonably straightforward even to a newcomer: just look for the colour and destination of the train.

GUIDED AND SELF-GUIDED TOURS Several companies run fleets of trolleys (quaint, wooden buses similar to old-style trams), with guided commentary, around the hotel area and the historic parts of the city, taking in most sights on the Freedom Trail. All of the routes on offer cover much the same ground. You can begin at any trolley stop. Tickets last a day, and you can get on and off where you like, then wait a few minutes for the next trolley. Additionally, Old Town Trolley Tours take in Cambridge. The same company runs a narrated JFK's Boston tour.

Boston By Foot (reservations not required) runs guided tours from May to October; for recorded information, tel: 617/367 2345.

BOAT CRUISES From spring until autumn, Boston Harbor Cruises (tel: 617/227 4321) operate whale-watching, harbour and themed Mystery and Summertime Blues cruises from Long Wharf by the New England Aquarium. The short cruise to the Charlestown Navy Yard is the most direct and pleasant way to approach it. The longer tour into Boston Harbour passes the airport and gains news of the 17th- and 18th-century fortifications on Castle Island and there is an impressive panorama of the skyscrapers. Boston By Boat is a shuttle that takes visitors to the Children's Museum, Computer Museum, Science Museum, USS *Constitution* and Aquarium in a continuous loop. The 80-minute Boston Duck Tours, from the Prudential Center (Apr–Nov), use brightly painted World War II amphibious vehicles. In addition to making a conventional ground tour of the city, they splash into the Charles for a river trip. Tel: 617/723 DUCK.

AIRPORT TRANSFERS See page 248.

AIRPORT TRANSFERS See page 248.

MORE TOURS

- Trolley tours round Boston include the Chocolate and Seafood trolleys – each with appropriate samples on the way.
- Guided walks are offered by Chinatown Tours (tel: 617/764 5656).
- Take the Orange Line to Stony Brook for the Boston Beer brewery and museum, home of Samuel Adams Boston ales; tours are Thursday, Friday 2pm, Saturday 12, 1, and 2pm, and Wednesday 2pm July and August.
- For baseball fans there are tours of Fenway Park, home to the Boston Red Sox (tel: 617/236 6666).
- The Federal Reserve Bank (tel: 617/973 3451), where old banknotes are destroyed, has free tours; visitors are given a bag of shredded money.

53

Don't even think of driving in Boston. With a map in hand, finding your way around on foot is easy

Boston

Events

For further information, contact the Greater Boston Convention and Visitors Bureau (see page 266).

January
Martin Luther King Day (18 January)
Chinese New Year (January/February), Chinatown: firecrackers, traditional music.

February
Black History Month, centred on Black Meeting House in Beacon Hill: plays, discussion, tours.
Boston Cooks, World Trade Center and Hynes Convention Center: billed as New England's premier culinary event, with dining, wine-tasting and entertainment.

March
Seafood Show, Bayside Exposition Center.
Spring Flower Show, Bayside Exposition Center: the third largest in the world.
St Patrick's Day Parade (mid-March): parade honouring Ireland's saint.

April
Boston Marathon (Patriot's Day), from Hopkinton to Boston: the oldest such race in America.
Patriot's Day Parade, City Hall to Paul Revere Mall.
Swan Boats, Public Garden: season begins with ceremony and first ride.

Late April/Early May
Ducklings' Day Parade, Beacon Hill, Public Garden: make way for the mallard family and costumed relatives.

May
Art Newbury Street: art, special exhibits, jazz and classical music.
MayFair: Book festival, Harvard Square.

June
Bunker Hill Day and Parade.
Dairy Festival (first week): cows make an appearance on the Common (a colonial law mandates this); ice-cream, butter-making, milking.
Cambridge International Fair, University Park, Cambridge.
Boston Globe Jazz Festival, various locations.
Harborlights Music Festival, Waterfront (June–September)

July
Boston Pops: free outdoor concerts at the Hatch Shell on the Esplanade.
Chowderfest, City Hall Plaza: sample a range of chowders produced by Boston restaurants and vote for the best.
Harborfest (week leading up to 4 July): celebration of Revolutionary War events in Boston Harbor, culminating in Revolutionary Era reenactments, military parades, fireworks and concerts.

August
Boston Seaport Festival, Charlestown Navy Yard.
Caribbean Carnival, Franklin Park.
August Moon Festival, Chinatown.

September
Cambridge River Festival.
Art Newbury Street (see May).
Boston Arts and Music Festival.

October
Columbus Day Parade.
Oktoberfest, Harvard Square, Cambridge.
Head of the Charles Regatta: major rowing event (the world's largest).
Mixfest, Free pop concerts in City Hall Plaza.

November
Holiday Happenings (19 November–24 December): holiday festivities, including Winter Wonderland and Sleigh Bell Parade.

December
Boston Tea Party Re-enactment, Tea Party Ship.
First Night Celebration: city-wide family celebration to ring in the New Year.
Newbury Street Stroll.
Tree-lighting Ceremonies at Prudential Center and elsewhere.

Part of the 4 July celebrations in downtown Boston

'Listen, my children, and you shall hear/Of the midnight ride of Paul Revere…' So begins Longfellow's *Paul Revere's Ride*, a ballad that was to turn a silversmith into America's favourite folk hero.

Until Longfellow's ballad was published in 1863, Paul Revere (1735–1818) was best known as a silversmith, though he dabbled in many things (see panel). An ardent patriot and experienced express rider, he frequently carried messages for the Sons of Liberty (see page 33). On 16 April 1775, Revere rode out to Lexington to warn patriot leaders Sam Adams and John Hancock that British troops in Boston were making plans to march to Concord to seize a cache of rebel arms, and to capture Adams and Hancock in Lexington on the way. A plan was made for another message to be relayed as the soldiers actually left town.

In case he was unable to escape from Boston himself, Revere asked the sexton of Old North Church, Robert Newman, to signal to Charlestown, across the Charles river, by holding up one lantern in the church steeple if the troops left by land (across Boston Neck), two if by boat (across the river). On the night of 18 April, the signal was duly given, and Revere got out of Boston and headed for Lexington. He was joined there by William Dawes, and as they rode on they met Sam Prescott. All three were captured by the redcoats. Only Prescott escaped and reached Concord.

The legend Most newspaper reports of the night's events did not even mention Paul Revere by name. The *New York Gazette* reported him dead. A century on, however, thanks to Longfellow, Revere stepped into the annals of history.

But Longfellow was a poet, not a historian, and so he used artistic licence to play around with the facts. He has Revere waiting for the signal in Charlestown; he also has him making the heroic ride alone; and he certainly does not reveal that Revere never reached Concord, only Prescott. But then 'Prescott' does not rhyme as easily as 'Revere'.

Left: Revere in middle age. Top: Revere as messenger

THE MAN
Paul Revere was born in Boston on 21 December 1735. A silversmith like his Huguenot father, he became one of the country's finest artists in silver, gold and copper. A remarkable man of boundless energy and talent, he also turned his hand to engraving and printing, often for propaganda purposes (see panel below). He made spectacles, surgical instruments and false teeth. After the War of Independence Revere manufactured sheet copper, some being used on 'Old Ironsides' (USS *Constitution*) and on the State House dome. Revere died in 1818, aged 83, and is buried in the Old Granary burial ground.

THE PROPAGANDIST
In March 1770, a street brawl got out of hand when some youths started throwing snowballs at British troops. The soldiers panicked, opened fire and five men were killed. Paul Revere plagiarised an engraving of the incident by Henry Pelham (to Pelham's annoyance), fuelling resentment against the redcoats or 'lobsterbacks', as the British troops were derisively called. The term 'Boston Massacre' was coined by Sam Adams.

Bronze bell cast by Revere, a distinguished bell-maker

55

Boston could be forgiven for quietly basking in its venerable past and resting on its glorious cultural laurels. But life here is as much about computers as culture and, in this capital of academia, the pace is intellectually challenging. Boston has its share of blue blood, but it is above all a dynamic, youthful city.

BRAHMINS AND BOSTON

The physical development of Boston is closely linked to the Brahmins. In 1795 the society portrait painter John Singleton Copley sold land on Beacon Hill to a group of entrepreneurs. On it Bulfinch built the prestigious Beacon Hill estate into which Boston's blue-blooded élite moved, leaving their homes in the old North End *en bloc*. Beacon Hill was one of three major hills to be levelled off, the soil being used to fill in the swampy 'Back Bay' area along the Charles river. By about 1870 the Back Bay had been developed and many of the Brahmins then moved on to its more grandiose houses.

The Christian Science Center, Prudential Center (left), and John Hancock Tower

High-rise and high-tech For many years the Custom House Tower was the only building in Boston higher than the State House dome. How different was the skyline then. In recent times, glassy skyscrapers and concrete office towers have risen rapidly one after the other to dwarf the elegant Victorian brownstone terraces of the Back Bay. The classic architectural image of Boston is the reflection of Henry Hobson Richardson's 1870s Romanesque-style Trinity Church in the glass windows of IM Pei's 1970s ultra-modern John Hancock Tower. And since IM Pei and his associates completed their commission to change the face of the blighted and downward-spiralling Boston of the 1950s and 1960s, a further proliferation of thrusting office towers has been occupied by financial and other leading institutions, and computer companies.

Boston today – together with Cambridge, across the river – is a high-tech place. Go to Harvard Square on a Friday or Saturday evening, and for every browser in the bookshops there are at least twice as many dads in the computer-ware shops showing their kids the latest educational software. It is not insignificant that Boston's Computer Museum (see page 68) is among the best of its kind in the world. Don't miss it – it's sensational.

In recent years, Boston and Cambridge may have become 'the Hub' (as Boston is known) of the computer industry, but this does not mean that their role as a leader in medicine has in any way diminished. The place is a hotbed of research – not for nothing has the Ether Dome, the Massachusetts General Hospital's operating theatre, where ether was first used as an anaesthetic, been completely submerged by modern buildings (it is open to visitors, if they can find their way through to it). As for education, it sometimes feels as if virtually everyone in town is somehow connected to the 67 colleges and universities on either side of the Charles River. The start of the academic year brings chaos; the streets seem to be full of walking mattresses, as 500,000 students move into their new accommodation. It is a city full of bright and lively people.

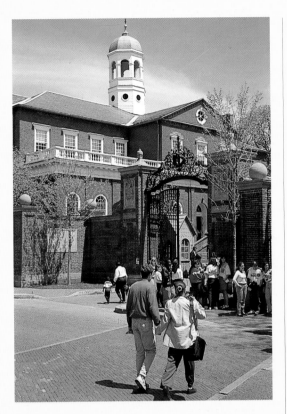

THE NEW ENGLAND HOLOCAUST MEMORIAL
Six glass and steel towers, 54ft tall and 4ft square, stand one behind the other in the gardens alongside Union Street, right beside the Freedom Trail and in an area of the city steeped in the history of human rights. The glass panels are etched with rows of numbers, a stark reminder of the 6 million Jews murdered by Nazis between 1933 and 1945. The paving stones are inscribed with quotations from Holocaust survivors and inside each tower steam rises through a grating placed over what appears to be a pit of glowing embers. The memorial is the work of architect Stanley Saitowitz.

57

The proliferation of academic institutions on either side of the Charles River means a huge student population: left, Harvard Hall, Harvard Yard, Cambridge

Boston Brahmins In the midst of all this ferment, a small but deeply significant element of Boston society calmly carries on with life just the way it has always done. These are the members of Boston's top families, the 'Proper Bostonians', the 'Boston Brahmins', as the city's Establishment was termed by Oliver Wendell Holmes in the 19th century. They trace their ancestry back to the 18th-century merchants and many claim to be related to early Puritan settlers (not, as is popularly misconceived, to the *Mayflower* Pilgrims, who landed not in Boston but in Plymouth and were definitely not so upper crust).

Certainly all are characterised by Puritan qualities of frugality and self-restraint, and a sense of superiority. Breeding, rather than money, has always been paramount. Indeed, the intermarrying of Boston's top families is surely matched only by that of European royals. A Brahmin is born with a name such as Adams, Cabot, Lowell, Bowditch, Appleton or Lodge, he is educated at Harvard (where else is there, after all?), he lives in the Back Bay and has a summer home in Maine.

In the 18th and 19th centuries it was the Brahmins who held all the power, and to a degree their blue blood continues to course through the city's veins today. Many of the financiers and businessmen in those downtown office towers are Brahmins; but perhaps it is families like the Kennedys (of Irish ancestry) and the intellectual élite who are the new generation of Brahmins?

BAR HARBOR BRAHMINS
Bar Harbor, in Maine, is where the proper Bostonian traditionally has his summer cottage. There is one page in the Bar Harbor telephone book on which every name, with just one or two exceptions, is that of a Boston Brahmin family.

LOWELL BRAHMINS
The story goes that there was some debate about whether or not a particular member of the Lowell family could be counted a true Brahmin, as he had not been born in Boston. 'Of course he is a Brahmin', pronounced his grandmother, 'he was conceived in the Ritz'.

Walk

The Freedom Trail: Part I

See map on pages 48–9 (yellow route).

Follow the red or brick line along the city pavements for colonial America's most historic walk. The route is the focus of Boston National Historical Park and passes many buildings associated with the Revolutionary War. Freedom Trail Players, in historic costume, patrol the trail to answer queries. Excellent free guided walks start every half-hour (in summer months) from the park visitor centre at 15 State Street opposite State subway station and the Old State House.

Boston Common▶, at the start of the walk, is a 44-acre, undulating grass expanse, formerly used as a pasture and parade ground. Follow the Freedom Trail across the Common up to the imposing State House with its gilded dome. Continue down Park

King's Chapel graveyard, where John Winthrop lies

Street to **Park Street Church** (1809), where William Lloyd Garrison made his first anti-slavery address in 1829 and where the song *America* was first sung in 1831. Adjacent is the **Old Granary Burying Ground**, containing graves from Revolutionary days, including those of John Hancock, Samuel Adams, Paul Revere and the five who perished in the Boston Massacre.

At the corner of Tremont and School streets, look inside **King's Chapel▶** (1754), the first Anglican church in Boston, and later the first Unitarian Church. It has especially well preserved furnishings, including white box-pews and a pulpit with sounding-board. A finely carved gravestone in the churchyard is that of Joseph Tapping (1678), depicting Father Time extinguishing the candle of Life.

The **Old Corner Book Store** (1712; now called Boston Globe Store), at the corner of School and Washington streets, was a literary meeting-house where the works of Longfellow, Stowe, Hawthorne and Emerson were first published. Today the store is largely devoted to books and maps on New England. Opposite is the **Old South Meeting House▶** (1729), a former Puritan house of worship, and at one time the largest public meeting-hall in the city. Here heated meetings took place as the British sought to impose their taxes on the colony. On 16 December 1773 Samuel Adams addressed some 7,000 citizens just before the Boston Tea Party (see page 33) and pronounced the immortal words 'Gentlemen, this meeting can do nothing more to save the country.' Threatened with demolition in the 1870s, the building was the first in Boston to be preserved solely for its historic importance. Today the building contains an exhibition focusing on the events leading to the Tea Party.

Further north along Washington Street, the **Old State House▶** (1713) has changed much over the years but externally is now restored to its original appearance, with the (renewed) British lion and unicorn flanking the gable above the balcony from where the Declaration of Independence was read to the public on 18 July 1776.

One-time meeting place for writers and thinkers

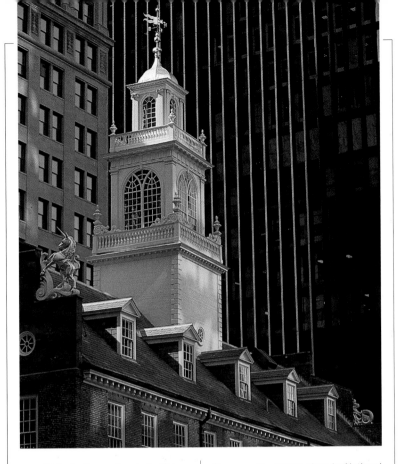

New, high-rise Boston dwarfs the Old State House

Today the interior is a museum devoted to historical exhibitions about Boston.

A neat circle of stones embedded in a road island beside the Old State House marks the site of the Boston Massacre (see page 32).

Nearby **Faneuil Hall▶▶** was dona-ted to Boston in 1742 by Peter Faneuil, the 'bachelor of Boston', who died a few months after the building's completion of 'an excess of good living'. The building contains the meeting-hall known as the 'Cradle of Liberty' (*admission* free) where, over the years, revolutionary protests, women's suffrage, slavery and every war except the 1990 Gulf War (the building was closed for renovation) have been discussed. The top floor contains regimental memorabilia of the Ancient and Honorable Artillery

Company (free tours given by National Park rangers every 30 minutes from 9.30 to 4.30). Behind Faneuil Hall is **Faneuil Hall Marketplace▶▶▶**, a lively scene, with shops, restaurants and buskers centred on Quincy Market and North and South markets.

A typically colourful scene in Faneuil Hall Marketplace

Walk

The Freedom Trail: Part II

See map on pages 48–9 (red route).

The second part of the trail leads from Faneuil Hall Marketplace, through the old Italian quarter of North End and past historic Charlestown Navy Yard to Bunker Hill. Some prefer to end the walk at Old North Church in the North End and take a ferry (from Long Wharf by the Aquarium), trolley or bus to Charlestown.

From Faneuil Hall Marketplace follow the trail along Union Street past the **Union Oyster House** (opened 1826), Boston's oldest restaurant, and the **Ebenezer Hancock House** (1767), home of John Hancock's brother, the deputy paymaster-general of the Continental Army. In the gardens alongside Union Street are the six glass towers of the **New England Holocaust Memorial** (see panel on page 57). Near by, the Haymarket is a great place for bargain fruit and vegetables on Friday and Saturday.

   North End▶▶ is one of Boston's oldest neighbourhoods. It has been home to wave after wave of immigrants. After the original 17th-century Puritan settlers came Irish refugees fleeing from the 1840s potato famine, then Jews from eastern Europe. Today the North End is the Italian quarter and has some of Boston's best restaurants.

Paul Revere House

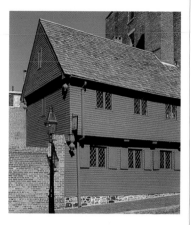

Something of a freak survival from the old town, **Paul Revere House**▶ (*Open* daily, except holidays, and Mon in winter) of about 1680, in North Square, was home to patriot Paul Revere (see page 55) and is Boston's oldest building. After Revere's time, the building functioned as a cigar factory, grocery, tenement and bank. Restored to its original appearance, the building now operates as a small museum.

   Photogenic **Paul Revere Mall** features the famous equestrian statue of Paul Revere against the magnificent steeple of **Old North Church**▶▶▶ (1723), where Robert Newman, the sexton, lit two lanterns on 18 April 1775 to warn the citizens across the river of British plans to cross by sea rather than by land via Boston Neck (see page 55). The church is a magnificent colonial survival, with a gallery, box pews and brass chandeliers; it is Boston's oldest church and has the tallest steeple.

   Copps Hill Burying Ground (1660) was used by the British as a vantage point for cannon while making preparations for the Battle of Bunker Hill. It is Boston's second oldest cemetery and has some fascinating early epitaphs. The headstone of Daniel Malcom (to the left if entering from

The North End, once a slum, is now a smart and lively district

Hull Street and found between the broken column commemorating Prince Hall and a circular path) records 'Here lies buried in a stone grave 10 feet deep. A friend to the Publick, an enemy to oppression', thus buried safe from British bullets. Though not an 'official' Trail site, **North End Garage Park**, on the left side of Hull Street, is of interest as the site of the famous Brink's robbery in 1950, which netted a record $2.5million; the FBI subsequently spent close on $29 million investigating it.

Across the road bridge is **Charlestown**, founded in 1629 and named after Charles I. It was razed by the British, and no house predates 1775. Charlestown was not incorporated into Boston until 1873. The trail continues to the entrance to **Charlestown Navy Yard▶▶▶** (see pages 66–7), today home of the warship the **USS *Constitution*▶▶▶** and the World War II destroyer **USS *Cassin Young*▶**, as well as the **USS *Constitution* Museum▶▶** and the Commandant's House.

Residential streets surround the **Bunker Hill Monument▶▶**, a tall obelisk that commemorates the first major Revolutionary War battle, fought on 17 June 1775. A 294-step climb is rewarded by an excellent view of the city. Musket firing takes place daily in summer and there is an exhibition inside the lodge.

'Old North', famous for the part it played in Paul Revere's ride

The Public Garden boasts the status of the nation's oldest botanical park

Walk

Back Bay

See map on pages 48–9 (orange route).

This tour wends its way through the elegant Victorian brownstone district of the Back Bay, where almost every doorway deserves attention, and past the two great high-level viewing platforms of Boston – the Prudential and Hancock towers.

Begin at the west side of the **Public Garden▶▶** (see page 73) and cross the walkway along the centre of **Commonwealth Avenue▶▶**, often rated as one of America's finest streets. This forms the central axis of the Back Bay, an area subject to an ambitious landfill project in the late-19th century when Parisian-style avenues were laid out on a grand scale and with an eye for symmetry.

Turn right into Berkeley Street. At 137 Beacon Street, to the right, **Gibson House▶** (*Open* 1 May–1 Nov,

Wed–Sun, plus weekends Nov–Apr; tours at 1, 2 and 3pm) is a wonderfully preserved example of the Back Bay brownstone, in pristine Victorian condition. Continuing west on Beacon Street, turn right at Dartmouth Street to take the footbridge over the highway to **Charlesbank Park**, a riverside strip popular with cyclists, sunbathers and joggers. The Hatch Shell, venue of outdoor concerts in summer, is to the right, while across the Charles river is the Massachusetts Institute of Technology (MIT) in Cambridge.

Return by another footbridge over the highway into Fairfield Street. Continue to Newbury Street, an inviting detour with its restaurants, sidewalk cafés and upmarket boutiques and galleries, and the **Newbury Street Mural** featuring historical and artistic figures. From Fairfield Street turn right into Boylston Street, cross over and go through the revolving doors and up the escalator into the **Prudential Center**, an undercover mall with 75 shops and restaurants. Walk straight ahead and at the Center Court turn right to the Prudential Tower. Take an elevator to the 50th floor for a panoramic view from the **Prudential Center Skywalk▶▶▶** (see page 72). Leave the Prudential Center through Huntington or Belvidere Arcade and

Back Bay statue of local maritime writer, Samuel Eliot Morison (1887–1976)

turn right outside to visit the **First Church of Christ, Scientist complex** immediately ahead. The long, low Broadcasting Centre to the right of a huge oblong pool houses **'A Light unto my Path', Bible Exhibit** (*Open* Wed–Sun. *Admission* free), which has an electronic map charting travels across the Holy Land and telephones telling the listener of assorted miracle healings. The skyscraper is the **Christian Science World Headquarters**. The **Christian Science Church►** (1906) is modelled on St Peter's in Rome and contains the largest pipe organ in the western hemisphere. Adjacent to the church (to its right) in a room in the publishing wing of the organisation, the

The Christian Science World Headquarters

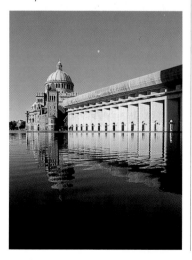

Mapparium►► (*Open* Mon–Sat 9–4.30; closed Mon in winter. *Admission* free), is a stained-glass representation of the globe as mapped in 1932–5. Looking from within the sphere (with the map appearing in concave form) you can see the whole globe in one visual sweep. The bizarre echo, with voices bouncing all around, makes this one of Boston's more offbeat experiences.

Return to the Prudential Center by the escalator leading up to Belvidere or Huntington Arcade. From Center Court take Back Bay Arcade to the Copley Bridge, a covered walkway leading over Huntingdon Avenue into Copley Place indoor shopping centre. Walk straight through on the first level, past the indoor waterfall, then just past the staircase go left down an escalator and cross the covered walkway over the road into the Westin Hotel lobby, at the far end of which take the escalator down to emerge into **Copley Square►►**. On its west side is the supremely dignified Renaissance Revival **Boston Public Library►►►** (1894), the first public lending library in the world, while on the north side the **New Old South Church** (1875), with its flamboyant exterior inspired by the North Italian Gothic style, can be admired. Physically the square is dominated by the huge skyscraper slab of the **John Hancock Tower and Observatory►►►**, with its viewpoint 60 storeys up (see page 70). Its glass reflects the magnificent nearby **Trinity Church►►►** (1877), the neo-Romanesque masterpiece of H H Richardson, with its sumptuously ornate interior which includes work by John LaFarge, William Morris and Edward Burne-Jones.

63

JOHN HANCOCK OBSERVATORY

The best place to see Boston

Beacon Hill

See map on pages 48–9 (green route).

This walk explores Beacon Hill's tight network of narrow residential streets ranged on a sloping site. The neighbourhood is a fascinating early 19th-century mixture of patrician and artisan homes. Intricate iron balconies, crisply proportioned brick façades and carefully preserved front doors are much in evidence. Portrait artist John Singleton Copley sold land here to the Mount Vernon Proprietors, who included the great architect,

Harrison Gray Otis House, built in post-Revolutionary 'Federal' style. A plain façade hides a supremely elegant interior

Charles Bulfinch, and the lawyer and orator, Harrison Gray Otis. Here and there you can see some of the original purple window glass imported from Hamburg in the 1820s which discoloured because of the presence of manganese oxide in the material. Another Beacon Hill quirk is that the gas lamps stay on all day.

Start from the north-east corner of the **Public Garden▶▶** (page 73) at the crossing of Charles Street and Beacon Street. Walk along Beacon Street eastwards. Number 45, built in 1805, was the last of three houses on 'the Hill' built for Harrison Gray Otis by

Charles Bulfinch. At number 33 lived George Parkman, the Harvard undergraduate who in 1849 ended up in several pieces in the laboratory of a Harvard professor of medicine; the sensational trial was the major scandal of Beacon Hill.

Opposite the **State House▶▶** (see page 73), the **Robert Gould Shaw and 54th Regiment Memorial** acknowledges the role played by the first black regiment in the Civil War. Shaw, himself white, lived at 44 Beacon Street and led his regiment from here. This is the start of the Black Heritage Trail (see page 66)

Turn left into Bowdoin Street. The column by the State House marks the site of the beacon which was erected here to warn the Puritans of Indians and foreign invasion and which gave the hill its name. The district was later to become a rough-and-ready jumble of disreputable bars and brothels, popularly known as 'Mount Whoredom'.

Turn left into Derne Street. From Hancock Street on the right, you can walk down to Cambridge Street and the first **Harrison Gray Otis House▶** (see page 68). If not visiting the house, continue instead along Derne Street and turn right into Joy Street, off which is Smith Court. The **African Meeting House** here is the oldest black church building still standing in the US and the birthplace of the anti-slavery movement, where William Lloyd Garrison and 12 others founded the New England Anti-Slavery Society. It houses the Museum of Afro American History. **Smith Court Residences** were typical homes of Beacon Hill's free black community who worked as servants in the 19th century.

Return along Joy Street and turn right into Pinckney Street, which was originally built to house service workers. Author Louisa May Alcott's family lived at **number 20**. **Number 24** (the 'house of Odd Windows') was converted by a relative of Ralph Waldo Emerson from a stable into a townhouse, while number 54 was the home of Nathaniel Hawthorne while working at Boston's custom house.

Detour right into Anderson Street and right again into **Revere Street**,

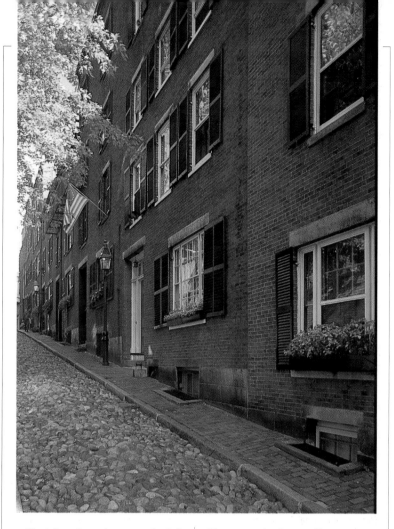

The more modest houses of lanes such as Acorn Street were built as servants' quarters

and look for a tiny entrance on the left between numbers 25 and 29. The house with columns at the end is a false façade, with a sheer drop behind.

Retrace your steps via Anderson Street to **Louisburg Square**, laid out in 1834–44 by Bulfinch. Louisa May Alcott spent her last two years here at number 10. America's oldest home-owners' association maintains the square itself.

Mount Vernon Street►►, on the south side of the square, is one of Boston's finest architectural pieces: Henry James called it 'the only respectable street in America'. Bulfinch's second Harrison Gray Otis house (1800) is at number 85, while the **Nichols House Museum►** at

number 55 (*Open* May–Oct, Tue–Sat 12–4.15; closed Jan, and Tue, Thu, Fri and Sun in winter), provides another opportunity to see a Bulfinch interior.

Follow Walnut Street into Chestnut Street, where abolitionist poet Julia Ward Howe resided at **number 13** in 1862 and penned *The Battle Hymn of the Republic*. Turn right into Willow Street and left into **Acorn Street►**, picturesquely cobbled and perhaps the city's most famous, although certainly not its grandest, residential street. Finish by exploring the shops and restaurants of **Charles Street**.

Boston Beer's award-winning brew

AFRICAN AMERICAN HERITAGE
The African Meeting House, 8 Smith Court, houses the Museum of African American History. The nearby Abiel Smith School, 46 Joy Street, tel: 617/742 5415, is home to the Boston African American National Historic Site and offers free guided tours of the Black Heritage Trail. Alternatively, the trail can be taken as a self-guided tour with a brochure available from the same organisation or from any tourist information point.

BOSTONIAN TERMS
The Black Maria was named after Maria Lee, who owned a disreputable hotel patronised by drunks and criminals. Police made frequent calls and took the offenders into the station by a 'paddy wagon', later renamed a 'Black Maria' to avoid disparaging the Irish population.

The term 'gerry-mandering' originated with Governor Elbridge Gerry, vice-president under James Madison, who re-apportioned electoral boundaries for his own advantage.

►►► Aquarium

See New England Aquarium, page 72.

►►   Boston Athenaeum   48C3

10½ Beacon Street
Open: year round, Mon 9–8, Tue–Fri 9–5.30; Sep–May, Sat 9–4; free tours Tue and Thu, 3pm with 24 hours' notice, tel: 617/227 0270. Subway: Park Street (Red and Green Lines).
Originating in 1807, this private library became the preserve of wealthy Boston intellectuals. In 1845 the Athenaeum moved into this Italian palazzo-style building. Classical statuary and choice paintings set a rarefied atmosphere. On the top floor the high-ceilinged Reading Room of 1915 has seven pairs of recessed bays looking over the Old Granary Burial Ground, while the Oval Room contains books from George Washington's library.

►►► Boston Public Library   48B2

Copley Square
Open: year round, Mon–Thu 9–9, Fri and Sat 2–6; Oct–May, Sun 2–6. Subway: Copley (Green Line)
A true palace of literature: when Charles Follen McKim's vast Renaissance-style edifice opened in 1895, it was America's first public library. Seemingly, no expense was spared: beyond the bronze reliefs on the entrance doors designed by Daniel Chester French – depicting female personifications of Music, Poetry, Wisdom, Knowledge, Truth and Romance – the sumptuous marble foyer is revealed, its grand staircases guarded by lions sculpted by Louis Saint-Gaudens. Seek out the colonnaded courtyard, the murals by John Singer Sargent, the huge reading room and the dioramas by Albert Wiggin of printmakers at work.

► Boston Tea Party Ship and Museum   49E2

Congress Street Bridge (adjacent to Children's and Computer Museums)
Open: daily, except 1 Dec–1 Mar. Bus: Courtesy shuttle bus from Quincy Market, at corner of State and Congress streets, in summer.
The ship moored here is a faithful replica of the brig *Beaver II*, one of the ships boarded in the Boston Tea Party protest (see page 33). You can put on quasi-Indian feather headgear and dunk a tea chest in the river, sample a cup of cold tea and visit the small museum. It is very much an audience-participation venture: you are summoned to attend a 'town meeting' such as happened (more or less) at the Old South Meeting House in 1773.

►►► Charlestown Navy Yard   49D5

Open: daily. Admission: free. Subway: North Station (Green Line), then a 10–15 minute walk; or bus 93 from Haymarket Station (Green Line); or MBTA Water Shuttle from Long Wharf by Aquarium Station (Blue Line). Trolley tours pass the Navy Yard.

Charlestown Navy Yard served the United States Navy from 1800 until 1974. Some 30 acres of the yard now form part of Boston National Historical Park. It has very much the atmosphere of a shipyard, and visitors may enter only a few buildings. Tours are at 11am during weekends and also at 2pm on summer weekdays. The Visitor Center gives out informative leaflets.

Restored to its full-masted glory, the frigate **USS Constitution**▶▶, the most famous of all the historic American warships, was built near by in 1797 and served in three wars. In the War of 1812, British cannon-balls bounced off the vessel, earning her the nickname of 'Old Ironsides', as she captured two sloops-of-war and sank two frigates. Maritime history is brought to life in the **USS Constitution Museum**▶▶, adjacent, for which there is an entrance fee (*Open* daily from 10). The museum displays paintings, models, and documents, as well as a number of interesting hands-on exhibits where you can try the ship's wheel or raise the sail. The **USS Cassin Young**▶ is a World War II destroyer that was hit by kamikaze raids at Okinawa. The **Commandant's House** (*Open* Mar–Oct, 1–4) is a Federal-style building that was once the home of the commanding officers of the Navy Yard from 1805 to 1976; the interior has been preserved as it was when it was last occupied. The **Boston Marine Society** (*Open* 10–3) is situated next to the prominent octagonal Muster House of 1852 and has three rooms filled with good nautical exhibits, including examples of model ships and paintings of maritime scenes.

Also in the Navy Yard site, the Bunker Hill Pavillion (*Open* Apr–Nov) has a 30-minute multimedia show *Whites of their Eyes*, plunging you into the Battle of Bunker Hill through costumed mannequins 'acting' the part.

CHANGING TIMES
More than 160 ships were built in Charlestown Navy Yard. Over the years numerous buildings have been added, including boiler-maker shops, a marine railway, New England's first granite dry dock and America's last surviving ropewalk. The yard expanded in the Civil War, and in World War II employed nearly 50,000 people. From the 1960s it specialised in the modernisation and overhaul of old vessels.

67

SUMMER SALUTE
The *USS Constitution* traditionally takes part in the annual Harborfest celebration and enters Boston Harbor on 4 July to fire a national salute, a role resumed in 1996 after dry-dock restoration. Throughout the rest of the year, cannon firing takes place daily at sunset, when the flag is lowered.

Below: USS Cassin Young *in the Navy Yard, Charlestown*

Boston

Having fun on the giant keyboard of the Computer Museum's walk-through computer

COMPUTER DINOSAURS
Some of the most fascinating exhibits in the Computer Museum are the machines of the past.
● In 1970 the first robot capable of reasoning about its actions was created: one drawback – it took half an hour to make a movement.
● A 1930s vision of the 1960s saw the future as an age when safe driving distance would be measured by radio control.
● On show is UNIVAC I, the first computer bought by a business in the US.

THE FOUNDER OF CHRISTIAN SCIENCE MOVEMENT
The First Church of Christ, Scientist was founded in Boston in 1879 by Mary Baker Eddy. Born in 1821 into a strict Calvinist family in Bow, New Hampshire, Mary became convinced of the power of prayer in healing after making a sudden recovery from a serious fall. She began to teach spiritual healing and in 1875 published her principal work, *Science and Health*. In 1908, aged 87, she founded the daily newspaper, the *Christian Science Monitor*. Published internationally by the Christian Science Publishing Society, it is relatively independent of the Church and is highly regarded.

▶▶▶ Children's Museum
49E2

300 Congress Street
Open: 10–5pm, plus Fri 5–9pm, when the entrance fee is reduced; closed Mon outside school vacations.
Subway: South Station (Red Line).
Adults will wish they were kids again when they see this interactive museum, one of the oldest and best of its kind anywhere. Venture aboard Boats Afloat, shop at the Super Mercado, look in at the Grand-parents' House, visit a Japanese home, play on a giant's desktop, climb a two-storey maze – and more.

▶▶ Christian Science Center and Mapparium
48A1

See page 63 and panel on this page.

▶▶ Computer Museum
49E2

300 Congress Street
Open: summer, daily 10–6; winter, Tue–Sun 10–5; closed Mon except school holidays. Admission: half-price Sun after 3pm.
Subway: South Station (Red Line).
The world's premier computer museum makes an excellent half-day visit for buffs and novices alike. On show are a gigantic walk-through mock-up of a computer, displays of robots and computers through the ages and over 160 hands-on exhibits illustrating the uses and impact of computers and computer networks.

▶▶▶ Faneuil Hall Marketplace
49D3

See page 59.

▶ Federal Reserve Bank Tours
See panel on page 53.

▶ Fenway Park Tours
See panel on page 53.

▶ FleetCenter Tours
48C4

Causeway Street (tel: 617/227 3200)
Open: daily, 10–4, year round.
Subway: North Station (Green and Orange Lines).
The Fleet Center is home to a branch of the Sports Museum of New England (see panel, page 171). Behind-the-scenes tours of Boston's state-of-the-art sports complex begin with a nostalgic look-back to the days when the home of the Celtics and the Bruins was next-door Boston Garden. Tours daily, 10–4 (tel: 617/624 1518).

▶ Harrison Gray Otis House
48C4

141 Cambridge Street
Open: Wed–Sun; last tour 4pm.
Subway: Bowdoin (Blue Line) or Charles Street (Red Line).
Dating from 1796, this fine Federal house was the first of three built on Beacon Hill for Harrison Gray and Sally Foster Otis. It houses the Society for the Preservation of New England (SPNEA).

▶▶▶ Isabella Stewart Gardner Museum   48A1

280 The Fenway
Open: Tue–Sun 11–5.
Subway: Museum (Green Line).
This magnificent museum is the creation of Isabella Stewart Gardner, the heiress of a wealthy New York family. The exterior of the building gives little hint of what lies within – a Venetian-style *palazzo* crammed with priceless art treasures and ranged around an exquisite four-storey courtyard in which architectural fragments are surrounded by ferns and flowers in season. Each room has a theme and is arranged as Mrs Gardner left it, giving an outstanding collection an appealing air of intimacy. As well as numerous works of art by Italian Renaissance artists, Dutch and Flemish masters and French Impressionists, there are ancient Egyptian artefacts, sculptures, ceramics, tapestries, a lace collection and furniture.

Concerts are held in the Tapestry Room on Saturdays and Sundays between September and May at 1:30pm (tel: 617/734 1359) and there is an excellent small café.

▶ John F Kennedy Library, New Museum   48C1

220 Morrissey Boulevard, Columbia Point
Open: daily 9–5.
Subway: JFK/UMass (Red Line) for free shuttle bus every 20 minutes, 9am–5pm.
This striking building, designed by IM Pei and scenically sited on the waterfront in the southern neighbourhood of Dorchester, is the nation's memorial to JFK. In the New Museum at the JFK Library the Kennedy era is re-created with replicas of the White House Oval Office, historical documents and films on JFK's life.
See panel for the adjacent **Commonwealth Museum**.

A STRONG CHARACTER
Isabella Stewart Gardner was the talk of the Back Bay. She wore diamonds in her hair and raised a few eyebrows by posing for her artist friend John Singer Sargent. Once she hired a boxer to perform at a ladies' tea party. She slept late in early-rise Boston. After her son died at the age of two, she suffered depression and took a trip to Europe. She returned to Boston a new woman; her Back Bay home became a fashionable salon, where she held glittering galas and balls, and she devoted much of her time to collecting art.

69

COMMONWEALTH MUSEUM
Next door to the JFK Library, this covers everything to do with the Commonwealth of Massachusetts. Changing and permanent exhibits feature Native Americans, immigrants, towns and cities, the political system, natural history and labour history (*Open* Mon–Fri 9–5, Sat 9–3. *Admission* free).

The splendid courtyard of the Isabella Stewart Gardner Museum, with its fountains, statues and flowers

Night-time view of the John Hancock Tower, an excellent observation point

LOCAL FINE ARTS

New England is well represented at the Museum of Fine Arts in the sections devoted to furniture. Among the pieces on show are a late-17th-century press cupboard from Wethersfield, Connecticut, with pillars painted black to resemble ebony, and two fine Newport chests of the mid-18th century. Silverware on display includes items by Paul Revere, and many of the museum's 19th-century pictures have a New England theme, such as Frederick Childe Hassam's Boston *Common at Twilight* and Winslow Homer's *Look-out – 'all's well'*.

▶▶▶ John Hancock Tower and Observatory
48B2

200 Clarendon Street (Copley Square)
Subway: Copley (Green Line) or Back Bay (Orange Line).
Boston's tallest building (built 1968–76), is a striking 60-storey slab of reflective glass designed by IM Pei and neatly reflecting adjacent Trinity Church. It suffered numerous teething problems just after completion when window panes repeatedly fell out and landed on the street below. On the top floor the Hancock Observatory offers, like the nearby Prudential Tower, superb panoramic views over Boston and the bay, to the highlands of Massachusetts, Vermont and New Hampshire (*Open* Mon–Sat 9am–10pm, Sun 12–10pm). You can see out of three sides only, but a recorded narration describes the view from one side and gives a general survey of the city's history. A model of Boston in 1775 is accompanied by a voice-over describing the events of that year and you can also listen in on the radio communication between Logan air traffic controllers and pilots landing and taking off.

▶▶▶ Museum of Fine Arts
48A1

465 Huntington Avenue
Open: Tue, Thu, Sat 10–4.45; Wed 10–9.45; Sun10–4.45. 'Pay as you wish' Wed 4–9.45. Subway: Museum (Green Line) or Ruggles (Orange Line).
New England's largest art gallery, often referred to as the MFA, is particularly noted for its Asian collection, of world-wide importance, and its European paintings.

Most of the ground floor is devoted to a wide-ranging selection of American paintings, furniture and decorative arts. The museum has an unrivalled collection of John Singleton Copley portraits, including John Hancock,

Samuel Adams and Paul Revere, in addition to his famous work *Watson and the Shark*. The Hudson River School landscape painters Albert Bierstadt, Fitz Hugh Lane and Thomas Cole, the American Impressionists Childe Hassam, Winslow Homer, Mary Cassatt and James McNeill Whistler, and New York's Abstract Expressionists are also well represented. A series of re-created period rooms provides a good insight into daily life in New England from the 17th to the 19th centuries. For other local themes, see panel on page 70.

Also on the ground floor is the largest collection of Japanese woodblock prints in the world, and some fine Indian miniatures and Islamic ceramics. The Nubian collection includes pottery, sculpture and fragments of furniture found in tombs and temples. Egyptian pieces include statues of King Mycerinus and Queen Khamerer-ebty II. The rooms devoted to ancient Greece have some fine red-figure vases and the Bartlett *Aphrodite*, while among the Roman treasures are frescoes from a house in Pompeii.

The bulk of the Chinese and Japanese collection is upstairs, as is European art. Among the high-lights here are J M W Turner's *Slave Ship* and Constable's *Stour Valley and Dedham Church*. An outstanding selection of French masters features works by Manet, Degas, Gauguin, Van Gogh, Renoir, Cezanne and Monet. The Firestone Silver Collection features pre-1789 French silver – rare items that escaped being melted down during the French Revolution.

▶▶▶ Museum of Science

48B5

Charles River Dam
Open: daily 9–5; Fri 9–9; school summer
vacations daily 9–7, Fri 9–9). Subway:
Science Park (Green Line).

One of the great science museums of the world, this has more than anyone could see in a single day. With over 450 interactive exhibits, it is a real hit with the children. At the **Theater of Electricity** you can watch high-voltage lightning sparks produced by the world's largest Van de Graaff generator. The **Observatory** delves into the unseen, including microscopic life and ultrasonic sounds, while **Earthworks** re-creates the process of gems growing beneath the Earth's surface. **Frontiers of Biotechnology** has interactive computers providing an introduction to genetics.

Two further attractions in the museum require separate admission; booking is strongly advised (tel: 617/723 2500). The **Charles Hayden Planetarium** gives tours of the New England skies and offers an intergalactic journey on its multi-media 'starship', as well as laser shows. The **Mugar Omni Theatre** has a wrap-around domed screen, 76 feet in diameter and as tall as a four-storey building. State-of-the-art projection and 84 speakers make it a far cry from the movie houses of the past.

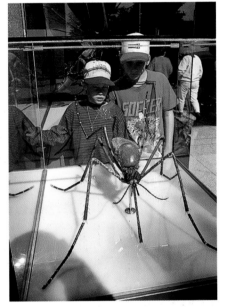

71

Explore the many faces of the world of nature at the Museum of Science

SPEAKING FOR FREEDOM

In Park Street Church in 1831, William Lloyd Garrison made his first anti-slavery speech, a landmark in the history of the abolitionist movement. From a cramped office in Washington Street he published the *Liberator*, an anti-slavery newspaper. His views incensed Brahmins and southerners alike and, after speaking for abolition in 1835, he was attacked by an angry mob. He sought refuge in the State House (then the city hall), and the mayor put him into the safety of a jail. The cause gathered support as slaves were smuggled to freedom through the so-called 'Underground Railroad'.

CHARLES BULFINCH (1763–1844)

America's first professional architect, Bulfinch was called on after independence to give Boston – with its wooden houses concentrated in narrow streets around the waterfront – an image better suited to its role as one of the world's most prosperous seaports. With resplendent public buildings such as the State House and a revamped Faneuil Hall, a dozen churches (only St Stephens, in the North End, still stands) and the development of Beacon Hill as an elegant residential area, Bulfinch radically changed the city's character. He then moved on to design the new Capitol in Washington, DC.

Whale watching with the New England Aquarium

▶▶▶ New England Aquarium 49E3

Central Wharf
Open: Jul–Labor Day, Mon, Tue, and Fri 9–6, Wed, and Thu 9–8, weekends and holidays 9–7; winter, Mon–Fri 9–5, weekends and holidays 9–6.
Subway: Aquarium (Blue Line).

A spectacular encounter with the underwater world. In 1998 the Aquarium acquired a new West Wing, with its exhibit Coastal Rhythms showing the marine and bird life of the coasts from New England shores to jungle lagoons. In the main gallery, you walk past a window onto the Aquarium Medical Center, where stranded sea creatures are treated. On the way up to the top of the ramp you will learn why fishes come in such a range of colours, shapes and patterns; you then spiral down beside a four-storey cylindrical water tank, with fish of every size – sharks among them – swimming around a replica coral reef.

Try to time your visit with a sea-lion show aboard the museum vessel *Discovery*. The Aquarium also runs whale-watching cruises and educational 'Science at Sea' tours on *Doc Edgerton*; for information, call 617/973 5281.

▶ Old South Meeting House 49D3
See page 58, and panel opposite.

▶ Old State House 49D3
See pages 58–9.

▶ Paul Revere House 49D4
See page 60.

▶▶▶ Prudential Center Skywalk 48A1
Prudential Tower, Prudential Center
Open: daily until 10pm.
Subway: Prudential (Green Line, E train).

Although scarcely Boston's best-loved building, the prominent Prudential Tower offers a superb view of the city from its Skywalk (50th) floor, 700 feet above the streets. On a really clear day, the 360° panorama stretches to the Berkshire Hills and to high points in New Hampshire and Vermont. As you walk around the gallery, various interactive displays and sound recordings highlight significant events and personalities from Boston's history. Both the Prudential and the John Hancock Tower are on the Back Bay walk (see pages 62–3).

▶▶ **Public Garden**　　　　　　　　　48B2

Subway: Arlington (Green Line).
Well-fed squirrels and pigeons populate this charming park, graced with statues and some 350 varieties of trees. Since 1877 pedal-powered swan boats have conveyed summer visitors across the pond, past weeping willows and beneath a scaled-down replica of the suspension bridge. Look for the bronze statuettes of a duck and eight ducklings, modelled on the heroes of Robert McCloskey's children's story, *Make Way for Ducklings*.

▶▶ **State House**　　　　　　　　　　48C3

Beacon Street
Open: Mon–Fri 10-4; free guided tour.
Subway: Park Street (Red and Green Lines).
Prominently sited at the top of the Common, the State House is the seat of government for the Commonwealth of Massachusetts. Road distances are traditionally measured from the gold-leaf dome. The State House was originally designed by Charles Bulfinch. Subsequently extended, the building has a rich marble interior. The entrance is through the **Doric Hall**. It leads to the **Nurses Hall**, hung with a trio of paintings by Robert Reid (*Paul Revere's Ride*, *James Otis Arguing Against the Writs of Assistance* and *The Boston Tea Party*), and into the circular Hall of Flags and main staircase. The **House of Representatives** contains the Sacred Cod, a wooden fish carving that is the symbol of Massachusetts. The **Senate Chamber** and **Governor's Office** are part of the original building by Bulfinch.

▶▶▶ **Trinity Church**　　　　　　　　48B2
See page 63.

▶▶ **USS *Constitution* Museum**　　　48C3
See page 67.

One of the famous and perennially popular swan boats in Boston Garden

73

MEETING-HOUSES AND CHURCHES
Old South Meeting House, with its Wren-inspired brick façade dating to 1729, replaced an earlier wooden meeting-house, built by Puritan settlers. These early colonists built their churches in the plain, square, meeting-house style, with a wooden spire or cupola and, inside, wooden panelling, box pews and galleries supported on wooden columns. Reflecting the unity of Church and State, the meeting-house often also served as town hall. It was not until the 19th century that new churches were built in such European-inspired styles as Gothic or Romanesque Revival.

HARVARD'S EARLY DAYS
In 1636 the Massachusetts Bay Colony allocated £400 to establish a college, originally for 40 students, to foster the Puritan ethic and to educate potential ministers. In the 18th century an endowment of £799 appeared. However, the headmaster stole half the money and fled.

Japanese print at the Arthur M Sackler Museum

Cambridge

Cambridge lies just across the Charles River from Boston, a short walk over the Harvard Bridge from the Back Bay. Yet it is a separate city – a commercial centre as well as a famous seat of learning centred on Harvard University and the Massachusetts Institute of Technology (MIT). At night, Harvard Square comes alive with buskers and bustle. It is the busy atmosphere and the shopping, dining and nightlife facilities rather than the physical appearance of Cambridge that attract visitors.

Cambridge was founded in 1630 as Newtowne and became the capital of the Bay Colony, being chosen for its protected site away from the exposed Boston peninsula. Harvard University was founded in 1636, and two years later Newtowne was renamed Cambridge after the English seat of learning. Following the battles of Concord and Lexington in 1775, provincial militias grouped on Cambridge Common to form the new Continental Army under the command of George Washington. Today Harvard University is one of the preeminent Ivy League establishments in the country (see pages 22–3).

The Massachusetts Institute of Technology was founded in 1861 as a 'society of arts, a museum of arts and a school of industrial science'. For the visitor it is of chief interest for its modern architecture and sculpture. In particular seek out two buildings by Eero Saarinen: the Chapel, which reveals a dramatic interior sparkling with dots of reflected light, and the Kresge Auditorium, with an eighth of a sphere forming a triangular shell over the rest of the structure.

▶▶ Harvard University Museums 74C2/3

The **Fogg Art Museum▶▶** and the **Busch-Reisinger Museum▶▶**, at 32 Quincy Street, are two museums in one, housing one of the most important and extensive art collections in the world (*Open* Mon–Sat 10–5, Sun 1–5; free on Sat 10–12). The Fogg covers art from western Europe and the US, featuring Italian Renaissance works by Simone Martini and Filippo Lippi, paintings by Dutch and Flemish masters and such 19th-century Americans as Homer, Whistler and Sargent; French Impressionists and Pre-Raphaelites are also represented. The Busch-Reisinger concentrates on art from northern Europe and Scandinavia, with Bauhaus artefacts and Expressionist paintings.

The **Arthur M Sackler Museum▶**, at 485 Broadway Street, is housed in an innovative, if controversial, candy-striped building by James Stirling known as 'Stirling's Zebra'. It contains beautiful and rare items from Asia and the ancient world, including Greek Attic vessels, carvings of deities, Indian and Persian miniatures, and the world's finest collection of Chinese jade.

Entrances to the Harvard University **Museums of Natural History** and **Peabody Museum▶** are at 24 Oxford Street and 11 Divinity Avenue (*Open* daily 9–4.30, Sun 1–4.30). Admission covers the four museums in this building. Much of it is the preserve of the specialist researcher, but the public mostly comes to see the unqique collection of glass flowers in the Botanical Museum, more than 700 items in all, representing giant cross-sections, roots, rotting pears and insects (see panel). A 30-minute tape tour guides you to the highlights. The other museums are devoted to zoology, including fossils, dinosaurs and the world's largest collection of spiders; archaeology and ethnology, and geology, with an attractive stone and gem collection. The Peabody includes a host of ethnological artefacts, including the Hall of the American Indian.

▶▶ Longfellow House 74A3

Henry Longfellow was 30 years old when he first saw this 1759 yellow clapboard mansion at 105 Brattle Street (*Open* Wed–Sun 10–4.30; for winter opening times, call 617/876 4492), and felt like a 'prince in a villa' just to lodge here. It was bought for him and his wife as a wedding present from his father-in-law; the couple enjoyed a happy marriage and had six children. Here he completed his translation of Dante, and penned *The Song of Hiawatha*, *Paul Revere's Ride* and *Evangeline*. Here he entertained Dickens, Twain, Emerson, Hawthorne and Wilde. Longfellow died here after living in the house for 45 years. His personal artefacts abound: there is his crowded study, with a book collection reflecting a passion for knowledge; a Steinway piano around which he enjoyed singing German *Lieder*, and the chair made from the 'spreading chestnut tree'. The house was one of several in Brattle Street built by wealthy Tories before the Revolution. During the siege of Boston George Washington made the building his headquarters.

HARVARD'S GLASS FLOWERS
George Lincoln Goodall, the first director of Harvard's Botanical Museum, wanted three-dimensional plant models for teaching purposes. He travelled to Dresden in 1886 to visit Leopold and Rudolf Blashka, father and son, who were specialists in supplying museums with glass sea creatures. In this way he established a year-round laboratory for scientific study. The final models were created by Rudolf to illustrate plant diseases.

75

Longfellow House, home to the poet from 1837 to 1882

JUST DESERTS?
Millionaire newspaper tycoon William Randolf Hearst achieved notoriety in his student days at Harvard, where he kept a pet alligator and gave personalised chamber pots to his instructors before being expelled. Similar gratitude was shown in 1764 when a student took a book from the library of Massachusetts Hall on the eve of its burning. On returning the volume he was thanked by President Holyoke, and then expelled for taking the book without permission.

The nation's oldest university, Harvard has become the wealthiest, too

Harvard and Cambridge highlights

See map on page 74 (yellow route).

This is a tour of Harvard University and historic Cambridge, encompassing the Common and the former home of the poet Henry Wadsworth Longfellow.

From Harvard Square Red Line subway station, walk north along Massachusetts Avenue to Johnson Gate, which gives access to **Harvard Yard**, the hub of the university. The first quadrangle, **Old Yard**, contains dormitories for freshmen and the oldest campus buildings; it was here that Washington gathered his troops against the British. To the left as you enter is **Harvard Hall**, a 1764 reconstruction of the original building endowed by John Harvard and

destroyed by fire. Adjacent is **Hollis Hall** (1762), whose students included Emerson and Thoreau. Dents in the steps in front of the hall were reputedly caused by the student

Leafy Harvard Yard

practice of placing cannonballs in fireplaces to radiate heat, and throwing them out in spring! On the right is **Massachusetts Hall** (1718), the oldest building of all, which numbers John and Samuel Adams among its luminaries.

In the centre of Old Yard the **John Harvard Statue** (1885), known as the 'Statue of Three Lies', is not quite what it seems. A student, not Harvard, was the model, and the inscription 'John Harvard, Founder, 1638' errs on two counts: Harvard was the benefactor, not the founder, and the university was founded in 1636.

Beyond **University Hall** (1816), designed by Charles Bulfinch, is **New Yard**, a quadrangle formed by Memorial Church (1931), Sever Hall (1880) and the **Harry Elkins Widener Library** (1913). The latter is the largest university library in the world and was endowed by the mother of Harry Widener, an avid collector of antiquarian books who perished aboard the *Titanic*. True to his mother's wishes, the building has been unaltered, and for a time all applicants were required to undertake a swimming test (Harry could not swim).

Memorial Church is dedicated to Harvard men who died in the two World Wars.

Leave the Yard and enter Quincy Street, opposite the concrete and glass **Carpenter Center for Visual Arts** (1963), the only building in the US designed by Le Corbusier. Turn left. Continue past the Fogg and Sackler museums to Cambridge Street. Cross to the other side and go left, past the

cathedral-like **Memorial Hall** (1874), built to honour all the Harvard men killed in the Civil War.

Carry straight on; cross Massachusetts Avenue at the traffic lights, then cross **Cambridge Common**, passing the war memorial. The Common formerly functioned as the focus for Cambridge's religious, social and political life. Three captured British cannons stand on the grass close to where Washington took command of the 9,000 men who had gathered to form the Continental Army. Washington's Elm (not the original tree) marks the spot.

Cross Garden Street by the traffic lights. To the left the **Old Burying Ground** contains the graves of the first eight Harvard presidents, and **Christ Church** (1761) was used as a patriot barracks after its staunchly Tory Anglican congregation fled before the Revolution – its organ pipes were pilfered for use as bullets.

Turn right along Garden Street, then left through the gate into **Radcliffe College**, which was founded as the Society for the Collegiate Instruction of Women in 1879, when Fay House (1807) was acquired. The college was incorporated into Harvard in 1894. Leaving Radcliffe, turn right along Brattle Street, known in the 18th century as Tory Row because of the British patriotism of its residents, as far as the **Longfellow House** (1759), described on page 75. Returning along Brattle Street, do not miss number 56, the home of Dexter Pratt, who was immortalised by Longfellow in *The Village Blacksmith* ('a mighty man is he, with large and sinewy hands'); the 'spreading chestnut tree' is no longer there.

Above: there's always entertainment in Harvard Square, whether it's eating out, listening to buskers – or watching a game of chess

Accommodation

The upmarket Lenox Hotel on Boylston Street

CITY FREEBIES
● Concerts at the Hatch Shell in summer.
● New England Conservatory concerts, some of which are held in the resplendent Jordan Hall (tel: 617/262 1120).
● Faneuil Hall Marketplace street entertainers and Faneuil Hall itself.
● Commonwealth Museum.
● Massachusetts State House.
● Ranger-led walking tour along the Freedom Trail.
● The Public Garden.
● The Harvard University Museums are free 10–12 Saturdays.
● Charlestown Navy Yard, including USS *Constitution* and USS *Cassin Young*.
● Christian Science Church and Mapparium.
● Tours of the Boston Athenaeum and Boston Public Library.

A visitor centre will help with finding accommodation

Accommodation

HOTELS Boston has world-class hotels right in the heart of the city. The principal hotel area begins at the Theatre District and extends westwards past the Prudential Tower towards Massachusetts Avenue. Although some of the larger streets in this area are visually uninspiring, by staying around here you are within easy walking distance of Copley Square and the start of the Freedom Trail at Boston Common. Other convenient hotels are found in the downtown and waterfront areas, and in Cambridge.

Boston is more expensive to stay in than is rural New England. At certain periods, especially during major conventions, it can be difficult to find a room, and rates are at a premium. At times like this, consider staying out of town and visiting Boston daily by public transport, for example from Salem or Concord (MA) using MBTA Commuter Rail – see 'Canny Planning', page 259. Weekends are less busy than weekdays, and accordingly rates tend to be lower. Since the converse applies in summer resorts such as the North Shore, Cape Cod and the islands, you can make substantial savings by visiting Boston at the weekend and making for the coast during the week. As elsewhere in the US, hotel rates do not usually include breakfast, and state and local room tax are added to the room charge.

BED AND BREAKFAST If hotels are too expensive, bed-and-breakfast (B&B) accommodation is a money-saving option. Several agencies organise hosted B&B accommodation, where you stay in someone's home. The most charming and convenient locations include the Back Bay, Beacon Hill and the North End. See page 268.

You may be able to find less expensive places by opting to stay further out from the city centre. The subway and rail systems take you to most further-flung locations, such as the suburb of Brookline, south-west of central Boston, which has numerous inexpensive bed and breakfasts. For those on a tight budget, the Boston International AYH Hostel (for address and telephone number see page 268) near the Prudential Center has dormitory accommodation; non-members can join on the spot.

Boston has a reputation as the most musical city in the United States, a reputation that rests almost entirely on its being the home of one of the finest ensembles in the world: the Boston Symphony Orchestra.

In October 1881 the BSO, or Boston Symphony Orchestra, gave its first concert, bringing to reality the dreams of the philanthropist and amateur musician Henry Lee Higginson of founding a permanent orchestra in his home town. For the first 20 years or so concerts were given in the Old Boston Music Hall, initially under the directorship of Georg Henschel and then under a series of German and French conductors.

In 1900 the orchestra moved into Symphony Hall, which to this day remains one of the world's most acoustically perfect venues. Symphony Hall also became the venue for the orchestra's hugely successful 'Promenade concerts,' which had begun in 1885, fulfilling Higginson's ambition to provide a 'lighter kind of music' in addition to more serious programmes. Later called 'Popular Concerts' and then 'Pops', these have remained a favourite springtime tradition under the auspices of the Boston Pops Orchestra.

The Koussevitzky era In 1924 the Russian-born Serge Koussevitzky, a man of extraordinary talent and dynamic personality, took over as musical director of the BSO. During his 25-years' illustrious leadership, the orchestra began regular radio broadcasts. Arthur Fiedler initiated the free Boston Pops Esplanade concerts that are still given in summer beside the Charles River, while from 1937 onwards the BSO took up a summer residency at Tanglewood, in the Berkshires (see panel, page 146).

'The aristocrat of orchestras' Charles Munch followed Koussevitzky in 1949, introducing American audiences to quantities of French music. In the 1960s, promoted under Erich Leinsdorf as 'the aristocrat of orchestras', the BSO made numerous recordings and tours all over the world.

With Seiji Ozawa as musical director since 1973, Higginson's 'great and permanent orchestra' has consolidated its worldwide reputation, commissioning new works from composers such as Hans Werner Henze and John Cage, and presenting soloists of the highest calibre, such as Yo-Yo Ma, Pinchas Zukerman and Itzhak Perlman.

Above and left: John Williams conducts the Boston Pops

CONCERT INFORMATION
The BSO season at Symphony Hall runs from the beginning of October to the end of April. Contact the Subscription Office, Symphony Hall, Boston MA 02115 (tel: 617/266 7575; fax: 617/638 9436). For the Tanglewood Music Festival, contact Symphony Hall, as above, or Tanglewood Ticket Office, Lenox MA 01240 (tel: 413/637 1940). For the Pops (May, June, 4 July and holidays) tel: 617/266 1492 for Symphony Hall or 617/ 266 2378 for concert information.

OPENING NIGHT
When Isabella Stewart Gardner opened her Venetian-style palace (see page 69) on New Year's Night 1903, her guests were entertained in the concert hall by 50 members of the Boston Symphony Orchestra. Afterwards, the doors of the hall were opened and guests had their first view of the ravishing courtyard, filled with flowering plants and lit by lanterns.

79

Boston

'And this is the city of
  Boston,
The land of the bean and
  the cod,
Where the Lowells talk
  only to Cabots,
And the Cabots talk only
  to God.'
– James Collins Bossidy,
toast at Holy Cross Alumni
dinner, 1910.

'I've never seen a Lowell
walk,
Nor heard a Cabot speak
  with God,
But I enjoy good Boston
  talk
And Boston beans and
  Boston cod.'
– R C H Bruce Lockhart, *In
Praise of Boston.*

*Eating al fresco at
Quincy Market against
the backdrop of Faneuil
Hall*

Food and Drink

As the birthplace of the humble baked bean, Boston is
nicknamed 'Beantown'. However, more sophisticated fare
– such as Maine lobsters, quahogs (large clams), chowders
and scrod (white fish) – is much easier to come by.

Faneuil Hall Marketplace is one of the best places to eat
cheaply. Food stalls in Quincy Market offer take-aways in
various forms – calzones, Middle Eastern pastries,
seafood, speciality milkshakes and swordfish kebabs –
but the market starts to close down after 9.30pm.

Options for leisurely meals include restaurants in Beacon
Hill's Charles Street, and in Newbury Street. Chinatown
has some excellent eating-places: some of the best offer bargain prices and with functional décor to match! The North
End can boast some of the highest-quality Italian food in
the Northeast, and although Bostonians as a rule tend to eat
early, it is possible to stop by in the early hours for a cap-
puccino or bowl of pasta. Bargain-priced food stands are
set up in the streets on Friday and Saturday, when you can
take your fill of pasta, battered calamari and mussels. The
Waterfront district also has several popular restaurants.

Cambridge has so much happening in the evening that to
dine out there is part of the Boston experience. A branch of
Au Bon Pain, a Boston-born sandwich bar chain, occupies
one side of Harvard Square. Popular with chess-players,
this is a pleasant point from which to watch Cambridge life
going by. Cambridge is strong on ethnic eateries, with
Portuguese fare along Cambridge and Hampshire streets
and good Korean, Creole and Indian restaurants.

Boston has some excellent beers: the Boston Brewery's
Samuel Adams ale and its variants are probably the best
known. Some pub-restaurants produce their own brew:
the Commonwealth Brewing Company, Cambridge
Brewery and the Boston Beer Works.

Boston means different things to different people. To some it means simply the Red Sox. Add the Celtics, the Bruins and the Boston Marathon and you begin to form a picture of a rich sporting tradition.

The Red Sox The ups and downs of Boston's baseball team are inextricably entwined in the fabric of Boston life. Strong men go misty-eyed at the mention of such legendary names as Babe Ruth, Jimmie Foxx, Carl Yastrzemski, Jim Lonborg, Ted Williams (the last major leaguer to bat over 400 for a season), Dick 'The Monster' Radatz or Roger 'The Rocket' Clemens (both of whom regularly pitched at over 90mph).

The skill of the Fenway Park pros is phenomenal, but to attend a college or local ballpark game, along with the mayor and the cheer leaders, is every bit as thrilling.

The Celtics and the Bruins Basketball was born at the YMCA in Springfield, Massachusetts, in December 1891. The invention of a physical education teacher, Dr James Naismith, to keep his students out of mischief in the winter months, it is the only major sport founded in the US. Naismith originally used two half-bushel peach baskets as targets, hence the name of the game.

Boston is home to the Boston Celtics, who won 11 of 13 titles between 1956/7 and 1968/9, making them one of the most successful teams in the National Basketball Association. If you look into almost any Boston backyard you'll find a group of young Celtics fans in the team's green and white colours emulating a Larry Bird jump shot. The Celtics share the FleetCenter (successor to the venerable Boston Garden, see page 68) with the Bruins, Boston's illustrious ice hockey team.

And more... Other great events in the Boston sporting calendar include the Boston Marathon, held in April. The first was held in 1897 with 15 runners; now over 9,000 take part. July sees the US Pro Tennis Championship and in October about 1,000 boats take part in a day of races in the Head of Charles Regatta.

TICKET INFORMATION
● The Boston Red Sox, Fenway Park, 4 Yawkey Way (tel: 617/267 1700, fax: 617/236 6640). The season runs from April to early October. For tours, tel: 617/236 6666.
● The Boston Celtics and Bruins, FleetCenter, 150 Causeway Street – by North Station (tel: (617/523 3030 for the Celtics and 617/931 2222 for the Bruins). Celtics' season runs from October to May, Bruins' from October to April. See page 68 for FleetCenter Tours which include a Boston Garden Highlights video and memorabilia.
● New England Patriots Football Club, Foxboro Stadium, Route 1, Foxboro (tel: 508/543 1776). The National Football League is in action from August to early January.

Fenway Park, much revered by Red Sox fans. It was built in the 1930s by the team's greatest benefactors, Tom Yawkey and his wife

Above left: the Friday and Saturday Haymarket – lively, lusty and colourful
Above right: altogether quieter, a bookstore near Tremont Street

BARGAIN HUNTING
Outlet shopping in New England is booming. The main places are Kittery, North Conway, Freeport, Fall River and Worcester; the last two of these can easily be reached by bus from Boston (see pages 16–17). However, some contend that the choicest bargains are to be had at sale time at such stores as Saks Fifth Avenue and Lord & Taylor in Boston.

MORE SHOPPING IDEAS
● Music: HMV, 1 Brattle Street, Cambridge; Tower Records, 360 Newbury Street.
● Secondhand books: Brattle Bookstore, 9 West Street, Cambridge (Park station).
● Antique maps: Eugene Galleries, 76 Charles Street.

Shopping

BACK BAY AND BEACON HILL If a competition was held to find New England's most chic shopping street, **Newbury Street** would be among the front runners. Running parallel to Commonwealth Avenue from the Public Garden through the fashionable district of Back Bay, the street has high-class designer shops, art galleries and boutiques (including Déjà Vu, selling used designer-label clothing for women) and makes for highly enjoyable window-shopping; Tower Records, on the corner of Mass. Avenue, is the largest in the US. In Beacon Hill, Charles Street is known for antiques.

The Shops at Prudential Center is a large, smart complex, connected to the Hynes Convention Center, the Sheraton Boston Hotel and, by footbridge, the Copley Place shopping centre and the Westin and Marriott hotels – all under cover. The 75 Shops at the Pru include shops for men, women and children such as Saks Fifth Avenue, Levi's, Chico's, Talbots Kids and Warner Brothers. There are also shoe and sports shops, gift shops and several restaurants. The 100-shop, two-level **Copley Place** is upmarket; here you will find Gucci, Tiffany, a Museum of Fine Arts shop and others. Again, there are restaurants, and a cinema. At 338 Boylston Street, the world's largest teddy bear marks the entrance to **FAO Schwarz**, the city's main toy store. Nearby, and also in Boylston Street, the Globe Corner Bookstore has a variety of New England books and maps.

DOWNTOWN CROSSING AREA There are over 300 retail stores around Summer and Washington streets, including the department stores of Macy's and Filene's; **Filene's Basement** is renowned for its bargain-price clothes. **Barnes and Noble** (395 Washington Street and 607 Boylston Street) is the city's largest discount bookseller.

OTHER BOSTON HIGHLIGHTS Chinatown is great for browsing, with markets, restaurants, gift shops and supermarkets, as well as Vietnamese, Thai and Cambodian stores. **Faneuil Hall Marketplace** is a top attraction, with 125 shops ranging from retailers such as the Disney Store to outlets for New England crafts and souvenir stalls. Its central hall, Quincy Market, offers a variety of places to eat, including Durgin's. By total contrast, the Haymarket is a no-frills fruit and vegetables market (Fridays and Saturdays only). Italian shops in the **North End** include some outstanding food stores and bakeries around Hanover and Salem streets.

The Boston Antique Center, with more than 100 dealers, is near Haymarket subway station at 54 Canal Street.

Good **museum shops** are found at the Children's Museum, Computer Museum, Museum of Fine Arts (also at Copley Place and Faneuil Hall Marketplace), the Peabody Museum in Cambridge (with a worldwide range of ethnic wares) and the Museum of Science.

CAMBRIDGE HARVARD SQUARE has a concentration of bookshops offering new and second-hand volumes. **WordsWorth** offers a wide range of books at discount prices. Bookshops remain open all evening and Sundays, and you are welcome to browse for hours. There are also numerous music shops and boutiques. The **Harvard Coop Society** (known as the Coop) on the Square is a department store and has book and music sections. There are more books for sale inside the MIT Coop at Kendall Square. From the square you can take the free shuttle service to the **CambridgeSide Galleria**, which comprises more than 100 shops and restaurants, including Sears (a large general store); the New England Sports Museum is in the same complex. For antiques, try the four-storey Cambridge Antique Market (201 Msgr O'Brien Highway, Lechmere subway); for crafts, Cambridge Artists Coop, 59A Church Street.

MORE SHOPPING Two good places for outdoor and hiking equipment are **Eastern Mountain Sports** at 1041 Commonwealth Avenue, Boston (also winter sports gear) and **Tent City** on 272 Friend Street near North Station.

Five miles west of the city centre on Route 9, the Mall at **Chestnut Hill** is a feast for the eyes, with over 100 stores, including Bloomingdales and Filene's. Concerts take place here at weekends. Take the Green Line (D train for Riverside) to Chestnut Hill station.

Further out of town, and accessible by commuter train, **Cape Ann**, **Marblehead**, **Ipswich**, **Essex** and **Newburyport** each have art galleries and antique shops.

BOSTON INVENTIONS
● Alexander Graham Bell invented the telephone in Sudbury Street, and the first telephone exchange followed in 1877.
● Charles Goodyear developed the vulcanisation of automobile tyres, in 1844.
● King Gillette invented the safety razor-blade in 1901.
● Other Boston innovations include the baseball catcher's mask, the polaroid film, the iron lung and the heart pacemaker.

Quincy Market, next to Faneuil Hall, dates back to the 1820s. Today, it is always an entertaining and lively place to be

BOSTON DINING PERSPECTIVES

Both the Prudential Tower and John Hancock Tower have stunning high-level views of the city by night. But the 52nd-floor Top of the Hub restaurant in the Prudential and the Bay Tower Room on the 33rd floor at 60 State Street allow diners to enjoy superb views at their leisure. Dinner cruises on the *Odyssey* from Rowes Wharf get a low-level but equally fascinating perspective on Boston.

Nightlife

There's a lot going on in Boston and Cambridge at night, although it is not an all-night city in the way New York is. The liveliest areas popular with visitors are Kenmore Square and Lansdowne Street (near Boston University), Harvard Square in Cambridge (by Harvard University), Copley Square and Boylston Place, and Faneuil Hall Marketplace. The Theatre District has a number of comedy clubs, and Roxy, an upscale nightclub. A little further out, Davis Square in Somerville has some lively nightspots.

LISTINGS AND TICKETS Full listings, covering theatre, concerts, cinema, bars and clubs, appear in the *Boston Globe* on Thursdays, the *Boston Herald* on Fridays, *The Improper Bostonian* (fortnightly; also includes restaurants) and Stuff@night, a guide to nightlife in the city. The website www.Boston.com has details of all kinds of events. For bookings and half-price tickets on the day of performance contact Ticketmaster (tel: 617/931 2000) or visit the BosTix ticket booth in Faneuil Hall Marketplace or Copley Square.

THEATRE The Theatre District, just south of Boston Common, has mainstream and avant-garde offerings. The Charles Playhouse in Warrenton Street is still showing the comedy whodunnit *Shear Madness*, America's longest-running play, in which the audience helps solve a murder mystery.

BARS AND CLUBS There's something for everyone in the Lansdowne Street/Kenmore Square area, where there are over 20 clubs offering everything from billiards to slam-dancing. Avalon is a hotspot for dancing, Mama Kin and Axis for rock and roll. Jillian's Boston offers pool, billiards and virtual reality games, Bill's Bar is funky and relaxed. Gay venues abound in the Kenmore Square, and also in the South End. Sunday night tends to be gay night; the Club Café (Columbus Avenue) is open all week.

The Bull and Finch, familiar to many from the TV series Cheers

Boylston Street has outdoor bars, such as the Cactus Club, which attract the younger set. In Somerville, Johnny D's in Davis Square has a welcoming crowd, good food and great music. In Beacon Hill, the Bull & Finch pub famed for its appearance in the TV series *Cheers* (filmed in Hollywood), is at 84 Beacon Street. Faneuil Hall Marketplace has plenty of piano bars, pubs, dance venues and comedy clubs to choose from.

Those who enjoy comedy will find Dick Doherty's Comedy Vault, 124 Boylston Street, Nick's Comedy Stop in the Theatre District and The Comedy Connection, at Faneuil Hall, are leading clubs of their kind.

JAZZ AND BLUES the Regatta Bar in the Charles Hotel, 1 Bennett Street, Cambridge, is a top-class jazz venue, hosting an annual festival from January to April; don't miss the Sunday Gospel Group brunch. The House of Blues, 90 Winthrop Street. Also in Cambridge, Scullers, 400 Soldiers Field Road, is a favourite, and Wally's, in Mass. Avenue, is a major attraction. In Somerville the Willows Jazz Bar, Ball Square in Broadway, with its smoky intimate environment, is for serious jazz lovers.

CLASSICAL AND LIGHT MUSIC The BSO (Boston Symphony Orchestra) performs at Symphony Hall from the start of October to the end of April (tel: 617/266 2378). The New England Conservatory gives free concerts from January to March, many in the glittering Jordan Hall, 290 Huntington Avenue (tel: 617/536 2412). The Boston Pops Orchestra performs light classics and popular favourites at Symphony Hall from May to July (see page 25) and in early July there is a series of free Boston Pops outdoor concerts at the Hatch Shell on the Esplanade (tel: 617/266 1492). From June to September the 'big name' Harborlights Festival is held in a 4,000- seater 'tent' on the Waterfront.

Boston Lyric Opera, New England's leading opera company, stages productions at 114 State Street (tel: 617/248 8811). Ballet performances are given at the Wang Center for the Performing Arts (tel: 617/482 9393), at 270 Tremont Street, and by Boston Ballet, at 19 Clarendon Street (tel: 617/695 6950).

The Charles Hotel's Regatta Bar provides a stylish ambience for an evening of jazz

85

BOSTON: FIRST BUILD-INGS IN THE THE U.S.
- First public school (Boston Latin School, 1636).
- US post office (1639).
- Lighthouse (1716).
- Chocolate factory (1765).
- Branch library (1871).
- Telephone exchange (1877).

OTHER BOSTON US FIRSTS
- Military training field (1631).
- First fire law, banning wooden chimneys (1632).
- Law against smoking (1633).
- Football game (Boston Common, 1862).
- Computer (Differential Analyzer at MIT, 1928)

MASSACHUSETTS

4

Lakeville
Canaan
Norfolk
Riverton
Old New-Gate Prison
Suffield
Falls Village
Winsted
Barkhamsted Reservoir
Granby
New England Air Museum
Enfield
Warehouse Point
Windsor Locks
Trolley Museum
Simsbury
Sharon
West Cornwall
Cornwall
Goshen
Canton
Avon
Bloomfield
Windsor
HARTFORD
Housatonic Meadows State Park
Cornwall Bridge
Torrington
Colllinsville
Litchfield Hills
Kent Falls State Park
Litchfield
Farmington
Wethersfield
Sloane-Stanley Museum
L. Waramaug
Warren
Newington
Glastonbury
Rocky Hill

NEW YORK

3

Kent
New Preston
Mount Tom State Park
Terryville
Plainville
New Britain
Bulls Bridge
Thomaston
Bristol
Kensington
Dinosaur State Park
Washington
Watertown
Wolcott
Southington
Portland
New Milford
Oakville
Plantsville
Middletown
Candlewood Lake
Woodbury
Middlebury
WATERBURY
Meriden
Higganum
Brookfield
Prospect
Cheshire
Durham
Naugatuck
Wallingford

2

Danbury
Housatonic
Seymour
Hamden
North Haven
Bethel
Woodbridge
Ansonia
Yale University
North Branford
Derby
Ridgefield
Redding
Shelton
Orange
NEW HAVEN
Madison
West Haven
Branford
Guildford
East Haven
Trumbull
Wilton
Milford
New Canaan
Westport
Stratford
Fairfield
BRIDGEPORT

1

Norwalk
Darien
STAMFORD
Greenwich
Long
Island

A   B   C

Red Mts
Canaan Mts
Farmington
Housatonic
781m

CONNECTICUT Named after New England's longest river, Connecticut extends some 90 miles west–east and 55 miles north–south. The state's rolling terrain is bisected by the Connecticut river, which flows south along a fertile valley into Long Island Sound. The shoreline has sandy beaches and quiet coastal towns, as well as more urbanised parts close to New York City. The coastal hinterland is a gentle plain, which rises further inland into forested uplands near the New York and Massachusetts borders. Connecticut is America's third smallest state (after Rhode Island and Delaware) and is densely populated. Yet the state has genuinely rural tracts that belie its proximity to the Big Apple. In all, two-thirds of Connecticut is rural, and most of that is forested.

Roseland Cottage in the quiet village of Woodstock

▶▶▶ REGION HIGHLIGHTS

Museums
Mystic Seaport *page 101*
Norwalk Maritime Aquarium *page 107*
Wadsworth Atheneum *page 95*
Houses
Lockwood-Mathews Mansion *page 107*
Mark Twain House *page 96*
Scenery, villages and small towns
Litchfield Hills *pages 98–9*
Wethersfield *page 97*
Universities
Yale *pages 103–5*

Connecticut

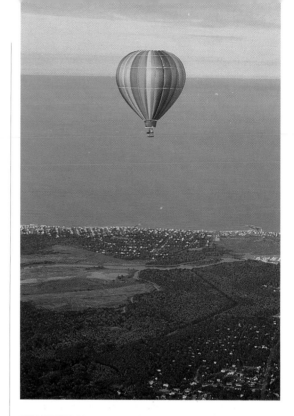

The coastal strip looks out across Long Island Sound, where the Gulf Stream entices tropical underwater marine life

THE NUTMEG STATE
Legend has it that local traders cunningly passed off wooden nutmegs as real ones, hence Connecticut's nickname.

'Here's to the town of
    New Haven,
The home of the Truth
    and the Light,
Where God talks to Jones
    in the very same tones
That he uses with Hadley
    and Dwight.'
– F S Jones, *On the Democracy of Yale.*

'Connecticut in her blue-laws, laying it down as a principle, that the laws of God should be the law of the land.'
– Thomas Jefferson, letter to John Adams, 24 January 1814.

THE HISTORIC HERITAGE The Connecticut River brought in the first Puritan settlers in the 1630s after Boston and Massachusetts had become too religiously intolerant for their tastes. Hartford, Windsor and Wethersfield were the original trio of towns they established, hence the three clusters of grapes on the state's coat of arms. These settlements merged to become the Hartford Colony, later named the Connecticut Colony. The Fundamental Orders of Connecticut, adopted in 1638, are widely held to have been the world's first written constitution of a democratic government – hence the state's official nickname, the Constitution State, on every vehicle licence-plate. Connecticut has also been named the 'Nutmeg State' – its inhabitants being 'Nutmeggers' (see panel) – and, during the Revolutionary War, the 'Arsenal of the Nation'. The state retains plenty of mementoes of those times.

Yankee ingenuity also made Connecticut the 'Gadget State'. This was the birthplace of the cylinder lock, the pay telephone, the steel fish-hook, the stone-crusher and the submarine torpedo. Samuel Colt's firearms company manufactured the famous .45 revolver and other guns in Hartford, while pioneer clock-makers Seth Thomas and Eli Terry had Thomaston and Terryville named after them. Eli Whitney devised interchangeable parts which effectively made him the father of mass-production. Charles Goodyear manufactured improved vehicle tyres and the first American copper coins were minted here. Even today, despite a decline in industrial activity, the state leans heavily towards manufacturing, including the output of ball-bearings, jet engines and nuclear submarines.

The state's oldest-established towns are found along the 253-mile shoreline and along the principal waterways, notably the Connecticut River. Early colonial days saw Yankee traders flourishing in ship-building, seafaring and commercial ventures at Mystic, Stonington, New London and elsewhere. The insurance industry that began in conjunction with this maritime activity gathered momentum. Today, insurance is still the state capital's *raison d'être.*

VISITOR ATTRACTIONS For the visitor, Connecticut's maritime heritage is an obvious attraction, and is admirably presented in the great museums of Mystic and Norwalk. But other industrial ports bordering Long Island Sound in the state's southwestern territory have only patches of interest; one such oasis is Yale University, an architectural treasure-house in New Haven. In the Hartford area, the former homes of Mark Twain, Noah Webster and Harriet Beecher Stowe can be visited. Off-beat whimsicality can be found at Gillette Castle, in the Connecticut River Valley, while the Lockwood-Mathews Mansion in Norwalk, the most sumptuous house of its day, foreshadows the opulent 'cottages' at Newport in Rhode Island. Fine art collections are found at Hartford, Yale University and New Britain, and in private houses such as the Hill-Stead Museum.

Elsewhere in the state, pristine white clapboard villages such as Litchfield, Wethersfield, and Farmington await discovery, grouped around their lovely village greens, each stubbornly refusing to concede to urbanisation. By the Massachusetts border is the state's highest terrain and most scenic drive, along the fast-flowing Housatonic river in the Litchfield Hills, an area well endowed with art and craft shops. The Connecticut and Housatonic rivers are both noted for fishing, the latter especially for trout, as well as for the more adventurous pursuits of tubing, canoeing and kayaking. Near Litchfield, the White Memorial Foundation has hiking, cross-country skiing, horseback riding and bird-watching. Connecticut also has some gentle drives through landscape dominated by cornfields, orchards, old barns and silos; one of the most scenic roads is Route 169 from Lisbon to Woodstock.

Several major venues exist for good spectator sport. The Hartford Whalers is a major-league hockey team. The sport of jai alai can be seen inexpensively at Milford (the biggest such venue in New England). Motor racing takes place at Lime Rock, and the annual Pilot Pen International Tennis Tournament is held at New Haven. The Canon Greater Hartford Open is an annual golf event.

CONNECTICUT SUPERLATIVES
● The Hartford Courant is the oldest established newspaper in the US (1764).
● The Connecticut river is New England's longest.
● The Rocky Hill–Glastonbury ferry has been operating since 1655, the longest continuous service in the nation.

89

Below: at Coventry, in the northeastern corner of the state, the Nathan Hale Homestead was built by the patriot's family in 1776, the year he was executed

Connecticut

Events

For further information contact the state tourist office (see page 266) or chambers of commerce.

January–March
Warm Up to Winter, Farmington Valley area: history and good food combine at museums and period homes.

May
Dogwood Festival, Fairfield.
Lime Rock Grand Prix, Lakeville.
Lobster Fest, Mystic Seaport: lobster served al fresco, on the waterfront.

June
A Taste of Hartford: food, comedy, music and more.
Farmington Antiques Weekend.
Yale–Harvard Regatta, New London.
Canon Greater Hartford Open, Cromwell: attracting top names in golf.

June–July
Barnum Festival, Bridgeport: parade and festival to honour PT Barnum.

July
Antique and Classic Boat Rendezvous, Mystic Seaport.
Guilford Handicrafts Exposition, Guilford.
Historic Homes Tour, Litchfield: houses open their doors to the public.
Riverfest, Hartford/East Hartford: 4 July river festival.
Blessing of the Fleet, Stonington.

August
Brooklyn Fair, agricultural fair.

Connecticut River Powwow, Durham: crafts, dancing etc.
Great Connecticut Jazz Festival, Moodus.
Outdoor Art Festival, Mystic: the streets close to traffic as the artists take over.
Pilot Pen International Tennis Festival, New Haven: a major men's professional tournament at Yale University.
Quinnehtukqut Rendezvous and Native American Festival, Haddam Meadows State Park.

September
Durham Fair, Durham.
Oyster Festival, Norwalk: tall ships, arts, crafts, oysters.
Woodstock Fair, South Woodstock: agricultural show, animals, crafts.

September–October
Mum Festival, Bristol: parade, arts, crafts, drama.
Walking Weekend, guided walks; state-wide.
Chowderfest, Mystic Seaport.

November
Thanksgiving Day Road Race, Manchester.

December
Christmas season, Mystic Seaport: Lantern Light Tours give a one-hour 'interactive play'.
First Night, Hartford: fireworks, procession, etc.

Mystic Seaport, venue for a variety of events and activities

Shelf clocks, the invention of Eli Terry, in the Clock and Watch Museum

EARLY CLOCK-MAKING
Connecticut's clock-making industry, now all but defunct, originated in the late-18th century. In 1792 Eli Terry began making his name and money by mass-producing wooden cogs at his water-powered mill in Connecticut, by standardising gears and by introducing interchangeable parts. Brass gears came in after 1800.

HILL-STEAD'S CREATOR
Theodate Pope (later Theodate Riddle) was primarily a self-trained architect who gained much of her initial experience when she engaged the firm of McKim, Mead and White to build her parents Hill-Stead as a retirement home. She played a large part in influencing the vernacular New England farmstead design, which incorporated elements of Georgian and Greek Revival styles.

Left: a carving in the Carousel Museum Below: architecture from Bristol's 19th-century heyday

▶ Bristol and Area   86C3

From the late-18th century until 1929 the neighbouring towns of Bristol, Thomaston, Terryville, Winsted and Waterbury played important roles as the centre of America's clock industry. Aptly, Bristol is home today of the **American Clock and Watch Museum▶▶** in an elegant post-Revolutionary mansion at 100 Maple Street off Route 72 (*Open* Apr–Nov). The collection is eclectic, charting the history of American horology. In all, the museum has 1,600 watches and 1,800 clocks. Look out for the re-created 1825 clock-maker's shop, and an 1860 novelty clock from New York featuring a lion's eyes going up and down in time to the tick. At 95 Riverside Avenue (Route 72), the **New England Carousel Museum▶** has over 300 antique carved horses and carousel chariots.

On Route 6, opposite the church at **Terryville**, the **Lock Museum▶** occupies a site close to the former Eagle Lock mills, which opened in 1854, some 20 years after the lock industry began in Connecticut. The display features around 20,000 items from a 1580s Spanish Armada chest to a 1920s lock-demonstrating machine used at trade shows.

East of Bristol, **Farmington▶**, has many Federal-style houses and has become a select satellite of Hartford. It was a key point on the underground railroad too, the village where the freed *Amistad* slaves awaited return to Africa (see panel, page 105). In the village, the **Stanley-Whitman House** has been carefully restored to its 1720 colonial appearance and contains period furnishings. The house has diamond-pane leaded windows and an overhanging upper storey. The nearby **Hill-Stead Museum▶▶**, a turn-of-the-century colonial revival home, exemplifies good taste. It belonged to industrialist Alfred Pope (see panel). The family adorned the interior with French Impressionist paintings, including two of Monet's *Haystacks* series and *The Absinthe Drinker* and *The Guitar Player* by Manet (*Open* Tue–Sun).

91

Connecticut

**GENEALOGY AT
MIDDLETOWN**
Middletown was settled in
1650 and prospered in
the late 18th century, as
ship-building and trade
with the West Indies made
it the richest community in
the colony. The town
attracts genealogists on
the trail of British and
European ancestors,
many of whom settled
here. The Godfrey Library
is the chief source of
information and has
records for the whole US
before the 1850s.

*The eccentric exterior of
Gillette Castle befits the
reclusive actor for whom
it was built*

▶ Connecticut River Valley   87D2

After its 410-mile journey along the New Hampshire-
Vermont border and through Massachusetts, the
Connecticut River finally crosses Connecticut itself before
flowing into Long Island Sound. The Connecticut scenery
along New England's longest river is pleasantly mild
rather than spectacular, but a scattering of good sights,
mostly in the county of Middlesex (at the southern end of
the river's course), makes it worth taking in. Antique
shops, art shows, country fairs, concerts and festivals are
thick on the ground along the entire valley.

SOUTH OF HARTFORD At the mouth of the river is **Old
Saybrook**, the earliest settlement in the valley; nearby
Essex is home to the Connecticut River Museum, pleasantly sited by the river. Though not extensive, the museum's displays illustrate ship-building and maritime life in
the context of the **Connecticut River Valley**. On show is a
replica of the *American Turtle*, the first submarine, a claus-
trophobic-looking one-man vessel invented to sink
British ships in the Revolution.

At Essex, the **Valley Railroad▶▶**, one of only two steam railways in New England (the other is at North Conway, NH) operates 1½-hour round trips to Chester and Haddam. Period carriages make it a nostalgic treat: original 1920s furnishings include padded armchairs in Pullman class and cane seats in standard. An optional extra is to stop off at Deep River for a connecting boat trip upriver to East Haddam. The **Ivoryton Playhouse** provides entertainment at nearby **Ivoryton**, where there is a **Fife and Drum Museum**, open at summer weekends.

Gillette Castle▶▶, high above the river, south of East Haddam, is a fantasy re-creation of Rhenish medievalism, or something approaching that style. It was built in 1914–19 for actor William Gillette, who was famous for his Sherlock Holmes performances, but, despite public prominence, was something of a recluse. A system of mirrors was placed so that he could watch from his bedroom for unwelcome visitors and decide whether to be indisposed, and his dinner table was almost comically small. His passion for railways led to the creation of a 3-mile railway (no longer existing, although one carriage is preserved) in the grounds. The castle's idiosyncrasies reveal themselves inside, its 24 rooms displaying wooden light switches, Javanese matting, walls made of field stones, light fittings made with pieces of bottle glass, and bizarre lock systems.

Horse and carriage rides are provided daily in summer at the castle, and at weekends during most of the rest of the year. A scenic approach to the castle is on the **Chester–Hadlyme ferry** (April to December). There has been a ferry here since 1769, making it one of the oldest such continuous services in the US. It is feasible to leave the car on the far side, cross the river as a foot passenger and walk up a path to the castle. **Selden Neck State Park**, devoid of facilities and accessible only by boat, is an ideal tonic for escapists who like to rough it. Canoe hire is available from below Gillette Castle.

At Middlefield, **Lyman Orchards** has been a family farm since 1741; its Apple Barrel Farm Store stocks a wide range of local produce.

Chester▶ is a village graced with an unblemished main street. Close by is the delightful **Goodspeed Opera House** (tours available; tel: 860/873 8668), with musicals usually

Passengers on the Valley Railroad's early 20th-century steam train enjoy views of the Connecticut River and valley

93

NEW ENGLAND'S LONGEST RIVER
Named by Algonquin people as the Quinnetukut ('the long river whose waters are driven by wind and tide'), the 397-mile-long Connecticut River flows from its source near the New Hampshire-Canada border through four states and is tidal from Hartford.

First charted by Dutchman Adriaen Block in 1614, the valley was by the 19th century an important cigar-tobacco-growing area, but as in much of New England, the forest has taken over Essex, which once had six shipyards, and other communities grew as river settlements. Ship-building, however, never recovered from a flood in 1936 and a hurricane two years later.

CRUISES

Deep River Navigation (tel: 860/767 0103 or 860/526 4954) offers trips from Old Saybrook and Hartford, in Long Island Sound and hour-long river voyages aboard the steamer *Becky Thatcher*. Camelot Cruises (tel: 860/345 8591) runs a sailing murder mystery cruise. *Sea Mist II* (tel: 203/488 8905), at Stony Creek, makes 45-minute trips around some of the 365 Thimble Islands; Money Island is where the pirate Captain Kidd reputedly used to draw in his boat.

AIR MUSEUM HIGHLIGHTS

Despite losing 23 vintage aircraft in a freak tornado in 1979 the New England Air Museum boasts a number of choice exhibits, including:
● 1911 Ernest Hall No. 1 Blériot: the same design of craft as that flown by pioneer aviator Louis Blériot when he made the first crossing from England to France in 1909.
● 1934 Marcoux-Bromberg Special: an R-3 racer which won a 150-mile contest in California in 1938 achieving an average speed of 265mph. It featured in the Clark Gable movie *Test Pilot*.

running for six or seven weeks, and audience participation on Wednesdays. You can arrive for a performance by boat, picnic on the lawn and have drinks at the interval on a balcony overlooking the river. A tiny one-room schoolhouse at **East Haddam** was where patriot Nathan Hale taught in 1773–4 and is open on weekend afternoons for a nominal fee. Its bell was made in Spain in AD 815 and is still in working order.

At Higganum, the **Sundial Herb Garden** is a compact but prettily contrived knot garden and topiary in 17th-century style, with miniature vistas opening up through its 'outdoor rooms'. It was created over a period of 20 years by an Irish and German couple who put on speciality teas (with English-style scones and clotted cream) and stocked a shop with a worldwide selection of herbs and spices.

Dinosaur State Park, on Route 91 at Rocky Hill (closed Monday), has in its exhibition hall some 500 dinosaur footprints in what was a shallow stagnant lake 185 million years ago. Life-size models, a diorama and a commentary flesh out the details, and there is a discovery room for children. If you bring your own plaster of Paris you can make casts of actual dinosaur prints. The impressions were uncovered in 1966 during building works.

For Hartford, see pages 95–7.

NORTH OF HARTFORD On Route 140 at **East Windsor**, the **Trolley Museum** dates from 1940 and claims to be New England's oldest. Volunteers run 'trolleys' (or trams) along a 1½-mile section of the former Hartford–Springfield Street Railway and have rescued old trolleys from other places: one was found in a scout camp being used as a laundromat. On Route 75 near Bradley Airport, the **New England Air Museum►** exhibits over 70 military and civil aeroplanes, from early biplanes to experimental fighters and modern home-built machines.

Old New-Gate Prison (*Open* May–Oct, Wed–Sun), off Route 20 in East Granby, retains its castle-like walls. The

Cruising on the Connecticut River near East Haddam

overgrown sandstone ruins have atmosphere, and children will enjoy exploring the mine. The prison dates from 1773, when it was built to provide prison labourers to work on the copper mine. This became the first state prison in the US in 1776, and British loyalists were jailed here during the Revolution. The opportunities this presented, with shafts providing convenient exits and the availability of gunpowder, proved irresistible, and a mass escape by British prisoners of war and Tories occurred in 1781. The prison was later abandoned in 1827.

▶ Foxwoods   87E2

Foxwoods Casino, on the Mashantucket Pequot Indian reservation, has become very big business (see page 125) – the largest casino in the US and a huge crowd-puller. It may not be everyone's idea of heaven, but the place is so bathed in commercialism as to be an experience in itself. Financed by some of the bucks cascading into the thousands of gaming machines, the **Mashantucket Pequot Museum and Research Center**▶▶ is on an impressive scale, featuring a re-creation of a Pequot village, a diorama depicting a caribou hunt scene, a re-created 1780 Pequot farmstead and site tours of the excavation of a 17th-century fort. Other attractions on site include the **Cinedrome 360° Theater**, the **Turbo Ride** and **Virtual Adventures**. Nearby on Route 2A at Uncasville, **Mohegan Sun** is another casino, a vast tentlike structure based on an Indian longhouse design.

▶▶ Hartford   86C3

America's insurance industry capital stands on the Connecticut river. Downtown is dominated by high-rise office buildings, the second tallest of which is the 527-foot **Travelers Tower**▶▶, offering a 37-mile view (tours by appointment May–October; there are 72 steps; tel: 860/277 0111). Virtually next door, at 600 Main Street, the Gothic Revival **Wadsworth Atheneum**▶▶▶ (*closed*: Monday; free Saturday morning and Thursday) was, in 1842, the first public art museum in the US (see panel). The original castle has been extended to form an architectural blend of five interconnecting buildings.

WADSWORTH ATHENEUM HIGHLIGHTS
A choice set of French Impressionist paintings includes Monet's *Beach at Trouville*, Matisse's *Woman with a Plumed Hat* and Van Gogh's *Self Portrait*. There are also important works by Thomas Cole and Frederic Church of the Hudson River School, as well as Caravaggio's *Ecstasy of St Francis* and Holman Hunt's *The Lady of Shalott*. Picasso, Dali, Warhol and Rauschenberg are also represented. Other rooms are devoted to applied arts: European porcelain, 17th- and 18th-century carved chests from Connecticut and Massachusetts, costumes, textiles and furniture.

95

Above left: a 'starburst' quilt in the Wadsworth Atheneum textile collection
Below left: local schoolmaster and patriot, Nathan Hale

Connecticut

CARILLON CONCERTS

Trinity College, a liberal, prestigious institution in Hartford, has a fine chapel modelled on the English Perpendicular (late Gothic) style and a Romanesque crypt. Carillon concerts are sometimes given.

INSURANCE

Hartford's insurance industry began in the 18th century to cover ship-owners against loss of vessels. After the decline of shipping in the area, fire insurance grew in importance in the 19th century. Today about 40 companies, including Etna, Travelers and CIGNA, are based here.

Hartford's State Capitol: its exuberant design reflects Victorian pride

Bushnell Park, the nation's first landscaped public space, cuts a green swathe across the centre of the city and counts a number of exotic rarities among its fine trees as well as a preserved carousel dating from 1914; a 1925 Wurlitzer organ provides the music. A grandiose brownstone structure known as the **Soldiers and Sailors Memorial Arch** (1886) honours citizens who served in the Civil War; its terracotta frieze depicts war scenes. In the park rises the gold-domed **State Capitol►**, built in 1878 to the design of Richard Upjohn and adorned externally with bas-reliefs of historic scenes. Its lavishly ornate legislative chambers, Hall of Flags and gaudy silver and gold marble hall are grand gestures of civic pride. There are free tours (Sep–Jun, Mon–Fri 9.15–1.15; Jul–Aug 9.15–2.15; also Sat, Apr–Oct 10.15–2.15), or you can just walk in and look round by yourself. Since 1988 the Capitol has been connected by a walkway to the new Legislative Office, an impressive addition in polished granite.

At 800 Main Street is the **Old State House►** (*Open* Mon–Sat. *Admission free*), designed by Charles Bulfinch, which served as the state capitol from 1796 to 1878 and then the city hall up to 1915. Today it contains exhibitions of early Connecticut and Native American life, and a visitor information centre. State memorabilia, including the 1662 royal charter and the Fundamental Orders of 1638, and a collection of Colt firearms are displayed at the **Museum of Connecticut History** at 231 Capitol Avenue (*Open* Mon–Sat. *Admission* free).

West of downtown, at 351 Farmington Avenue, is the red-brick Gothic **Mark Twain House► ► ►** (reached by bus E from the central transit station in Hartford). Samuel Clemens, alias Mark Twain (see pages 46–7), stipulated that his 19-room house should be unique. His personality still pervades what a local newspaper in 1874 described as 'the oddest house in Connecticut if not in the whole of America'. Here he wrote *Huckleberry Finn*, *Tom Sawyer* and five other major works up to 1891. Many of the original family pieces survive, including the items ranged on a mantelpiece, about which he used to tell stories to entertain his children. Each of these items had to feature in his story,

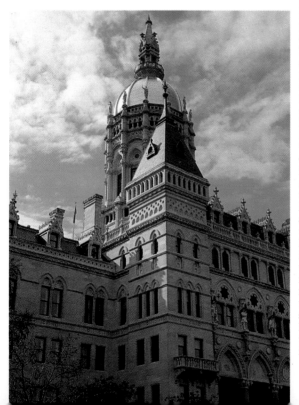

and he had to start over again if he missed anything out (*Open* daily, Memorial Day–15 Oct, and Dec; rest of the year Wed–Mon).

Immediately adjacent is the **Harriet Beecher Stowe House►**, the home of the author of Uncle Tom's Cabin (see pages 46–7) from 1873 to her death in 1896; most of the contents are not original. Harriet Beecher moved here while the Twain house was being built; at that time the neighbourhood was known as Nook Farm and comprised a small literary colony (*Open* daily, except Mon in winter).

At 950 Trout Brook Drive, **West Hartford**, is the Science Museum of Connecticut, which has animal and planetarium shows and several hands-on exhibits. At 227 South Main Street is the **Noah Webster House►**, the birthplace of the author of *An American Dictionary of the English Language* and *The American Speller* and has absorbing Webster memorabilia (*Open* daily in summer, except Wed; other seasons, afternoons only). On the north side of the city, at 200 Bloomfield Avenue at the University of Hartford, the **Museum of American Political Life►** (*Open* daily except Mon) charts political campaigns, women's rights and prohibition movements from the time of George Washington.

Off I–91 at exit 26, the town of **Wethersfield►►**, settled in 1634, is one of the earliest settlements in the state. Its charming historic district, the state's largest, includes early 18th-century sea-captains' homes set along Broad Street, a huge, long green with houses set back. The **Webb-Deane-Stevens Museum►**, on Main Street (*Open* May–Oct, Wed–Mon; weekends only in winter), comprises three restored houses. At the Webb House General George Washington and the Comte de Rochambeau planned the final campaign in the Revolution, leading to the British defeat at Yorktown in 1781.

More period charm and a fascinating early kitchen are found in the **Buttolph-Williams House** of 1692, on Broad Street (*Open* Wed–Mon). The **Keeney Memorial Cultural Center** has information and changing exhibitions on local history. Main Street ends at **Cove Park**, where one 17th-century warehouse survives from the days when Wethersfield was a port on the Connecticut River before it changed course.

Mark Twain's house, in the Nook Farm district of Hartford

THE CHARTER OAK
A royal charter of 1662 gave a measure of independence to the Hartford colony; but in 1687 the new royal governor insisted it should be returned. At the meeting held to discuss the matter, the candles were suddenly extinguished and the charter vanished. It remained hidden (reputedly) in an oak tree for two years until the governor returned to England. In the 19th century Hartford's famous Charter Oak, as it had come to be known, was felled. Numerous items are said to be made from it, including the chair of the lieutenant-governor in the State Capitol.

Drive

Early autumn in the Litchfield Hills

by the late Eric Sloane. He considered these objects as 'symbols of American heritage, worthy of at least the same recognition as the popular current sculpture made from American junk'. He himself was a landscape painter and his studio has been re-created. Remains of an iron furnace in the grounds recall a vanished local industry. **Kent Falls State Park** is a roadside picnic stop-off, with pools for swimming where water tumbles down a 200-foot flight of natural steps. **Housatonic Meadow State Park** has picnic benches with a riverside setting and is popular with anglers. Just north, a sign on the west side of the road marks the start of the Pine Knob Loop Trail, leading up to a summit with a fine view. At **West Cornwall**, cross the covered bridge over the Housatonic River.

Take Route 128 east to **Goshen** then Route 63 to **Litchfield▶▶**, the first National Historic District declared in the state and widely regarded as one of the finest towns in New England. In its heyday it was an industrial centre, with grist- and sawmills, iron forges, tanneries, fulling mills, carriage- and clock-makers and hatters' shops. During the Revolution it became a depot for military stores on roads linking Connecticut with the Hudson River Valley. The obvious legacy of the past is the wealth of Federal-style architecture along North, West, South and East streets, which radiate from the town's prominent and much-photographed Congregational Church (1829) on the spacious green.

The Litchfield Hills

See map on pages 86–7 (yellow route).

A 64-mile tour of the highlands of Connecticut, taking in the best of the Housatonic Valley and the picture-postcard town of Litchfield. The autumn colours are superb.

Start from **New Milford**, with its attractive green, and where the Atelier Studio Gallery features work by over 100 artists. Take Route 7 north past **Bulls Bridge**, which boasts one of only two covered bridges in the state still open to motor traffic (off Route 7 to the left). The scenery becomes increasingly unspoilt and rugged along the **Housatonic Valley▶▶**, known for trout-fishing and canoeing.

At **Kent** there are more antiques and crafts shops, and the **Sloane-Stanley Museum▶** (*Open* May–Oct, Wed–Sun) exhibits bygone country tools collected

A good place for an overnight stop is in this inn at Torrington

In the middle of town, the **Litchfield Historical Society**▶ maintains an archive library and a museum. By a genealogical fluke the Society inherited the world's largest collection of pictures by Ralph Earl, who was an eminent portrait painter in the US in the 18th century. The collection contains examples of Litchfield County furniture from the days when the area was a major craft-producing centre. Close by, the **Tapping Reeve House** of 1774 (*Open* May–Oct, daily except Mon) belonged to Judge Tapping Reeve, who in 1784 built America's first law college – a primitive, single-room, unheated structure – in the grounds. A small exhibition commemorates its history and graduates, who included vice-presidents Aaron Burr and John C Calhoun.

Route 202 west passes the entrance to **Mount Tom State Park**▶, where a 1-mile trail leads to a tower at the 1,325-foot summit and a pleasant local view. At the junction with Route 45, divert north-west a short distance to take in **Lake Waramaug**▶, idyllically set beneath hills, and offering boating, swimming, picnics and camping; the far end of the lake has a tiny beach. Close by the lake, **Hopkins Vineyard** provides free tours and tastings.

Route 202 takes you back to New Milford. An optional detour is via Route 47 to the **Institute for American Indian Studies**▶ at Washington. It has Algonquin arts and artefacts from up to 10,000 years ago. Highlights include a longhouse, a 17th-century Native American village and a simulated archaeological site.

Litchfield, an example of the perfect New England town

If there is one image that first-time visitors to New England bring with them, it is of white clapboard houses grouped round a village green, overlooked by the tall, white spire of a wooden church and set in rolling countryside against a backdrop of flaming, autumnal trees.

100

A CHANGING FACE

The New England village did not always present the face that is so cherished today. What is now a neat, attractive green, with its bandstand and war memorial, was once an unsightly, scrubby piece of common land. The clapboard house was not always archetypal white; until idealisation set in during the 19th century, houses were painted in a range of colours: reds, russets and blues. Even that icon, the tall, white church spire, has not always been there – many were added in the 19th century.

FARM BUILDINGS

While houses within the village itself are nowadays most often white, old wooden farm buildings are traditionally a deep red in colour. Particularly in the colder areas of New Hampshire and Maine, farm buildings are connected, so that the farmer can go from barn to shed to kitchen to house protected from the weather. (This also means, however, as many have learned to their cost, that fire too can move swiftly from barn to shed to house.)

The truth is that the New England village lives up to every expectation, serene as any calendar picture. The ingredients are always much the same. Facing on to a green is the white timber church, most often Unitarian or Congregationalist. Then there is the country store, a treasure chest that every visitor must delve into, selling anything from freshly made doughnuts and gourmet local products to cans of kerosene and farmers' rubber boots.

Larger villages often have a number of other, individually owned and equally enticing shops, selling clothes, gifts, books or crafts. Then there will be the town hall, seat of local government. And filling in the gaps around the green, and lining the roads leading to it are the timber-built houses that typify New England, usually painted white but occasionally traditional dusky shades. Some may fly the Union flag, many have a seasonal wreath of dried flowers on the door. One or two of these houses may be 'inns', private homes that offer accommodation and meals. Often dating back to colonial days and furnished with antiques, inns are a delightful way to enjoy the charm and hospitality of a New England village. Every village also has its burial ground, a plot of land set apart from the church or meeting-house.

The village way of life Because the houses are of timber, the local fire brigade is often a focus of social life, organising parades and, along with the churches, events such as barbecues and ice-cream socials. The green is a setting for regular flea markets and, during the Christmas season, for the tree which, like others, is decorated with white lights. Some villages boast a theatre.

Village scenes: (top) autumn in Cohasset, MA, and (right) winter in Sudbury, MA

▶▶▶ Mystic

Mystic Seaport▶▶▶ is placed by the Mystic River, where numerous boat and ship yards flourished before decline set in during the 1880s. The museum features an admirable re-creation of life in a late 19th-century coastal community with period buildings that include a drug store, sailor's tavern and printing press. Over 400 small craft make up the largest such collection in the world, while among the larger ships which you can board are the *Charles W. Morgan* (1841), the last surviving American wooden whaler. A replica of *Amistad*, the notorious slave ship (see panel, page 105) is being built for the year 2000 using traditional techniques and authentic materials. Indoor exhibits include displays of scrimshaw and figureheads.

Mystic Marinelife Aquarium▶▶▶ is one of New England's largest. Much emphasis is placed on state-of-the-art viewing: in addition to the spectacular marine life displays – which include the world's largest artificial beluga whale habitat – you can take a simulated dive to the bottom of the ocean and experience the sounds as you descend. The Jason project (to open by 2000) will allow visitors to watch broadcasts of underwater journeys through kelp forests, deep water canyons and coral reefs – and even to see the resting-places of the *Titanic*, *Bismarck* and other shipwrecks. There are seal, eagle and whale-watching cruises in season (tel: 860/572 5955). Ocean samples are studied in Project Oceanology at Groton (see page 107).

The town of Mystic has a row of captains' houses by the waterfront and a drawbridge (raised hourly, Apr–Oct), and a specialty shopping area called **Olde Mistick Village**, replicated to look like the original colonial settlement. More delightful shoreside archi-tecture awaits at **Noank**, a lobstering and oystering village, with views of Fisher's Island (NY), where Abbot's, something of a Connecticut institution, sells ocean-fresh lobsters straight from the boat.

The **Denison Homestead** on Pequotsepos Road has been restored in the styles of five eras, from colonial times to the 20th century (*Open* Memorial Day–Columbus Day week-ends, Thu–Sun 1–5pm) .

101

Masted sailing vessels moored on the Mystic river

STONINGTON'S SURVIVALS
Stonington, Mystic's coastal neighbour, also has several charming 18th- and 19th-century homes set in tree-lined streets. Settled in the mid 17th-century, it became a whaling, sealing and ship-building community.

MYSTIC CRUISES
Educational cruises, with a naturalist on board, can be taken on the windjam-mer *Argia* (tel: 860/536 0416). You can cruise on the SS *Sabino*, the last operating coal-fired steam-er in the US, or try the *Resolute*, a 1917 motor launch. Or sail the *Breck Marshall*, a catboat. Tel: 860/572 0711.

Life in a 19th-century seaport re-enacted at Mystic Seaport

HISTORIC HAMBURGERS
Not many fast-food establishments get on to the National Register of Historic Places. However, family-run Louis' Hamburgers in Crown Street, New Haven, made it by dint of being the birthplace of the American hamburger in 1900. Louis' retains its original grilling equipment. This is puritanical cuisine: toast, burger, lettuce and tomato only – strictly no ketchup or mustard. The turn-of-the-century fittings and Tiffany lamps are a far cry from McDonald's too.

▶▶▶ New Haven   86C2

Although it would take courage to rate the relative academic standards of Yale University at New Haven and Harvard University at Cambridge, Yale by far outstrips Harvard for visual interest for the day visitor. Imitations of the medieval universities of Oxford and Cambridge in England are Yale's architectural hallmark. However, Yale and New Haven have little of the student–town interaction found between Harvard and Cambridge.

Founded in 1638 by the Puritans as an independent colony, New Haven is today a major cargo port, with a profusion of galleries, upmarket shops and good restaurants along Chapel Street.

MUSEUMS Natural history displays make up the bulk of the **Peabody Museum▶▶** (*Open* daily). Most popular is the dinosaur collection, including the first discovered specimens of *Brontosaurus* and *Stegosaurus*. The *Deinonychus*, or 'Terrible Claw', inspired the vicious Raptor in the movie *Jurassic Park*. In the Hall of Mammals, an 11,000-year-old ground sloth (found in a tar pit in New Mexico) is remarkable for still having part of its skin and hair attached. Elsewhere, the museum displays Egyptian and Polynesian artefacts, geology exhibits, natural history dioramas and birds, and has a discovery room for children. At 1080 Chapel Street, the **Yale Center for British Art▶▶** (*Open* Tue–Sun. *Admission* free) has a magnificent collection of works by Turner, Hogarth, Constable, Reynolds and others, and puts on special exhibitions, talks and films (for details, tel: 203/432 2800). Less well known is the **Yale Collection of Musical Instruments▶**, at 15 Hillhouse Avenue, where 800 instruments include antique keyboards and entertaining oddities such as a 19th-century Italian-made Russian horn with a representation of a snake's head whose tongue vibrates when it is played (*Open* Sep–Jun, Tue, Wed and Thu 1–4). The **Yale University Art Gallery▶▶** at 1,111 Chapel Street (*Open* Sep–Jul, daily except Mon. *Admission* free), founded in 1832, has especially fine sections devoted to European paintings, a reconstructed Mithraic shrine, and a representative collection of American paintings and decorative arts.

THE UNIVERSITY Tours of **Yale University▶▶▶** from 149 Elm Street are provided free by students at 10.30am and 2pm on weekdays; 1.30pm at weekends.

The university was founded at Branford in 1701, moved to Old Saybrook the same year and then to New Haven in 1716. Yale is the only collegiate university in the US, with students attached to the 12 colleges that belong to the university; the system is modelled on Oxford and Cambridge universities in England. Some 300 students live in each college, plus 100 freshmen on Old Campus.

In the present century, the architect James Gamble Rogers gave Yale an 'Oxbridge' look with his Georgian and Gothic-style buildings. To age the buildings, tiles were buried under different soils so that they would discolour and their edges become chipped. Acid was poured on the stonework, and glass was deliberately broken and releaded. Niches were left empty, as at Oxford and Cambridge, where so many statues have been stolen or otherwise destroyed through the ages.

The Green dates from colonial days when Puritan settlers laid out the town in neat squares, including this grazing ground. On one side, Phelps Gate leads into the **Old Campus**, where **Connecticut Hall**, built in the 1750s, is the oldest university building. The patriot Nathan Hale, industrialist Eli Whitney and lexicographer Noah Webster were students here. Hale's statue was made in 1914 by a sculptor who had no idea of his subject's true appearance, so a handsome Yale student was used as a model. The Theodore Dwight Woolsey statue is the only true likeness in the courtyard; his right foot is polished by students who rub it for good luck in their exams.

Above left and below: Yale University is an architectural showpiece, with buildings by leading 20th-century architects rubbing shoulders with Gothic Revival and Georgian creations

103

WHERE THE SHOWS BEGAN
From 1938 to 1976 New Haven's Shubert Theatre was the favourite venue to première new productions before transferring to Broadway. Début shows and plays have included *Oklahoma!*, *My Fair Lady*, *Blithe Spirit*, *The Sound of Music*, *A Streetcar Named Desire*, *Long Day's Journey into Night* and *Annie Get Your Gun*. WC Fields, the Marx Brothers, Sarah Bernhardt and Marlon Brando have all graced its stage. The theatre reopened in 1983 and gives performances between October and May. Tours are given Sep–Jun, Mon–Fri (tel: 203/624 1825).

Connecticut

Above: home of the Yale Repertory Company
Right: Harkness Tower, a High Street landmark

SPORTING SPECTACULARS

Football in autumn at the Yale Bowl has been a major feature of New Haven life since 1913. Once every two years Yale and Harvard, the two old Ivy League rivals, battle it out in 'The Game'. Tennis superstars compete each August at the Pilot Pen International Tennis Tournament. At Milford, jai alai, a Basque sport similar to squash, takes place (matinees Sat–Mon; evenings Mon, Wed–Sat) from June to December. Although it is watched mainly for gambling, it is exciting and the entrance fee is nominal.

Beyond the Old Campus, the neo-Gothic **Harkness Tower** (1920), the country's tallest free-standing tower when built (221 feet), was modelled on Boston Stump in Lincolnshire, England. Around its clock are sculptures of the eight great men of Yale: Nathan Hale, Eli Yale, Jonathan Edwards, Samuel FB Morse, Noah Webster, Eli Whitney, James Fenimore Cooper and John C Calhoun. **Wrexham Tower** was modelled on St Giles Church, Wrexham, Wales (where Eli Yale is buried), while **Pierson College's** tower is based upon the design of Philadelphia's Independence Hall. **Davenport**, ex-President Bush's college, displays the ubiquitous Gothic treatment on the street frontage but its courtyard is in a very different Georgian style.

The art deco **Hall of Graduate Studies** (1932) resembles a miniature New York skyscraper with its chequered motif and flat relief. President and Hillary Clinton attended the **Law School,** opposite, whose stonework displays carvings of cops and robbers. Part of the building was inspired by King's College, Cambridge, England. The **Sterling Memorial Library**, known as the 'Cathedral of Knowledge', looks intentionally like a medieval European cathedral, with cloisters decorated with stone carvings (one showing a student with a book of nude pictures and a glass of ale) and telephones booths masquerading as confessionals; the 'altar' is the main desk. There is also a large mural depicting a Mary Magdalene-like figure of Mother Yale holding the Book of Truth, with an orb of light. To the right are three men representing Art, Literature and Philosophy (then, as now, these are the principal subjects that are studied at the university).

Woolsey Hall, a large circular building, is the venue for concerts by student and visiting musicians. In the courtyard beyond is the **Beinecke Rare Book and Manuscript Library**, perhaps the most memorable of the modern buildings at the university. The library's ingenuity is revealed inside: the outer shell of Vermont marble shields a skyscraper-like stack of priceless books and manuscripts from the sun's ultra-violet rays, while halon gas is used to protect the contents from fire. The library is best seen on a sunny day when the translucence of the marble is apparent. There is no admittance to the stacks themselves, but a complete Gutenberg Bible of 1455, one of only 22 known, is displayed in the public area. Outside, you look down into the **Sculpture Garden**, a compact landscape of geometrical shapes formed in white marble by Isamu Noguchi (the library desk has a leaflet outlining the artist's ideas).

A windowless building close by is home to secret university societies, such as President Bush's Skull and Bones Society. Note how the **President's Office** is purposefully smaller than the other buildings: administration is seen as less important than academic life. In **Berkeley College**, Cross Campus Lawn is reputed to be the birthplace of the game of frisbee, first played here by students using plates, which evidently had aerodynamic qualities.

OUT OF TOWN At Ansonia is **General David Humphreys House**, home of the aide to General Washington and the first US ambassador (*Open* Mon–Fri. *Admission* free). It is a museum with a difference, presented as a hands-on, late-18th-century experience, in which visitors dress up, spin, cook, and make bread and chowder in the manner of the period.

The **Eli Whitney Museum** at 915 Whitney Avenue, Hamden (*Open* Wed–Sun), pays tribute to the inventor of mass-production and charts 200 years of industrial development in the New Haven area. Over 100 restored trolleys can be found at the **Shore Line Trolley Museum** at 17 River Street, East Haven, from where you can take a 3-mile trolley ride.

North-west on Route 69 is **Shepherd's Farm**, a dairy farm whose Jersey herd provides the raw material for a celebrated ice-cream made on the premises. Further on, a sign on the left leads to the **Whitlock Book Barn** (*Open* Wed–Mon), which has countless used and antiquarian tomes, maps and prints crammed into two old turkey-brooder houses.

105

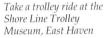

Take a trolley ride at the Shore Line Trolley Museum, East Haven

NEW HAVEN'S STRONGHOLD
On 5 July 1779, 3,000 British and German Hessian troops were sighted in Long Island Sound. They succeeded in capturing the important port town of New Haven, but only after astonishing resistance from just 19 patriots ensconced at Black Rock Fort on the east side of the harbour. This fortification was rebuilt as Fort Nathan Hale and served in the War of 1812. It has since been restored and is open from Memorial Day weekend to Labor Day free of charge.

A DRAMATIC TRAINING CENTRE

The Eugene O'Neill Theater Center at Waterford has been the training ground for hundreds of American actors; Meryl Streep and Al Pacino have been among them. Here, during the Playwright's Conference in July (drama) and August (musicals), you can watch new works in various stages of production. Performances are inexpensive, and the producer may substantially vary the presentation from one day to the next. You can listen in on rehearsals for free (Open daily except Sundays; at other times of the year, you can see students rehearse and perform).

▶ New London   87E2

The seafaring town of New London has a mixture of gracious houses with lawns sloping to the water's edge and a brick-built port area. The latter has numerous survivals from its whaling days, which are also commemorated in the Maritime Museum inside the **Custom House**. The door timbers of this building were taken from the USS *Constitution*, the historic fighting ship of the War of 1812 (see page 67).

Captains of industry lived in Greek Revival mansions in Whale Oil Row (1832), which, together with the imposing railway station, echo former prosperity. Starr Street (1835) is strikingly uniform, its houses recently revamped. The **Joshua Hempsted House** (1678) and **Nathaniel Hempsted House** (1759) are typical of their period and are open to the public. Other notable survivals are the Burial Ground (1653), the New London County Courthouse (1784) and Union Station (1888). Incongruous beneath the huge I-95 viaduct, **Ye Olde Towne Mill** (free) originally dates from 1650 and retains its water-wheel and some historic documents.

On the harbour, a statue of the young Eugene O'Neill pays a belated tribute to the playwright, who was once held in popular esteem as no more than a drunken reprobate. His father bought **Monte Cristo Cottage▶**, close by the water, in 1880 and the summers spent here made a great impression on Eugene. The house (open to the public) was the setting of his autobiographical drama *Long Day's Journey into Night*.

The **US Coast Guard Academy**, situated opposite Connecticut College, trains aspiring coast-guards from the age of 18. Below the visitors' centre in the grounds, the famous tall ship *Eagle*, where sea skills are taught, can be boarded free of charge on Sunday afternoons when in port. Ironically for a vessel which has become a symbol of the US, it was built by the Germans in 1936, captured and brought back after World War II.

The US Coast Guard cutter Eagle, a square-rigger used by the Coast Guard Academy as a training ship

Ocean Beach Park, Waterford, a few miles south of New London

BATTLESITE MARKER
A granite obelisk of 1830 above the east bank of the Thames by Fort Griswold marks the site of the Battle of Groton in 1781, the only British victory in Connecticut. Climb the 160 steps for views of Long Island.

Across the Thames river is the naval base of **Groton**, no great beauty in itself but offering a free tour of the **USS Nautilus▶** (*Open* Wed–Mon 9–5, Tue 1–5), the world's first nuclear submarine, and film shows about life on board. At Niantic, the **Children's Museum of South Eastern Connecticut** has plenty to keep youngsters occupied. At Waterford, mini golf, a 1-mile boardwalk and a water-slide are to be found at **Ocean Beach Park**. **Rocky Neck State Park**, 3 miles west of Niantic, has a crescent beach, and is good for swimming, fishing and scuba diving. There are also facilities for picnicking and camping.

SEA ADVENTURE CRUISES
Project Oceanology, based at Mystic Marinelife Aquarium (tel: 860/572 5955), operates 2½-hour trips from Groton to Ledge Light in summer. Participants set lobster pots, examine fish life and mud samples, and learn about marine pollution. Captain John's (tel: 860/443 7259) runs whale-watching and deep-sea fishing excursions from Waterford. At South Norwalk cruises depart for Sheffield Island Lighthouse (tel: 203/838 9444), which guarded Norwalk Harbor from 1868; its ten rooms are open to the public.

▶▶▶ **Norwalk**   *86A1*
This oystering town is home to the **Maritime Aquarium▶▶▶**, one of New England's most ambitious maritime museums. Housed in an old brick foundry, the museum features everything about the human and natural life of Long Island Sound, where even tropical fish can live because of the presence of the Gulf Stream. Its aquarium leads visitors through the inshore world of salt-marsh habitats and out to sea, with curved glass tanks and video selections explaining aspects of the ocean. Sharks and striped bass feature in the largest tank. Other displays include oyster boats, Long Island boats, diving equipment and boat-building. Hands-on activities make the atmosphere distinctly lively, with opportunities to design your own boat and to work out how sail and wind interact. Children can try out water flows and more in the 'Wet Lab'. Check ahead for details of lectures, events, cruises and demonstrations (tel: 203/852 0700); bookings are recommended for the IMAX movie theatre, with its screen as tall as a six-storey building.

Close by, at 295 West Avenue, the astonishing **Lockwood-Mathews Mansion▶▶** was the ostentatious 1860s precursor to the mansions of Newport (see pages 216–18) with its cavernous frescoed rooms, inlaid doors and magnificent staircase. Its semi-restored state (see panel) lends it an atmosphere of faded grandeur verging on the theatrical. Upper rooms give a good idea of the mansion's former glory and contain a wide-ranging collection of 19th-century music-boxes.

REBIRTH OF A MANSION
The Lockwood-Mathews Mansion was built for LeGrand Lockwood, who lost his fortune in a Wall Street crash in 1869. The house was sold to the Mathews family, then taken over by the city in 1938. The contents were sold, the floors covered with linoleum and the rooms used to store voting machines. Narrowly avoiding a threat of demolition in 1959, the mansion has been reunited with some of its former contents. Restoration began in 1966 but will take many years to complete.

▶▶▶ **Yale University**   *86C2*
See New Haven, pages 102–5.

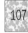

Maine

Near Somesville on Mount Desert Island: the island has been popular with artists and summer visitors since the mid-19th century

Madawaska
Fort Kent
Frenchville
Van Buren
Dickey
Guerette
Hamlin
Eagle
Lake
Limestone
Caribou
Fort Fairfield
CDN
Portage
Presque Isle
Allagash
Wilderness
Waterway
Ashland
Mars Hill
689m
Norway Bluff
516m
Bridgewater
Saddleback Mt
Knowles
Corner
*Chamberlain
Lake*
Baxter
State
Park
Smyrna Mills
Houlton
*Chesuncook
Lake*
Patten
1606m
Mt Katahdin
Island
Falls
1109m
*Boundary
Bald Mt*
Ripogenus
Reed
*Moosehead
Lake*
Rockwood
Millinocket
Danforth
*Chiputneticook
Lakes*
Jackman
*Indian
Pond*
Gulf Hagas Gorge
Macwahoc
Vanceboro
Coburn
Gore
1109m
Greenville
**Katahdin
Iron Works**
Mattawamkeag
Topsfield
1203m *Kibby Mt*
*Flagstaff
Lake*
Monson
Brownsville
Junction
Milo
Lincoln
Springfield
Snow Mt
Stratton
891m
Moxie Mt
Dover-
Foxcroft
Howland
Princeton
Calais
Western Lakes
Region
Carrabassett
Valley
Bingham
Bradley
Wesley
**Reversing
Falls**
*Passamaquoddy
Bay*
Perry
**Grafton
Notch**
Rangeley
Kingfield
Skowhegan
Newport
Dexter
Orono
Aurora
Eastport
*Campobello
Island*
*Mooselookmeguntic
Lake*
Farmington
Pittsfield
Bangor
Brewer
Machias
East Machias
Lubec
Newry
Bethel
Rumford
Livermore
Falls
Waterville
Buckspor t
*Graham
Lake*
Cherryfield
Columbia
Falls
Cutler
White
Mountain
National
Forest
Waterford
Norway
Belfast
Blue
Hill
Ellsworth
Milbridge
Jonesport
Harrison
AUGUSTA
Castine
Bar Harbor
Birch Harbor
Bridgton
Camden
*Acadia
National
Park*
Fryeburg
Auburn
Lewiston
Union
Rockland
*Penobscot
Bay*
Stonington
Cornish
Sebago Lake
Brunswick
Wiscasset
Isle au Haut
Waterboro
*Desert of
Maine*
Bath
Port Clyde
Gorham
Freeport
Yarmouth
Boothbay Harbor
Pemaquid Beach
Sanford
Saco
Casco Bay
Portland
Popham Beach
Biddeford
Old Orchard Beach
Kennebunkport
South
Berwick
Wells
Ogunquit
Kittery
York

NEW HAMPSHIRE

St John
Allagash
Aroostook
Penobscot
St Croix
Kennebec

95

0   40   80   120 km
0   20   40   60 miles

MAINE The summer vacationland of Maine is slightly larger than all the other New England states put together and has the lowest population density. Even with a massive influx of summer visitors to the coast there are still places where you can find remoteness. Easily the most crowded part is from Camden to the New Hampshire border; even here there are areas of quiet charm if you are prepared to seek them out, but development along and around Route 1 is dense and often disappointingly drab. Further up the coast, and including most of Mount Desert Island is **Acadia National Park**, the jewel in the crown and the coast's only appreciable hilly area. Beyond that, the crowds thin out substantially. Even then, the intricate coast is elusive, except from a boat: drivers won't see much of it, and access on foot is limited.

Augusta is the state capital, but **Portland** is the cultural epicentre, and the only place that feels like a big city. Freeport and Kittery are factory-outlet shopping towns.

TREES AND MORE TREES With forests covering 17 million acres, Maine is nicknamed the Pine Tree State. About 90 per cent of the land is forested, and Maine has for long lived off its appreciable timber supplies. The state is also referred to as Downeast, as the prevailing wind pushes sailing boats eastwards 'down' the coast. The term 'Downeaster' refers to any Maine-built ship.

Many Maine villages are now gentrified, but pockets of Downeast atmosphere remain at numerous fishing villages and coastal settlements. Distances between towns increase as you head north or east, and the towns get smaller and roads emptier. Inland, paper companies own vast tracts of Maine's forests; many of the roads are private. Today paper-making accounts for nearly 35 per cent of the state's total value of manufactured products.

On the few public roads in the big forests, you will encounter huge and somewhat terrifying lumber trucks every few minutes or so, which have right of way (and should be given a very wide berth).

Rocky shores and dark coniferous trees typify the coast of Acadia National Park

▶▶▶ REGION HIGHLIGHTS

EARLY DAYS The state was settled by European explorers from early times. In the early 1600s, French and English settlers established themselves on the St Croix and Kennebec rivers respectively. Charles I then gave the territory to Sir Ferdinando Gorges and made him Lord of New England in 1635. The Massachusetts Colony purchased Maine, which remained part of Massachusetts until becoming an independent state in 1820.

From colonial times up until the latter part of the 19th century, Maine supported a flourishing ship-building industry. America's first sawmill was built in 1634 at South Berwick and by 1840 this number had increased to 1,400. Maine has produced more wooden sailing ships than any other state in the Union.

Sebago Lake offers boating, swimming and fishing

Maine salt-of-the earth

LUMBER FACTS
● From the 1630s to 1850s sawmills made use of the 'sash saw', an up-down moving frame. A later invention was the circular-saw blade.
● Winter is the best season for felling, when the sap is down.
● In former times logs were placed on ice-covered lakes or rolled down to streams or rivers to be carried toward the sea each spring. As sawn logs could not be floated, sawmills were located close to shipping ports.

BLUEBERRY BOUNTIES
Blueberries are harvested by a special rake, boxed on three sides. Cherryfield, the 'blueberry capital of the world', and Machias are the main processing centres.

Native Americans used to dry the berries for winter rations, and used them in healing potions.

MAINE TRAITS Inhabitants of Maine have a reputation for being frank and down-to-earth. They keep their cool and don't always smile at strangers (an off-putting attitude to some).

Maine is one of the nation's poorest states. While that may seem hard to believe as you scan the antique and crafts shops in the smart resorts of Penobscot Bay, Kennebunkport, Ogunquit and elsewhere, the remoter areas see younger people drifting out of the state and there are high unemployment rates (particularly in the Native American reservations). Much employment is seasonal. Tourism is the biggest earner – hence the slogan 'Vacationland' on car licence-plates. Crowds flock to the coast in summer and, in the fall, foliage and winter sports draw visitors inland.

MAINE AT WORK Agricultural labourers spend August and September working on the wild blueberry harvest. Maine produces 90 per cent of the nation's output of this fruit, which grows mostly in Washington County in the state's eastern corner. Potatoes are the largest crop in the state, with over 20 million hundredweight harvested each year. From late October to early November, the Christmas wreath industry is at full swing. Maine has just the right type of balsam fir brush for this purpose, and the finished product graces the doors of many American homes.

Because of the harsh winters, the fishing and packing industries operate at maximum capacity when the weather allows it. Some three-quarters of the nation's lobsters come from Maine. Lobster is a ubiquitous menu item; even McDonald's restaurants offer lobster sandwiches in their Maine branches in summer. Meanwhile, Rockland, Prospect Harbor and Lubec are major centres for sardine canning.

Events

For further information contact the state tourist office (see page 266) or chambers of commerce.

January
Sugarloaf USA/Carrabassett:
Children's Festival Week: fireworks, torchlight parade and pool parties.

February
Western Mountain Winter Wonderland Week, Bethel: balloon and sleigh rides, dog sledding.
Annual National Toboggan Championship, Camden: races, chowder challenge, numerous events.
International Snowmobiles Festival, Caribou.

March
Ice-fishing Tournament, Rockwood, Moosehead Lake.
New England Sled Dog Races, Rangeley.
Log Drivers Bean Cookout, Island Falls: torchlight parade, bonfire and other events.

April
Fishermen's Festival, Boothbay Harbor.
Kenduskeag Stream Canoe Races, Bangor: whitewater open-canoe races.
Maine Maple Sunday, statewide: sugar houses demonstrate the production of 'liquid gold' maple syrup.

May
MooseMania, Rockwood: month-long moose-related activities and events.

June
Rodeo and Country Weekend, Farmington.
Windjammer Days, Boothbay Harbor: schooner races.
Acadian Festival, Madawaska: dance, food, music, heritage.

July
Bar Harbor Music Festival: classical and popular music (summer series).
Camden Garden House Tour: houses and gardens open to the public.
Clam Festival, Yarmouth: the biggest festival in Maine, with carnival, seafood, crafts, fireworks, children's parade, and other events.
Great Schooner Race, Blue Hill.

August
Blueberry Festival, Machias: harvest celebration.
Indian Day Celebration, Perry: Pasmaquoddy crafts, dancing, meals, traditional games.
Retired Skippers' Race, Castine.
Maine Lobster Festival, Rockland: a feast of Maine's most succulent crustacean in its busiest fishing port.

September
Blue Hill Fair, Blue Hill: on the Labor Day weekend.
Bluegrass Festival, Brunswick.

October
Living History Days, Leonard Mills, Bradley: water-wheel and sawmill demonstrations, horse and buggy rides, antique costumes.
Harvestfest, York: colonial celebration.
Fryeburg Fair: Maine's largest agricultural fair.

November
Lighting of Nubble Lighthouse, Long Sands Beach, York.
Christmas United Maine Craftsman Show, Bangor.

December
Christmas Prelude, Kennebunkport.

A maple sugaring demonstration at the big agricultural fair held annually in Fryeburg

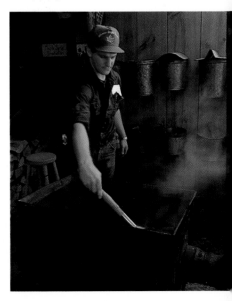

ACADIA TRIPS

Horse-and-carriage tours can be taken from Wildwood Riding Stables from Memorial Day to October (tel: 207/276 3622). Sailing trips on *Blackjack* run four times daily from Northeast Harbor (tel: 207/288 3056), while two-person glider rides leave from Bar Harbor Airport on Route 31 (tel: 207/667 SOAR). For mountain tours: Acadia National Park Tours (tel: 207/288 3327) and Oli's Trolley (tel: 207/288 9899). Cycling on the traffic-free carriage roads and on the Loop Road is possible; for rentals, Acadia Bike & Canoe, 48 Cottage Street, Bar Harbor (tel: 207/288 9605).

▶▶▶ Acadia National Park   108B2

This scenic national park is dominated by the 1,530-foot granite form of **Cadillac Mountain▶▶▶**, the highest point on the US Atlantic coast. While no one can expect solitude in high summer, Acadia is undeniably the most rewarding place for hiking on the entire New England seaboard. It gives outstanding opportunities for observing wildlife, both flora (boreal northern and temperate southern species) and fauna.

In 1919 Acadia became the first national park east of the Mississippi. Mount Desert Island (the major part of the national park, connected to the mainland by bridge) was endowed a 57-mile system of scenic carriage roads by John D Rockefeller, Jr. He considered Mount Desert Island 'one of the great views of the world' and donated more than 10,000 acres to the national park. Meanwhile, Bar Harbor became the summer society rival of Newport, Rhode Island, as the Astors, Rockefellers, Vanderbilts, Fords and others ensconced themselves here for the season. In 1947, a fire destroyed more than 60 of the millionaires' 'summer cottages'. Today everything is very much visitor-oriented.

VISITING ACADIA In July and August, **Bar Harbor** (outside the park boundary) becomes one of the busiest points on the Maine coast. It is the most practical place for

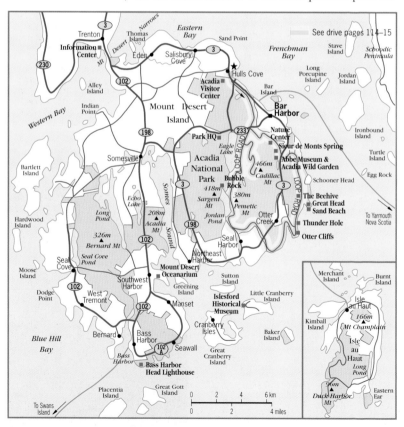

accommodation, eating and shopping, as well as a starting point for whale-watching cruises, bicycle hire, kayaking tours and sailing trips. Ferries sail from here for Nova Scotia. In the town are the Natural History Museum, the Oceanarium, the Wendell Tiley Museum of Bird Carving and the Bar Harbor Historical Museum.

Route 3 makes a drab entrance to Acadia, a virtually unbroken strip of motels, malls and amusement parks, but things soon get better. Most visitors concentrate on the east side of Mount Desert Island by following the **Park Loop Road►►►** (see pages 114–15).

The west side is much quieter and less dramatic, but tempting as an escape from the crowds, with few views from the wooded summits. Bass Harbor, Bernard, Southwest Harbor and Northeast Harbor are typical Maine fishing villages, and not particularly touristy. **Echo Lake** is good for swimming by virtue of being warmer than the waters on the coast. **Northeast Harbor** is a starting point for cruises into the Sound and out to the Cranberry Isles. From the village the **Sargent Drive** (cars and bicycles only) skirts the east side of **Somes Sound►►**, the East Coast's only fjord, carved by glaciers then flooded by the sea. An undemanding 2½-mile walk from Route 102 up Acadia Mountain on the sound's western side offers an outstanding view. **Bass Harbor Head Lighthouse** (1858) ranks among Maine's most photogenic lighthouses and can be reached by car.

Route 186 leads to **Birch Harbor** where you can follow the one-way coastal loop road to **Schoodic Point►**, which gives views of Mount Cadillac.

Acadia's furthest-flung outpost, **Isle au Haut►**, lies in Penobscot Bay and is reached by ferry from Stonington (no cars taken; tel: 207/367 5193). Quiet trails wind through the island's spruce forests and along its rugged shores; there is a small campsite. Ranger-led excursions are offered to **Great Cranberry Island. Little Cranberry Island** has a free museum covering maritime and local history. Ranger-led walks, often with a natural history content, are given free of charge in the park. Trailheads are mostly well-marked from the road.

With temperate and sub-Arctic species, such as this wild iris, Acadia is a rich hunting ground for naturalists

INFORMATION SOURCES
Thompson Island Information Center can help with accommodation and campsites, while the national park Visitor Center provides information and hiking maps.

For information and reservations, contact Acadia National Park, Bar Harbor, ME 04609 (tel: 207/288 3338); for camping reservations, tel: 1-800/365 2267. Between June and October the park publishes Acadia Beaver Log, a free newspaper listing ranger-led tours, cruises and walks.

113

Bar harbor.

From the loop road views extend across tiny bays and miniature cliffs

Drive

Acadia's Park Loop Road
See map on page 112.

This scenic (mostly one-way) 27-mile road skirts Cadillac Mountain and provides a series of views that encapsulate the stunning beauty of Acadia. Although the loop can easily be driven in two hours or so, it merits a full day so that some of its trails can be experienced to the full. It may also be undertaken as a

Some of Mount Desert's early summer residents (in 1913) presented the US government with lands which in 1919 were declared a national park

bicycle tour (there are several bike-rental shops in Bar Harbor), although some may find the traffic at peak times mars enjoyment. Parking is rarely a problem as you can stop anywhere on the right-hand side of the two-track road along its one-way section. Week-long or seasonal passes must be bought on entering the park; entrance is free for US citizens over 62 or registered as having disabilities.

The **Hulls Cove Visitor Center▶** marks the start of the Loop Road and has a diorama of the park and a film show about Acadia's natural history.

The **Acadia Wild Garden▶**, created by the Bar Harbor Garden Club in co-operation with the national park, demonstrates the range of wild flowers and vegetation that can be found in contrasting sites such as beach, bog, mountain heath and mixed woodlands. Immediately adjacent are the Nature Center, the **Sieur de Monts Spring** and the **Abbe Museum▶** of Indian artefacts, which tells the story of the local Native American inhabitants before the Frenchman Samuel de Champlain discovered Mount Desert Island in 1604.

One of the toughest walks, definitely not for vertigo-sufferers, is the **Precipice Trail▶**, which ascends lofty crags by means of rungs and ladders. In recent years, peregrine falcons have been nesting here and consequently the trail has been closed in the summer months. **Sand Beach▶**, the only sandy beach in the park, has great beauty but the water stays decidedly cool on even the hottest August day. If you turn right out of Sand Beach car park along the road, the trailhead for the **Beehive Trail▶** is almost immediately on the

Silver birch trees growing behind the sandy shore of Sand Beach

left. The short but strenuous path makes a spectacular ascent. There is an easier (less interesting) route which may be taken as a safe descent. Go right at the first path junction, and from the summit go forward, following signs for the Loop Road.

Exquisite views can be enjoyed from the **Ocean Trail▶** (3.6 miles there

and back), one of the most scenic easy walks in the national park. It runs closely parallel to the road, along the cliffs between Sand Beach and Otter Point. **Thunder Hole**, beside the road, needs bad weather to look its best, when the waves are tossed into the rock niche and the spray slants across its entrance. Otherwise it is little more than a minor chink in the coastline with pleasant rocks on which to sit.

The **Gorham Mountain Trail▶** offers further spectacular high-level views which are similar to those on the Beehive Trail (you can make a longer walk along the ridge to take in the Beehive), but the trail itself is less demanding. Just below the trail is Cadillac Cliff, an overhanging rock with a small cave.

Where the one-way traffic ends, you can detour south past **Seal Harbor**, a sandy beach, to **Northeast Harbor**, from where you can take a cruise (see panel on page 112). Alternatively, continue north to **Jordan Pond▶**, which has nature trails through the woods and along the lakeside. A longer scenic trail encircles the entire lake. The half-mile trail to South Bubble Summit, a 768-foot protuberance with a fine panorama, passes **Bubble Rock▶**, a classic glacial 'erratic' (deposited boulder), balanced precariously on its side.

The summit road to **Mount Cadillac▶▶▶** needs careful timing for the best of the light and the view, both of which can significantly change in quality for better or worse within a few minutes. When conditions are right you can see as far as Mount Katahdin (5,267 feet), Maine's highest point, located inland in distant Baxter State Park. Hikers who want the satisfaction of reaching a similar viewpoint without the crowds should follow the Dorr Mountain Trail, a short distance east of Sieur de Monts Spring.

So prolific was the lobster in the days of the early colonists that they would catch it with hooks or spears in shallow waters and feed it to chickens and prisoners. Today lobstering is one of New England's proudest traditions and the king of seafood is dispatched to top restaurants across the world.

116

LOBSTERING LORE

Each harbour has its own close-knit society, one that guards its trade fiercely. Fishing territories are strictly defined, by tradition, and each fisherman's buoys are painted in his own colours. Trespass and you may find, as one Portland fisherman did in 1993, a bomb in your trap. The scalloper who drags his nets and scoops along the ocean floor and falls foul of a lobster pot or two won't find a warm reception either.

FOR A CLOSER LOOK

Several ports operate trips on lobstering boats in summer months, including Bar Harbor, Boothbay Harbor and Ogunquit in Maine, and Gloucester in Massachusetts. Remember to take warm clothes.

Lobster pounds are the best place to enjoy the day's catch – straight from the sea

The tradition The American lobster, *Homarus americanus*, lives along the Atlantic coast between Labrador and North Carolina, being particularly plentiful off the coast of New England. Trapping on a commercial basis began in southern New England by 1800. By the mid-1800s the hoop net had been introduced, which meant lobster could be caught without damage, and Maine, by now heading the trade, was transporting live lobsters in sailing 'smacks' to New York and Boston, where they were boiled and sold on the streets. The Maine fishery also supplied no fewer than 23 canning factories with smaller, less saleable lobster. Canning ceased at the turn of the present century, but lobstering is still a vital part of the coastal economy, not only attracting tourists but also providing work for local industry producing the boats and the slatted trap that, with modifications, has been used for decades.

The catch Harbours bobbing with boats and wharves stacked high with traps and buoys reveal little of the tough life the 'trapper' leads. In all weathers he heads out to his line of buoys (pronounced 'boo-ies') at daybreak and winches up the strings of pots. Many trappers have up to 50 traps per string and 1,000 traps in all. Each lobster is measured to ensure it is of legal size; 'keepers' are typically 10 inches long overall, 1–1½ pounds in weight and about five years old. The bait (dead fish) is renewed, the lobster pots are returned to the ocean floor, and then the catch is turned in to the dealer. It's no easy way to make a living.

▶ **Augusta** *108A2*

Maine's state capital is not a place that routinely attracts visitors, but it has a handful of good sights justifying a brief detour. The town lies on the Kennebec river at the site of an early Pilgrim colony. Along the river extends the green swath of 34-acre Capitol Park. Above stands the prominent **State House▶**, dating from 1832 but extended twice since Charles Bulfinch designed it. The façade is original, although the dome replaced a cupola in the early 1900s. The building is open in normal office hours (*Open* Mon–Fri). Wall panels provide a self-guided tour to its function and history. Next door, the **Maine State Museum▶** presents attractive displays covering various aspects of the state's industry and life from the Ice Age to the present. Lumbering and ice-harvesting, two of the city's former mainstays, feature in the 'Made in Maine' displays, together with exhibits of the state's ship-building, sardine-canning and farming industries.

Fort Western▶, the oldest wooden fort in the US (1754), occupies the site of a Pilgrim trading post established near the river in the 1620s. The need for the fort arose from the colonists' nervousness of the French and Indians. It was never besieged and it became a trading post during its 12-year history as a fort. Its design was that of a typical New England fort, with a 100-foot-long main house. William Harvard, the commander, made the fort his home from 1766 to 1810, which is why it has survived; today it is presented as a house rather than a barracks. Reconstructions of the stockade blockhouses, with replica cannons and guns, date from 1921. Cannon firing takes place at weekends, and guides in period costume show visitors round (*Open* Memorial Day–4 July, daily 1–4; 4 July–Labor Day, Mon–Fri 10–4, Sat, Sun 1–4; Labor Day–Columbus Day, weekends 1–4).

Out of town, the **Matthews Museum** at Union comprises a collection of bygones, including a schoolroom, a horse-drawn hearse, a cooper's shop, a colonial kitchen, spinning and weaving items, and farm tools.

The Federal-style Blaine House (1833) in Augusta is the official residence of the state's governors

117

THE BIRTH OF MOXIE
The locally popular soft drink known as Moxie began life at Union, near Augusta, in 1885. Its inventor, Dr Augustin Thompson, originally sold it as Moxie Nerve Food. The Matthews Museum in the village has an interesting collection of memorabilia.

Above and below right: ships' figureheads and marine art feature among the indoor displays at Bath's maritime museum

KING OF BANGOR
Stephen King, the author, lives in West Broadway, Bangor, and his fans frequently track him down. Many of his novels and films have a local setting. Betts Bookstore in Main Street specialises in Stephen King books and memorabilia.

LUMBER CAPITAL
In the 19th century Bangor was the world's largest lumber-exporting centre. The industry peaked in 1872, when 2,200 ships entered Bangor via the Penobscot river in a year, but the timber supply waned and ship-building declined as paper-making assumed an important role in the state. At Bradley, off Route 178, the Maine Logging Museum at Orono stands on the site of Leonard's Mills (1790). It features a working water-powered sawmill, a sawing demonstration, a trapper's cabin and more. For opening times, tel: 207/581 2871.

▶ **Bangor**   108B2

Bangor is more a commercial centre than a visitor destination. Although victim of a fire in 1911 and much redeveloped in the 1960s, the city retains some fine buildings, notably along Broadway, High Street and the streets leading off. The **Thomas Hill Standpipe** in Summit Park is a unique contribution to Bangor's skyline. Built in 1897, this water-tower observation point is floodlit at night. The **Historical Society** operates a museum in a Greek Revival house at 159 Union Street (*Open* Mar–mid-Dec, Tue–Fri 12–4; Jul–Sep, also Sun) and runs bus tours round the city (Jul–Sep, Thu and the first Sat of the month).

Bangor's heyday is chronicled in the **Old Town Museum** on North 4th Street (*Open* Wed–Sun 1–5pm. *Admission* free). At the I–95 and I–395 intersection, the **Cole Land Transportation Museum** boasts over 200 vehicles, including snow-ploughs and logging trucks from old Maine (*Open* May–Nov).

▶▶ **Bath**   108A1

Bath's **Maine Maritime Museum and Shipyard**▶▶, at 243 Washington Street, is the most ambitious museum of its kind in the state. It occupies the last surviving wooden ship-building yard in the nation, used by Percy & Small from 1897 to 1920. The *Wyoming*, the largest ever sail vessel used in the country, was built here. Inside the Maritime History Building, a museum display tells the story of Maine's seafaring past from the days of the early explorers to 20th-century tourism and fishing. The museum possesses over 200 paintings and drawings, 250 models and 100 boats.

In the Percy & Small shipyard you can see apprentices at work restoring and building wooden boats on weekdays. Five of the original buildings survive; displays include small craft and the story of lobstering. Tours of the shipyard, available at no extra cost, are highly recommended.

Special cruises usually take place on Tuesdays, in addition to a regular programme of 50-minute narrated boat trips on *Hardy II*. The latter pass the Bath Iron Works, the state's largest industrial employer, and a major shipyard. It is usually possible to board vessels by the museum piers, including the *Sherman Zwicker*, where you can get an idea of the tough life endured by the Great Banks cod fishermen.

▶▶▶ Baxter State Park *108B3*

The park is one of the more accessible parts of Maine's unpopulated mountains and forests. Wild flowers, hiking, geology, whitewater rafting, cross-country skiing, moose-spotting, hunting, canoeing and fishing are among its attractions.

Baxter Peak (5,267 feet) is the summit of **Mount Katahdin▶▶** and marks the northern end of the 2,035-mile Appalachian Trail to Georgia. It is the highest point in Maine and probably the only mountain in the state to have remained bare of trees since glaciation. Several trails lead to the top, including the famous **Knife Edge Trail**, which edges its way along a sharp glacial ridge, or arête. Two cirques (glacial hollows) flank the Knife Edge, which is just 3 feet wide in places and with dizzy drops on either side of up to 2,000 feet. The trail is strictly for experienced walkers in calm weather conditions.

Great Basin is the finest of seven cirques on the mountain; the Chimney Pond Trail from Roaring Brook campsite gives access. Outstanding for its arctic wild-flowers, the Tableland has abundant evidence of freeze-thaw weathering processes on the rocks scattered over it.

Other notable trails include **Doubletop Mountain**, **South Turner**, the **Owl** and **The Brothers**. Moose may often be seen at **Big** and **Little Niagara Falls**.

Southwest of Baxter State Park, the West Branch of the Penobscot river has its moment of glory as it gushes though **Ripogenus Gorge▶▶** (access by unpaved road). Over a mile long, the gorge has almost vertical sides up to 200 feet high, with the rock strata exposed like a school textbook diagram. It can be seen on foot or by whitewater rafting or canoeing.

Further south, near Brownville Junction, is **Gulf Hagas▶▶**, another magnificent canyon best reached from Lloyd Pond. Here, the West Branch of the Pleasant River tumbles over five waterfalls, a memorable sight when in full spate in spring. Allow six hours for the hike.

The Lumberman's Museum (*Open* summer, except Jul and Aug), at **Patten**, has ten buildings that tell the story of the state's lumber industry. There is also a museum of bygones at the paper-producing town of **Millinocket**.

AN INDUSTRIAL GHOST TOWN
Gulf Hagas canyon can be included in a visit to the site of the Katahdin Iron Works, signposted off Route 11 south of Millinocket. Now a state memorial park, it retains kilns and a stone furnace as reminders of a mining town which in the 19th century produced almost 2,000 tons of raw iron per year and employed nearly 200 men.

CAMPING AT BAXTER
For information about camping in Baxter State Park, contact Baxter State Park Authority, 64 Balsam Drive, Millinocket, ME 04462 (tel: 207/723 5140). Reservations are advisable in summer as the numbers of campsites and lean-tos (simple shelters) are deliberately restricted.

Baxter State Park is remote, but one of the best places in Maine for moose-spotting

Maine

SUNRISE CANOEING
A memorable way to enjoy the wildlife and scenery of the Western Lakes area is to take a dawn canoe trip. Look for advertisements in Rangeley, for instance, for a guided trip that offers the chance to watch beavers and moose, and be serenaded by birdsong as the mists rise.

MOSS GARDEN
A few minutes' walk from Moose Cave in Grafton Notch State Park (signposted from the lay-by on Route 26) is this little fairy-tale clearing. A silvery carpet of reindeer moss (*Cladonia rangifera*), an exquisite erect ferny lichen, is interspersed with other mosses, some cool green and smooth, others darker and upright. With the tiny pine seedlings, it looks like a miniature forest.

New England cameo: rocking chairs and a pumpkin on a porch of a house in Bethel

▶▶ Bethel and the Western Lakes   108A2

The Western Lakes Region, stretching north from Sebago Lake up to the lakes and mountains around Rangeley, includes some of New England's most beautiful countryside, with forested hills rolling down to crystal lakes and rivers. The further north you go, the more remote and wild it all becomes. It offers excellent opportunities for walking, camping, fishing, golfing, sketching and moose-spotting. In summer there is boating of all sorts on the lakes and rivers, in winter every type of snow-sport and in autumn, of course, the brilliant foliage.

At the heart of the region is **Bethel▶**, a classic New England small town with craft shops, inns and restaurants. Near by is the Sunday River ski resort (see page 229). Alongside the road that passes the resort from Newry is one of Maine's most photographed covered bridges, **Sunday River Bridge**, built in 1870. Northwest of Newry is **Grafton Notch State Park▶▶**, an area of gorges, waterfalls and mountains, where walks range from short hikes such as Screw Augur Falls Gorge to challenging trails up Table Rock. North-east of the papermill town of Rumford, **Kingfield** has an absorbing rainy-day option in the Stanley Museum (*Open* 1–4, Tue–Sun; *closed* Apr and Nov), with items relating to the Stanley family, whose early 20th-century work encompassed steam-powered cars, violin-making and photography. Nearby, **Sugarloaf Mountain▶▶**, Maine's highest peak (4,237 feet) and a winter sports resort, merits taking the chairlift even outside the skiing season for the far-ranging views from its treeless summit.

Rangeley▶ is the hub of the Rangeley Lakes region, which offers canoeing, sailing, swimming, fishing and walking. The town has hotels, restaurants, campsites and sports shops (for rentals and licences), and a spectacularly sited golf course. The Rangeley State Park has chalets, picnicking and boat-launching areas.

South of Bethel is **Fryeburg**, a canoeing centre (with hire shops) famed for its agricultural fair in October. **Harrison**, set between Long Lake and Crystal Lake, is a another good centre for the outdoor enthusiast. Famous for its trout and land-locked salmon fishing, **Sebago Lake▶▶** is ringed with small towns offering plenty for the watersports enthusiast.

*Boothbay Harbor is a
busy boating resort as
well as an active
fishing port*

**VISITING MONHEGAN
ISLAND**
In 1614 Captain John
Smith landed here, and
settlers followed 11 years
later.
   Trips are offered from
Boothbay Harbor by Balmy
Days Cruises (tel: 1-
800/298 2284), and from
New Harbor by Hardy Boat
Cruises (tel: 1-800/278
8346).

121

▶ **Boothbay Harbor**   108B1

Settled in the 17th century and developed for tourism from
the 1870s, Boothbay Harbor is the largest boating harbour
north-east of Boston, as well as a busy resort town packed
with boutiques and galleries. The self-proclaimed 'boating
capital of New England' offers over 50 daily cruises, the
best choice in Maine – including seal-, whale- and puffin-
watching trips, deep-sea fishing expeditions and tours of
the coast and islands. By the Lobsterman's Co-op, the Sea
Pier Aquarium is stocked by local fishermen and contains a
good variety of species from the Gulf of Maine.

   On the east side of Route 27, near its intersection with
Route 1, **Boothbay Railway Village** is a village theme park
encompassed by a railway, where an original narrow-
gauge train hauls you through woods inhabited by garden gnomes. There is a collection of re-erected buildings
to explore (a blacksmith's shop, an old fire station, a
village school and more). For the most part, you can only
look inside the buildings from the entrances.

   Some 10 miles offshore, **Monhegan Island▶▶** is only
1½ miles across at its widest, but has surprising variety,
including some 400 species of wildflowers. The Cliff Trail
runs the length of the island and there are fine walks in
the balsam-scented Cathedral Woods, as well as 160-foot
cliffs on the east side. The island is partly developed for
visitors, with shops and restaurants. Monhegan's impressive ocean panoramas made the island a popular artists'
haunt: Rockwell Kent and Edward Hopper are among
those who have come and painted the scene.

   Across the inlet east of Boothbay Harbor is one of the
loveliest parts of Maine's seaboard, **Pemaquid Point▶▶**,
which is graced by wave-sculpted rocks and wind-
battered ledges. Pemaquid Point Light (1827) presides
over the scene, while the former lighthouse-keeper's cottage functions as a museum of commercial fishing and a
small art gallery, open in summer. At nearby **Pemaquid
Beach▶**, a sand beach rare for these parts, is the Colonial
Pemaquid Restoration, the excavated site of an early 17th-
century mariners' settlement, with an adjacent museum.
Fort William Henry is a replica of a 1692 fort and forms
part of a state park.

RAFTING
New England Whitewater
Center operates raft trips
on the Kennebec, Dead
and Penobscot rivers
between April and
October: Box 669,
Millinocket, ME 04462
(tel: 1-800/766 7238).

*Lobster fishing has been a
vital earner in Maine
since the 19th century*

Massachusetts Hall, Bowdoin's oldest building, dates from 1799

RECORDED FOR POSTERITY
The substantial film and video heritage of New England is being preserved by Northeast Historic Film, which operates from a restored 1916 cinema building in Bucksport, within sight of the massive form of Fort Knox. The exhibition 'Going to the Movies' looks at the movie-watching tradition from the early days (*Open* free 9–4 weekdays. For information about showings tel: 207/469 0924, or e-mail oldfilm@acadia.net; there is a website at www.acadia.net/oldfilm/.

FOREIGN VISITORS
Visitors to Campobello Island must bring their passports. Citizens of Australia, United Kingdom, New Zealand and Eire need no visa, but should be sure not to surrender their visa-waiver forms. Tell the passport-control officer that you intend to return the same day. Drive over International Bridge or take a ferry from Eastport via Deer Isle.

▶ **Brunswick**   *108A1*

Bowdoin College▶, in the centre of Brunswick, was founded in 1794 and counts among its former students the writers Henry Wadsworth Longfellow and Nathaniel Hawthorne, and President Franklin Pierce. Two fine museums (both free) flank the attractive campus green. Hubbard Hall, a tall and prominent tower, houses the Peary-MacMillan Arctic Museum, which tells the story of these two former students, who made the first successful expedition to the North Pole in 1909. Displays feature three rooms of sleighs, guns, equipment and writings. To the right of Hubbard Hall, the Art Museum has American colonial and federal portraits (among them Gilbert Stuart's painting of Thomas Jefferson), paintings by Winslow Homer and classical antiquities.

In town, the Pejepscot Historical Society maintains three museum properties. The Italianate **Skolfield-Whittier House** at 161 Park Row (*Open* summer 10–3, Tuesday to Friday; 10–4, Saturday), was closed up and forgotten about from 1925 until 1982, and inhabited by a sea-captain. It contains exotic items he brought back from his voyages and family possessions spanning three generations. Its north side houses the free **Pejepscot Museum** (local history and genealogy). The **Joshua L Chamberlain Museum** (*Open* summer, 10–4, Tuesday to Saturday) commemorates the college professor who achieved fame as the hero of Little Round Top in the Civil War Battle of Gettysburg.

▶ **Bucksport**   *108B2*

This small port on the Penobscot river is busy with tankers off-loading petroleum products and picking up coated paper manufactured locally. Route 1 crosses the Penobscot by Waldo-Hancock Bridge, affording a spectacular view of the formidable **Fort Knox▶▶**. Not to be confused with its more famous namesake in Kentucky, the fort was built between 1844 and 1869, originally because of the British threat from Canada. It was never completed but saw activity in the Civil War and Spanish American War of 1898. An annual Civil War encampment, with costumed actors and cannon firing, enlivens the fort on two weekends in July and August. Take a torch for exploring the inside of the structure (in restoration).

►► Campobello Island
(New Brunswick, Canada) — 108C2

Franklin D Roosevelt's 'beloved island', where he found rest and freedom from care, is just over the Canadian border, but his family summer house is jointly maintained as an International Park by the US and Canada. The park comprises 2,800 acres of deep forest, bogs, stone and sand beaches, ocean-side trails and viewpoints in addition to the house. Maps are available from the visitors' centre near International Bridge. (See also panel, page 122.)

The **Roosevelt Cottage►►** is in Dutch colonial style, and retains the original furniture. The atmosphere is comfortable and personal rather than grand, with the president's umbrellas and books put out as if the great man had just stepped outside. The adjacent visitor centre shows a film on Campobello and the Roosevelts (cottage and visitor's centre *open* daily, May–Oct. *Admission* free). Next door, the opulent **Hubbard Cottage** was home to Gorham and Sara Hubbard, an insurance businessman and a concert pianist who became friends of the Roosevelts. The cottage is open to the public.

Roosevelt spent his boyhood summers at a cottage on the adjacent site, which his father built in 1885 (demolished in 1951). His family later made the existing building the summer home.

Many roads on the 9-mile-long island are unpaved, but are passable in dry conditions. The northern tip offers a fine view, and whales can often be seen. **Friar's Head Outlook►►** (signposted between International Bridge and the Roosevelt Cottage) commands an impressive view of Passamaquoddy Bay.

On the way to Campobello, **Lubec** is the last village in Maine, and is noted for sardines and smoked herring. Aptly, it is home to the Old Sardine Village Museum, with displays including canning equipment, boats, a sheet-metal shop and a company store (*Open* Jul–Aug, Wed–Sun afternoons only; Jun and Sep weekends only).

To the south, **Quoddy Head►** marks the easternmost point of the US mainland. **West Quoddy Light**, built in 1858, sends out a 20-mile beam. A 4-mile trail along high cliffs provides opportunities for spotting whales.

THE BELOVED ISLAND
Franklin Roosevelt had a full and energetic life as a boy during family vacations on Campobello Island. In 1920 he received the vice-presidential nomination but was defeated. In 1921, at the age of 39, while on a boating trip here, he was suddenly stricken with an illness that was later diagnosed as polio, causing permanent paralysis. After becoming US president in 1921 he did not return to Campobello until 12 years later, and made only two subsequent visits. His wife Eleanor and their children came frequently.

123

Roosevelt's house on Campobello Island

One of New England's most familiar lighthouses, West Quoddy Light

'In 1492 Native Americans discovered Columbus lost at sea!', reads the T-shirt slogan. And not long afterwards these so-called 'American Indians' met the first European colonists on the shores of New England. This was a meeting of two cultures, which to this day are as different as chalk from cheese.

A PROUD TRADITION
Keeping the tradition of basket-making alive is important to the preservation of Indian culture. The Maine Arts Commission has developed a programme through which basket-makers pass on their skills to apprentices. These works of exquisite craftsmanship may be bought at crafts festivals and through co-operatives or shops.

A Passamaquoddy native of Maine

124

Windsong, a Massachusetts Wampanoag who does not live on an Indian reservation, is a deeply spiritual man. For his traditional, sacred rituals he needs eagle feathers. But the eagle is a protected bird and only Native Americans living on registered land are entitled to their feathers. This lack of awareness of the spiritual needs of another culture is, he says, typical of a white man's society brought up on images of peace-pipe-smoking Indians who raise one hand and call out 'How!', images that have more to do with Hollywood than real life.

Cultural and social issues For hundreds of years the Native People of the eastern United States have mixed with other elements in society – with blacks and, in more recent decades, with whites. Yet, although there is a degree of integration that may not exist in the western states of the US, where reservations are often enclaves of poverty and social disintegration, there is considerable resentment – on both sides.

In the workplace, for instance, Native Americans once felt a bitter sense of discrimination as they were overlooked for promotion. Now, however, anti-discriminatory regulations mean that this can no longer happen legally, and the pendulum has swung so far that the playing field is somewhat more even. Nevertheless, the clash of cultures remains and in many instances the archetypal, conscientious and diligent Yankee may find the Native American frustratingly casual.

Today there is far less social distinction between Native Americans and other Americans. Yet the Native American culture continues to be widely celebrated, notably with the opening in 1998 of the ambitious Mashantucket Museum and Research Center at Foxwoods, Connecticut (see page 95), built at the cost of $135 million.

Staking a claim

So regulations are bringing Native Americans closer to full integration into New England society. At the same time, the tribes are actively reasserting their own rights. In Maine the Penobscots and Passamaquoddy have long fought for legal control of fishing, mineral and forest rights on their lands. In Vermont the Abenaki threaten legal claims on much of the land. But the hottest issue concerns the Mashantucket Pequots in Connecticut.

In 1992 the Pequots, a tribe that had all but died out, opened Foxwoods High Stakes Bingo and Casino (see panel). It currently brings in more than $1 million daily on slot machines alone. It is the largest casino in the western hemisphere, a vast operation through whose ever-open doors pass 40,000 Americans a day, some bussed in for two hours from New York and Boston. Awaiting them are the 1,500 clattering slot machines, the bingo rooms and the blackjack, craps, baccarat, roulette, acey-deucey, money wheel, pai gow poker and chuck-a-luck, to name but a few of the table games. In an area of dire unemployment, Foxwoods is now one of the biggest employers. Moreover, Connecticut's coffers are fatter by well over $100 million per year, as a result of a deal with the governor whereby 25 per cent of slot machines takings are handed over in exchange for a monopoly control of all gaming machines in the state. Foxwoods looks after its employees well, but along with jobs it brings traffic, noise and, potentially at least, some of the less desirable members of society to the neighbourhood. Now its owners plan to buy more land, annexing it into sovereign Indian land and thereby removing it from local control and, significantly, state and federal tax rolls. This is cause for deep concern in the nearby villages and for bitter resentment amongst some of New England's tax-payers.

Top: spinning the wheel at Foxwoods
Left: a Connecticut Algonquin

125

SOVEREIGNTY OF LAND

A tribe that is federally recognised can assume responsibility for its own internal control. The Pequots, for instance, have established their own police force, housing authority, ambulance and fire service, as well as their own court system. They also have their own water supply and sewage system. No federally recognised tribe pays state or federal taxes. This means that cigarettes and alcohol can be sold more cheaply on a reservation than elsewhere.

PLAYING THE GAME

Federal law allows recognised Indian tribes to conduct gambling if the state in which they live allows gambling. Connecticut allows fund-raising, non-profit 'casino nights' (for example church bingo evenings) and the Pequots took advantage of this, opening Foxwoods Bingo in 1986. It began to make a profit and the state of Connecticut sued them. The case went to the Supreme Court, where the state lost. The Pequots obtained investment capital from Malaysia and opened the casino. In 1993 Rhode Island, not liking the possibility of a similar temple to gambling, repealed its law allowing fund-raising bingo.

Almost extinct 100 years ago, the puffin has recently been making a come-back in the Gulf of Maine

WILDLIFE SANCTUARY
Moosehorn National Wildlife Refuge, 5 miles north of Calais (pronounced 'Callous', itself north of Eastport on Route 1) on the Charlotte Road, consists of 23,000 acres of bogs, woods and marshes, inhabited by 216 species of birds, plus moose, deer, bear, beaver, mink and woodchuck (groundhog). Some 50 miles of roads and trails are open to hikers.

► Eastport *108C2*

This is small-town Maine at its most seductively peaceful, far removed from the crafts-designer shops and tourist crowds of the more frequented parts of the coast. Eastport's population numbers under 2,000 but is rated important enough to have its own city hall. High, Ray, Washington and Water streets contain an attractive mixture of architectural styles, from colonial to Victorian.

In the town itself, seek out Raye's Mustard, the last stone-ground mustard mill in America, a legacy of the days when mustard was used as a preservative. In the summer months (afternoons only), you can visit the local history museum, which is housed within the old Sullivan Barracks (1809). The garrison surrendered to the British in the War of 1812 without a shot being fired.

RAYE'S MUSTARD

CONTENTS: MUSTARD SEED, TURMERIC & SPICES, VINEGAR.

Net Wt.

Choice Quality SINCE 1903

12 oz.

SALT FREE

ALL NATURAL • STONE GROUND
AGED IN THE BARREL

J.W. RAYE & CO., INC. P.O. BOX 2 EASTPORT, MAINE 04631

The town, sited on Moose Island and linked by causeway to the mainland, is a sardine, granite, timber and processed-paper port. It lies on **Passamaquoddy Bay►►**, site of the world's largest lobster pound, and notorious for treacherous waters that include fast incoming tides and great changes in water levels. Old Sow, the world's second largest whirlpool, can be seen from the car ferry to Deer Island. The curious tidal phenomenon of **Reversing Falls**, where the current goes in the contrary direction to the tide at certain times of day, occurs near Pembroke (for directions see panel opposite). Two dams near Lubec are all that remain of an abandoned scheme begun in 1919 to harness tidal energy from the bay.

A little further south, **Cobscook Bay State Park** has two trails, one leading to the coast, the other along the creek.

There are ferry connections to **Deer Island**, connecting with another ferry for **Campobello Island►►** (see page 123). At the far end of Deer Island a free ferry crosses to L'Etete on the Canadian mainland.

In the former lumber town of **Machias**, the **Burnham Tavern►** on High Street (dating from 1770) is eastern Maine's oldest building. Here patriots planned the capture of the British schooner *Margaretta* on 12 June 1775, after the British captain had ordered locals to take down their liberty pole. This was the first naval battle of the Revolution, the 'Lexington of the Sea'. Now a museum, the tavern has Revolutionary-era furnishings and items from the British vessel.

On Route 92, half a mile from town, the Maine Wild Blueberry Company produces around 20 million pounds of berries a year; free tours (weekdays in summer, best by appointment; tel: 207/255 8364) show the processes of cleaning, freezing and grading

Revolutionary memorabilia is displayed in the Burnham Tavern, Machias

the berries. Route 191 leads through the town of **Cutler**, where the lobster hatchery is open to the public in summer. Route 187 reaches **Jonesport**, a typical Downeast fishing village, linked by bridge to Beal Island, where clams are raised. A causeway gives access to the Mud Hole Trail (from Black Duck Cove), with good views across to the islands.

▶ **Ellsworth**   *108B2*

An unassuming small town on the way to Bar Harbor, Ellsworth has a fine First Congregational Church (1846), thought to be Maine's best example of a Greek Revival church. The steeple is a faithful fibreglass replica. The Old Hancock County Buildings, on Cross Street, are in similar style. The Big Chicken Barn, on Route 3 in town, is Maine's largest antiquarian bookstore and antique shop.

Just out of town is the **Colonel Black Mansion▶** (*Open* Jun–mid-Oct), built in 1824–8 by land agent Colonel John Black. This charming Georgian home has original furnishings, a fine circular staircase and delightful formal gardens. The old carriage house contains old sleighs and carriages.

Out on Route 3, the **Birdsacre Sanctuary** covers 100 acres, with trails leading past ponds and nesting areas. The Stanwood Homestead Museum here is dedicated to pioneer ornithologist Cordelia Stanwood.

Lamoine State Park▶, on Route 184, has excellent views of Mount Desert Island and a safe beach. At Columbia Falls, just off Route 1, is **Ruggles House▶** (*Open* 1 Jun–Oct), which dates from 1818 and was inhabited until 1920. The house is noted for its 'flying' staircase (supported only at the top and bottom); the woodcarving on the staircase was executed with a penknife over a three-year period.

GRANITE MEMENTOES
On Route 1 between Calais and Robbinston are 12 granite milestones erected by James Shepherd Pike in 1870. Pike, a lumberman, abolitionist, ambassador and writer, had a summer residence in Robbinston. By measuring the circumference of his cartwheels, he placed the stones to check the speed of his horses.

REVERSING FALLS
The 'Falls' take some finding. Turn off Route 1 at Pembroke, taking the road to the right of the post office. Very soon turn right and then left (signposted to the shore), then, after 3.2 miles, turn right past a cemetery. Bear left at a T-junction with a dirt track. Continue for 1.4 miles, then fork left beyond a covered picnic bench up on the left: the car park is just beyond.

127

The 1817 Tisdale House, now Ellsworth's City Library

LL BEAN

This famous store started as a humble one-man mail-order operation and has since boomed. In 1912 Leonwood Bean marketed his invention, the Maine Hunting Shoe: 'designed by a hunter who has tramped the Maine Woods for the past 18 years. They are as light as a pair of moccasins with the protection of a heavy hunting boot.' Today the store sells over 6,000 products. It is still largely mail-order, but there are factory outlets at Ellsworth, ME, and North Conway, NH.

Above: Freeport is home to the popular mail-order clothing company, LL Bean

Penobscot Bay has long been busy with boats, both large and small

►► Freeport 108A1

Freeport, Maine's biggest visitor attraction along with Acadia National Park, consists of a main street lined wall-to-wall with factory shopping outlets. There are over 100, and most of the time sale prices are offered somewhere. Serious shoppers journey up here from New York and even further to make Christmas purchases.

It is a matter of dispute whether Freeport is really such good value (compared to North Conway for instance), but the choice (candles, kids' clothes, maps and guides, crafts, sports equipment, soap and so on) is impressive. Although village-sized, Freeport is crammed with shoppers transporting bulging carrier bags, and the traffic and car parks are on an urban scale. Maps showing locations of the stores are given away at Bean's and other shops. Freeport has inns, motels and B&Bs as well as a beach, and is the starting point for ocean cruises.

Outside Freeport, the **Desert of Maine►** is a curiosity. This really is a small desert, an eye-opening example of 18th-century bad farming practice, where the soil was depleted and massive erosion followed. Entire farm buildings and trees were engulfed in the dunes, and tell-tale tree-tops still protrude like small bushes. From May to Columbus Day a tour is provided of this odd tribute to human failure.

South of town, live osprey and seals may be spotted from **Wolf Neck Woods State Park►**, which has trails and wooded shores as well as some unusual rock formations. At **Bradbury Mountain State Park►** a 20-minute trail to the summit leads to views over Casco Bay, while other paths head along the bay and Harraseeket river.

►► Penobscot Bay 108B2

The biggest indentation in Maine's coast, Penobscot Bay and its islands offer some of the loveliest panoramas along New England's seaboard. Boating has been big here for centuries. The Penobscot river once supplied over 20 towns with timber for ship-building, and today the ports are busy with pleasure and commercial craft. Rockland and Camden are the busiest boating areas; Camden is much prettier and more of a resort. Be warned, though: the sprawl along Route 1 is unsightly, and in summer driving along it is no pleasure.

THE WEST SIDE Port Clyde, situated on the west side of the bay, is the departure point for ferries making crossings to **Monhegan Island►►** (see page 121). On the way to the town you pass through Tenants Harbor, a typical fishing village complete with lobster boats moored in the harbour.

Further north, **Owls Head Transportation Museum►►** opens year-round, and displays New England's largest collection of pioneer vehicles from the early 20th century. They include a number of vintage bikes, early horseless carriages and gas-powered cars. A schedule of events features airshows, and motorcycle and tractor meets.

Nearby **Rockland**, New England's biggest distribution centre for the lobster industry and a major sardine port, has a workaday atmosphere. The local processing of seaweed gives the place a wholesome whiff.

The **Old Conway Homestead and Museum**, Route 1 and Conway Road (*Open* Jul–Aug, Tue–Fri 10–4) is an atmospheric 1770s farmhouse and barn with farm tools, a blacksmith shop and a maple-sugar house (with sugaring demonstrations in spring).

On the move at Owls Head Transportation Museum

129

THE BEANS OF EGYPT, MAINE
No relation to the Beans of Freeport, the Bean family of Egypt was a fictitious invention of novelist Carolyn Chute. Her book *The Beans of Egypt, Maine* (1985) is the saga of a violent and primitive family, prisoners of rural poverty in the woods of Maine. Despite its bleak setting, the novel has moments of black humour.

BAY ISLANDS
Penobscot Bay's main islands make attractive hiking or cycling country. Vinalhaven, the largest at 14 miles long, and Islesboro (12 miles long) have accommodation but no camping is allowed. North Haven and Matinicus both have accommodation and camping by permission. Isle au Haut is part of Acadia National Park (see pages 112–13). For Monhegan Island, see page 121. Islesboro is reached by ferry from Lincolnville Beach; North Haven, Vinalhaven and Matinicus from a car ferry at Rockland. For details, call the Maine State Ferry Service (tel: 1-800/529 3939).

Maine

CASTINE'S MILITARY PAST

Castine had a strategic importance and was fought over by the French, Dutch, British and Americans for nearly two centuries. Above the Maine Maritime Academy are the grassy ramparts of Fort George, built by the British in 1779 to protect Canadian interests and the last fort they abandoned at the end of the Revolutionary War. It retains its moat and earthworks.

Crammed into the **Shore Village Museum►►**, at 104 Limerock Street, Rockland, is the largest collection of lighthouse lenses and lighthouse paraphernalia in the US, plus coastguard buoys, bells, ship models, navigational instruments, Civil War memorabilia and 19th-century costume dolls (*Open* daily, 1 Jun–15 Oct, 10–4; donations requested). Also in Rockland is an outstanding art collection at the **Farnsworth Art Museum and Homestead►►** (*Open* Nov–May, Tue–Sat 9–5, Sun 12–5). The display of art is rotated and features Maine and New England art and artists, including the three generations of the Wyeth family. Winslow Homer's *Girl in a Punt* is one of the best-known works. The 19th-century Greek Revival homestead of William A Farnsworth, the lime baron who endowed the museum, has period décor in its 12 small rooms.

Andrew Wyeth had a studio at the **Olson House** on Hathorn Point Road, Cushing (*Open* Jun–Oct, 11–4). He depicted the owner, Christina Olson, in front of the house

The bold and bright Romance of Autumn by George Bellows (1882–1925), on display at the Farnsworth Art Museum in Rockland

in *Christina's World*, one of the most evocative of all American paintings.

Rockport► has a charming village centre, little changed from the 19th century, which overlooks a marina, old lime kiln and oceanside park. The best of **Camden►** lies off busy Route 1: Chestnut and Bayview streets are conspicuously attractive. Crafts shops and traffic jams are the norm in summer, with window-shoppers spilling off the sidewalks. The village keeps going all year, with events, a community theatre, an opera house and a winter carnival.

Mount Battie is the crowning glory of **Camden Hills State Park►►►** (*Open* 1 May–1 Nov), where a toll road winds up to the top for a glorious view of the bay and towards Acadia, and over the strikingly empty hinterland. Hikers can walk 25 miles of park trails; it takes 1–1½ hours to ascend the mountain on foot.

Searsport is Maine's 'antiques capital', well endowed with shops and flea markets. **Penobscot Marine Museum**▶▶ (Open Memorial Day weekend–15 Oct) chronicles the maritime history of Penobscot Bay. Searsport once specialised in building trading ships, and several captains' houses (including the Fowler-True-Ross House) survive from those times. The museum is on several neighbouring sites; one ticket covers tham all. The main building has a notable collection of maritime art, a remarkable film of a 1929 voyage around Cape Horn in a hurricane and a quaint assemblage of 200 butter dishes collected by a captain's wife. Other buildings display small craft, whaling and scrimshaw, and ship-building.

THE EAST SIDE By complete contrast this side of Penobscot Bay has few attractions but has a quiet charm of its own by virtue of its inaccessibility. A causeway links Deer Isle to the mainland, with the sleepy fishing village of Stonington at its southern tip, where ferries leave for Isle au Haut in Acadia National Park (see pages 112–13). **Blue Hill**▶▶ rises to 934 feet just north of the village of the same name: from the village take Route 15 north, then turn right into Mountain Road; the trail starts on the left-hand side and ascends for a view over Acadia and Penobscot Bay. An easier viewpoint to reach is the Caterpillar Hill picnic area a mile south of the junction of Routes 15 and 175.

Castine▶▶, one of the most attractive villages in the state, has some gracious early 19th-century homes, with plaques recording their history, in Main and Perkins streets. By the common is the First Parish Church, begun in 1790 and eastern Maine's oldest church. At shore level, lawns slope to the water's edge and there are two museums. The entire village has been designated a National Historic Site (see panel opposite). Berthed here is the *State of Maine*, a former troopship used by the adjacent Maine Maritime Academy for training merchant midshipmen. Regular tours are given round the ship; for hours, call 207/326 4311.

Crockett Cove Woods Preserve is a 100-acre site maintained by the Nature Conservancy and comprising coastal spruce woods and a miniature bog. A self-guided trail leads visitors around the preserve, and brochures are available from the entrance registration box.

A NOSTALGIC SIDE-TRIP At Belfast, the Belfast & Moosehead Lake Railroad (tel: 1-800/392 5500) runs narrated two-hour trips to Brook in 1920s Pullman cars. This is a 25-mile round trip (it is extended to 33 miles in the autumn), and you get 'ambushed' by comic bandits on the way. A critically acclaimed theatre shares the train station, located near the water's edge. The railroad operates at weekends in spring, daily except Monday in summer; there are autumn foliage specials on Friday and at weekends.

131

WINDJAMMER VACATIONS Companies in Penobscot Bay offer vacations on schooners known as windjammers (see picture below). Participants stay for the week and can enjoy sailing trips lasting from two hours to several days on tall-masted wooden sailing ships (some are magnificent 19th-century restorations). You can hoist the sails, take a turn at the wheel and help navigate. Anyone sailing alone in the Boothbay or Penobscot Bay areas should have plenty of experience and be able to read a nautical chart.

Camden has the largest fleet of windjammers

For lovers of the great outdoors, New England has something for everyone, whether lone fishermen or families, adventurous young or 'active seniors'. From spring to autumn there is first-rate hiking, cycling, fishing and golfing. There are watersports from sailing and wind-surfing to canoeing and whitewater rafting.

CANOEING

The Appalachian Mountain Club (AMC) publishes *Quiet Water Canoe Guide, New Hampshire/Vermont* and *River Guide, Central/Southern New England.* Contact AMC, PO Box 298, Gorham, NH 03581 (tel: 603/466 2721). Canoes can be hired and trips operate from dozens of places, including the Rangeley Lakes area, ME; the Lamoille and Batten Kill rivers, VT; the Saco river at Conway, and the Connecticut river at Hanover and Balloch's Crossing (all in NH). Information leaflets are available locally.

Hiking and biking Walking, or as Americans call it, hiking, is on marked trails (see page 257). All state parks have clearly signed trails, and notice-boards often indicate length and difficulty. Trails range from easy to extremely challenging, but with vast areas of New England covered in forest, the terrain is not always particularly varied.

New Hampshire's White Mountains make superb hiking territory (see page 208). The lakes and forests of Maine's Kennebec Valley and the Western Lakes and Mountains are popular for hiking and biking. Bicycles can be hired in many places. Naturalists will enjoy the trails in Baxter State Park. As with several other ski areas in Maine, Vermont and New Hampshire, Sunday River in Maine has a network of mountain-bike trails using the ski-lifts. The Cape Cod National Seashore has 40 miles of hiking and cycling trails; the Berkshires is another favourite area. Nantucket, MA, and Block Island, RI, have miles of biking paths.

Fishing and golfing Anglers can find excellent fishing opportunities throughout New England. Lake Champlain, 100 miles long, has dozens of public access points for fishing for lake trout, land-locked salmon, bass, walleye and the brightly coloured, tasty pumpkinseed. The lake is also superb for ice-fishing, an increasingly popular winter sport.

From mid-April to the end of October there is excellent fishing for landlocked salmon and trout in the lakes and ponds of New Hampshire and areas of Maine such as Bethel and Rangeley, the Winthrop Lakes, and around The Forks and Jackman in the north. Vermont's Northeast Kingdom region is especially popular. The region also has numerous 'backwoods' ponds, remote and lovely beaver ponds teeming with brown trout and needing a map to reach them. The 397-mile-long Connecticut River is a scenic, peaceful waterway, a delight for anglers.

New England's spectacular natural scenery makes a glorious backdrop for hundreds of public golf courses. Hire of clubs and carts is easy to arrange. Some of the most magnificent courses are offered by grand resort hotels such as The Balsams at Dixville Notch, NH, the Mount Washington in

Anywhere in New England, fishing provides beautiful scenery: above, near the Mohawk Trail

the White Mountains, or Tory Pines, set in the Monadnock region, all with panoramic views. Outstanding courses in Vermont include the Woodstock Inn Resort as well as clubs in Stratton and Manchester Village (The Equinox). In Connecticut try Lyman Orchards in Middlefield and the Richter Park or the Hilton in Danbury. There is a fine course near Rangeley in northern Maine and in the Berkshires Cranwell is an old country hotel with a splendid course.

Watersports There is good sailing from many places around the coast. Newport, Rhode Island, former home of the America's Cup, and the Penobscot Bay section of the Maine coast are the best-known areas (but beware, much of the Maine coast has odd currents and is not for the novice – see panel, page 131). Inland, Lake Champlain and the bigger lakes in New Hampshire and Maine are popular for sailing, sailboarding, canoeing and windsurfing, and most have boats for hire. The Connecticut River and the Housatonic provide plenty of opportunities for easy canoeing. Canoeing is a wonderfully peaceful way to explore the remoter areas of northern New England, offering intimate encounters with beaver, moose and other wildlife (see panels, opposite page and page 120).

Whitewater rafters await the spring run-off, when the rivers start to swirl and swell. Mecca is The Forks, in Maine, where several companies organise trips down the Kennebec, Dead and Penobscot rivers. In the far north, experts relish the challenges of the Allagash Wilderness Waterway. In Vermont, whitewater rafting trips operate on West river. There is rafting on seven rivers from Conway, New Hampshire, and in western Massachusetts there are rafting centres on the Deerfield river.

FISHING
Licences may be obtained from town clerk offices, local sporting shops or the state Fish and Wildlife Office (see below).

Vermont Fish and Wildlife Department, 103 South Main Street, Waterbury, VT 05676, publishes a *Guide to Fishing* leaflet.

Other useful addresses for further information on fishing:
● Connecticut Department of Environmental Protection, 79 Elm Street, Hartford, CT 06106.
● Maine Department of Inland Fisheries and Wildlife, 284 State Street, Augusta, ME 04333.
● Massachusetts Division of Marine Fisheries, 100 Cambridge Street, Boston MA 02202.
● New Hampshire Fish and Game Department, 2 Hazen Drive, Concord, NH 03301.
● Rhode Island Division of Fish and Wildlife, Government Center, 4808 Tower Hill Road, Wakefield, RI 02879.

THE APPALACHIAN TRAIL
The Appalachian Trail (2,144 miles) stretches from Maine, through New Hampshire, Vermont, Massachusetts and Connecticut, continuing south to Georgia. Road access makes it easy to cover short stretches. The Appalachian Mountain Club estimates that of some 2,000 to 3,000 who attempt the trail each year, only 10 per cent complete it.

CASCO BAY

Casco Bay is the largest deep-water haven on the Atlantic coast; the islands that protect the bay are said to number 365. The first secret war conference between Churchill and Roosevelt took place in a battleship off Long Island in the bay, when the Atlantic Pact was signed. Several fortifications can be spotted on the islands, including forts Scammel, McKinley and Gorges. South Portland is the water terminal for the Portland–Montreal pipeline. Crude oil super-tankers from South America and the Middle East are common sights.

Brewed in Portland

CRUISES FROM PORTLAND

Casco Bay Lines' mailboat run is the longest such operating service in the US, stopping at the islands of Cliff, Chebeague, Long, Little and Great Diamond. The company also provides cruises to Bailey Island (tel: 207/774 7871). Eagle Tours (tel: 207/774 6498) offer seal-watching and fishing trips, as well as cruises to Eagle Island.

►► Portland 108A1

Maine's largest city prospered as a port on the basis of its accessibility to Europe. Its decline after World War II was reversed by a revival in fortunes, spearheaded by the revitalisation of the Old Port Exchange district, with its uniform grid of red-brick streets rebuilt in the 1860s after a disastrous fire. This part of the city is pleasant for walking, and has restaurants, boutiques and speciality shops. Portland's face is unmistakably urban, but the city has good cultural attractions. Commercial Street runs along the harbour, where you can join cruises (see panel).

The **Portland Museum of Art►►**, in Congress Square, houses one of New England's finest art collections. The American collection includes Maine scenes by Winslow Homer, Andrew Wyeth, Marsden Hartley and Rockwell Kent. European art features sculpture by Henry Moore and Rodin, and Impressionist and Cubist works. The museum is closed Monday, with late nights on Thursday and Friday; gallery tours are at 11 and 2 daily (for current opening hours, tel: 1-800/639 4067).

Next door, the **Children's Museum of Maine►**, 142 Free Street (*Open* daily; until 8pm on Fri; free admission 5–7pm Fri), ranks among the best of its kind in New England.

At 485–9 Congress Street is the **Wadsworth-Longfellow House►**, the childhood home of Henry Wadsworth Longfellow, America's most popular 19th-century poet. His family was comfortably well off but not wealthy, and in the house are numerous family possessions and portraits (*Open* Jun–Columbus Day, Tue–Sat, 10–4). Longfellow was inspired to write several poems about Portland, including *The Lighthouse, My Lost Youth* and *The Ropewalk*. He penned *The Rainy Day* in the house.

Portland Observatory, at 138 Congress Street, was built in 1807, and is a rare example of a signal tower on which signal flags would be flown to identify incoming vessels.

Victoria Mansion►►, on the corner of Danforth and Park streets, is an ornate Italianate brownstone house, built 1858–60 and reflecting northern European taste. The interior is a lavish showpiece, with plasterwork made to resemble wood, an intricate eye-catching chandelier, painted walls and ceilings, and a Moorish-style smoking room (Open Memorial–Labor Day; Labor Day–Columbus Day weekends only; closed Mon).

Tate House, 1270 Westbrook Street (*Open* May–Oct, Tue–Sat 10–4, Sun 1–5) is a fine colonial-period house with a riverside setting and 18th-century herb garden. A worthwhile free visit is the **Neal Dow Memorial**, at 714 Congress Street, a Federal mansion of 1829 which belonged to a leading figure in the temperance cause (*Open* Mon–Fri 11–4).

Fort Williams Park► occupies a fine section of rocky coast south of the city. Adjacent to the fort, Portland Head Light (1791) is the oldest lighthouse in Maine and inspired Longfellow. A museum in the lighthouse-keeper's quarters tells its story (*Open* Jun–Oct; weekends only in Nov, Dec, Apr and May). Lighthouse devotees may also like to visit nearby **Two Lights State Park**. Not far away, artist Winslow Homer made his home at Prout's Neck (also open).

► **Wiscasset**   *108B1*

On the Sheepscot river at Wiscasset is one of the most evocative sights on Route 1: the two huge wrecks of the *Hesper* and *Luther Little*, the world's last four-masted schooners, here since the 1930s. Every 4 July they are set alight, and their eventual demise seems on the cards.

Fort Edgecomb► (*Open* May–Labor Day in daylight hours) is reached by turning off Route 1 on the east side of the river bridge and is a well-preserved octagonal wooden blockhouse built in 1808–9. It was one of four defensive forts on the Lincoln County coast. Although there is nothing to see inside, the riverside setting is magnificent.

In town, at Lee and High streets, is **Castle Tucker** (*Open* Jul–Aug, Tue–Sat 11–4) a grand house built in 1807 by Judge Silas Lee and later modified, and now displaying 19th-century furnishings. In Federal Street, the **Old Lincoln County Jail** (*Open* daily except Mon in summer), was built in 1811 and in use until 1953. Visitors can see the cells and jailer's house.

Rail and sail excursions run from Wiscasset (see panel below)

RAIL AND SAIL
Combined rail and sail excursions from Wiscasset from May to October are offered by Maine Coast Railroad (tel: 1-800/795 5404). The excursion train features restored 1920s and 1930s carriages, and the cruise explores the Sheepscot river and passes Fort Edgecomb.

LONGFELLOW'S TRAGEDY
On Longfellow's marriage to his cousin, Fanny Appleton, in 1843, her father presented the house in Cambridge, Massachusetts (see page 75) to the couple as a wedding present. She died 18 years later when her hoop skirt caught fire while melting sealing-wax to preserve locks of her children's hair. Henry grew a beard to cover the physical scars incurred while trying to save her, but remained emotionally scarred.

The hulks of two schooners, built around the end of World War I, dominate the scene at Wiscasset

*Hancock Warehouse,
York, dates from the mid-
1700s and is still used as
a boathouse today*

BLOWING CAVE
Located between Walker
Point and Cape Arundel,
just east of Kennebunk-
port, this sea cave is a
curious phenomenon. As
waves enter it, air is
trapped and compressed;
as the water recedes, the
trapped air is released,
sometimes sending out a
spray of sea-water.
Unfortunately it is difficult
to see this happen as the
cave is only really
accessible at low tide,
but it is fun to explore just
the same.

IN LOVE WITH THE PAST
Elizabeth Perkins and her
mother fell in love with
their house in York and
spent their summers
there. Proud of their New
England heritage and
ancestors, the Perkins
crammed the house with
antiques and furniture,
creating a comfortable
rather than historically
accurate house for enter-
taining and holidaying.
Elizabeth took an interest
in preserving York and
was responsible for saving
the schoolhouse and
wooden bridge. She loved
collecting antiques, and
installed old-fashioned
beams and panelling for
effect in the dining room.
Both women's ashes are
in the garden.

*Elizabeth Perkins House,
transformed into an
idyllic weekend retreat
by a wealthy New
York family*

▶▶ **York and Kennebunkport**   *108A1*
York is a composite place: just off Route 1 lies historic
York Village, alone worth at least half a day to explore.
Along the shoreline are Long Sands Beach (popular for
surfing) and the famous Nubble Lighthouse (also known
as Cape Neddick Lighthouse), built in 1789 on York
Beach, which itself retains a graceful 19th-century air.
York Harbor is a small area between the old village and
the beaches.

THE OLD YORK HISTORICAL SOCIETY SITES These
include a number of buildings, some with tours conducted by interpreters, others self-guided. Tours start on the
hour; the last are at 4pm. **Jefferds Tavern** (1754), where
you buy your ticket, features displays about York and is
often filled with the aroma of hearth-side cooking. Next
door, the **Old Schoolhouse** (1745) has a small exhibit on
schooling and apprenticeship in Maine.

Made from two colonial houses put together, the
Emerson Wilcox House▶ is presented in a variety of periods, from the 1765 parlour to the 1930s dining room. The
bedroom possesses the oldest known complete set of
American bed-hangings, done in crewel work in 1746
and in pristine condi-
tion (with the origi-
nal spelling mistakes
in the words of a
hymn worked into
the design).

The Old Gaol▶, in
use from 1719 to
1860, took in about 14
prisoners per year;
interpreters fill in the
facts and legends. Jail
quarters and the
jailer's chambers are
on show.

The **Hancock Ware-
house▶**, once owned
by John Hancock,
occupies a charming
spot on an unspoilt

creek, near a wooden bridge. A replica of an 1880s gundalow (a flat-bottomed boat) is often on the river here. The warehouse is the last commercial colonial building in town, and is still used as a working boathouse. It houses a small exhibition on ship-building, timber, shipping, farming and lobstering.

By the York river, the **Elizabeth Perkins House▶▶** is a fascinating example of the Colonial Revival style – a colonial house kitted out during the 1920s to 1940s in an idealised conception of the colonial style itself. Its transformation began in 1898 when the Perkins bought the (then four-roomed) 18th-century farmhouse (see panel on page 136).

ELSEWHERE ALONG THE COAST The yachting and fishing village of **Kennebunkport** is the home and former Summer White House of ex-President George Bush, who used to jog along the beach (often with scores of red-faced reporters and photographers in tow). His house at Walker's Point can be seen from the sea-front, otherwise memorable for its swing-bridge. On Route 9A/35, the Wedding Cake House is a particularly fetching yellow and white confection.

The **Brick Store Museum▶**, at 117 Main Street, Kennebunk (*Open* Tue–Sat; closed Sat in winter), is a fine local history museum with rotating exhibits on both maritime and social history, and on the decorative arts. Three miles north of Kennebunkport, the **Seashore Trolley Museum▶** (*Open* May–Nov) has the world's largest collection of trolleys (trams), and offers a chance for you to take a nostalgic ride.

Route 1 in this area is packaged-fun country. At York itself is the **Wild Kingdom** (with zoo and amusement park). The **Wells Auto Museum** has more than 130 vintage automobiles as well as an entertaining assembly of antique arcade games, nickelodeons and other items; it is open in summer. Saco is home to **Funtown**, the **Maine Aquarium** and **Aquaboggan Water Park**. **Old Orchard Beach**, on the coast, has a sandy shoreline and is densely developed with fast-food outlets and amusements; Palace Playland is a major attraction whose seaside rides are reminiscent of New York's Coney Island.

Ogunquit is an upmarket resort village, and was once an artists' colony. Cove views are available from a pretty swing-bridge leading to Perkins Cove, and from a mile-long coastal path known as Rustic Way. Ogunquit's Museum of Art is open in the summer months, and there is a summer theatre season.

Kittery▶ has similar factory shopping outlets to Freeport (see page 128); there are over 100 such discount stores along Kittery's 'miracle mile', offering savings of up to 70 per cent.

WEBHANNET RIVER MARSH
The marsh, off Route 1, is an important bird habitat. Species include the scarce piping plover, a small buff and white bird with a black band around its neck. Ducks, grebes, loons, gulls and herons may also be seen at the marsh.

BEACHES
Beaches in this area are safe for swimming and the water is clean. The main ones are Long Sands Beach at York; Ogunquit, one of the best in Maine, stretching 3 miles; Goose Rocks at Kennebunkport, a favourite with families; and Kennebunk Beach.

137

Travel through time at the Trolley Museum near Kennebunkport

MASSACHUSETTS Even apart from the attractions of
Boston and Cambridge (see pages 48–85), there is plenty
in the rest of Massachusetts to excite the curious traveller.
The state is the cradle of modern America and as such is
packed with history. In 1620 the Pilgrim Fathers landed at
Provincetown, some 600 miles further north than they
had intended (they were bound for Jamestown in
Virginia) before finally establishing themselves at
Plymouth. In 1775 the first shots of the American
Revolution sounded at Lexington and Concord. In the
19th century the first large-scale textile mills appeared in
Lowell, heralding the birth of industrial America.
Massachusetts is seen as a centre of political and intellec-
tual thought: great names associated with the state
include Ralph Waldo Emerson (1803–82), Henry David
Thoreau (1817–62), Herman Melville (1819–91), Emily
Dickinson (1830–86), Louisa May Alcott (1832–88), Edith
Wharton (1862–1937) and John F Kennedy (1917–63).

ALONG THE COAST Early settlers ensconced themselves
along the coast, often referred to as the North Shore and
the South Shore, with Boston at the pivot. Today the coast
is a place for summer relaxation, though the sheer

Autumn colour on the Mohawk Trail

numbers of visitors trying to get away from it all can be self-defeating. North Shore towns are select and picturesque, notably Salem, Marblehead, Rockport (on Cape Ann) and Newburyport. Each makes a feasible day trip from Boston, with good public transport links. Of these, Salem has the most to see, with its gruesome episode of the witches persecution told at a number of venues in a variety of styles.

On the South Shore, Plymouth is a pleasant town with several mementoes of the pioneer days, most notably the re-created Pilgrim village at Plimoth Plantation and the *Mayflower II*. Cape Cod needs time to appreciate fully, although quirky Provincetown is an entertaining day out by ferry from Boston. Ideally, Cape Cod should be seen out of high summer, and the trip should include visits to the islands of Martha's Vineyard and Nantucket, both haunts of the rich but remarkably different in character; in particular the towns of Oak Bluffs and Nantucket have their very own, inimitable period atmospheres. New Bedford, the whaling port that succeeded Nantucket, looks unappetising as you speed through its industrial outskirts on the I-195, but its old centre has atmosphere and a good whaling museum.

The huge granite blocks of a pier at Rockport on Cape Ann, mementoes of a former local granite industry

'Listen to the surf, really lend it your ears, and you will hear in it a world of sound: hollow boomings and heavy roarings, great watery tumblings and tramplings, long hissing seethes, sharp rifle-shot reports, splashes, whispers, the grinding undertone of stones, and sometimes vocal sounds that might be the half-heard talk of people in the sea.'
– Henry Beston, *The Outermost House* (1927), written in a coastal shack on Cape Cod.

HEADING INLAND Concord and Lexington lie just beyond the western suburbs of Boston; in addition to the Revolutionary battle sites, there is a rich literary heritage to explore at Concord. Worcester, a large industrial city, deserves a look for its Armory and art museum.

Of much more mainstream appeal is the evocation of 1830s New England at Old Sturbridge Village – sheer pastiche, but convincingly done and atmospheric when not too crowded. Even the farm animals resemble authentic early 19th-century breeds.

Up to the late 18th century New England extended only as far west as the Connecticut River (known here as Pioneer Valley), where you will find an academic centre, the so-called Five Colleges Area, plus the industrial centres of Holyoke and Springfield. There are some good walks along the river, with abrupt cliff edges in places. Historic Deerfield is the best sight in the valley. Here the

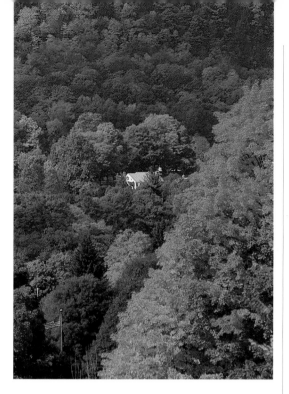

Massachusetts

Spectacular autumn views at Shelburne Falls in western Massachusetts

mile-long village street has none of the period-clad actors found in Old Sturbridge, but some will find the uncommercialised and slow-going atmosphere appealing.

THE FAR WEST Massachusetts now extends west of the Connecticut river into Berkshire County, which borders New York state. This hilly and predominantly rural region has much to offer in the arts: Tanglewood hosts the premier summer musical event in Massachusetts, and is the summer base of the Boston Symphony Orchestra (see page 79). Artist Norman Rockwell (see page 150) is remembered near Stockbridge by an excellent museum, and at Chesterwood the house and studio of sculptor Daniel Chester French makes an absorbing visit. Hancock Shaker Village gives a fascinating insight into the virtually vanished lifestyle of the Shaker sect.

TRUSTEES OF RESERVATIONS A useful source of information for exploring the further-flung sights of Massachusetts is the handbook published by The Trustees of Reservations. Established in 1891, this is the world's oldest preservation society. It owns over 70 houses and areas of countryside, including woodlands, gorges, waterfalls and wildlife refuges throughout Massachusetts. Members are admitted to most properties free of charge and to the remaining few at reduced rates. Information and membership details can be obtained from 572 Essex Street, Beverly, MA 01915-1530 (tel: 978/921 1944).

Massachusetts

Events

The dates of festivals vary from year to year. Book in advance for popular events, such as the Tanglewood summer concerts. For further information contact the state tourist office (see page 266) or chambers of commerce.

April
Daffodil Festival, Nantucket: flower show and vintage cars.
Re-enactment of the Battle of Lexington and Concord.

May
Brimfield Antique Flea Market, Brimfield: New England's prime antiques event.
Seaport Festival, Salem: crafts, walks, exhibitions and children's activities.

June
Craft Fair, Old Deerfield.
Jacob's Pillow Dance Festival, Becket: renowned modern dance event (until August or September).
St Peter's Fiesta, Gloucester: Blessing of the Fleet; fireworks, parade, music.

Plymouth Rock, the stone on to which the Pilgrim Fathers are supposed to have stepped when they came ashore from the Mayflower

Tanglewood Music Festival, Lenox: Boston Symphony Orchestra concerts (until August or September).

July
Barnstable County Fair, East Falmouth: major Cape Cod event.
Brimfield Antique Flea Market.
Lowell Folk Festival: music, crafts.
Mashpee Pow Wow: Native American festivities, contests and food.

August
Annual Teddy Bear Rally, Amherst: dealers, teddies' hospital, entertainment, contests.
Fall River Celebrates America, Fall River: ships, boat races, fireworks.
Feast of Blessed Sacrament, New Bedford: the country's largest Portuguese festival, with the Blessing of the Fleet, food, dance and a parade.
Marshfield Fair.
Martha's Vineyard Agricultural Fair.
Waterfront Festival, Gloucester: pancake breakfast, Yankee lobster bake, whale watching.
Waterfront Festival, Newburyport: art, crafts and entertainment.

September
Brimfield Antique Flea Market.
Harwich Cranberry Festival, Harwich: country and western music, fireworks and parade spread over 10 days.
The Big E, West Springfield: New England's great state fair.

October
Haunted Happenings, Salem: magic, witches, costume parade and candle-light tours at Halloween.
Topsfield Fair, Topsfield: oldest continuous fair in USA. Includes a pumpkin weigh-in.

November
Thanksgiving Day Celebration, Plymouth: Pilgrims' procession, Thanksgiving service and dinner.
Bright Nights at Forest Park, Springfield (until January).

December
Christmas Shoppers' Stroll, Nantucket: carol-singing, theatre, house tours.
First Night Celebration, Cape Cod, Lowell, Newburyport, New Bedford, Northampton, Pittsfield, Quincy, Salem, and Worcester: New Year fun.

▶▶▶ Berkshire Hills 138A2

The Berkshires is the hilliest and western-most part of Massachusetts and was a fashionable summer resort area for wealthy urbanites in the late-19th century. Summer nowadays is busy with arts events, with some 300,000 people attracted to Tanglewood (see page 146) for the Boston Symphony Orchestra summer concert series alone. The area's autumn foliage brings in more crowds later on in the year, and there are opportunities for downhill and cross-country skiing enthusiasts in winter. Compulsive antique-shop browsers may like to head for the area around Route 7 between South Egremont and Ashley Falls. Many of the museums and houses close between mid-October and late May.

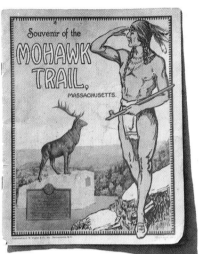

THE MOHAWK TRAIL AND THE NORTHERN BERKSHIRES

The **Mohawk Trail▶**, the country's first designated Scenic Road (opened 1914), follows Route 2 for 63 miles from the Pioneer Valley to the New York state border. The trail dates back to 1663 when the Pocumtuck tribe invaded Mohawk Territory by creating this route over the mountains from Deerfield, MA, to Troy, NY. Much of it is unspoilt even today, although motels and 'Indian trading posts' (with racks of plastic totem poles and the like) straggle the highway in places. **French King Bridge▶** is a scenic crossing of the Connecticut river, the first point on the trail worth stopping for; the river is 140 feet below. Further west,

Shelburne Falls▶ is known for its Bridge of Flowers, an old trolley bridge graced with colourful blooms. Near the Salmon Falls weir, jagged rocks in the river attract swimmers and picnickers. The road passes the **Hail to the Sunrise Monument**, erected in 1932 by tribes and councils of the Approved Order of Red Men, showing a Mohawk with arms outstretched.

Signs soon begin to announce 4 miles of steep gradients and sharp curves, culminating spectacularly at **Hairpin Turn▶▶**, a fine outlook. Go north along Route 8 towards Clarksburg for **Natural Bridge State Park**. Waters tumble through a small chasm gouged out by glacial meltwater and spanned by a natural bridge. Adjacent is an abandoned white marble quarry.

The Mohawk Trail passes through some spectacularly rugged scenery – and there are plenty of reminders of its origins Left: the 'Hail to Sunrise' memorial at the entrance to the Mohawk Trail State Forest

143

INFORMATION FOR THE BERKSHIRE HILLS
For further information contact the Berkshire Visitors' Bureau, Berkshire Common, Plaza Level, Dept MT, Pittsfield, MA 01201 (tel: 413/443 9186, or toll-free 1-800/BERKSHR). *Berkshires Week* is a free weekly listings magazine containing information on state parks, campgrounds, sights, children's activities, shopping and events; it is available at all chambers of commerce.

Aerial view of Williamstown in the Berkshires

THE HOOSAC RAILROAD TUNNEL
This 4.7-mile tunnel near Adams, in the northwest corner of the Berkshires, was constructed in 1851–75 and was the first project of its kind to use nitroglycerine for blasting out the rock. The project was costly, both in terms of money ($24 million) and lives (195 workers perished). It gained the nickname of the 'Bloody Pit' and, not surprisingly, is alleged to be haunted.

Mount Greylock▶▶▶, the highest peak in Massachusetts at 3,491 feet, was named after Chief Grey Lock who hunted here. A road climbs to the top for a grand view over three states. Church spires dominate **North Adams**, a red-brick mill town. The museum at Western Gateway Heritage State Park narrates the history of the Hoosac Railroad Tunnel (see panel). Away from the Mohawk Trail, the cotton-mill town of **Adams** has legacies of the 18th century, most significantly the atmospheric Quaker Meeting House of 1782 on Friend Street.

Founded as West Hoosac in 1750, elegant **Williamstown▶▶** owes its name to Ephraim Williams, who left money for the founding of an academy, stipulating that the town must take his name; the academy opened in 1791, becoming Williams College two years later. Today it is among the top liberal arts institutions in America. The superb **Sterling and Francine Clark Art Institute▶▶▶** (*Open* Tue–Sun. *Admission* free) is noted for French Impressionist and American paintings, as well as British silverware. The **Williams College Museum of Art▶** (*Open* Tue–Sun. *Admission* free) possesses 11,000 works ranging from 9th-century Assyrian stone reliefs to Andy Warhol's last self-portrait. The **Hopkins Observatory** contains a museum and planetarium, open during term time and on occasions during the summer.

The town of **Pittsfield** has been a paper-mill centre since the 19th century and is the largest town in the Berkshires region. Art galleries exhibiting local work include Pittsfield Arts League (2 South Street), Radius Gallery (137 North Street) and Berkshire Artisans (28 Renne Avenue). **Berkshire Museum▶** (39 South Street) includes art of the Hudson River school, dolls, early electric inventions of the Stanley Electric Company and domestic bygones. The Crane Paper Company's **Wahconah Mill** manufactures paper on which the American currency is printed. At Dalton, east of Pittsfield, the **Crane Museum**, within the 1844 Old Stone Mill, tells the story of American paper-making (*Open, summer weekdays, 2–5. Admission* free). On the outskirts of Pittsfield, off Holmes Road, **Arrowhead** (tours Memorial Day–Labor Day, 10–4.30) was the home of Herman Melville and family from 1850 to 1863. The furniture is not original but is contemporary. The house contains the room where Melville wrote *Moby Dick* (1851).

Renoir and Degas, part of the notable French collection in the Sterling and Francine Clark Art Institute

The region's best-preserved Shaker village, active from 1783 to 1960, **Hancock Shaker Village▶▶▶** is a living museum, worth a full day's visit if you want to catch the various events held here (*Open* third week in May–third week in Oct, 9–5; plus guided tours Apr–late May, late Oct–end Nov, 10–3; tel: 413/443 0188). Originally called the 'City of Peace', the village is famous for its round stone barn. The museum's craftsmen and craftswomen continue to live out the Shaker lifestyle (see pages 148–9), tending historic livestock breeds, maintaining an authentic herb garden and demonstrating Shaker cooking.

TRUE CONNOISSEURS
When Williamstown's Sterling and Francine Clark Institute opened in 1955 a unique collection came under the public gaze for the first time. The display was gathered by Robert Sterling Clark (1877–1956) thanks to a family fortune amassed by the Singer sewing machine empire. While living in Paris from 1911 to 1921 he married Francine Clary, who shared his passion for art; during this time he added many paintings by late 19th-century French artists. Painters represented include Homer, Sargent, Pissarro and Monet.

The round barn (dating at least back to 1830) at Hancock Shaker Village. People came from far and wide to study its ingenious design

MUSIC AT TANGLEWOOD

The Tanglewood Music Center, a training centre for musicians, is the summer home of the Boston Symphony Orchestra (see page 79). The open-sided Music Shed is the main concert hall; it is cheapest to sit on the adjoining lawn for concerts (the sound does carry). Open rehearsals take place at 10:30am on Saturdays; you can eavesdrop from the lawn at other times, since members of the public are admitted into the grounds. Whilst there you can visit the Little Red House, a reconstruction of the house in which Nathaniel Hawthorne wrote *The House of the Seven Gables* (1851) and *Tanglewood Tales* (1852–3); inside is a free museum, open in summer.

STOCKBRIDGE WALKS

Just south of Stockbridge, off Park Street, boulder-strewn Ice Glen is so called because of the presence of ice crystals well into summer; a trail climbs up to Laura's Tower for a three-state view.

Three miles south of Stockbridge, on Route 7, the Monument Mountain Reservation overlooks the southern Berkshires, with trails encountering rock outcrops, caves and a hillside strewn with quartzite boulders. William Cullen Bryant waxed lyrical in a poem about the mountain: 'the beauty and the majesty of the earth, spread wide beneath'.

THE SOUTHERN BERKSHIRES An amiable small-town atmosphere envelopes **Lenox►**, well located as a base for exploring the southern Berkshires. In the late-19th century the estates formed rural summer retreats for the wealthy; one such was **Tanglewood** (see panel), near Lenox, originally owned by the Tappan family. Another was **The Mount►**, in Lenox, summer residence of the writer Edith Wharton (see page 46) from 1902 to 1911. A sledding accident at Lenox was the basis of her novel *Ethan Frome* (1911). The restored **Lenox railway station** (1902) also evokes the period; the Berkshire Scenic Railway maintains a model railway, a short section of track and a shop.

Norman Rockwell (see page 150) put **Stockbridge►►** on the map with his depiction of Main Street. At the heart of the village is the Red Lion Inn, dating from 1773 and sporting the sign of George III.

Even older is the **Mission House►** (*Open* Memorial Day weekend–Columbus Day and holidays, Tue–Sun 10–5), the only elegant house in a wilderness when built in 1739 for a Congregationalist minister; its furniture is original and there is a display on the Native American

Chesterwood, the summer home of sculptor Daniel Chester French

Daniel Chester French's statue of the seated Abraham Lincoln

community of Stockbridge. Across the street, Merwin HouseP (Open summer, Tue, Thu, Sat and Sun 12–5; owned and operated by SPNEA – see page 68) is a Federal-style brick house built around 1825, furnished in turn-of-the-century style.

Located just outside town, the **Norman Rockwell Museum▶▶▶** holds the world's largest collection of original works by the hugely popular artist. About a quarter of the works are on display at any one time. The reconstructed studio has Rockwell's art books, easel and many props familiar from his paintings.

Chesterwood▶▶ (*Open* daily, May–Oct; signposted from the west end of Main Street, Stockbridge), was the summer home of sculptor Daniel Chester French from 1898 ('I live here six months of the year – in heaven. The other six months I live, well – in New York'). Tours take in his studio and house (see panel).

The best opportunity to glimpse inside a fashionable summerhouse in the Berkshires is at **Naumkeag▶▶** (*Open* late May–Columbus Day, Tue–Sun). Built in 1885 by Stanford White for the Choates, it still retains some of the family's eclectic possessions. Fletcher Steele later modified the gardens to create terraces with a stepped waterfall.

The **Berkshire Botanical Garden▶** (*Open* May–Oct; Route 102 west of the intersection with Route 183) is compact but varied, with a herbarium of dyer's and medicinal herbs, rock garden, lily pond, day-lilies, shrubs and wildflowers. July and August are the best months to visit.

Bidwell House▶, in Monterey (*Open* Memorial Day–mid-Oct, Tue–Sun and holidays, 11–4), is a Georgian house built for a minister; it has original features and is furnished according to an inventory of 1784.

At Great Barrington the **Albert Schweitzer Center** is a museum and library dedicated to the humanitarian and winner of the 1953 Nobel Peace Prize. The town is popular with antiques hunters.

Colonel John Ashley House▶, Ashley Falls (*Open* Memorial Day–Columbus Day, Wed–Sun and holidays in summer, 1–5; weekends in spring. *Admission* free), is a quintessential colonial house of 1735 where Ashley and others drafted the petition against Britain in 1773 known as the Sheffield Declaration. In 1781 Ashley's slave, Mum Bett, was the first slave to win her freedom, doing so under the new constitution.

The pools below **Bash Bish Falls▶▶** (a fine waterfall) are excellent for swimming. They can be reached from the lower car park (beyond the New York State sign). Near by is **Mount Everett State Forest▶**.

DANIEL CHESTER FRENCH
America's most prolific sculptor, French produced some works of worldwide renown, including his first commission, the *Minute Man* (completed in 1875 and made from 10 army cannons melted down for the purpose) at Concord, the John Harvard statue at Harvard University and the Lincoln statue in Washington, DC.

147

MORE TRAILS IN THE BERKSHIRES
October Mountain State Forest, off Route 20 near Lee, is Massachusetts's largest state forest, with 50 campsites and many trails, including the walk to Schermerhorn Gorge. To the south of Tyringham Center are good hill walks on Tyringham Cobble and the McLennan Reservation, the occasional haunts of coyotes, bob cats, black bears and wild turkeys.

The 2,035-mile Appalachian Trail, from Georgia to Maine, crosses the length of the Berkshire Hills south to north.

The Shaker religious sect is now almost extinct but, in today's complex world, the purity of its followers' way of life, the simple, functional design of their architecture and furniture, and their herbal medicines and organic farming methods have an increasing appeal.

SHAKER YOUR PLATE
In the summer and autumn, visitors to Hancock Shaker Village can partake of a candlelight dinner. The Shaker practice of silence during meals is not observed, and the sexes may mix, but the dishes are taken from Shaker cookbooks. Guests should note an extract from Rules for Visitors: 'At the table we wish all to be as free as at home, but we dislike the wasteful habit of leaving food on the plate'. Hence the American expression 'shaker your plate'.

The kitchen at Hancock, efficient and elegant

Named because of the trembling some members experienced during worship, the Shakers were a persecuted offshoot of the Quakers in England. In 1774 their founder, Ann Lee, led eight followers from Manchester, England, to America, where religious liberty was firmly upheld, and settled near Albany, New York. Their beliefs and practices soon attracted interest and converts, and by the mid-19th century there were 18 Shaker communities in New England, New York and the Midwest, with about 6,000 members in all.

The Shakers were originally called the United Society of Believers in Christ's Second Appearing and believed that the millennium, a thousand years of heaven on earth, had arrived with Mother Ann. The fundamental principles laid down by Mother Ann were communal living, separate from 'the world', and celibacy. In the belief that Mother Ann was the female aspect of God, her followers shared leadership and work equally between men and women. Tasks indoors and out were put on a rota so that no one had to endure the unpopular jobs for too long (such as looking after the small boys sent by their parents to learn a trade in the Shaker community).

'Hands to work and hearts to God' The Shakers aimed for perfection in all they turned their hands to. Adapting the Yankee work ethic to fit their religious ideals, they became renowned for their industry and ingenuity. Their numerous inventions include the circular saw, a rotary harrow, a threshing machine, an automatic hay-seeding device, a non-drip paint can and the flat broom.

The Shakers were also immensely practical and kept the house very clean (this was heaven on earth, and there is no dust in heaven). This explains the ubiquitous wooden peg rails for hanging clothes, kitchen utensils, mops and their ladder-backed chairs; the built-in, floor-to-ceiling wardrobes (no need to sweep underneath or dust on top) and the beds on rollers for ease of sweeping; it also accounts for the striking efficiency of their kitchens, and the famously progressive round barn at Hancock, Massachusetts (see page 145).

In the belief that a sound soul needs a healthy body, the Shakers ate well (their recipes are famous); they also made a wide range of herbal medicines. Assiduous gardeners, they were the first to market seeds, an enterprise which developed into a most successful industry.

Villages such as Hancock (left) are preserved for posterity

Shakers and 'the world' The Shaker communities adopted orphans. They also took in children indentured to the society by their parents in order to learn a trade, many of whom later joined the communities. Converts were also made from the many visitors who came to the villages, for while separation from the world was a basic principle, Shakers were happy to sell their goods to the 'world's people' – brooms, chairs, boxes, baskets, seeds and cloaks (specially woven in bright colours for society ladies to wear to the opera).

Numbers peaked in the 1840s but, in the decades that followed, began to decline; restrictions were put into force on adoption, and the pacifism Shakerism stood for and which had attracted converts, went out of favour. Celibacy began to take its toll in falling numbers and communities could not compete with mass-production of goods.

Today, only a handful of Shakers are left, living in the town of Sabbathday Lake, Maine. They generally continue to live the traditional Shaker life, worshipping devoutly, selling their goods at fairs, farming their land (though they are more likely to be seen wearing Levis for hoeing the vegetables than the long skirts or white shirts and black waistcoats still worn for services). Tours can be taken around the village, but most buildings may be seen from the outside only. At Canterbury and Lower Shaker villages in New Hampshire (see pages 192 and 195), and at Hancock village in Massachusetts (see page 145), the old buildings are preserved in recognition of the purity and ingenuity of the Shaker contribution.

SHAKER ARTEFACTS
Oval boxes, baskets and furniture, in particular the chair, exemplify the clean, simple lines of Shaker design and their perfect craftsmanship. Everything was made purely to serve its function, without any embellishment. The chair is sturdy, but light – so it could be hung up out of the way – with a straight ladder-back. The chairs' back legs were fitted with a 'button tilter', a swivel device designed to prevent wear on floors. The reproduction of Shaker artefacts is a burgeoning industry and the Shaker villages sell beautiful examples.

THE GIFT OF SONG
Singing and dancing was, and is, an integral part of the Shaker service of worship and 10,000 or more of their songs have been collected. Many are based on English and early American folk tunes. Aaron Copland borrowed the Shaker 'Simple Gifts' melody for his Appalachian Spring, scored for a Martha Graham ballet in 1944:
''Tis the gift to be simple, 'tis the gift to be free,
'Tis the gift to come down where we ought to be,
And when we find ourselves in the place just right,
'Twill be in the valley of love and delight.'

'Without thinking too much about it in specific terms, I was showing the America I knew and observed to others who might not have noticed.' Norman Rockwell's portrayal of scenes from everyday life touched the nation's soul and made him one of America's most popular illustrators.

150

Born in New York in 1894, Norman Rockwell was given his first freelance commission by the magazine publishers Condé Nast, at the age of 17. In 1916 he took some paintings to the art editor of the *Saturday Evening Post*, the most widely circulated magazine in America, and thus began a partnership that was to turn Norman Rockwell into a household name, and his works into national treasures. Over the next 47 years he illustrated 317 covers for the Post, each one eagerly awaited by its readers.

The American dream In almost photographic detail Rockwell depicted childhood scenes, family scenes and small-town scenes, each tinged with affection and gentle humour: the family outing in the car, the boy who discovers his father's Santa Claus costume, a visit to the optician, the signing of a marriage licence. When he moved with his wife Mary Barstow and their three sons to Arlington, Vermont in 1939, the neighbours were 'exactly the models I need for my purpose – the sincere, honest, homespun types that I love to paint.' And it was just these people that he depicted in the famous wartime series of posters – 'Freedom of Speech', 'Freedom of Worship', 'Freedom from Want' and 'Freedom from Fear' – inspired by President Roosevelt's Four Freedoms Proclamation of 1941.

In 1953 the family moved to Stockbridge in Massachusetts, where Rockwell lived and worked right up to his death in 1978. His works include illustrations for calendars, such as the Boy Scout Calendar, covers for other magazines, advertisements and greetings cards, as well as oil paintings and portraits.

Rockwell's work has always been a touch too sentimental for the fine art buffs, but among ordinary people for whom he captures American life as it was always meant to be, Norman Rockwell remains as popular as ever.

Top: Triple Self-Portrait (1960)
Above: 'Freedom from Want'

WHERE TO SEE HIS WORK
The largest collection of Rockwell originals is in a museum near Stockbridge, Massachusetts (see page 147). The old carriage house he converted to a studio has been moved to this site from his Stockbridge home. In Vermont, Rockwell's hometown of Arlington has a display of prints in a 19th-century church, and in Rutland the Norman Rockwell Museum has an exhibition covering his career (open all year).

*Cape Ann's rocky shore-
'line has long appealed to
summer visitors and
artists*

**BIRDSEYE'S FROZEN
FOODS**
Clarence 'Bob' Birdseye
(1886–1956) created the
frozen-food business from
Gloucester after observ-
ing, on an expedition to
Labrador in 1914–17, that
local people ate fish,
meat and vegetables that
they had frozen months
before. In 1925 he
developed a quick-freezing
system for commercial
use and helped to found
the General Seafoods
Company in Gloucester,
selling frozen foods to
consumers in Springfield,
Massachusetts. Birds Eye
is now a household name
and the original plant in
Commercial Street is still
in operation.

▶▶ Cape Ann   *139D3*

Abutting the northern extremity of Massachusetts Bay,
Cape Ann harbours many charming fishing ports, as well
as idiosyncratic historic buildings and coastal views
much depicted by artists. There are good bathing beaches
and shops for browsing. Weekend traffic winds slowly
along Routes 127 and 127A, and parking can be very
difficult, particularly in Rockport. A rail service from
Boston's North Station and Monday to Saturday bus
services provide feasible alternatives.

Manchester has an attractive harbour and clean sands at
Singing Beach (the rail station is a short walk away).

Gloucester▶ is a starting point for whale-watching trips
and is also a working fishing port – founded in 1623 it is
America's oldest. Fine beaches draw crowds at summer
weekends. Artist Fitz Hugh Lane (1804–65) lived in the
three-gabled granite house on the waterfront, and the
nation's largest collection of his work is exhibited with
fishing industry displays at the **Cape Ann Historical
Society▶**. Living artists' work can be seen in the thriving
Rocky Neck Art Colony and at the North Shore Arts
Association's exhibition centre.

THE MIGHTY HAMMOND
The massive 8,200-pipe
Hammond organ at
Hammond Castle was
built to play automatically
because, ironically, Dr
Hammond, the inventor,
was not musical enough
to play the instrument
himself. The immense
sound of Bach's Toccata
and Fugue, often played to
tour groups, is astonish-
ingly powerful. There is a
programme of concerts
given here.

Hammond Castle Museum▶▶ in
Gloucester (*Open* summer, some winter weekends, 10–4; for details, tel:
798/283 7673) is a sham medieval
folly perched just above the shore;
home of the inventor John Hays
Hammond Jr, the eye-catching edifice was built around the
Hammond organ in the Great Hall
(see panel). The castle comprises
a labyrinth of small rooms and
passages adorned with
Renaissance treasures, a
library with a 'whispering
ceiling' that picks up the
slightest sounds, and a
courtyard graced by a
Roman sarcophagus.

*The Gloucester
Fisherman by Leonard
Craske looks out to sea*

Fishing floats adorn the wall of Motif No 1 (above), the 1884 fishing shack by Rockport harbour (top)

THE PAPER HOUSE
North of Rockport, off Route 127 at Pigeon Cove, is this all-paper building constructed between 1922 and 1942 by Elis F Stenman as an experiment. He invented a special paste for the purpose and used some 100,000 newspapers: the furniture included a piano, a clock, a radio cabinet, chairs and a desk. The walls are made of diamond-shaped blocks, with the headlines still legible. Stenman's wife created the bead curtains from old magazines.

A short drive southwards along the coast, though still in Gloucester, is the fantasy retreat of **Beauport►** with its warren of 40 rooms, many of them devoted to historical themes (*Open* mid-May–mid-Oct, Mon–Fri, plus weekends in Sep and Oct; owned and operated by SPNEA – see page 68). The house was built, and periodically enlarged, between 1907 and 1934 by interior designer Henry Davis Sleeper. It is full of quirky visual effects, windows with coloured glass, and bottles, antiquites and curiosities – including a secret staircase. The Pine Kitchen, recalling the simple homes of the colonial era, contrasts with the Octagon Room, elegantly French in spirit, or the Belfry Bedroom, which is sheer chinoiserie. The road continues southwards to **Eastern Point Lighthouse** at the east side of Gloucester Harbor.

Picturesque **Rockport►►** is the most visited place on Cape Ann. The harbour scene epitomises coastal New England and includes the fishing shack known as 'Motif No 1', one of the most photographed and painted buildings in all America. **Bearskin Neck**, the heart of the old village, is a mixture of craft shops and toytown-scale fishing huts turned into homes with tiny front gardens.

Within the 54 acres of **Halibut Point State Park►►** is a fine panorama where a dwarf forest gives way to heathland and scrub, with drops to a rocky shore.

Essex stakes a claim as 'king of the clam'. It has lobster shacks, seafood restaurants, fishing-tackle shops and over 60 antique shops. The Shipbuilding Museum expounds on 300 years of the industry in Essex. Boat trips up the Essex river give opportunities for bird-watching, while Crane's Beach at **Ipswich** ranks among the North Shore's finest.

All the way up the coast, lighthouses stand as symbols of New England's maritime history. The Coast Guard has now automated the light stations, but they remain a unique and cherished part of New England's heritage.

One of the earliest acts of Congress, signed by George Washington in 1789, provided for a programme of construction and maintenance of lighthouses, beacons, buoys and public piers. Both immigrants and traders were vital to the development of the American nation and the safe navigation of their ships was crucial.

Unique landmarks Constructed of anything from wood or granite to concrete or iron, every lighthouse is different.

The tall New London Harbor Light was built in simple colonial style by the British, while Portland Breakwater Light (1855) is in the Greek Revival style, its height typical of the shorter lighthouses found in ports. Portland Head Light, probably the most painted and photographed on the coast of New England, stands 80 feet high above the cliffs. Owls Head and Pemaquid Point in Maine are also photogenic. The red and white stripes of West Quoddy Head will be familiar to many. At Fort Point the wooden fog-bell house still stands, one of the last of its kind. Boston Light is America's only offically manned lighthouse and the oldest station in America. Anyone interested in lighthouses should visit the Shore Village Museum in Rockland, Maine (see page 130).

Keeping the lights shining The heroic keepers have passed into history, and today many lighthouses are in poor repair. There is, however, mounting interest in preserving them and lighthouse cruises operate from Bath's Maritime Museum and Portsmouth, New Hampshire.

GET-AWAY
For a 'unique romantic adventure' – and a taste of what life was like for the keeper and his family – you can book bed and breakfast at Rose Island Lighthouse in Narragansett Bay (also available for longer spells, with record-keeping and maintenance chores). Contact Rose Island Lighthouse Foundation, PO Box 1419, Newport, RI 02840 (tel: 401/847 4242). Similarly, you can spend the night in the lightkeeper's quarters on the Monomoy Islands, a wildlife refuge (Cape Cod Museum of Natural History, PO Box 1710, Brewster, MA 02631; tel: 508/896 3867), or in Isle au Haut lighthouse, Acadia National Park (Keeper's House, PO Box 26, Isle au Haut, ME 04645).

153

FOR MORE INFORMATION
Contact the Lighthouse Depot, PO Box 1690, Wells, Maine 04090, or call 1-800/758 1444.

TALES OF HEROISM
Most famous of all New England's keepers was Ida Lewis (1842–1911) who took over from her father at Lime Rock Light in Newport, Rhode Island, when he was paralysed by a stroke. She became an expert oarswoman and over half a century saved dozens of lives.

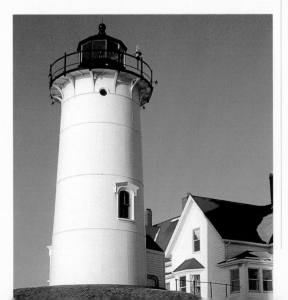

Winter comes to Nobska Light, Falmouth, Cape Cod

Massachusetts

CAMEOS OF NATURE
Cape Cod has several
nesting areas for plovers
and terns. Diamond-back
terrapins, an endangered
species, lay eggs in Sandy
Neck Beach, Barnstaple.
Some 90 per cent of the
rare Plymouth gentian,
found by ponds, grow on
Cape Cod. Much of the
hinterland between the
two coasts consists of
infertile dwarf forest,
characterised by pitch
pine and scrub oak: coy-
otes have moved in since
the late 1980s. Wild
cranberries proliferate.
Bog plants, such as
bladderwort, pitcher plant
and sundew, thrive on the
salt marsh.

154

*Hyannis, for shops,
ferries to the islands
and round-the-harbour
cruises*

▶▶▶ Cape Cod and the islands   *139E1*

Cape Cod▶▶ is a busy vacation resort. Off season you may have the majestic, unspoilt beaches more or less to yourself, but in July and August traffic grinds along the roads, beach car parks fill up early in the day and accommodation is pricey. It's not touring territory and it has few major sights, yet it really is worth going out of your way if you are a nature-lover, or like a stay-put holiday with boat trips and mild pottering thrown in.

Physically the Cape is low-lying, covered with dwarf forest and cranberry bogs, and edged by marshes and sandy beaches. It is often likened to a bent arm: severed at the shoulder by the Cape Canal, with most of the popula-tion around the biceps portion (or Upper Cape); as it turns north (the Lower Cape) the peninsula narrows to curve round at Provincetown. The towns on the south side vir-tually roll into one anonymous mass. The waters on the Atlantic side are cool but often good for surfing; the bay side (facing north and west) is calmer and warmer.

THE UPPER CAPE: SOUTH COAST Family-style attrac-tions (see page 245) are abundant on the much-developed south coast. Routes 6 and 28 cross the **Cape Cod Canal**. For a longer look at this waterway, completed in 1914 and possessing a rare vertical rail lift (for hoisting the tracks up to allow shipping through), look out at water level from the largely reconstructed **Aptucxet Trading Post Museum** in Bourne. Also on site are reconstructed 18th-century salt works and a railway station specially built for President Grover Cleveland who summered here.

Although much expanded, **Falmouth▶** preserves its conspicuously pretty village centre and green. The Falmouth Historical Society maintain a handsome 1790 house, subsequently home to Elijah Swift, who pioneered

The Glass Museum at Sandwich displays items from the town's 19th-century factory

the local whaling industry. A museum in the grounds honours local lady Catherine Lee Bates, author of *America the Beautiful* (1893).

Like Falmouth, **Woods Hole▶** is a ferry port for Martha's Vineyard and Nantucket (see pages 160–3). The National Marine Fisheries Aquarium is stocked with local species, while Woods Hole Oceanographic Institution museum has displays on the wrecks of the *Titanic* and *Bismarck*.

At the Old Town Hall in Main Street, Hyannis, the **JF Kennedy Museum** has displays of JFK's vacation days on the Cape with family and friends at Hyannis Port.

Visitors may join an oceanographic cruise from Woods Hole

155

THE UPPER CAPE: NORTH COAST The north shore is more genteel and historic; Route 6A is the Cape's 'antiques road'. **Pairpoint Glass Works** on Sandwich Road, Sagamore Bridge, is the oldest glass-manufacturer in America, with glass-blowing demonstrations on weekdays.

Sandwich▶ has a charming centre, with a church and pond. Dexter Grist Mill (1640) still produces corn meal for sale and Hoxie House is a 1675 saltbox; both are open and stand by Shawme Pond, a haunt of waterfowl. The 1641 Wing Fort House has heirlooms and period pieces, and is the oldest house in America continuously lived in and owned by the same family. The **Glass Museum▶** has items made by the defunct Boston Sandwich Glass Company. **Yesteryears Doll Museum** is one of the largest collections of its kind in New England. **Thornton W Burgess Museum** commemorates the creator of the children's stories *Peter Cottontail* and *Old Mother Westwind*.

The **Heritage Plantation▶▶** (*Open* daily, mid-May–late Oct) is a delightful museum of Americana displaying custom-made cars, model soldiers, Currier-and-Ives pictures, toys and old tools. The setting is enchanting: the extensive grounds are planted with over 125 varieties of rhododendron, which bloom in May.

At **Brewster▶** the Cape Cod Museum of Natural History has hands-on exhibits for children and runs outings (including trips to the Monomoy Islands; tel: 1-800/ 479 3867). Close by, the Fire and History Museum has a gleaming array of over 30 vintage fire-fighting devices.

Continued on page 158.

MARINE RESEARCH
Since the 1870s the pleasant shoreside village of Woods Hole has been home to three important marine research establishments: the National Marine Fisheries Science Center and Aquarium, the Marine Biological Laboratories and the Woods Hole Oceanographic Institution (WHOI). The latter exists to study rivers, coasts, sea beds, marine life, currents, pollutants and other aspects of the oceans. In season daily oceanographic cruises are run from here on the *Oceanquest* (tel: 1-800/37 OCEAN). This is an excellent introduction to the study of the sea, enabling participants to use plankton nets and microscopes under the guidance of a scientist.

Pembroke
Bryantville
Duxbury
Gurnet Point
Kingston
Plymouth Bay
Halifax
Plymouth
Plympton
Manomet
44
Cape Cod
Carver
Middleboro
South Carver
Lakeville
Cedarville
495
Great Herring Pond
West Wareham
Long Pond
Cape Cod Canal
Sagamore
Buzzards Bay
Wareham
25
Sandwich
Sandy Neck
Heritage Plantation
Rochester
Onset
Bourne
Aptucxet Trading Post Museum
West Barnstable
Monument Beach
6
140
Marion
Pocasset
Forestdale
Mashpee Pond
195
Acushnet
North Falmouth
Hatchville
Mashpee
Centerville
Craigville
Mattapoisett
28
Osterville
Fairhaven
Cotuit
NEW BEDFORD
Buzzards
West Island
West Falmouth
Ashumet Holly Res & Wildlife Sanctuary
New Seabury
Wilbur Point
Bay
28
Teaticket
East Falmouth
Great Neck
Falmouth
Round Hill Point
Falmouth Heights
Nantucket
Woods Hole
Nonamesset Island
Elizabeth Islands
Naushon Island
Vineyard Haven
Oak Bluffs
State Lobster Hatchery
Joseph Sylvia State Beach
Penikese Island
Pasque Island
Vineyard
Lagoon Pond
Cedar Tree Neck Sanctuary
Cape Poge
Nashawena Island
Sound
North Tisbury
Felix Neck Sanctuary
Cuttyhunk Island
Edgartown
Chappaquiddick Island
West Tisbury
Tisbury Great Pond
Edgartown Great Pond
Muskeget
Menemsha
Katama
Wasque Point
Channel
Gay Head
Chilmark
Squibnocket
Long Point Wildlife Refuge
Squibnocket Pond
Martha's Vineyard
No Mans Land

0   5   10   15   20 km
0   5   10 miles

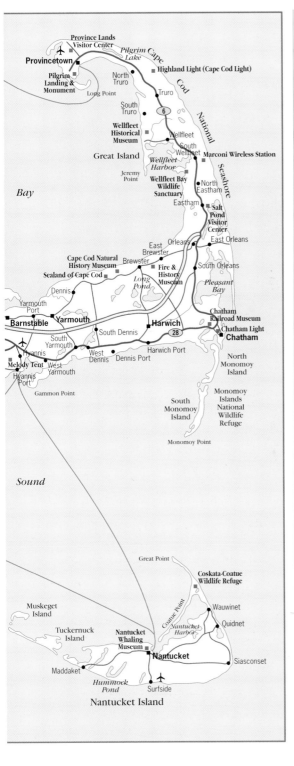

Province Lands
Visitor Center

Pilgrim **Cape**
Lake

Provincetown

Highland Light (Cape Cod Light)

Pilgrim
Landing &
Monument

North
Truro

Cod

Long Point

Truro

South
Truro

6

National

Wellfleet
Historical
Museum

Wellfleet

Great Island

South
Wellfleet

Marconi Wireless Station

Wellfleet
Harbor

Seashore

Jeremy
Point

Wellfleet Bay
Wildlife
Sanctuary

North
Eastham

Bay

Eastham

Salt
Pond
Visitor
Center

Orleans

East Orleans

East
Brewster

Cape Cod Natural
History Museum

Brewster

Fire &
History
Museum

South Orleans

Sealand of Cape Cod

Long
Pond

Pleasant
Bay

Dennis

Yarmouth
Port

Chatham
Railroad Museum

Barnstable

Yarmouth

Harwich

Chatham Light

South Dennis

Chatham

South
Yarmouth

28

Hyannis

West
Dennis

Harwich Port

North
Monomoy
Island

Melody Tent

West
Yarmouth

Dennis Port

Hyannis
Port

Monomoy
Islands
National
Wildlife
Refuge

Gammon Point

South
Monomoy
Island

Sound

Monomoy Point

Great Point

Coskata-Coatue
Wildlife Refuge

Muskeget
Island

Wauwinet

Coatue Point

Quidnet

Tuckernuck
Island

Nantucket
Whaling
Museum

Nantucket
Harbor

Nantucket

Siasconset

Maddaket

Hummock
Pond

Surfside

Nantucket Island

*Cape Cod National
Seashore*

Massachusetts

Provincetown, overlooked by the belfry of the 1861 Center Methodist Church

BEACHES

The National Seashore beaches are all suitable for families; a pass covers admission to all six of them (free out of season or after 5pm). To reach Coast Guard Beach it is best to take the free shuttle bus from the car park signposted for that beach; car parks are often full in July and August. There are numerous town beaches (fee payable). Le Count Hollow and White Crest are known for surfing. Cahoon Hollow for surfing and partying. Newcomb Hollow and Longnook are quiet family beaches. First Encounter Beach at Eastham is where the *Mayflower* landed, to be greeted by friendly Native Americans.

THE MONOMOY ISLANDS

Nature-lovers should not miss a visit to the Monomoy Islands, formed of a barrier beach south of the elbow of Cape Cod. North Monomoy has dunes, beach grass, migrating birds and a large summer population of eastern shore birds, while South Monomoy is much larger and has a wide range of flora and fauna, including deer and seals. Other sites for observing nature include Falmouth Ponds, Ashumet Holly and Wildlife Sanctuary (Falmouth), Sandy Neck (Barnstable), the beech forest at Provincetown and West Harwich Conservation Area.

Continued from page 155.

THE LOWER CAPE The best scenery on the Cape is found here, especially along the 40-mile **National Seashore▶▶** with its superb beaches and cliff-like dunes. The area is famous for its plant and bird life.

Salt Pond Visitor Center▶ is useful for information on natural history, trails and ranger-led walks; it is also the start of the **Nauset Marsh Trail▶**. The **Rail Trail**, an inland course of some 20 miles, passes ponds, salt marshes, pine woods and cranberry bogs; it is open to cyclists, horse-riders and hikers.

The site of **Marconi Wireless Station** was abandoned in 1920 and only concrete foundations now remain, though a model explains how the first overseas radio message was transmitted from here in 1901 to Cornwall, England. **Cape Cod Light**, the Cape's oldest lighthouse, dates from 1857 and sends out a 20-mile beam.

On the west coast, **Wellfleet▶** is prettily sited overlooking an intricate pattern of marshy creeks and a marina. To its west, the trail along the sandy spit known as Great Island (4 miles each way) has remote beauty.

At **Province Lands Visitor Center▶** (tel: 508/487 1256), an observation platform gives a panorama of the invasive dunes resulting from the removal of trees, overgrazing and the subsequent loss of topsoil.

PROVINCETOWN Sand spills on to the road and is whipped up by the wind as you approach **Provincetown▶▶**. On 11 November the Pilgrim Fathers first touched American soil here in 1620. The Pilgrims' arrival, and the signing of the Mayflower Compact, are commemorated by the **Pilgrim Monument▶▶** (modelled on the belltower of the town hall in Siena, Italy), 252 feet high and the nation's tallest granite structure. From the top the Cape spreads out like a map and Boston's towers can be seen on a clear day. The adjacent museum (entry covers both sites) exhibits scrimshaw, toys, a fire engine and items relating to the Arctic explorer Admiral Donald MacMillan.

Provincetown (known as 'P-town') is commercialised and touristy but fun, with shops ranging from the tasteful to the outrageous. The subtle lighting effects of sun and water have drawn numerous artists, including Edward Hopper, Jackson Pollock, Robert Motherwell and Mark Rothko. The town's galleries include the Provincetown Art Association Museum, the Fine Arts Work Center and the Provincetown Gallery Guild.

Provincetown has a strong theatrical heritage: Eugene O'Neill had his first plays performed here, and Richard Gere, Marlon Brando and Al Pacino have all acted at P-town. The artistic and theatrical ethos has gone hand in hand with the establishment of one of the East Coast's largest gay communities.

Accommodation is plentiful, and the town is easy to walk around. Trolleys tour the sights, and horse and trap tours leave from the town hall.

Stained-glass shop in Provincetown

CRUISES AND TRIPS

Whales can be seen around Steelwagen Bank – boats from all over the Cape, and from Boston, Plymouth and the North Shore, head over here. Passenger-only ferries connect Provincetown with Plymouth (tel: 1-800/242 2469) and Boston (tel: 617/457 1428). Scenic flights can be made on a classic 1930 Stinson Detroiter plane (tel: 508/487 0240). Fishing and sightseeing cruises leave from Hyannis, Provincetown, Falmouth and elsewhere. Cape Cod Canal Cruises depart from Onset (tel: 508/778 2688), while Water Safaris at West Dennis offer the only river cruise on the Cape (tel: 508/362 5557).

Extending 2 miles north from Edgartown, Joseph Sylvia State Beach flanks calm, mild waters

GETTING AROUND
Cycle hire is available at ferry ports. A public bus network connects most places, and tour buses meet the ferries. Petrol is expensive: fill up on the mainland.

WILDLIFE SANCTUARIES
● Cape Poge Reservation – salt marsh, ponds and red cedar uplands with a range of wildlife.
● Felix Neck Wildlife Sanctuary – trails, wildfowl ponds, salt marshes and an interpretation centre.
● Cedar Tree Neck Sanctuary – good for wildlife spotting from trails and has coastal views.
● Long Point Wildlife Refuge – butterflies and moths, spring and fall bird migrations; birds of prey.

MARTHA'S VINEYARD The English explorers, John Brereton and Bartholomew Gosnold, landed on **Martha's Vineyard►►►** in 1602, and Gosnold named the island after his daughter, Martha. Brereton remarked on the 'incredible store of vines and the beautie and delicacie of this sweet soil'.

The East Coast's largest warm-water resort island is about three times the size of neighbouring Nantucket (see page 162). The rich and famous have summered here for many years: President Clinton has repeatedly taken his vacations here and singers Carly Simon and James Taylor are among those who own houses on the Vineyard.

Variety is a key feature in the island's places, architecture, people, weather and scenery. The north shore is craggy, the south shore sandy with a heathy hinterland speckled with ponds. Inland a dwarf forest of scrub oak blankets much of the scene. Weather is remarkably localised; often one part of the island can be basking in bright sunshine while another is cloaked in a hot, humid mist (a 'smoky sou'wester').

Most of the island's beaches are privately owned. The main public beaches are Joseph Sylvia State Beach, between Edgartown and Vineyard Haven (no surf, ideal for families); Katama (facing the Atlantic, good surf, strong swimmers only); Moshpu (by Gay Head cliffs, with surf); Oak Bluffs Town Beach (convenient, though often crowded, family beach); and Menemsha (small and quiet).

AROUND THE VINEYARD At the western extremity of the island, the village of **Gay Head** has a sizeable Wampanoag community (hence the Native American crafts shops). **Gay Head cliffs►►** are a tumbled mass of multi-coloured clay, a spectacular natural landform of great geological interest with an excellent beach at the base accessible by road. The fishing village of **Menemsha▶** has retained a weather-beaten character, with little hint of gentrification. An excellent fishmarket is found among the tiny shacks in the harbour. You can take the ferry from here to Cuttyhunk in the Elizabeth Islands, where a monolith commemorates the first European settlement in America.

Immaculately preserved **Edgartown▶▶**, haunt of millionaires, gained its prosperous look when sea-captains from the whaling days built handsome Federal-style homes. The Old Whaling Church of 1843, an outstanding example of Greek Revival architecture, has been converted into a performing arts centre; walking tours begin from here (for details, tel: 508/627 8619). Vincent House (open to the public) dates from 1672 and is the oldest building on the island. The town centre is usually busy with window-shoppers admiring the jewellery stores and upmarket boutiques.

Endowed with the longest beach on the Vineyard (scenes from the movie *Jaws* were filmed here), **Oak Bluffs▶▶▶** is a period-piece resort where the Methodists held their first summer camp in 1835. By 1850 some 12,000 people were attending the Sabbath meetings at the open-sided tabernacle. Tents were replaced by charming 'carpenter Gothic' gingerbread houses, each adorned with ornate filigree work. There are now more than 300, with no two quite alike. One house is open as a museum.

Vineyard Haven (Tisbury)P is a big yachting and boat-building centre, and possesses a state lobster hatchery. A fire destroyed much of the town in 1883 but Greek Revival houses survived along William Street. Ritter House Museum expounds upon times past. Crafts such as scrimshaw are exhibited in the Old School House Museum. The Seaman's Bethel (1892) was the place of refuge for seamen; gifts from those who survived storms and shipwrecks are displayed.

GETTING TO THE ISLANDS
● The Steamship Authority (tel: 508/477 8600) runs ferries from Woods Hole to Vineyard Haven and Hyannis to Nantucket, plus inter-island services.
● Hy-Line Cruises run from Hyannis to Oak Bluffs (tel: 508/778 0404).
● Cape Island Express Lines operate from New Bedford to Vineyard Haven and Nantucket (tel: 508/997 1688).
● Island Commuter Corporation runs a summer service from Hyannis and Provincetown to Oak Bluffs, taking about 35 minutes to the Vineyard and 2 hours 15 minutes to Nantucket from Hyannis.
● Cape Air (tel: 1-800/352 0714) is among several airlines serving the islands.

161

Victorian gingerbread cottages at Oak Bluffs, built on land still leased from the Camp Meeting Association

NANTUCKET The island of **Nantucket▶▶▶**, 30 miles off the Massachusetts mainland, deserves the accolade 'a step back in time'. The town (also called Nantucket) is preserved down to the last paving stone, and the handsome houses evoke the prosperity of the whaling days. Like Martha's Vineyard, this is a millionaires' vacationland, but while the larger island is considered the territory of the newly rich, Nantucket is more the haunt of rich Yankees who choose not to flaunt their wealth, and is certainly less developed. **Nantucket▶▶▶** town preserves an air of genteel perfection. On cobbled Main Street the oldest houses include the Three Bricks, built in 1836–8 by Captain Joseph Starbuck for his sons. The tower of the Congregational Church offers a good view of the island. Shops tend towards artiness and good taste (although at a price), antique shops abound and there are weekend antique auctions. Center Street's shops have traditionally been run by women (dating back to the time when captains' wives had time on their hands). A local speciality is the Nantucket Lightship, a woven basket into which is inserted a scrimshaw disc.

One ticket gets you into all Nantucket's museums, though apart from the Whaling Museum these are modest in scale. Housed in a former whale oil refinery, the **Whaling Museum▶▶** displays artefacts related to past whaling days, including the ship's logs of the *Essex* (the vessel immortalised in *Moby Dick*), sailors' souvenirs, a finback whale skeleton and scrimshaws.

Local history collections form the basis of the **P Foulger Museum**. The **Museum of Nantucket History▶** covers the complete timescale from the distant geological past to the present day; a model shows how the island's coastline is changing. **Hadwen House▶**, built in imposing Greek Revival style in 1845, belonged to the same man who owned the refinery that is now the Whale Museum; it has Federal, Empire and Victorian furnishings. A four-vane **windmill** (1746) still grinds corn today.

The little **Life Saving Museum** covers the work of the United States Life Saving Service. Both the **Old Firecart House** (vintage fire-fighting equipment) and the **Old Gaol** are open free of charge. The **Quaker Meeting House** was built in 1838, though Quaker worship on the island goes back to 1690. Simply furnished, the **Jethro Coffin**

TOURING NANTUCKET
Ferry boats (see panel on page 160) bring you directly into Nantucket town where there are plenty of taxis. In addition to public bus services, Gail's Tour runs a 1 hour 45 minute bus tour from Federal Street Visitor Center at 10am, 1pm and 3pm (tel: 508/257 6557). Bicycles can be hired; cycling the island's quiet roads and cycle paths is a pleasure. Numerous boat trips depart from the wharves in Nantucket town. Walking tours (tel: 508/228 5585) start from the Atheneum Library Garden in India Street at 11am and 4pm.

House of 1686 is the oldest on the island and gives a good idea of an early settler's home.

BEACHES At its maximum dimensions, Nantucket is 14½ miles long by 3½ miles wide. The northern beaches are sheltered and the waves usually gentle, while the south-facing ones have plenty of surf and are strictly for strong swimmers.

Smaller beaches in and around Nantucket town have shallow waters and are suitable for children. Jetties Beach, good for watching boats and migrating birds, is an easy walk from the town (or take a shuttle bus), past the lighthouse on Brant Point; sailboards can be rented at the beach. Further west, Dionis is a family beach.

On the south side are Surfside (public bus service) and Nobadeer beaches (the latter popular with teenagers). Madaket Beach, at the western tip, has stunning sunsets. Siasconset Beach, served by bus, has some surf.

FURTHER AFIELD The former fishing village of **Siasconset►** (pronounced 'Sconset') has tiny shacks with names such as Doll's House and La Petite Cottage, though house prices are astronomical. In the 1930s Hollywood stars, such as Clark Gable and Carole Lombard, summered here. Near by, Sankety Head Golf Club has a 15-year waiting list for membership!

The **Coskata-Coatue Wildlife refuge►**, at the north-eastern tip of the island, is shaped like a fish-hook and formed of a huge barrier beach. Wind and sea have sculpted a remote and wild place; the refuge includes around 10 miles of shoreline, as well as ponds, forest, salt marshes, and tidal creeks.

Nantucket's southern beaches such as Surfside take the full force of the Atlantic surf

THE INLAND SCENE
Nantucket's hinterland is mostly scrub oak, with patches of heath and cranberry bogs. Altar Rock (111 feet) is the island's highest point. The lack of mammalian predators makes the island suitable for ground-nesting birds such as northern harriers, short-eared owls, least terns and piping plovers.

A WHALING TRADITION
Settled by the English in 1659, Nantucket rapidly took off as the New World's premier whaling centre, and by 1775 the export of whale oil, ambergris and whalebone meant that Nantucketers accounted for over a third of the hard currency earned in New England. The demise in Nantucket's whaling industry after 1842 was hastened by the emergence of the whaling port of New Bedford (see page 172), and by the collapse of the British market for whale oil with the advent of gas lighting.

Waterfront scene, Nantucket town

From the rocky inlets and myriad islands of the north through sandy beaches and salt marshes southwards to the dunes of Cape Cod, the coast of New England supports an exceptionally rich and diverse plant and animal life. Opportunities abound for visitors to observe it all at close hand.

Top: dolphins may well join in a whale-watch cruise

WHALE-WATCHING CRUISES
In the 19th century the hunting of whales was a principal source of revenue for New England; nowadays whale-watch cruises have taken over as a burgeoning industry. In summer, boats leave from many ports, including Barnstable Harbor and Provincetown (Cape Cod); Boston, Plymouth, Gloucester, Newburyport (MA); Portsmouth (NH); Kennebunkport and Bar Harbor (ME). Qualified naturalists give commentaries while furthering research. Trips usually take half a day and go well out to sea. You may need warm clothes – and seasick pills.

MARINE STUDIES
A number of excellent aquariums are listed on pages 244–6 where visitors can get a close-up view of many of the creatures of the deep. For more serious naturalists, the Oceanographic Institute at Woods Hole, Cape Cod, is an international centre for marine research offering study cruises. Similar cruises also run from Mystic, CT. The Shoals Marine Laboratory on Appledore Island in the Isles of Shoals, NH, offers courses for naturalists (details from Shoals Marine Laboratory, G-14Y Stimson Hall, Cornell University, Ithaca, NY 14853-7101).

Whales and dolphins In the Gulf of Maine is a chain of rocky ledges and underwater sandbanks. Tidal currents around their edges are constantly churning up the plentiful nutrient-rich algae. The tiny crustaceans that feed on this green-algae soup are in turn the diet of the slim, silvery, 6-inch sand eel (or sand lance), the primary food source for several species of whale. Every summer hundreds of humpbacks come up from the Caribbean to feast in these rich feeding grounds. And every summer thousands of people go out to sea for a close-up look at these captivating creatures.

There is a good chance of seeing the massive but sleek and speedy fin (or finback) whale (they grow to over 65 feet) and the smaller (less than 30 feet) minke whale. The most commonly seen, and the most fascinating in its behaviour, however, is the humpback. Anything up to 50 feet in length and over 40 tons in weight, humpbacks will be seen raising their flukes, or tails, out of the water and then lobbing them down with a splash. They will roll on to their sides for a bit of flipper-slapping and, most exciting of all, will 'breach' or jump vertically out of the water. Each humpback has a distinctive black-and-white pattern on its fluke, enabling researchers to identify and name individuals.

Just as engaging as the antics of the whales is the sight of a school of white-sided (and occasionally white-beaked) dolphins surfing the waves alongside the boat. Porpoises too are sometimes spotted, while the harbor seal is fairly common near port. Seabirds to look out for during the May to September whale-watching season include Wilson's petrel, great shearwater, gannet, herring gull and cormorant.

The American lobster *Homarus americanus* differs from the common or European lobster in the fearsome size of its claws. The cutter claw is used to grab and cut food (some lobsters being right-handed, some left-handed), while the broader, crusher claw is used to crush it. A nocturnal creature, of mottled green, yellow and black (it turns red only when cooked), the lobster lives on the floor of the ocean feeding mainly on clams, sea urchins and fish. Several times a year it outgrows and sheds its shell.

Bog and marsh life The New England coast has several areas of salt marsh. Hampton Harbor and marshes are New Hampshire's largest salt marsh, rich in birdlife. Look out for piping plover, whimbrel, short-billed dowitcher, black skimmer, least sandpiper, sanderling, snowy egret, osprey and great blue heron. In Maine, the Wells National

Estuarine Sanctuary at Laudholm Farm has marked nature trails along the marsh, while Scarborough Marsh Nature Center, just outside Portland, runs guided nature walks and canoe tours (summer only). From Essex, Massachusetts, you can glide up the Essex river salt-water estuary in a glass-bottomed boat. Two-thirds of the fish caught off this coast have fed on the insects, larvae and other rich pickings of the salt marsh 'pantry'.

Plants thriving in salt marsh habitats include sea lavender, sea aster, seaside and grass-leaved golden rod, cockleburr, beach grass (or 'compass grass', because it sways in the wind) and 'salt marsh hay', used by early colonists for cattle food, and the protected salt reed grass (Spartina cynosuroides).

Another plant that thrives on a combination of peat and sand is the cranberry. In September/October the extensive cranberry bogs of Cape Cod, Nantucket and the Plymouth area are flooded and the berries are shaken loose to float to the surface in a most spectacular sea of red. One of the trails from the Cape Cod Natural History Museum at Brewster winds through a cranberry bog.

BLOWING BUBBLES
One humpback whale eats up to 2 tons of food per day (about 250,000 sand eels). Uniquely among whales, humpbacks blow a 'bubble net' below and round a shoal of fish, then rise to the surface with mouth open wide to swallow hundreds of fish in one gulp.

165

Left: a great blue heron keeps a beady look-out

A LOOK AT PUFFINS
Hunted for their meat, eggs and feathers for over 300 years, puffins were virtually extinct in Maine by the late 1800s. Since the 1970s the National Audubon Society has successfully encouraged the re-establishment of colonies in the Gulf of Maine. Boat trips may be taken from Rockland, Boothbay Harbor and other Maine ports to nesting colonies on Eastern Egg Rock, Matinicus Rock and Machias Seal Island, in the Gulf of Maine. The best time is during June and July or the beginning of August.

Salt reed grass, found in Cape Cod's salt marshes, is now a protected species

Massachusetts

The sun goes down on Columbia Street, Fall River

166

THE BORDEN MYSTERY
The mystery of who killed Andrew and Abby Borden has never been solved. Lizzie (their daughter) was tried but acquitted for lack of evidence. This did not stop the nation drawing its own conclusions, which were expressed in satirical verse:
'Lizzie Borden took an axe,
And gave her mother forty whacks,
When she saw what she had done
She gave her father forty-one.'

THE CON-SOCIATE FAMILY
The Fruitlands community attempted to create a new Eden. Property was owned in common, and technology and animal products were shunned (ploughing had to be done by hand). A leading member was Bronson Alcott, whose daughter Louisa (author of Little Women) was only ten when she was exposed to the regime's cold-bath rigours. A conflict between Charles Lane – who urged Bronson Alcott to become celibate – and Mrs Alcott may well have contributed to the decline of the community.

FRUITLANDS PERSONA
Others at the Fruitlands community included Joseph Palmer, persecuted for his unfashionable beard: he was picked on in a scuffle and refused to pay a $10 fine so went to jail for a year. Samuel Bower was an Adamite (a nudist), while Samuel Larned allegedly lived one year entirely on a diet of crackers, the next on nothing but apples.

► **Fall River**   *139D1*

In its heyday Fall River was one of the great textile producing centres of the world. Today many mills survive, some empty, some as sewing-machine sweatshops and some as factory-shopping outlets. Though not picturesque, the town is set dramatically beneath the I-95 viaduct over the Taunton river.

The town's waterfront attractions begin with the **Fall River Heritage State Park** (*Open* daily, except Mon in winter. *Admission* free) which charts the chequered mill history of the town, its labour disputes and its demise, and includes a film show on Fall River's social history. The tower gives a view over the harbour and its ships.

Close by, **Battleship Cove►►** features historic battleships which you can board and explore at will. The mightiest of all the vessels on display is the *Massachusetts*, known as 'Big Mamie'; she served in 35 battles and carried a crew of 2,300. USS *Joseph P Kennedy, Jr* was built in Quincy, Massachusetts; everything has been left out as if the ship is sailing. Meanwhile 1950s music throbs and Morse signals beep in the submarine USS *Lionfish*, which evokes the cramped lifestyle for the 76 crew members. Walk under the I-95 viaduct for the **Marine Museum**, which presents a history of steamers and steam power as well as a model of the ill-fated *Titanic*, used by Twentieth Century Fox for the 1953 movie.

The **Fall River Historical Society►** (*Open* Tue–Fri 9–3, summer weekends 1–4; closed in winter) maintains a Greek Revival granite mansion at 451 Rock Street, moved in 1869 to its present location and redecorated in French Empire style. Exhibits include art, toys, china, glassware and material on the mysterious and much publicised murder of Andrew Jackson Borden and his wife Abby in 1892 (see panel).

►► **Fruitlands Museums**   *138C3*

Fruitlands (in the town of Harvard, northwest of Boston) owes its present form to Clara Endicott Sears who lived in a house (now gone) by the road and who created the museums between 1914 and 1947. The site comprises four buildings. The **Fruitlands Farmhouse** was used by the Con-Sociate Family, a utopian transcendentalist community which existed for seven months in 1843 (see panels). The rural retreat was chosen for its contemplative setting overlooking mounts Monadnock and Wachusetts. Thoreau manuscripts are on display.

Shaker House (1794), used as an office by Harvard Shakers (extant 1791–1919), is now furnished with Shaker items. The **American Indian Museum** displays headdresses, pottery, painted leather, baskets and clothing. The **Picture Gallery** features Hudson River School artists and portraiture (*Open* Tue–Sun, and Mon during holidays).

▶▶▶ Lexington and Concord *138–9C3/D3*

The names of Lexington and Concord are inextricably linked with the events that sparked off the American Revolution in 1775 (see pages 32–3 and 55). The historic sites where these events took place are all marked along the 4-mile road that links the two towns (see below).

In the 19th century Thoreau, Emerson, Hawthorne and Louisa May and Bronson Alcott all lived at Concord, and their homes give a fascinating insight into a remarkable circle of intellectual and literary talent (see also page 46).

THE BATTLE ROAD At Lexington, a flagpole stands on the triangular Green near the statue of Captain Parker. Guides sporting hats in Minute Man style give tours on the Green (tips appreciated). On Patriots Day (the Monday nearest to 19 April) you can witness battle re-enactments, both here and at Concord's North Bridge. Behind the church the Burying Ground contains 17th-century gravestones.

The Lexington Historical Society (*Open* Mon–Sat 10–5, Sun 1–5) maintains three historic buildings.

At **Buckman Tavern▶** the American militia gathered before dawn prior to the battle on the Common. A bullet hole is visible in the front door. The **Hancock-Clarke House▶** was in the parsonage of the Reverend Jonas Clarke in 1775. Patriots John Hancock (Clarke's cousin) and Samuel Adams were staying here on the eve of the battle, when Revere and Dawes alerted them of the British approach. The house contains the drum which William Diamond sounded to rally men to assemble in two lines on the Green prior to the firing of the first shot. The **Munroe Tavern▶**, a mile from the centre of town, was used by the British as a field hospital on their retreat (*Open* Fri–Mon).

THE FIRST SHOT
On 19 April 1775 the British marched into Lexington on their way to Concord where they planned to seize a store of arms and ammunition. Revere and Dawes rode to Lexington to alert the colonial militia. By the time the 700 British – under Lieutenant-Colonel Francis Smith and Major John Pitcairn – had arrived, Captain John Parker and 77 American militia were waiting in two lines on Lexington Common. It will never be known who fired the first shot in the confusion, but the British ignored orders not to return fire and they shot at the fleeing Americans, killing eight.

167

Fruitlands Farm, an early, short-lived commune, is now a museum complex dedicated to the idealists who set it up

THE ADVANCE TO CONCORD

After the skirmish at Lexington, the British advanced to Concord where they started to burn military supplies. The American militia saw the smoke and hastened to save their town. The opposing ranks met at North Bridge and the British fired. With Major Buttrick's words 'Fire, fellow soldiers, for God's sake, fire!' the Americans returned a volley and forced the British to retreat. At Lexington, Lord Percy met the British with reinforcements and the fighting intensified.

'When [the British] got about a mile and a half to a road that comes from Bedford and Bilrica they was waylaid and a great many killed. When I got there there was a great many lay dead and the road was bloody.'
– Amos Barret (1752–1829), recalling in 1825 the Battle of Old North Bridge.

Orchard House, home to novelist Louisa May Alcott

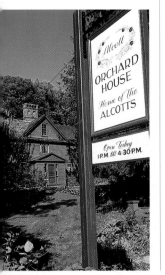

On the way out of Lexington, the **Museum of Our National Heritage▶** on Route 2A (*Open* daily. *Admission* free) has permanent and changing exhibits on American history; Lexington is featured in the display entitled 'Let it Begin Here'.

A self-guided historical trail begins from the **Fiske House** site, explaining how the silence was shattered at Ebenezer Fiske's Farm that fateful day. Part of the original Lexington–Concord road here is an unpaved track, giving an idea of its appearance in 1775. Virtually adjacent, the **Battle Road Visitor Center▶▶** has guided walks and talks, and an excellent film dramatisation re-creating the events leading up to the battle. The **Paul Revere Capture Site** is marked by a memorial. **The Captain William Smith House** was the residence of the captain of the Lincoln Minutemen. **Hartwell Tavern** has been restored to its appearance in 1775, when it played the role of the community meeting-place; here volunteers now re-create colonial life (*Open* Wed–Sun).

At **Concord**, an obelisk marks the spot where the first British soldier fell on 19 April 1775 at the **Old North Bridge Battle Site▶▶**. Adjacent is the famous Minuteman statue sculpted by Daniel Chester French (see page 147). Ranger talks and activities are scheduled in summer through the nearby National Historical Park Visitor Center (*Open* all year. *Admission* free), which has historical displays, a video and a diorama of the Lexington–Concord road.

CONCORD Founded in 1635, Concord has numerous 17th- and 18th-century houses, many with date plaques. In the 1850s Concord was a stop on the underground railroad for escaping slaves. One-hour walking tours at weekends and holidays begin at 12:45pm from the information booth. Canoeing on the Concord river is also popular.

At the **Concord Museum▶▶** Revolutionary exhibits include the lantern from Old North Church and a diorama of the battle at Old North Bridge. Ralph Waldo Emerson's study has been installed here, complete with his books and rocking chair, and there is a Henry Thoreau collection. Archaeological finds, communion silver, samplers and costumes are also displayed.

LITERARY CONCORD The **Ralph Waldo Emerson House►** (*Open* Thu–Sat 10–4.30, Sun 2–4.30), has been restored and is furnished very much as it was in the time when the author lived here, from 1835 to 1882.

Orchard House►► (*Open* daily, except in winter) was the home of the Alcotts; the six members of the family feature in Louisa May Alcott's novel, *Little Women* (1868), written and set here. The Alcotts used to host an 'at home' every week, with music, singing and acting. They were then a poor family and the present comfortable appearance of the house owes much to Louisa's writing income. Mary's room contains several of her sketches, some drawn on the walls. Next door, the former Concord Summer School of Philosophy, extant 1880–8, was established by Louisa's father, the transcendentalist Bronson Alcott.

Nathaniel Hawthorne lived for a period near Orchard House at **The Wayside►** (*Open* Apr–Oct, closed Mon), which he purchased from the Alcotts.

Minute Men relive the Revolution at North Bridge, Concord

'By the rude bridge that arched the flood
Their flag to April's breeze unfurled,
Here once the embattled farmers stood
And fired the shot heard round the world.'
– Written for the dedication of the 1836 monument at Concord by Ralph Waldo Emerson.

'To outsiders, the five energetic women seemed to rule the house, and so they did in many things; but the quiet scholar, sitting among his books, was still the head of the family, the household conscience, anchor, and comforter, for to him the busy, anxious women always turned in troublous times, finding him, in the truest sense of those sacred words, husband and father.'
– Louisa May Alcott, *Little Women* (1868).

The **Thoreau Lyceum**, headquarters of the Thoreau Society, gives lectures and classes. A furnished replica of his famous cabin at Walden stands in the grounds.

The Old Manse►►, next to North Bridge (*Open* Mon–Sat 10–4.30, Sun 1–4.30; closed Tue in winter), was built by William Emerson in 1769 or 1770. His grandson, Ralph Waldo Emerson, wrote *Nature* (1836) while living here. The house was also rented out to Nathaniel Hawthorne and his wife, Sophia, for three years. All the possessions are original, including Hawthorne's tiny desk and nearly 3,000 books. Sophia loved to paint in the dining room, and she etched the writing and the dates on the windows.

Sleepy Hollow Cemetery is situated just off Route 62 (Bedford Street). At Author's Ridge are buried Emerson, Thoreau, Hawthorne, Louisa May Alcott and Daniel Chester French.

Thoreau made regular visits to **Great Meadows**, now a designated National Wildlife Refuge with headquarters at Weir Hill. This wetland is an important wildlife habitat, with well over 200 migratory and nesting bird species recorded.

At **Walden Pond Reservation**► Thoreau observed nature and faithfully recorded 'the progress of the seasons' in a journal he kept while living in a cabin. Pieces of the cabin have long since been turned into letter-openers and other souvenir items for devoted admirers. Visitors in the 19th century used to sign stones and leave them on a cairn on the site of the structure. There is a trail around the edge of the lake.

Further afield, the **Gropius House**►► (*Open* 1 Jun–15 Oct, Fri–Sun, plus first full weekend of each month, Nov–May; tours: 12, 1, 3 and 4pm; 68 Baker Bridge Road, Lincoln; owned and operated by SPNEA – see page 68) was designed by the architect Walter Gropius (1883–1969), founder of the Bauhaus School of Design. Built in 1938, this house is a remarkable synthesis of tradition and innovation, ahead of its time in the use of acoustical plaster, chrome, welded steel, glass blocks and other modern materials.

At Framingham, south of Concord, **The Garden in the Woods** (*Open* 15 Apr–31 Oct, Tue–Sun; last admission 4pm, May 7pm) is the botanical garden of the New England Wildflower Society. It covers 45 acres and is planted with a mixture of wild native flowers, shrubs, ferns and trees.

The Old Manse, Concord, where writers Ralph Waldo Emerson and, later, Nathaniel Hawthorne lived and worked

'I went to the woods because I wished to live deliberately, to front only the essential facts of life, and see if I could not learn what it had to teach and not, when I came to die, discover that I had not lived.'
– Henry David Thoreau, *Walden* (1854).

▶▶ Lowell   *138C3*

When they were first built in the 19th century, Lowell's textile mills were the wonder of the age and a landmark in the early industrialisation of America (see pages 36–7). Today, after a long decline, Lowell has cleaned up its 6 miles of canal and its mills to become a much-cited example of successful urban regeneration.

The **Lowell National Historical Park Visitor Center▶** (free) explains Lowell's social and industrial history through audio-visuals and exhibits. The park itself offers free ranger-led tours lasting 90 minutes and also operates a free trolley shuttle to the Boott Cotton Mills Museum (see below). An inexpensive 2½-hour **canal and trolley bus tour▶▶** (eight times daily) heads along the Pawtucket Canal, past guard locks where the water levels were measured, to the **Pawtucket Falls**, a 32-foot drop in the Merrimack river which provided power for all the mills; now it generates hydroelectric power, supplying electricity to 120,000 homes. Those wishing to explore on foot should pick up the booklet for the Lowell Waterpower Trail. The Mack Building has a Water Power Exhibit.

The fully restored Boott Cotton Mills at Lowell offer an insight into the life of a major textile manufacturing town

171

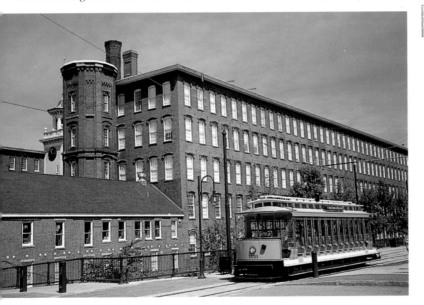

At **Boott Cotton Mills Museum▶▶** earplugs are provided to counter the deafening clatter of the 88 looms. An excellent exhibition includes a model of the mill, plus videos of the 1912 strike and the reminiscences of mill workers. The **Boott Gallery** has changing exhibits of paintings and photographs, and chronicles Lowell in the Civil War.

By Boott Mill the **Working People Exhibit▶** (*Open* Wed–Sun 10–4. *Admission* free) shows the life of the first mill girls, who were well looked after, and of the bleaker conditions of the immigrants who followed. Near by, the mills at Lawrence were the largest in the world when built; the **Lawrence Heritage State Park** (tours May to November) merits a two-hour visit.

NEWBURYPORT'S ECCENTRIC

Former resident Timothy Dexter proclaimed himself 'the Greatest Man in the East'. He wrote a book entitled A Pickle for the Knowing Ones, nicknamed 'the Foe of Grammar' by its detractors because it was so illiterate. One critic said it would be read 'when Shakespeare and Milton are forgot... but not until'. Dexter arranged a mock funeral for himself, then caned his wife because she did not shed sufficient tears. In the early 1800s, his Newburyport garden was adorned with statues of great men, allegorical figures and Native American chiefs. These he transformed with paint into new characters when the old ones fell from fashion.

Once a busy whaling centre, New Bedford is now home to the East Coast's largest fishing fleet

▶ New Bedford   139D1

The fishing and manufacturing town of New Bedford retains an attractive old town at its heart, recalling its heyday as America's greatest whaling port. The whaling industry began in 1765 and by the 1840s there were some 10,000 seamen working here, pushing rival Nantucket into second place in the whaling league. Melville enthused about the town and some of the patrician houses he referred to in his whaling epic, *Moby Dick* (1851), can still be seen along County Street (for example the Rotch-Jones-Duff House and Garden Museum). The decline in whaling was sparked by the loss of numerous whaling ships at sea and by the discovery of petroleum, which gradually superceded whale oil as a fuel for use in oil lamps. The town remains the nation's busiest fishing port.

The **Seamen's Bethel**, with its boat-shaped pulpit, was frequently visited by mariners before they set out on a perilous voyage; it was also the setting for a chapter in *Moby Dick*.

Close by, the **Whaling Museum▶▶** (*Open* daily) occupies an 1821 mansion. Among a fine array of model ships is the world's largest: an 89-foot-long half-size replica of the New Bedford whaling bark Lagoda. Scrimshaw, fishing gear, figureheads, harpoons and paintings are exhibited; William Bradford's huge 19th-century canvas, *Sealers Crushed by Icebergs*, was the first to depict the harsh reality of the life of seal-hunters. Toys, samplers, dolls and glassware are also displayed.

The **Fire Museum** (Bedford and South Sixth streets) has antique fire-fighting equipment. Two vessels on the waterfront are the retired Lightship on State Pier (*Open* Jul, Aug) and the schooner *Ernestina*, an 1894 fishing vessel once used for Arctic expeditions (State Pier; now available for sailings).

The village shoe-maker at work in Old Sturbridge

▶ Newburyport   *139D3*

Newburyport, pleasantly situated on the Merrimack estuary, is one of the most popular day-trip destinations on the North Shore. It is a centre for fishing and whale-watching trips as well as for excursions along the Merrimack itself. It also has a seductive selection of antique shops and boutiques.

The **Custom House Maritime Museum▶** (*Open* Apr–Dec), located within the granite Custom House, has displays covering 300 years of nautical history. Much of the town was rebuilt in brick after a fire. **High Street** has the finest architectural survivals, including the **Cushing House Museum▶** (*Open* Tue–Sat; tours 10–3; closed in winter), a three-storey brick house of 1808 with many reminders of the town's maritime heyday.

Out of town, **Plum Island Beach▶▶** has 10 miles of sands and incorporates Parker River Wildlife Refuge, prolific in birdlife; in high season, this peninsula often fills to capacity quite early in the day.

173

▶▶▶ Old Sturbridge Village   *138B2*

Old Sturbridge Village opened 1946 and is arguably New England's most memorable re-creation of yesteryear. Actors in period dress play the part of the villagers and craftsmen who would have inhabited a typical New England settlement of the 1830s. The village green is flanked by several venerable buildings brought from all over New England and re-erected here. There is a bank, meeting-house, shops, a saw mill and more; a variety of ramshackle outbuildings, 19th-century cattle breeds and vociferous roaming chickens help compound the time-warp illusion (*Open* daily except Mon in winter; for details of special events, tel: 508/347 3362).

A TRIP FROM NEWBURYPORT
From the Custom House Maritime Museum you can take a boat trip to Lowell's Boatshop at Amesbury, where boat-building has been carried out since 1793 and where the flat-bottomed dory was invented. Paint encrustations, hanging like stalactites from the ceiling in the paintroom, are testimony to the long history of the site, which is very prettily located and recalls the early seafaring days of New England.

▶ Pioneer Valley 138B3

In pioneer days the Connecticut River in Massachusetts marked the western frontier of New England. Until westward expansion began in the 19th century this was stock-farming country, and many trees were felled to feed the kilns making bricks to build the mills in Holyoke and South Hadley. The valley today is broad and tame but some drama comes from the basalt ridges, where vertical splits in the rock have formed exciting cliffs and slopes. The valley's sedimentary rocks have also preserved same 200-million-year-old dinosaur footprints. These, along with fossil plants and petrified ripple marks of a prehistoric pool, can be seen at the **Dinosaur Footprints Reservation** on the west bank of the Connecticut River near Holyoke (Route 5).

COLLEGE NUANCES
Holyoke, Northampton and Amherst form the Five Colleges Area, the state's biggest concentration of academia west of Boston and Cambridge. Amherst College is prestigious, high-class and preppy. The nearby University of Massachusetts (UMass) is a state university with a good academic reputation. Prestigious Smith College, Northampton, is an all-women's college; traditionally Smith girls date Amherst boys. Hampshire College is expensive and ultra-liberal. Mount Holyoke College, in South Hadley, is America's oldest women's college (founded 1837) and counts Emily Dickinson among its most distinguished alumnae.

174

The campus of Amherst College, founded in 1821

Holyoke itself is reached by driving north from Springfield (see page 187). Here, a modest Volleyball Hall of Fame (free) commemorates the birthplace of the sport. At **South Hadley** the Mount Holyoke College **Art Museum▶** is one of the oldest collegiate museums in the country and contains classical and Egyptian artefacts as well as American paintings. The summer festival features student theatre and concerts by student and visiting artists.

Hadley Farm Museum (*Open* Tue–Sun, May–Oct. *Admission* free) houses rural bygones, including the first broom-making machine, and offers teas on the porch on Saturday afternoons.

The main entrance for **Holyoke Range Park▶▶** and **Skinner State Park▶▶** is off Route 47 at Hadley. From here the park road winds up to a famous viewpoint over a loop in the river, painted by Hudson River School artist Thomas Cole as *The Oxbow* in the 1830s. Basalt columns known as Titan's Piazza add to the drama, and mounts Monadnock and Tom are in sight. Folk, jazz and classical concerts are given at the summit cabin in summer.

Mount Tom, south of Northampton, is equipped for year-round activity, with skiing, two water rides, a wave pool and a chair-lift to the summit. **Northampton▶** itself is a lively college town. **Smith College** has an arts museum begun in 1879 featuring European masters, the Hudson River School, and 20th-century sculpture (*Open* Tue–Sun, except Jun–Jul: Wed and weekends only). **The Words and Pictures Museum▶** in Main Street pays tribute to comic-book art, including that of the local co-creators of the Teenage Mutant Ninja Turtles (*Open* daily, except Mon and Wed, and until 8pm on Fri and Sat).

AMHERST The attractive college town of **Amherst▶**, built around a sloping common, makes one of the best bases for exploring the Pioneer Valley. The **Emily Dickinson Homestead▶** (280 Main Street; *Open* May–Oct, Wed–Sat 1.30–3.45; advance booking essential, tel: 413/542 8161) was the home of the poet (see page 176). The world's largest collection of Dickinson memorabilia forms a display and archive in the Jones Library and is open free of charge when the archivist is there (tel: 413/256 4090); it also incorporates a large collection of material relating to Robert Frost. Next door, the **Strong House** (1740) has rooms in a range of styles including colonial and Victorian (*Open* May–Oct, Wed and Sat, 2–4).

In Amherst College, the **Pratt Museum** exhibits natural history while the **Mead Art Museum▶** shows ancient art European sculpture and paintings and works by American masters. Just outside town, the University of Massachusetts has concerts during the academic year.

CONTINUING NORTH The architectural highlight of the Pioneer Valley, **Historic Deerfield▶▶** is a beautifully pre-served historic village displaying a variety of domestic buildings from early colonial times. First settled in 1669, the village grew rich on beef farming. Today it is a living village-cum-museum but, thanks to its residents, it is one of the best documented places in the country. Currently 14 houses are open for tours that last approximately 30 minutes. Combined entry tickets are valid for a week and open-ing times are staggered; guided walking tours and horse-and-carriage tours are also available.

Near by, off Route 116, **Mount Sugarloaf State Reservation▶** has a road to the top where fine views extend from a rocky cliff.

175

Dwight House, an early 18th-century house which, like others in Deerfield that are open to the public, displays a fine collection of furniture

is, and my heart, and all t
and my heart, and all t
And all the meadows wic
ure you count, should I
Some one the sum could

In 1886 Emily Dickinson died in the house in which she had been born, in the village of Amherst in Massachusetts, a lyric poet unknown and unpublished. Her sister found 1,775 poems and numerous letters that revealed an original and exceptional talent. Equally extraordinary is the life led by this 'New England mystic'.

ide.
[fo
d te
ill t
vell

'There's a certain slant of
    light
On winter afternoons,
That oppresses, like the
    weight
Of cathedral tunes.

Heavenly hurt it gives us;
We can find no scar,
But internal difference
Where the meanings are.

None may teach it
    anything,
'Tis the seal, despair,
An imperial affliction
Sent us of the air.

When it comes, the
    landscape listens,
Shadows hold their
    breath;
When it goes, 'tis like the
    distance
On the look of death.'

'It's all I have to bring to-
    day,
This, and my heart beside,
This, and my heart, and all
    the fields,
And all the meadows wide.
Be sure you count, should
I forget,
Someone the sum could
    tell,
This, and my heart, and all
    the bees
Which in the clover dwell.'

After her father died in 1874, Emily Dickinson left the grounds of her house only once, when her nephew next door died

The recluse Emily Dickinson was born in 1830 into a household dominated by her puritanical father, a lawyer and treasurer of Amherst College. Described by a schoolfriend as demure and shy but witty, she began to write poems when she was in her 20s, sewing them into little booklets. During her most productive year, 1862 (the height of the Civil War), she wrote 356. She tried unsuc-cessfully to interest a newpaper editor, Samuel Bowles, in her work, and in 1862 she asked a young man of letters, T W Higginson, for an opinion. He did not recommend pub-lishing, although they remained correspondents, and from then on she refused to consider publication.

After the mid-1860s Dickinson's output waned and she began to withdraw from the world, seeing few friends. By the late 1860s she had become known as an eccentric recluse, always dressed in white, who never left the grounds of her home (see page 175). From the mid-1870s she was increasingly saddened by the deaths of many dear to her.

The poetry Emily Dickinson's themes of love, death and nature are treated with an intensity and a sensitivity surprising for one who led such a secluded life. The poems and letters of the late 1850s and early 1860s reveal intense emotions, probably focused on a married Philadelphia clergyman, Charles Wadsworth. In her years of retreat, one person she did see was Otis Lord, an old family friend, and drafts of letters from these latter years suggest a tender and pas-sionate relation-ship. Her poems, like her letters, are composed with scrupulous artistry: words are pared down to an epigram-matic minimum, rhythms are often irregular to assist expression of thought, and the rhymes themselves are sometimes imperfect.

▶▶▶ Plymouth
139D2

Hallowed as the birth-place of modern America, where the Pilgrim Fathers first established themselves, Plymouth preserves the spirit of the early years. Apart from Plimoth Plantation (see page 179), the attractions are small-scale, but the town has become a place of historic pilgrimage and the **Pilgrim's Path**, a designated walking route, will lead you around the town's historic sites.

Despite a dearth of evidence that they ever landed here, **Plymouth Rock▶**, beneath its classical canopy, is, in any event, nicely symbolic of a nation that likes to think of itself as built upon a rock. *Mayflower II▶*, close by, is a faithful replica of the 104-foot-long ship in which the Pilgrims crossed the Atlantic, with period-clad actors telling the story of the 66-day voyage. The cramped conditions leave you wondering how the 102 Pilgrims dealt with frayed tempers on their long journey. The original *Mayflower* returned to England in 1621 and was broken up a few years later.

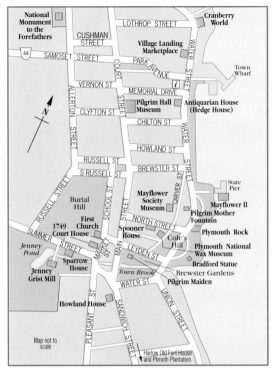

Across the street, on Cole's Hill, a sarcophagus of 1921 contains the remains of some of the Pilgrims while a monument honours Chief Massasoit of the Wampanoag tribe, who befriended the Pilgrims. Adjacent, the **Plymouth National Wax Museum** (closed during winter) has 26 tableaux and 120 characters telling the story of Plymouth's beginnings.

North Street leads away from the sea from here and has some fine houses. Most notable is the **Mayflower Society Museum▶** (*Open daily in summer, Fri–Sun in spring and autumn*), high-ceilinged and with a magnificent flying staircase that is supported only at top and bottom. Edward Winslow, a Pilgrim descendant, built the house in 1754 and Lydia Jackson married Ralph Waldo Emerson in the east front parlour in 1835. **Spooner House** at 27 North Street has five generations of family possessions. **Hedge House▶** (1809), opposite Town Wharf, is a Federal-style home of a 19th-century merchant shipowner, one Thomas Hedge, and displays China trade porcelain, dolls, costumes, quilts and toys.

The Mayflower Society Museum, Plymouth

177

Pilgrims and Native Americans share an authenticated 17th-century meal at Plimoth Plantation

The **Pilgrim Hall Museum▶** (*Open* daily), designed by Alexander Parris (architect of Boston's Quincy Market) focuses on the Pilgrims and their voyage. Paintings show their embarkation and landing, and there are items thought to have been brought to America as part of the Mayflower's cargo, including the cradle of Peregrine White, born on the voyage. The Lower Hall contains artefacts relating to the Plymouth Colony, featuring paintings, furniture, tools and clothes.

The 1749 **Court House and Museum** (*Open* summer. *Admission* free) is notable as America's oldest wooden courthouse. The reconstructed court room was saved from demolition during major redevelopment in the 1950s. A vintage piece of 1828 fire-fighting equipment is displayed. **Sparrow House** is the oldest surviving dwelling in Plymouth (*Open* Thu–Tue). The house dates from 1640 and has characteristic leaded window panes and period furnishings; pottery demonstrations are given inside.

Howland House▶ (*Open* daily, Memorial Day–Columbus Day, then weekends until Thanksgiving) is the only house where Pilgrims actually lived; *Mayflower* passengers John and Elizabeth Tilley Howland resided here and had ten children. The building was enlarged in 1750. A path along the river leads to the **Jenney Grist Mill**, America's first public utility, set up by the Pilgrims in 1636. The exterior is very picturesque, with a waterwheel still churning over the water. Along Sandwich Street is **Harlow Old Fort House** of 1677, restored to its 17th-century appearance.

The **National Monument to the Forefathers▶** is an outstanding example of 19th-century statuary,

ROUND AND ABOUT
The Plymouth Rock Trolley Company gives narrated tours of Plymouth every 20 minutes and you get on and off for the price of one ticket. Whale-watching from Plymouth is offered by Captain John Boats, Town Wharf (tel: 508/746 2643). A ferry goes from Plymouth to Provincetown and buses run between Boston and Plymouth.

Plymouth

commemorating the Pilgrims. A gigantic central figure of Faith flanked by Law, Education, Liberty and Morality stands high on elevated ground. Bas reliefs depict the Departure from Delfthaven, the Landing of the Pilgrims, the Treaty with Massasoit and the Signing of the Mayflower Compact. Etched in granite are the names of the 102 *Mayflower* passengers.

Ocean Spray, makers of cranberry juice (exported worldwide), shows its wares at **Cranberry World▶** (*Open* 1 May–30 Nov, daily 9.30–5; plus 5–9 Jul and Aug. Admission free). Displays explain cranberry growing and harvesting, and there are vintage Ocean Spray TV commercials. Free samples of a range of cranberry-based juices await at the end. This is one of New England's greatest freebies, especially on a thirst-inducing summer's day!

Plimoth Plantation▶▶▶ is an impressively faithful reconstruction of the original Pilgrims' village, 3 miles south of the landing site (Open Apr–Nov, 9–5). The '1627 Village' has all the authentic elements: partly thatched wooden dwellings, straw on the ground, wood-smoke, cow dung, blankets hung out to dry in a yard. Dressed in period costume, interpreters answer visitors' questions as if they were Pilgrims, not tourist guides, and the authenticity extends to the carefully researched 17th-century accents. One woman talks of midwifery as she spins wool, a man tells of his voyage and another explains the schisms in the Church of England. Even the chickens resemble the breeds the settlers would have had.

Also re-created here is the homesite of a native Wampanoag who acted as counsellor to the new settlers. The gentle, peace-loving Wampanoags traded with the Pilgrims but some were later taken as slaves.

'Down to the Plymouth Rock, that had been to their feet as a doorstep Into a world unknown – the corner-stone of a nation.'
– Longfellow, *The Courtship of Miles Standish* (1858).

'Neither do I acknowledge the right of Plymouth to the whole rock. No, the rock underlies all America: it only crops out here.'
– Wendell Phillips, Speech at dinner of the Pilgrim Society at Plymouth, 21 December 1855.

179

PLYMOUTH CRANBERRIES
Plymouth County has some 12,000 acres of cranberry bogs, set within impermeable clay-lined kettleholes and dependent on supporting wetlands for their survival. In spring the bogs look like a sea of light pink flowers. The petals fall off in mid-July, leaving a green berry which ripens spectacularly to a brilliant red and is harvested a few weeks after Labor Day. Plymouth Colony Winery, near Plymouth, claims to be New England's original cranberry winery. Cranberry juice and vodka are mixed to create the 'Cape Codder' cocktail.

Visit Cranberry World to learn about cranberry growing and harvesting

Weak and weary from an uncomfortable nine-week voyage, an intrepid band of 102 English men and women arrived in Plymouth in the winter of 1620. About one-third had been driven out by their radical Puritan faith. All had hopes set high on a new life.

BLOWN OFF COURSE?...

Tradition has it that the Pilgrims, who set off heading for the James River in Virginia, were blown off course and ended up in the Cape Cod area. However, the chances of an experienced mariner such as Christopher Jones not knowing he was 120 nautical miles too far north are remote. First, he would certainly have known the latitudes of all American east coast landmarks; secondly, the astrolabe, a forerunner of the sextant, enabled navigators at that time to calculate all north and south distances with precision.

...OR A CHANGE OF MIND?

Descendants of David Thomson have claimed that when the *Speedwell* needed repair work and she and the *Mayflower* unexpectedly called at Plymouth, the Pilgrim leaders spoke there with David Thomson about New England. The indications are that Thomson, who had been there more than once but never further south than Cape Cod, might have recommended the Plymouth area, where his friend Squanto lived. Did the Pilgrims then change their minds about Virginia?

The Mayflower, an English merchant ship before she was hired to transport the Pilgrims

Puritans and Separatists At a time when the English monarch was also head of the Church in more than just name, dissenting from the Anglican Church was a treasonable offence. While some Puritans attempted to reform the Church of England, one group decided in 1608 to flee to Leiden in Holland, a centre of Protestantism, to escape persecution. These Protestant Separatists lived rather discontentedly in Holland for some 12 years before deciding to start a new life in America. They managed to secure finance from a group of London investors for a pilgrimage that would take them to a land where, according to all reports (and there had been many by then), they could find a better life as well as religious freedom.

The Leiden Separatists bought a small ship, the *Speedwell*, in which they sailed from Holland to Southampton, England, where they met up with the *Mayflower*. Some of the *Mayflower's* passengers were also Puritan Separatists, but the majority were sent by the London stock company to ensure the venture's success, men such as the military officer Miles Standish (hero of Longfellow's long poem *The Courtship of Miles Standish*). Both ships set sail from Southampton, but the

Speedwell proved unseaworthy and had to be abandoned at Plymouth in Devon, and her passengers crammed on to an already crowded *Mayflower*, which set sail once again on 6 September 1620.

Arrival in America Amazingly, the ship and her passengers survived a 66-day journey that was not without storms or near-disasters, and land was sighted on 9 November. On the 11th, the *Mayflower* dropped anchor

Top: Miles Standish makes a treaty with the Native Americans
Above: the Pilgrim Fathers give thanks after landing

at what is now Provincetown on Cape Cod. A meeting was held on board and a famous document, the 'Mayflower Compact', was drawn up by the Pilgrim Fathers (as they were only much later called) under the leadership of William Bradford. Under the terms of this agreement, the settlers promised obedience to the minority of Pilgrim leaders and, despite its one-sidedness, it remained in force until the settlement joined with Massachusetts Bay Colony in 1691.

A reconnaissance party then sailed along the coast to Plymouth, with its safe harbour, running water and corn-fields already cleared by the Wampanoag. It also had high ground from which the colonists could defend themselves against possible attacks from Native Americans, Spanish and French traders or fishermen. On Christmas Day the men began to build their new homes.

Settling in By the end of that first winter, half of the *Mayflower's* passengers had died. The weather was harsh, the colonists were weak from the journey, food supplies were low and crops not yet established. It was a tough time, until the spring came and, with it, friendly contact with members of the Wampanoag people. Like so many other Native Americans, the Wampanoag had been decimated by epidemics of European disease that had come with the traders, but one of the survivors was a man named Squanto. He had been to England (see panel opposite) and was prepared to help the colonists.

The Pilgrims and their fellow settlers had come with a diversity of skills and interests, but most were craftsmen and not used to making a living from the land. Nevertheless, with guidance from the Wampanoag and the arrival of more goats, cattle and other goods with further colonists from England, the Plymouth settlers became self-sufficient within a few years, and by 1640 their numbers had swelled to about 3,000.

SQUANTO
In 1605 an English captain, George Weymouth, captured five Wampanoag men, including Squanto, and took them back to Plymouth in England. Here they became friendly with David Thomson, an apprentice to a ship's doctor. In 1607 the doctor, Thomson and the five Wampanoag joined Sir John Popham's expedition to Sagadahoc, the men acting as inter-mediaries between the Native Americans and the English. Squanto made several more similar trips.

THANKSGIVING
Thanksgiving Day, celebrated across the country with turkey and pumpkin pie, traditionally originated in the autumn of 1621, when the first colonists invited the Wampanoags to join in a three-day festival of thanksgiving for their first successful harvest. Nineteenth-century romancing turned it into a New England institution, and in 1863 Thanksgiving Day was made a national holiday by President Abraham Lincoln.

A calm evening on Quabbin

▶ Quabbin Reservoir   *138B3*

One of America's largest reservoirs, Quabbin supplies water to half of Massachusetts and its zigzag form effectively divides the state into eastern and western halves. The reservoir has a 118-mile shoreline and many islands. Some 2,500 homes were lost when it was built and 7,500 bodies from 34 cemeteries were reinterred. For the tourist its scenic attributes make it worth a detour: an excellent view is from **Quabbin Summit▶▶** at the southern end, where a tower looks to Mounts Tom, Lincoln, Monadnock and Wachusett. To locate the tower follow signposts past Winsor Dam. The reservoir offers outstanding freshwater fishing (boat hire is available for anglers) and there are nine trails, including the ¾-mile summit trail from Quabbin Hill Lookout.

North of the reservoir, at North New Salem, the Swift River's middle branch roars along **Bear's Den▶**, a gorge with rushing waterfalls embraced by granite cliffs which are cloaked with hemlock trees. Supposedly this was a Native American haunt in 1675 during the wars against the white settlers.

JOHN QUINCY ADAMS
An advocate of strong federal government during his presidency, Adams was previously the US minister in The Hague, Berlin, St Petersburg and London. As secretary of state to James Monroe he formulated in 1823 the Monroe Doctrine, which defined any European colonial ambitions in the Western World as a threat to American peace and security. He was also a lawyer and in a landmark case successfully defended the Mendi Africans who were taken aboard the slave ship *Amistad* and mounted a rebellion against their captors (see page 105).

▶ Quincy   *139D2*

Quincy (pronounced 'Quinzee') is known as the 'City of Presidents' because John Adams (America's second president) and his son, John Quincy Adams (America's sixth) were both born here, in 1735 and 1767 respectively. The **Adams Mansion▶**, a large clapboard house, was home to four generations of the Adams family and now displays family pieces and paintings. In the garden, the 1870 Stone Library contains presidential books and manuscripts. Both John and John Quincy Adams were born in 17th-century saltbox farmhouses near by, forming, with the mansion, the **Adams National Historical Site**, the earliest surviving presidential birthplace. The **Adams Academy**, built on the site of John Hancock's birthplace, is now the home of the Quincy Historical Society. The National Park Service Visitor Center (opposite City Hall on Hancock Street) has brochures on historic Quincy, with information about the Quincy Homestead, the Josiah Quincy House, the Quarry Museum, and the United First Parish Church and Crypt, where two presidents and their wives are buried. Quincy can be reached from Boston by the Red Line to Quincy Center.

In 1692 the village of Salem, in the Massachusetts Bay Colony, suddenly found itself in the grip of an infamous witchcraft hysteria. It was a brush with the devil that that would leave its mark for ever.

Tituba's secret Reverend Samuel Parris came to Salem after working as a merchant in the Caribbean. He brought back a slavegirl, Tituba, who was put in charge of Parris's daughter Betty and her cousin Abigail Williams, girls at the impressionable ages of nine and 11. Innocently, Tituba would tell them stories of her own voodoo culture, so very different from the starchy Puritan ethic the girls were brought up on. They were gripped. Soon they were bringing others into Tituba's 'circle' – but for fear of eternal damnation they had to keep it all secret. Betty, however, could not cope with the divided loyalties, and it began to show in her behaviour. Abigail, jealous of all the fuss now being made of Betty, mimicked her 'fits' and one by one the other girls began to writhe and scream similarly.

'Spectral evidence' In 1692 most of the world believed in witchcraft, and to the Puritans of Salem this was the only explanation for the girls' behaviour. But who was it who was bewitching them? The hunt was on. Tituba and others were put under pressure, false confessions were made, innocents incriminated. Things got out of control. Prisons were bursting with suspects (even the wife of the governor of Massachusetts, William Phips, was accused), and 19 'witches' were actually hanged. But everything hinged on 'spectral evidence', the evidence given by the bewitched girls that they were afflicted by a spectre, or the devil, in the image of someone else.

Eventually, in October, Increase Mather and his son Cotton, leading Puritans, and others protested that this meant that it was on the testimony of the devil that justices were condemning people to death. Governor Phips brought the trials to an end, prisoners were released and convictions annulled. The girls were discredited – and Tituba was able to renounce her confession.

183

Top: Tituba and the girls
Above: the title page of Cotton Mather's account of the trials

THE CRUCIBLE
The names of Tituba, Abigail and many of the other personalities involved will be familiar from American playwright Arthur Miller's play *The Crucible* (1953), based on the Salem witch trials. A French film, *Les Sorcières de Salem*, was made of the play. A remake of the film, 'The Crucible' was shot in 1995 on location on Hog Island, located off Ipswich, MA. The film stars Daniel Day-Lewis and Winona Ryder.

An all-too-common sight in 1692: a 'witch' is arrested

Map: Salem

*The Puritan Roger
Conant founded Salem in
1626; his statue can be
found in front of Salem
Witch Museum*

▶▶▶ Salem and Marblehead   139D3

Salem's notorious witch-hunts of the past are only one aspect of the town. Its prosperity, brought about by trading (in particular with China), has left the town with a rich architectural legacy and a particular wealth of Federal-style houses.

That the witch trials (see page 183) amounted to a puritanical persecution of innocent women is hardly remembered here in the ghoulish array of trinkets and souvenirs, all featuring witches in pointed hats. At least the museum-type attractions aim for rather more authenticity.

History Alive! Cry Innocent – The People Versus Bridget Bishop▶ is worth catching (tours daily at 11:30, 1:30 and 3pm only, Jun–Oct); this theatrical reconstruction of a witch trial is set in the Old Town Hall, with its faded classical grandeur and courtroom atmosphere. The audience plays the role of a 17th-century Puritan jury asked to judge the woman's guilt. The **Witch Dungeon Museum** also starts with a short two-person theatrical presentation, setting the scene for the persecutions, before embarking on a brisk but informative tour of the reconstructed dungeons.

The **Witch House**▶ is a fine example of a mid-17th-century house, with period furniture. It belonged to Jonathan Corwin, one of the witchcraft trial judges. It was here that witches were examined for bodily defects. In the **Salem Witch Museum** (presentations every half-hour), 13 tableaux are lit to spin the witchcraft yarn; the dummies are not particularly lifelike and the commentary is over-sensationalised in tone, but the story is gripping.

TRADING AND MARITIME LEGACIES Founded in 1626, Salem was once America's sixth largest city. So widely was the name of Salem known at the peak of its trading activity (1790–1807) that many overseas merchants thought Salem was a country and America just a part of it. At the **Salem Maritime National Historic Site▶** (free) you can see three surviving wharves (there were once over 50). Elias Hesketh Derby, America's first millionaire, established Derby Wharf (1762), and his brick Georgian home, Derby House, can be visited along with the unfurnished Narbonne-Hale House. In the 1840s Nathaniel Hawthorne worked as a surveyor in the Custom House (1819): you can peer into his 'cobwebbed and dingy' office, still used up to 1937. Behind is the Scale House (1829) where goods were weighed and taxed.

While Hawthorne worked here observing the life of Salem, he lived in a house in the grounds of his cousin's 17th-century mansion, **The House of the Seven Gables▶▶**. A secret staircase, a look-out window for observing ships in the harbour, and numerous odd corners and nar-

row passages add to the romance of the house that inspired Hawthorne to write his famous novel (1851) of the same name. Hawthorne's birthplace, the Retire Becket House of 1655, and the Hooper-Hathasay House of 1682 are on the same site.

185

Above: The House of the Seven Gables, inspiration for Hawthorne's novel Left: ship's figurehead in Salem's Peabody Essex Museum

The Peabody Essex Museum▶▶▶ (*Open* daily, Memorial Day–31 Oct) celebrates three centuries of Salem trade with an outstanding collection of model ships and maritime art, as well as period rooms, pictures of old Salem, witchcraft exhibits and a splendid array of ships' figureheads. Out-side are an 1830s shoe shop and the 1684 John Ward House. The adjacent Andrew-Safford House (1819) was, in its day, the most expensive house ever built (not open).

Chestnut Street▶▶ has been called America's finest street. The Stephen Phillips Memorial Trust House at number 34 and the Ropes Mansion (1727), around the corner at 318 Essex Street, are both open in summer. Salem Common was a pasture and drill ground.

Pioneer Village, a short drive to the south (Open late May–mid-Oct), is a re-creation of old Salem, with gardens, farm animals and crafts as well as costumed actors playing the roles of 17th-century Puritans and acting scenes from Hawthorne's *The Scarlet Letter* (1850).

'Halfway down a bystreet of one of our New England towns stands a rusty wooden house, with seven acutely peaked gables facing towards various points of the compass, and a huge, clustered chimney in the midst ... The aspect of the venerable mansion has always affected me like a human countenance, bearing the traces not merely of outward storm and sunshine, but expressive also of the long lapse of mortal life, and accompanying vicissitudes that have passed within.'
– Nathaniel Hawthorne, *The House of the Seven Gables*

Massachusetts

Marblehead, once a busy trading port, is today popular with yachtsmen

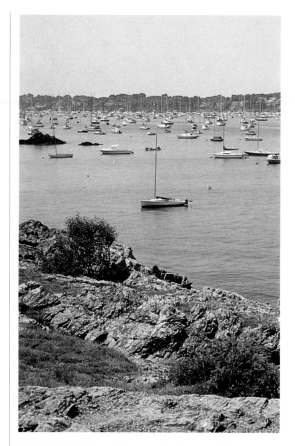

GETTING AROUND
Salem is easily reached from Boston's North Station; trains are frequent and inexpensive (with discounts for round trips) and take 30 minutes. Trolley buses tour Salem every half hour and there is also a free shuttle bus. However, the sights can easily be taken in on foot, and Salem is a delightful town for walking. A red line marks the walking route linking the historic sights (but omits Chestnut Street); free brochures are available from the National Park Visitor Center in Museum Place or from the Chamber of Commerce in the Old Town Hall.

TRADE WITH CHINA
The China trade began when Derby's ship, the Grand Turk, dropped anchor at Whampoa in 1786. By 1800, traders from Salem and Marblehead were a common sight in Canton, the only Chinese port open to them. All sorts of exotic items turned up in America as a result of this trade. From East Africa came ivory, gold, ostrich feathers and hippopotamus teeth; from the West Pacific appeared semi-precious corals and mother-of-pearl; from the Far East, ceramics, textiles, tea, coffee, spices, sugar and Japanese artefacts were landed.

MARBLEHEAD▶▶ This handsome coastal town is located just to the east of Salem and can be reached by bus 441 from Boston or Salem. Like Salem, it prospered on trade. Its tightly knit, irregular 18th-century streets have a salty charm that evokes coastal England. Today it is a wealthy commuter satellite, known for boating, antique shops and boutiques.

At **Public Landing** you can join cruises around the harbour and buy lobster, sea bass and stripers off the boats. Fort Sewell, a small fortification built for the War of 1812, Fountain Park and Crocker Park all overlook the bay. Some 600 Revolutionary War soldiers are buried in the **Old Burial Ground**. In **Abbot Hall** (the town hall) hangs Archibald Willard's famous painting, *Spirit of '76*, epitomising the patriotic spirit of the Revolution. The **Jeremiah Lee Mansion▶** (*Open* summer) has altered little since it was built in 1768; its wooden exterior was made to resemble stone in an attempt to look English.

A causeway road links **Marblehead Neck**, skirted by a loop road; affluent New Yorkers have built summer houses here in various styles such as French château and English Tudor. Chandler Hovey Park is at the northern tip of the Neck and overlooks the bay at Marblehead Light. The best sandy beaches are at Beverly; West Beach has 3 miles of sand while Dane Street Beach is smaller.

► **Springfield**   *138B2*

This major industrial city sits at the southern end of the Pioneer Valley (see pages 174–5) and deserves a visit for its museums (*Open* Wed–Sun 12–4). Combined entry to four of them, all situated by the Quadrangle, is available. The **Connecticut Valley Historical Museum** details the history of the valley from 1636. Dinosaur exhibits, an aquarium, a planetarium and the story of early aviation in Springfield are attractions at the **Springfield Science Museum**. The George Walter Vincent Smith Art Museum is an excellent collection of Victoriana, armour, Hudson River School paintings and an outstanding collection of Chinese cloisonné. The Museum of Fine Arts features French Impressionist works among its European paintings. At Springfield Armory National Historic Site► Washington set up the first arsenal in America. In 1873 the 'Trapdoor' Springfield Rifle was invented here (the model 1903 was used by the US Army in World War I). The arsenal closed in 1968 and now

INDUSTRIAL LEGACY
The Blackstone River Valley close to Worcester was a busy mill district in the 19th century. Mill owners provided jobs, schools, housing, churches and stores for their workers, who included refugees from Europe seeking religious and personal freedom. Industrial competition from the South eventually spelt economic decline. Some old mill villages survive, such as Hopedale and Whitinsville, while the Willard House and Clock Museum at Grafton honours the Willard brothers, clock-makers in the 18th century.

187

Worcester: museum visitors can choose between armoury (left) or fine art (below)

contains perhaps the nation's finest collection of firearms.

In 1891 Dr James Naismith devised the game of basketball in Springfield. At 1150 West Columbus Avenue the **Naismith Memorial Basketball Hall of Fame►** pays homage to the sport's great players, teams and coaches with reverent displays of photos and mementoes, as well as 'virtual reality'. Interactive exhibits include the chance to participate in a shoot-out (Open daily).

► **Worcester**   *138C2*

A busy industrial and commercial centre, and New England's second largest city, Worcester has two notable museums. The **Worcester Art Museum►►►** (*Open* Wed–Sun) 55 Salisbury Street) boasts works from the ancient world, European art from the Renaissance to the 20th century, and American masters including Whistler, Homer, Copley, Sargent and Edward Hick. The **Higgins Armory Museum►►** (*Open* Tue–Sat 10–4. Sun 12–4; 100 Barber Avenue) is spectacularly housed in a gallery modelled on the hall of a medieval Austrian castle, and displays a collection of weapons and armour from all over the world. For details of Worcester Common shopping outlets, see page 16.

0   20   40   60 km
0   10   20   30 miles

CDN

4

916m
Deer Mt
Connecticut
Lakes

Lake
Francis

Colebrook   Beaver Brook
Falls   Dixville
1061m   Notch

North
Stratford   Dixville Peak
Errol

VERMONT

1128m
Sugarloaf Mt

Groveton   Milan

MAINE

Lancaster   1268m
Mt Cabot

Berlin

3

St.
Whitefield   Gun   Jefferson
City   Highland   Gorham

Littleton   Bretton   1917m
Bethlehem   Woods   Mt Washington
Cog Railway

Lisbon

93   1600m   Crawford
Mt Lafayette   Notch   Jackson

Woodsville   Franconia Notch   Glen

North Conway

1466m   White   Bartlett
Mt Moosilauke   Lincoln   Mountain   Conway

Woodstock   King Pine
Ski Area

National Forest

Wentworth   Center
987m   Sandwich   Tamworth

Smarts Mt   Plymouth   Squam   Moultonborough
Holderness   Lake

Center Harbor   Castle in the Clouds

2

Hanover   Ruggles   Meredith   Lake
Lebanon   Mine   Winnipesaukee

Lower Shaker Village   Bristol   Weirs
Beach   Wolfeboro

89   Grafton

Saint-Gaudens NHS   New   Laconia
Cornish   Grantham   London   Danbury   Alton

Sunapee   Andover   Belmont   Farmington

Claremont   Sunapee   93   Shaker
Village

Newport   Rollins   Canterbury   Rochester
Mount Sunapee   Bradford   State Park   Pittsfield
State Park   Somersworth

Charlestown   Contoocook   Northwood   Dover

Alstead   Henniker   Hopkinton   CONCORD
Deerfield   Durham   Portsmouth

Marlow   Hillsboro   Suncook   Newmarket   Odiorne Point

Antrim   Epping   Wallis Sands

1

Harrisville   MANCHESTER   Rye Beach
Keene   Greenfield   93   Exeter   Hampton Beach

Dublin   Kingston   95
Marlborough   Peterborough   Derry   Seabrook Beach

965m   Merrimack   America's
Mt   Jaffrey   Stonehenge
Fitzwilliam   Monadnock   Milford   Nashua
West Ridge   Cathedral   Hudson
of the Pines

MASSACHUSETTS

A   B   C

The Union Church and
covered bridge at Stark
(both 1850s) in northern
New Hampshire

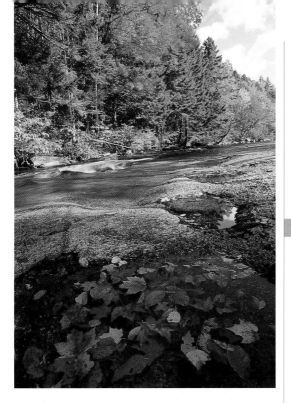

Fall foliage in the White Mountains

NEW HAMPSHIRE The state's triangular form extends 168 miles north to south and 90 miles west to east at its maximum dimensions. In shape and size, it is an inverted form of Vermont, although its population, nudging a million, is almost twice as high.

THE LAND AND PEOPLE By repute, New Hampshire inhabitants are independent, hardworking, conservative and proud of their state and its history. They are also thrifty, and somewhat suspicious of government. One typical manifestation of this die-hard New Hampshire attitude is that there are no income or sales taxes: much state revenue comes instead from 'sin tax' on liquor (hence you can only purchase alcohol at state liquor stores), and from tobacco and gambling. Another is that the state is unique in the Union in that any resident has the right to raise an issue at the state capitol for discussion. 'Live free or die', words first uttered in the Revolution by Colonel John Stark, form the most cut-and-thrust of all state mottos. New Hampshire was the first state to vote in favour of the Declaration of Independence.

Despite its nickname 'The Granite State', New Hampshire does have areas of good, fertile land, particularly in the river valleys. Agriculture, together with forestry, ranks third in the state's economy after manufacturing and tourism. With a decline in the number of dairy farms in recent years have come changes in farming methods, including the replacement of animal-feed crops with strawberries, flowers and other produce.

New Hampshire

New Hampshire

Industry, however, is New Hampshire's economic mainstay, and its factories employ a higher proportion of the population than those in New York. Textiles have declined drastically in New Hampshire since their economic heyday in the 19th century. Machinery, paper, pulp, plastics and electronics are now important in the industrial heartland in the southern part of the state centred on the Merrimack Valley.

Tourism is another state money-earner. Locals will tell you that New Hampshire has better maple syrup than Vermont and the best autumn foliage in New England. It certainly does have the distinction of possessing New England's tallest mountains, and the merit of having lakes, uplands, forests and the coast all within an hour or two's drive.

Ask a New Hampshire native if he's lived there all his life and he'll reply 'not yet'

VISITOR HIGHLIGHTS The **White Mountains** in the north of the state are New England's tallest and finest uplands. This prime territory for leaf-peeping, scenic drives and hiking has attracted artists, writers and intellectuals since the early 1800s. Today it is busier than ever, and shopping outlets, motels and theme parks have sprung up around its edges. As is the case elsewhere in New England, many of the visitor attractions, however, are only open in the May to October season.

Views from the Kancamagus Highway in the White Mountains present some of New England's finest shows of autumn colour

Summer crowds also head for the Seacoast and Lakes regions of New Hampshire. The state's first colonial settlers came to the **coast** in 1623 and eked out a living supplying timber to the English. In 1679 New Hampshire became a separate royal colony from Massachusetts. Today, **Portsmouth** continues as a commercial port. The town itself has the state's biggest concentration of historic houses.

Elsewhere the 18-mile seaboard is given over to pleasure-seeking. Apart from a short, empty stretch at its northern end it is almost entirely developed, with summer cottages, motels, fast-food outlets and motels culminating in the 3-mile boardwalk at Hampton Beach.

The lakes number about 1,300 in all, including the smaller 'ponds'. **Lake Winnipesaukee** is the largest and the most obviously commercialised, but is still very attractive with abundant islands and tempting boat excursions.

The **Mount Monadnock region** in the south-west has a bucolic charm belying its nearness to the urbanised parts of New England. Bumpy backroads set a slow pace in the vicinity of Mount Monadnock itself, where the sleepy villages have quintessential white clapboard and trim greens. The mountain itself gives a view over six states and has long attracted visitors; in 1860 there was a 'half-way house' and a 'summit house'.

'…New Hampshire has One each of everything as in a show-case.' – Robert Frost, *New Hampshire* (1937).

Events

For further information contact the state tourist office (see page 266) or the local chambers of commerce.

January
Loon Mountain Independence Day Weekend, Lincoln.
Jackson Winter Carnival, Jackson.

February
Great Rotary Fishing Derby, Meredith.
Dartmouth Winter Carnival, Hanover.
World Championship Sled Dog Derby, Laconia.

March
Rockingham Park Craft Festival, Salem.
Spring Mania, Attitash Mountain, Bartlett.

April
Aprilfest, Cannon Mountain, Franconia.

May
Sheep and Wool Festival, New Boston.
New Hampshire Lilac Festival, Lisbon.

June
Market Square Celebration, Portsmouth.
Old Time Fiddlers Contests, Lincoln and Stark.
Seacoast Jazz Weekend, Portsmouth.

July
Nascar Winston Cup Race, at NH International Speedway, Loudon.
Wolfeboro Antique Fair, Wolfeboro.
Antique and Classic Boat Show, Laconia.

August
League of NH Craftsmen's Fair, Mount Sunapee State Park.
Balloon Rally, Pittsfield.
Attitash Equine Festival, Bartlett.
Candlelight Tour of Historic Homes, Portsmouth.

September
Riverfest Celebration, Manchester.
Seafood Festival, Hampton Beach.
NH Highland Games, Loon Mountain.

October
Harvest Day, Canterbury Shaker Village, Canterbury.
Fall Foliage Festival, Warner.
Sandwich Fair, Sandwich.

November–December
Traditionally Yours, Jackson.

December
Dickens Holiday Celebration, Hanover.
Candlelight Stroll, Strawbery Banke, Portsmouth.
First Night Celebrations (New Year's Eve) Concord, Portsmouth, Wolfeboro, Claremont, North Conway and Keene.

On the shores of Lake Sunapee, an all year round resort

Canterbury Shaker Village, now a museum, was a celibate religious community, relying on conversion and adopting orphan children

A PREHISTORIC MYSTERY

Also known as Mystery Hill, America's Stonehenge comprises chambers with massive capstones, stone walls, standing stones, a sacrificial table and a 'speaking tube'. Various monoliths align with the pole star and the summer solstice. What connection all this had to solar and lunar events is uncertain, but its purpose may well have been astronomical and/or ceremonial.

192

The Shakers believe that every artefact should be perfectly made, to last a thousand years

▶ America's Stonehenge 188B1

This enigmatic 4,000-year-old site at North Salem may not quite emulate its more famous English namesake but is a genuine prehistoric relic (see panel). From Boston leave I-93 at Exit 3 and take Route 111 east to Island Pond and Haverhill Road. Go south on Haverhill Road to the entrance on the right (*Open* weather permitting, daily, Apr–Nov; call for hours on 603/893 8300).

▶▶ Canterbury Shaker Village 188B2

Just north of Concord, this pristine example of a Shaker community, established in the 1780s, is the sixth of 18 such villages in order of founding. The last surviving female inhabitant, or sister, died in 1992, but the village has been preserved intact, with a meeting-house (note the separate entrances for men and women), fire station, schoolhouse, herb garden, dwelling house (with a bell cast by Paul Revere) and a remarkably well-preserved steam-powered laundry. The Shakers here were progressive in outlook: they had the first telephone and first car in the area, and converted to electricity in 1910, five years before the state house in Concord.

The guided tour takes a look at Shaker inventions, which include the wide-headed brush, an early washing-machine, knitting-machines, an automatic hayseeding device and a self-sealing front door. Craft workshops, including herbal crafts, broom-making and box-making, are held in season. For more on the Shaker way of life see pages 148–9. (*Open* daily, May–Oct, weekends only in Apr, Nov and Dec. Tours last 90 minutes, starting on the hour.)

▶ Concord 188B1

Not to be confused with Concord, Massachusetts (see pages 168–70), this commercial and administrative centre is the state capital of New

Hampshire. Visitors are most likely to come for the **Christa McAuliffe Planetarium►►** (for times and reservations (tel: 603/271 STAR), named after the Concord astronaut and schoolteacher who died instantly in the ill-fated take-off of the *Challenger* space mission. The planetarium is one of the world's most technologically advanced. It offers a number of programmes, in which you may see our galaxy from inside and outside in a simulated voyage through space, and home in on close-ups of the moon and the planets. It holds an Astronomy Day Celebration in May, as well as a monthly SkyWatch.

One of a number of granite public buildings downtown, the **State House►** was erected by prisoner labour in 1819 and much enlarged subsequently, although the legislature still meets in the original chambers. With 400 representatives it is the fourth largest such assembly in the world (after the government assemblies of Britain and India, and the US Congress). Murals and some 200 portraits of New Hampshire dignitaries adorn the inside, as well as 88 tattered Civil War flags in the entrance hall. There are free weekend tours on the hour between 10am and 2pm; during the week you guide yourself with the aid of a leaflet available at the desk.

In Eagle Square, close by the State House, the **Museum of New Hampshire History** (*Open* Tue–Sun) is where the renowned 1852 Concord Coach is on display (see panel). **The New Hampshire Historical Society** (free), across from the State House, maintains changing displays looking back on the state's past. The **Coach and Eagle Trail** is a self-guided walk taking in points of interest in the city centre (free pamphlets available from the State House and from the Chamber of Commerce, 244 North Main Street). The **League of New Hampshire Craftsmen**, a state-wide handicraft association, has its headquarters and a gallery at 205 North Main Street.

Out of the downtown area at 14 Penacook Street at the end of North Main Street, the **Franklin Pierce Manse** (*Open* mid-Jun–Labor Day, Mon–Fri, 11–3) was the home from 1842 of the 14th president and contains a number of family pieces. Pierce had a somewhat nondescript political life, and a tragic family one: two of his children died in infancy, then his third was killed in a railway accident aged 13, two months before his inauguration in 1853. As a consequence of this his wife could not face public appearances and his cousin had to stand in as first lady.

Concord's up-to-the-minute planetarium

193

THE CONCORD COACH
Concord's history of coach-making dates from 1827 when J Stephen Abbot, coach-builder and wheelwright, completed the first Concord coach. He forged a partnership with Lewis Downing, and together they created 14 types of Concord coach, as well as numerous kinds of other recreational and commercial vehicles. Their company produced 3,000 coaches, some of which were used by the Wells Fargo Company in the pioneering days of the West.

Pick your own fruit in Canterbury – and in many other places

Winter, with deep snow covering much of the region, is very different in New England from summer. Christmas and First Night, a New Year's Eve festival that originated in Boston's bicentennial Independence celebrations of 1976, are very special times.

194

Top: Christmas at Faneuil Hall, Boston
Above: snow and a welcoming wreath on the door – all part of the spirit of a New England Christmas

CHRISTMAS WREATHS
One small but thriving industry in the economically impoverished area of northern Maine is the making of decorative Christmas wreaths. Based on a particular type of balsam fir, they are sold all over eastern America.

First Night Buttons – passport to Boston's New Year's Eve celebrations

Christmas As soon as Thanksgiving Day is over, Christmas trees, lights, wreaths and garlands start going up all over the towns and villages. The month of December is filled with festivities, from lantern-lit sleigh rides to readings of Dickens. To highlight just three: in Portsmouth, New Hampshire, there is a Candlelight Stroll round the houses of Strawbery Banke Museum, each decorated in its own period style; lantern-bearing guides in 19th-century costume lead evening tours in Mystic Seaport Village, Connecticut; and Old Sturbridge Village, Massachusetts, celebrates a colonial-period Christmas.

Summer visitors who want to see what a New England Christmas is like should be sure to look inside one of the dozens of Christmas shops that stay open all year round. Plastic trees hung heavy with colour-co-ordinated bows, baubles, enamelled cut-outs and crystal Santas glitter against the fake snow and piped carols. There are rolls of ribbon by the dozen, tiny stars by the yard, garlands and wreaths ready-made or in kits. Displayed amongst it all are little groups of 'Snowbabies', 'Carolers', Annalee dolls (see panel on page 196), nutcrackers and miniature Christmas villages – collections to build up and arrange under the tree or on the mantelpiece. There may even be a Nativity scene.

First Night This colourful and exciting, non-alcoholic community festival has become a well-established tradition that is spreading rapidly to dozens of towns throughout New England and elsewhere. Between the afternoon carnival procession and the midnight fireworks on New Year's Eve, there are scores of different indoor and outdoor 'happenings'. For the cost of a First Night Button (badge), families and friends, often wearing masks or fancy dress, wander the streets imbibing jazz, dance, theatre, puppets, ice carvings, store-front tableaux and many other entertainments.

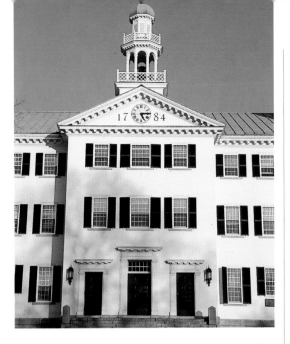

Dartmouth College, the only Ivy League college in northern New England

DARTMOUTH'S BEGINNINGS
Dartmouth College was founded in 1769 when the Congregational minister, Eleazar Wheelock, gained a charter from the governor of New Hampshire to educate Native Americans in a log hut. The college's first sponsor was the 2nd Earl of Dartmouth, the secretary of state for the colonies under George III.

► **Hanover**   *188A2*

In Hanover, on the Connecticut River, the town centre is dominated by the 265-acre campus of prestigious **Dartmouth College►**, an Ivy League establishment (see pages 22–3). Notable among the college buildings grouped around the maple-shaded green are the colonial-style **Baker Library** (1928) and **Dartmouth Hall** (1784). The **Hood Museum** has a small but choice art collection (*Open* Tue–Sat 10–5, Wed until 9, Sun 12–5. *Admission* free). The **Hopkins Center** features year-round music performances, plays, movies and other cultural events.

South of town towards Windsor, the **Saint-Gaudens National Historic Site►►**, off route 12A at Cornish, marks the summer home of Augustus Saint-Gaudens (1848–1907), one of America's foremost sculptors. Many of his works are on show, both in the garden that was his passion and in his studio. Pieces include copies of the *Shaw Memorial*, which stands on Boston Common opposite the State House, and the *Adams Memorial*, installed in Washington, DC. (*Open* last weekend in May to end of Oct.)

East from Hanover, by Mascoma Lake, the **Lower Shaker Village** retains 13 Shaker buildings of the former nearby Enfield community (1781–1923) and includes a craft shop and a small museum of Shaker artefacts (*Open* mid-May–mid-Oct and winter weekends). The nearby feast ground on Mount Assurance was chosen for its view of the lake. Further on, at Grafton Center, a signpost points up a bumpy road to the **Ruggles Mine►** (*Open* mid-May–mid-Jun, weekends 9–5, then daily until mid-Oct). This abandoned mica, feldspar, beryl and uranium mine (see panel) is an expensive visit for what is offered, but the site is dramatic. Entrance is through a rock tunnel into a huge open-cast mine, from which a number of man-made caverns and underground ponds can be explored (a torch is advisable).

MICA AT THE RUGGLES MINE
The flexible, flaky material known as mica, which is found abundantly in the Ruggles Mine, has high resistance to heat. It was formerly used to glaze stove-fronts and lanterns, and to carry wires in electric toasters. The owners claim over 150 types of minerals have been found at the mine. Visitors can rent hammers and take home souvenir chunks of rock.

The motif
of
Annalee's
dolls

ANNALEE'S DOLLS

Back in 1934 Annalee Thorndike made her first doll, the first of many thousands of felt and wire creations, which with their hand-painted faces and rosy cheeks, have gained something of a cult status. Near Meredith in the Winnipesaukee region is the Annalee Doll Museum and shop, on the original manufacturing site. The museum exhibits some pre-World War II specimens, including the first doll ever produced (in 1934; early examples can fetch $2,000 nowadays). The gift shop sells a variety of mice in top hats, Christmas shepherds, baseball players and fishing boys.

At the foot of Mount Sunapee, Lake Sunapee is popular for water sports

►► Lake Sunapee 188B2

The Sunapee area offers unspoilt lake and mountain scenery, and a good alternative for those who find Lake Winnipesaukee too commercialised. The state beach on Lake Sunapee is a narrow sandy strip, ideal for families with small children as the water is shallow and the beach shelves very gently. The M/V *Mt Sunapee II* cruises the lake, with two narrated tours daily (tel: 603/763 4030). The **John Hay National Wildlife Refuge**, Newbury, is a former estate of a diplomat's summer mansion, with fine grounds sloping to the lake and containing wild alpines. **Mount Sunapee►►** towers over the lake. Its ski-lift operates all year, and the summit café offers a huge panorama encompassing Mad River Glen (73 miles) and Mount Washington (75 miles). Walks from the top include the 1,000-yard trail to a cliff high above spectacularly sited Lake Solitude. At the base of the chair-lift is the site of the League of New Hampshire Craftsmen's Craft Fair in August.

Mount Kearsarge► (2,937 feet), in Rollins State Park, has a straightforward trail up its south side (reached by road from Warner). The walk up takes 20–30 minutes; the view from the top takes in the White Mountains. **Mount Kearsarge Indian Museum** (Exit 8 off Route 89 near Warner) explores the world of the North American Indians with exhibits of baskets, fishing artefacts, canoes and quiltwork (*Open* daily, May–Oct, weekends Nov and Dec).

►► Lake Winnipesaukee 188B2

New Hampshire's largest lake is the centre of a busy vacation area whose fortunes were boosted considerably by the movie *On Golden Pond*, filmed at adjacent Squam Lake. Its shoreline is very irregular and the charming views ever-changing, although the small Victorian resort communities that fringe it are of limited interest. The best way to appreciate it is to take a cruise on the M/S *Mount Washington* (May–Oct; tel: 603/366 5531).

Ellacoya State Beach is suitable for families, with a narrow sandy strip; the water is clean and there is a boat launch for lightweights. **Weirs Beach**, with the main

Aerial view of Moultonborough in the Lakes Region

SPEEDWAY
New Hampshire International Speedway (tel: 603/783 4931) is a big state revenue earner on Route 106 north of Canterbury. Races take place in the 75,000-seater stadium.

197

steamer pier, is the most commercialised point on the lake. It is a far from sedate boardwalk village thick with fast-food stands, motels and family-oriented action (see panel), but retaining a quaintly antique array of 1950s home-made slush kiosks and amusement arcades. One of New England's last drive-in movie theatres (an endangered species) is here too. **Meredith Bay** hosts a summer theatre, while **Center Harbor** has a Children's Museum for ages two to ten.

The **Science Center of New Hampshire**▶ (*Open* 1 May–1 Nov), off Route 113 near Holderness, is a wildlife sanctuary for rescued animals of New Hampshire. It is nicely done, with a ¾-mile trail leading past enclosures. Live animal demonstrations, with a naturalist, take place twice daily, and there are lots of hands-on activities for children, including microscopes and quizzes. In addition to the main trail, there is a 1-mile trail up to Mount Fayal which offers a view of **Squam Lake**. From July to September, the Center also runs nature cruises on the lake for sightings of loons and other wildlife (for details, tel: 603/968 7194). Cruises are also operated by Squam Lake Tours (tel: 603/968 7577).

Quieter, traditional towns include **Center Sandwich** and **Wolfeboro**▶. Both have crafts shops and historical museums. The nearby **Castle in the Clouds**▶, built in 1911–14 for millionaire Thomas Plant, is a turreted hilltop house with whimsical interior features, including an octagonal elm-panelled dining room. However, it is the setting that is most memorable. The shuttle bus which takes you up also visits the Castle Springs mineral-water bottling plant. Be prepared for crowds.

At **Tamworth** is the Barnstormers Theater, New Hampshire's oldest professional summer theatre. Tamworth itself glimpses Chocorua Lake, while nearby **White Lake State Park** has a beach with canoe and rowing-boat rentals.

FAMILY FUN AT WEIRS BEACH
The Winnipesaukee Railroad runs diesel trains along the lakeside from here, with dinner specials in the evening. There are also two open-air water parks, one called simply Water Slide; pay for a batch of rides, or for two hours, or for the whole day. The Surf Coaster lies away from the beach and is pricier, but also has a wave-machine surf coaster. The latter also runs a crazy-golf course. Across the road, another company operates go-karts and a baseball pitching machine.

Seaplane rides are a popular way of enjoying the autumn foliage

SEAPLANE RIDES
FOLIAGE FLIGHTS

198

MONADNOCK CHECKLISTS
Because the forest on Mount Monadnock was burned off around 1810, the views from the upper trails are particularly fine. The open terrain here gives rise to some rare semi-alpine flora, including mountain cranberry, mountain golden rod, mountain sandwort and cinquefoil. Fauna includes moose, black bear, white-tailed deer, grey fox, red fox, woodchuck, porcupine, opossum and raccoon.

Andrew Wyeth is one of several artists with New England connections on show at the Currier Gallery

ROUTES UP MOUNT MONADNOCK
Numerous routes lead up the mountain from Monadnock State Park headquarters at Jaffrey, where free maps are available. The most popular and easiest are the White Cross and White Arrow trails (3–4 hours there and back). The Pumpelly Trail is the longest at about 5 hours' walking time. The Spelman Trail, which heads up a breath-taking series of schist rock ledges to reach Pumpelly Ridge, ascends 1,000 feet in half a mile and is the steepest. The Red Spot Trail is perhaps the most scenic. For a very full but rewarding day's walking, make a circuit by taking any trail via Bald Rock to the summit and return via Pumpelly Ridge.

▶ Manchester 188B1

In the 19th century the thriving Amoskeag Mill made Manchester the world's largest cotton cloth-producing centre. Today it is a commercial and manufacturing city, but the **Currier Gallery of Art▶▶** makes the city worth a visit. The collection includes European and American masters, with paintings, sculpture and decorative art from the 13th to 20th centuries (*Open* daily, except Tue; late night on Fri). The gallery also organises tours of the 1950 Zimmerman House, designed by Frank Lloyd Wright (*Open* Fri–Sun; advance booking only, tel: 603/626 4158).

South of town, the **Robert Frost Farm▶** at Derry was the poet's home from 1900 to 1911 (see page 209). Here he 'wrote more than half of my first book, much more than half of my second and even quite a little of my third'. He later visited it to find it a scrap yard, and it was only after his death that his daughter Lesley Frost Ballantine restored it. The locality was the setting for Frost's 'Stopping by Woods on a Snowy Evening'. (*Open* daily in summer, weekends in spring and autumn.)

▶▶ Mount Monadnock Region 188A1

Mount Monadnock▶▶▶, America's most climbed peak, rises to a modest 3,165 feet, but by virtue of its isolation from New England's other high spots it gets one of the grandest views in the Northeast. The surroundings are relatively unfrequented and make a good getaway from the Boston area for those seeking accessible, low-key relaxation. Walking, kayaking, canoeing, covered-bridge spotting, leaf-peeping, skiing and antique-hunting lead the pursuits.

Only reached on foot, the mountain that stands alone on the plain demands a substantial walk to the top (see panel). Rock formations to look for include the Imp, the Sarcophagus (a boulder transported and dumped on Pumpelly Ridge by glaciers in the Ice Age) and the Doric Temple (a set of composite stone blocks). The summit view on a clear day takes in points more than 100 miles away and extends to the White Mountains, to the Boston skyscrapers and over every New England state.

Peterborough is home to the MacDowell Colony, begun by composer Edward MacDowell (1861–1908), whose best-known works include his second piano concerto and the piano solos *To a Wild Rose* and *New England Idyls*. After his death the Colony was for 40 years directed by his widow; it offers artistic seclusion to artists, composers and writers, but only a small part is open to the public. Those attracted here have included Leonard Bernstein,

Thornton Wilder, Aaron Copland and Virgil Thomson. Wilder's play, *Our Town*, was set in Peterborough and became one of the cornerstones of American drama. Theatrical traditions are maintained by the Peterborough Players with their summer theatre, and the Marionette Theater (tel: 603/924 7585), which specialises, most unusually, in opera performed by marionettes to recorded music. Fans of vintage diners should seek out the Peterborough Diner in Depot Street. **Miller State Park▶▶**, off Route 101 east of Peterborough, has road access for vehicles to the summit of Pack Monadnock (2,300 feet), plus picnic sites and a summit loop trail. You can walk up (1½ miles) by following the Wapack Trail from Route 101.

Blink and you'll miss **Dublin**. Along its sleepy main street is the headquarters of the *Yankee Magazine* and *Farmers' Almanac*, two famous New England-based publications; tours of the premises are given on weekdays. West of town, Dublin Pond is the haunt of blue herons and offers a town beach with water-slides, sailing, windsurfing and swimming. Close by, Friendly Farm (*Open* daily in summer, weekends in autumn) operates a petting farm for children, with a range of farmyard animals and milking demonstrations. Near by, **Harrisville▶** has a pretty pond and a cluster of old mill cottages; Harrisville Designs demonstrate old weaving methods (*Open* Tue–Sat. Admission free).

Keene is a commercial centre rather than a tourist town, but has some dignified 19th-century homes. The Horatio Colony House Museum, at 199 Main Street, is a pleasing Federal-style house of 1806. The Children's Museum has displays on different parts of New England, including colonial life and a 'typical' village.

West of Keene by Route 9, an easy ¾-mile loop trail follows Wilde Brook through deep **Chesterfield Gorge** (*Open* weekends. *Admission* free). **Rhododendron State Park▶**, at Fitzwilliam, comes into spectacular bloom in mid-July and has views of Mount Monadnock. **Fitzwilliam** itself has a concentration of antique shops, while at **West Rindge** Ed's Country Auction offers rural antiques, domestic junk and copious local colour (Saturdays in summer at 10am; winter at 6pm). Near Rindge is the **Cathedral of the Pines▶** (*Open* year round, 9–5; see panel).

199

Mt Monadnock, seen from Dublin

Over 80 per cent of New England is covered in forest. The woods, a mixture of hardwoods and softwoods, are home to an exciting variety of wildlife species. Seeing moose or beaver can be a holiday highlight, and in summer the sound of songbirds is sensational. There are also areas of enchanting alpine flora.

'BRAKE FOR MOOSE...'

'...It could save your life'. So read the road signs in New Hampshire. Every year there are scores of collisions between moose and cars on forest roads. A moose can severely damage not only the car but, quite possibly, the driver too. If you see a moose at the side of the road, try not to startle it and go carefully – moose are unpredictable. Dark brown in colour, they are difficult to see in the dark.

POISON IVY

Poison ivy is common throughout eastern North America and is poisonous to touch. Its leaves have three leaflets, green turning to red/purple, and it has white berries. If you so much as brush against the plant, its poison can cause blistering and great discomfort (it can even rub off from a dog's coat on to your leg). Clothes worn a year after contact can cause poisoning. Don't go into undergrowth and always wear socks and long trousers if you are going near wild vegetation. If you brush against it, wash its poison off quickly; don't scratch the infected area or rub your eyes. Severe allergies are rare.

New England has two National Forests: the White Mountains National Forest, which covers much of New Hampshire and creeps over the border into Maine, and the Green Mountain National Forest, in Vermont. Both are laced with trails. Away from the coastal strip, Maine too is heavily forested – and dotted with thousands of lakes. Its most northerly areas are predominantly soft-wood, managed by timber companies. The softwoods are mainly pine, spruce and fir, while sugar maple, yellow birch, aspen and paper birch are New England's dominant hardwoods.

Forest fauna The largest of the forest animals are moose, black bear and white-tailed deer. The deer are ubiquitous and hunting them is an autumn ritual. The black bear stands almost 3 feet high and is fairly frequently seen making its clumsy way through the woods of Maine, New Hampshire and, occasionally, Vermont. They are usually harmless (but see panel, far right). The animal that attracts most attention, however, is the moose. There are numerous organised moose-watching trips (information available locally) and you may well see one as you drive around (they like the salt that runs off the roads), particularly in northern Maine, the most northerly parts of the White Mountains and along the Kancamagus Highway. Baxter State Park is one of the best places in New England for moose. The most likely time of day to spot moose is at dawn or dusk, especially near ponds or marshes. A full-grown male moose can be 6 feet tall at its shoulders, weighing over half a ton, and has huge antlers to boot – give such an animal a wide berth. Moose are most ungainly creatures, with a long,

White-tailed deer are a fairly common sight

pendulous snout and a hairy dewlap. They eat grasses and often stand in lakes.

Smaller forest animals include raccoon, chipmunk, marten, woodchuck and porcupine. Red squirrel, coyote, red fox, lynx, muskrat, skunk and snowshoe hare are fairly common. Beaver activity in rivers and lakes is always fascinating. Their lodges (houses of sticks and mud) are up to 6 feet high, and the dams, similarly built, are amazing constructions. The beaver's favourite food is bark – look out for sticks that have been neatly stripped and gnawed. The beavers themselves are usually seen at dusk or dawn, giving themselves away with a slap of their tails as they dive.

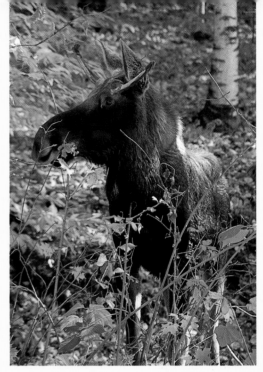

Mountain birds Even if you cannot identify all the songbirds, you will enjoy the songs that fill the woods in spring and summer. Many of the birds are migratory. The most common include blackpoll and Nashville warblers, ruby- and golden-crowned kinglets, pine siskin, raven, blue jay and chickadee, Maine's state bird and familiar to Europeans as a member of the tit family. The loon, a diver sometimes heard calling from the lakes of New Hampshire, is reputedly the oldest bird species on earth.

Alpine flora There are over 8 square miles of alpine zone in the White Mountains. On Mount Washington the treeline occurs exceptionally low, at 1,400 feet. Climb it (see page 208) and you will notice the trees become more and more stunted. Dense mats of vegetation called *krummholz* (German for 'twisted tree') cover the ground.

Above the treeline, in the alpine zone, 100 different alpine flowers that are unique to Mount Washington, Labrador and the Arctic grow among lichens, sedges and mosses. The dwarf cinquefoil (*Potentilla robbinsiana*) is endemic to Mount Washington. Other alpine flowers that may be found here and in the alpine areas of the Katahdin range in Maine's Baxter State Park include mountain aster, alpine violet, alpine bearberry, moss plant, mountain brook saxifrage and goldthread.

This young moose is one of many that inhabit the remote northern forests

BEAR ESSENTIALS
Black bears are shy, preferring to stay away from people and unlikely to do any harm. Nevertheless, it is wise to be careful with food as the smell attracts them and this is when injuries may occur.
● Never feed bears.
● Don't leave food scraps lying around or throw them into a camp fire.
● Store food (and any clothes soiled with food) in sealed containers in the boot of the car or in a tree (so the bears can't damage your car).

FRAGILE FLORA
Remember that some of the flowers that have adapted to the biting winter winds and the poor soil take up to 25 years to flower for the first time, so mind where you put your feet. The best time to see wild flowers is from mid-June to August.

Settled in the 1630s, Strawbery Banke was named after the strawberries that once grew wild there

STRAWBERY BANKE
In its early days, Strawbery Banke was a prosperous merchants' centre. Later, the Puritans came and, in 1653, changed the name to Portsmouth, which sounded less frivolous. Having escaped an urban renewal plan in 1958, the grid of old streets of the 1690s has been restored. The 42 houses show the lifestyles of its inhabitants through the ages.

NEW HAMPSHIRE CRUISES
Cruises to the nine islands constituting the Isles of Shoals and whale-watching trips are popular excursions. Operators around Portsmouth include:
● Portsmouth Harbor Cruises (tel: 1-800/776 0915).
● The Isles of Shoals Steamship Co (tel: 1-800/441 4620).
● New Hampshire Seacoast Cruises (tel: 603/964 5545).
● The Atlantic Fishing Fleet, which operates the Atlantic Queen II (at Rye Harbor; tel: 603/964 5220).

▶▶ **Portsmouth and the coast** *188C1*

PORTSMOUTH Occupying the northern end of New Hampshire's short coastline, **Portsmouth**▶▶ was the most important colonial town north of Boston. It has an English look, with a fine legacy of red-brick 18th- and 19th-century houses, many built for prosperous sea-captains. Along the waterfront you can see one of the swiftest flowing navigable rivers in the world.

The original colonial settlement in the harbour was **Strawbery Banke**▶▶, one of New Hampshire's leading historic attractions (see panel). All but one of the houses, plus a re-erected four-seater privy, stand on their original sites. (*Open* May–Oct for self-guided tours, and two weekends in December for Candlelight Strolls, which also take place one night in August.)

Portsmouth Historical Society, with the Society for the Preservation of New England Antiquities, maintains a number of 18th-century houses (*open* Jun–Oct) scattered around town (the Portsmouth Trail connects each of these historic sites). If you intend to visit more than one, pick up a Portsmouth Passport for reduced admission.

In 1962 the **Warner House**▶▶ (*c*1716) became the first house in the US to be registered as a National Historic Landmark (following the restoration of the White House in Washington, DC, an action that promoted an awareness of house preservation). It was Portsmouth's first brick house, the work of John Drew, an English builder. The house retains numerous English features in its panelling and furniture. Folk-art murals date back to the time of construction; one of them (once covered up) shows English patriotic sentiment with its portrayal of a redcoat. Outstanding among the furnishings is a Portsmouth-made high chest on the upstairs landing.

The **Moffat Ladd House**▶ (*open* daily), a three-storey blue and white building of 1763, stands amid pretty English-style gardens with grass steps. In them William Whipple, a signatory of the Declaration of Independence, planted what is now the state's tallest horse-chestnut tree. The house has fine Portsmouth furniture, eye-catching wallpaper that was hand-painted in Paris in 1819 and a tunnel in its kitchen that supposedly led to the wharf! Its spacious entrance hall is modelled on the

English style. The **Wentworth Gardner House**, located at 50 Mechanic Street (*open* Tue–Sun, 1–4), is a Georgian structure of 1760, and is noted for the quality of its interior carved woodwork, tiled fireplaces and painted wallpaper.

Two other houses have historical connections: the **Tobias Lear House** (*open* Wed, 1–4) was the birthplace of George Washington's private secretary, Colonel Tobias Lear, while the **John Paul Jones House** was the lodging of the revolutionary commander Jones while his frigate *Ranger* was being refitted in the port.

A state-of-the-art interior of 1807 is found in the **Rundlet-May House** (owned and operated by SPNEA – see page 68), featuring a contemporary roasting oven, Portsmouth furniture and foreign wallpaper, while the **Governor John Langdon House** of 1784 (also an SPNEA property) has fine carving, Portsmouth furniture and landscaped grounds.

In Albacore Park, Market Street, is the **USS *Albacore*** (*open* 1 May–Columbus Day), a navy submarine in service from 1953 to 1972 (see panel).

Horse-and-carriage tours of the old town start from the church. The **Children's Museum** at 280 Marcy Street provides a variety of hands-on activities for youngsters of all ages (*open* daily, except Mon out of summer and school vacations).

THE COAST Just out of town, **Odiorne Point State Park►** covers 350 acres of duneland, the largest tract of undeveloped land on the 18-mile New Hampshire coast, and provides views of the harbour. The World War II fort here is one of a number of historic harbour defences. The Science Center (free) features aquariums showing tide-pool and salt-marsh ecology. There is also a fine drive on Route 1B to **New Castle Island►** (also known as Great Island), which has old homes, forts and lighthouses. The remainder of the New Hampshire coast is almost entirely built up, except for a few patches of marshy hinterland, but there are good state beaches at **Wallis Sands**, **Jenness** and **North Hampton**. **Hampton Beach** has a long sandy beach but is very commercialised with an extensive boardwalk, amusements and fast-food outlets. **Water Country**, New England's biggest water park, is on Route 1 some 3 miles south of Portsmouth.

PORTSMOUTH FURNITURE
Portsmouth's proximity to vast stands of inland timber and its ice-free harbour made it a major centre of ship-building, house construction and furniture-making in the 18th century. The town prospered, the ships' captains built grand mansions, and a market for quality furniture was born. Foreign influences moulded taste and fashion in furniture, notably through the skills of immigrant craftsmen from England. New styles were born; reversed curves, scrolled pediments and cabriole legs appeared. Black walnut was the rage; stained maple was a simulation. John Gaines III and Joseph Davis led the way with flamboyant styles, Gothic and Chinese pieces appearing in the 1760s.

203

REVOLUTIONARY SUB
During her 19 years in service, the USS *Albacore* is one of a number of submarines to have been built in the Portsmouth naval shipyard, founded in 1800 as the first US government shipyard and still in use. The vessel never fired a weapon. She was a prototype submarine which boasted new hull design, sonar system and dive brakes. A memorial garden nearby pays tribute to crew and officers who perished in submarine service.

Portsmouth's waterfront: boats have taken visitors to the Isles of Shoals from here since the mid-19th century

EARLY CONSERVATION DAYS

The Weeks Act was passed in 1911 and introduced the National Forest system. The White Mountains were the first such forest area to be designated, affording protection after the removal of many trees in the region. The soil erosion and washdown that had occurred had worried politicians who spent vacations here, and political pressure for change followed.

▶▶▶ The White Mountains   *188B3*

The White Mountains are the highest and most dramatic uplands in New England. This is the region's finest area for mountain walking and in season draws crowds to its ski slopes and fall foliage display. The main accommodation areas are the purely functional resort towns around the White Mountains proper. These places are well geared to tourism but not strong on character.

North Conway is highly rated by many for its outlet shopping malls (also known as Mount Washington Valley), which get particularly busy on rainy days in high

Winter in the White Mountains: Echo Lake

The Mount Washington Cog Railway puffs its way up an uncomfortable but scenic 1¼-hour ascent over fragile-looking viaducts and up 37-degree gradients

season. Woodstock and Lincoln are best placed for exploring the Kancamagus and Franconia areas. Bethlehem in the far north-west is particularly noted for its architectural gems.

WHITE MOUNTAIN SIGHTS Mount Washington▶▶▶, New England's tallest (6,288 feet) and extremely windswept mountain, soars high above the rest of the Presidential Range. Numerous hiking routes lead up the slopes, but the most popular ways up are by the toll road (guided tours by van also available) and the **Mount Washington Cog Railway**▶▶, the world's oldest tourist railway (runs May–Oct; for reservations, tel: 603/278 5404, or 1-800 922 8825). At the summit, the view extends to Boston and the Atlantic Ocean. There was once a succession of grand hotels at the top; today only the Tip Top House survives (preserved as a museum; free), while the rest is a stark miscellany of masts and huts, together with an observatory and a small museum. Visitors making the trip by railway only have 20 minutes at the summit to ensure a seat on the return.

The **Robert Frost Place**▶, in a remote spot near Franconia, is the 50-acre farm where the New England poet (see page 209) dreamt he 'could live cheap and get Yankier and Yankier'. The tiny house contains original manuscripts and Frost's own writing table. **Clark's Trading Post**▶, near Lincoln, was set up by a family of collectors in the 1920s. Included is a reconstructed New England Street, the museum (with working musical boxes, vintage slot machines and peep-shows), and a topsy-turvy 'haunted house'. Black bears perform three times daily, while the railroad around the grounds gets held up by 'bandits'.

At Glen, **Heritage-New Hampshire**, a look at the state's past using tableaux of selected historical titbits, is like walking through a huge stage set. Actors explain their lives – one as a trapper, another in a mock-up of 18th-century Portsmouth. It finishes with a simulated train ride. Next door, **StoryLand** is a well thought out children's theme park. There is a Mexican village, and rides that include flying clogs and a log-boat trip down water-slides.

Two other theme parks, both at Jefferson, are **Santa's Village**, including 'Santa's summer home' with similar rides to StoryLand, and **Six Gun City**, with a water-slide and Wild West adventure. **Whale's Tail** (Route 3, North Woodstock) is a water park. **Attitash Alpine Slide**, at Bartlett, features 'wet and wild water-slides', plus a scenic chair-lift, horseback riding and a golf-driving range.

Continued on page 208.

'Men hang out their signs indicative of their respective trades; shoe makers hang out a gigantic shoe; jewelers, a monster watch; and the dentist hangs out a gold tooth; but up in the mountains of New Hampshire God Almighty has hung out a sign to show that there He makes men.'
– Attributed to Daniel Webster, on the Old Man of the Mountain, Franconia Notch.

THE WORLD'S WORST WEATHER
Because of a funnel effect, Mount Washington gets the full brunt of three continental storm systems. The fastest winds ever recorded (231mph) have occurred here: a 10mph breeze further down becomes an 80mph blast at the top. Some 175 feet down, the ground is permanently frozen. These unusual conditions give rise to 63 alpine flower species. The mountain has claimed many lives: below the summit, on the right of the railway, a wooden sign and cairn mark the spot where 23-year-old walker Lizzie Bourne died of exhaustion in 1855.

Drive

The White Mountains

See map on page 204 (yellow route).

This 94-mile loop tour is perhaps the most scenic mountain drive in New England. It takes in the Kancamagus Highway and Franconia Notch, and provides opportunities to drive up to the magnificent viewpoints on Cathedral Ledge and Mount Washington. Watch out for moose, which often stray on to the roads, and keep the petrol tank topped up.

From North Woodstock take Route 112, the **Kancamagus Highway▶▶▶**, famous for its fall foliage and with choice but scattered views. Beyond **Loon Mountain ski area**, with its gondolas and outdoor activities, there are particularly fine roadside panoramas from the Pemi Overlook (with its view of mounts Kancamagus, Osceola and Loon) and from **Kancamagus Pass Overlook** (with Mount Kancamagus prominent).

Covered bridge over The Flume in Franconia Notch

Numerous trails start from the road, including a short path to **Sabbaday Falls▶**, a trio of waterfalls tumbling and twisting into a deep chasm, and another to **Champney Falls▶**.

Passaconaway Historic Site: Russell-Colbath House (*open* Jul and Aug, 9–4:30, but may vary. Admission free) is a tiny cottage formerly occupied by Ruth Colbath, the 'hermit woman' postmistress whose husband walked out without explanation one night. She waited 39 years for him and left a light burning each night, but died in 1933 before his return. The Swift river flows over great boulders at **Rocky Gorge**, where a short loop trail leads to Falls Pond. A short distance east, also by the road, Lower Falls is designated for swimming and picnicking. At the next left turn take Dugway Road, leaving Route 112 to dodge the traffic jams of North Conway. **Conway** has a pair of covered bridges.

Turn left to Echo Lake and Cathedral Ledge▶▶▶. The small lake (a state park with a small, roped-off swimming area) is magnificently sited beneath the huge granite outcrop of Cathedral Ledge, a popular cliff for rock-climbing. A road ascends the top of the ledge, and a path leads out to a dizzy view.

Further north, via Glen, the Summit of **Mount Washington▶▶▶** is approached on foot, by toll road or by cog railway. Retrace your drive to Glen then follow Route 302 to the **Mount Washington Hotel**, New England's largest wooden building, the last surviving of 15 grand hotels in the White Mountains and still laced with period atmosphere (see pages 40–1).

To the west, the **Franconia Notch road (I-93)▶▶▶** carves its way through awesome scenery. The drama unfolds fully from above: take the cable-car up **Cannon Mountain▶▶**, where the ½-mile Rim Trail looks down 2,500 feet into the valley and into New York State. By the cable-car station, the **New England Ski Museum** (*open* winter, Fri–Tue. *Admission* free) has displays of archive photographs and equipment of various periods, plus a multi-screen slide show about skiing history.

From I-93 you can glimpse the famous **Old Man of the Mountains**, a rock outcrop some 40 feet tall which displays the uncanny profile of a human face. There is roadside parking for northbound traffic, and a short trail from a parking lot to Profile Lake for southbound traffic. **The Basin▶**, a 30-foot-wide pothole, was gouged out by glacial meltwater and is one of a number of attractive features passed on the popular Cascade Brook Trail. Better known still is **The Flume▶▶**, a dark, steep-sided chasm that keeps cool on the hottest of summer days and becomes laden with 30–40 feet of ice in winter, when the wooden walkways are dismantled. A fine waterfall tumbles into its far end.

At North Woodstock, it is worth diverting west on Route 112 to **Lost River▶▶** (closed in winter). The board-walk trail, through caves created by tumbled boulders and along a series of waterfalls, is tortuous and exciting, and requires good footwear. The river disappears at points into the caves, which can be explored by ladder. This remote spot was discovered by two brothers on a fishing trip when one fell into the top entrance of a cave and had to be rescued.

Take a diversion on a cable-car for bird's-eye views

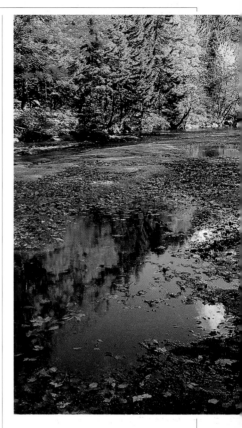

Glorious colour is guaranteed in the autumn

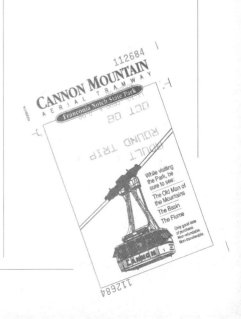

Zealand Notch is between Whitewall Mountain to the east and Zealand Ridge to the west, which provides a magnificent walk up to the 1,395m summit of Mount Guyot

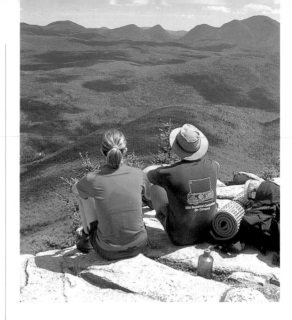

PLANNING AND PREPARATION

National Forest information centres have free leaflets detailing the main trails, and sell hiking maps. The De Lorme Trail Map gives an overview of trails, with 250 descriptions. For serious hiking, the Appalachian Mountain Club (AMC) publishes the definitive guide to mountain walks and maintains a network of mountain huts. Reservations recommended (tel: 603/466 2727; website www.outdoors.org). Free shelters are open on a first come, first served basis. Since even the easy trails tend to be rocky, good boots with tough soles are recommended.

HIKE HINTS

● Drinking stream water is discouraged, as the parasite giardia is prevalent. This causes symptoms similar to dysentery.
● Parts of the White Mountains are designated as wilderness areas, where no vehicles, fires, bicycles or radios are allowed, and camping must be at least 200 feet from the trail.
● The Appalachian Trail is marked in white on rocks and trees. Side trails into it are blue; other trails are yellow. Two blazes together denotes a junction. A pile of sticks across a trail means that that trail is closed.

208

Continued from page 205.

WHITE MOUNTAIN WALKS The White Mountains are amply laced with trails of all degrees of difficulty. The Presidential Range has the highest summits. **Mount Washington** is popular but must not be underestimated; a recommended ascent is from Pinkham Notch and up Tuckerman's Ravine. Ask at the Appalachian Mountain Club (AMC) here first about conditions. Another rewarding hike is the **Zealand Trail** to the Zealand Falls AMC hut (3–3½ hours there and back). From the AMC building at Crawford rail depot on Route 302, an easy climb up **Mount Willard** follows a well-graded trail, an old carriage road, which takes in ledges and cliffs above Crawford Notch Zealand Campground (allow 2–2½ hours).

Along the Kancamagus Highway, photogenic **Mount Chocorua** can be approached from the trailhead leading to **Champney Falls**. The less demanding 3-mile **Boulder Loop Trail**, starting at Covered Bridge Campground, offers views from high rock ledges. Easier still is the Lincoln Woods Trail from Hancock Campground, which follows the course of an old railroad and gives river views before reaching Franconia Falls (allow 4 hours).

North-east of Glen, Town Hall Road leads into Slippery Brook and becomes a dirt road. Further on is the trail encircling lonely **Mountain Pond**, set beneath Slope Mountain. One of the best ridge walks above the tree-line is along the **Franconia Ridge Trail**, reached from Lafayette Campground on I-93 (allow 5 hours). Ascend via the Falling Waters Trail and climb Mount Lincoln (5,089 feet); descend via the Bridal Path. **Mount Kearsarge North** (3,268 feet) is a 2,700-foot climb, north of North Conway, taking roughly 3 hours each way.

For a very arduous day's walking (for experienced and fit hikers only) an exceptionally fine route is from Route 16 south of Gorham up **Mount Jefferson**.

Further ideas for short walks are covered in the drive on pages 206–7.

The poet Robert Frost is best known for his simple themes, his language and his rhythms. His appeal lies in his sharp observation of daily rural scenes, which he describes in conversational language, but with delicacy and a hint at deeper meanings. In setting and in character, his poetry is deeply rooted in New England.

Early days Robert Frost's father, William, a teacher and newspaper editor, was a New Englander. His mother, Isabell Moodie, also a teacher, was born in Scotland, of Orkneyan origin. Robert was born on 26 March 1874 in San Francisco, where his father was working on a newspaper, but after his father's death he was taken back to New England, aged 10.

Frost's mother was to exert a strong influence, teaching him and his sister and encouraging the enjoyment of literature. He briefly attended both Dartmouth College in Vermont and, later, Harvard, but gave up to teach and to write poetry. In 1900 he began working on a farm in Derry, New Hampshire, given him by his grandfather (see page 198). Farming was to be a recurring theme of his life, one never taken very seriously as a living, but something that brought him close to nature and, in particular, botany.

'The voice of New England' Some of Frost's best-known poetry was written in Derry, but he received no recognition there. In 1912 he moved with his wife, Elinor Miriam White, and their children to Britain, to live in Beaconsfield, Buckinghamshire. During this time, two collections of poems written in Derry, *A Boy's Will* and *North of Boston*, were published in Britain, and to great acclaim.

After the outbreak of World War II, Frost returned with his family to America, unexpectedly famous. He bought another farm, in Franconia, New Hampshire (see page 205), and began a long association as teacher and poet-in-residence with several academic institutions, including Amherst College in Massachusetts.

Four times Pulitzer Prizewinner, Robert Frost died in Boston in 1963, almost 90 years of age.

Top: the poet's grave in Bennington
Above: Robert Frost on his 85th birthday
Below: the Robert Frost Farm in Derry

'I'd like to get away from earth awhile
And then come back to it and begin over.
I'd like to go by climbing a birch tree,
And climb black branches up a snow-white trunk
Toward heaven, till the tree could bear no more,
But dipped its top and set me down again.
That would be good both going and coming back.
One could do worse than be a swinger of birches.'
– From 'Birches'

Yachting is big in Rhode Island, and Newport in particular

RHODE ISLAND Officially this is Rhode Island and Providence Plantations, the state with the longest name but the smallest area, roughly 48 miles by 37 miles at its maximum dimensions. The state capital, Providence, lies at the northern end of Narragansett Bay, a scenic 28-mile inlet which is speckled with islands and which almost splits the state in two. The hinterland is low lying. To the east it is densely urbanised and industrialised, while to the west it is more rural, with pockets of solitude such as the 2,600-acre Great Swamp. But it is the intricate coastline, measuring 419 miles, that most attracts visitors. Rhode Island is one of the finest sailing areas on the East Coast, and the state proudly proclaims itself as 'America's first resort'. Its major island, Block Island, has an open terrain with cliffs and a rolling countryside that remind some visitors of Scotland.

The state's remarkable architectural legacy includes 20 per cent of all the nation's Registered National Historic Landmarks. Most famous of all are the Newport mansions, the summer 'cottages' of magnates of the coal and railroad age, but there are also fine earlier survivors. Both Newport and Providence have impressively intact colonial districts. A ferry service enables Providence, Newport and Block Island to be enjoyed without a car; call Interstate Navigation on 401/783 4613

211

EARLY DAYS Rhode Island began as a haven in a time of religious intolerance. Roger Williams, a clergyman, founded the state in 1636 after being expelled from the Puritans' Massachusetts Bay Colony for his heretical views. Williams and his followers established a settlement on the banks of the Moshassuck river and named the place Providence, as God's providence was thought to have led them there. In 1644 he travelled to England and gained a charter, reinforced in 1663, uniting the various settlements in the area as the Colony of Rhode Island and Providence Plantations. The charter gave the inhabitants a degree of independence and 'full liberty in religious commencements'. Hence the state became a sanctuary for religious refugees. Jews and Quakers came to Newport, and their presence made a significant contribution to the town's success. The Native American population declined after 1676 when an unsuccessful attempt by Philip, king of the Wampanoags, led his people, the Narragansetts and Nipmucks, in a war against the English colonists.

Rhode Island was the first colony to declare its independence from Britain (May 1776) but the last to become a state (1790); it celebrates 4 May as well as 4 July. Providence became a commercial centre with the boom in shipping and trade. The China trade, pioneered by John Brown of Providence, and the Triangle Trade (see page 34) enhanced the state's prosperity. In 1793, the opening of Slater's Mill at Pawtucket initiated the mass-production of textiles, a landmark in America's industrialisation. Skilled immigrant workers, notably from Britain, Ireland, Italy and French Canada, heralded an expansion of the cities and the start of the state's tradition of industrial excellence.

Events

March
Irish Heritage Month. Month-long, city-wide celebration of Irish Heritage. Newport.

April
Blithewold Gardens & Arboretum Annual Spring Bulb Display, Bristol.

May
May Breakfasts: over 100 state-wide.
Gaspee Days, Warwick: arts and crafts festival, with colonial encampment.

June
Used Boat Show, Newport.
Quonset Air Show, North Kingstown.
Festival of Historic Houses, Providence: private houses and gardens specially open for tours.
Annual Great Chowder Cook Off. Best chowder competition. Newport.
Annual Newport Outdoor Art Festival.
Block Island Race Week.
Annual Big Easy Bash, West Greenwich.
Festival of Historic Houses, Providence.
Convergence Art Festival, Providence.

July
Bristol 4th of July Parade: the nation's oldest (1785).
Newport Music Festival: two weeks of classical music in the mansions.
Miller Lite International Hall of Fame Tennis Championships, Newport: major professional men's grass court tennis tournament.
Wickford Art Festival, Wickford: one of the East Coast's oldest, largest, and best.
Black Ships Festival, Newport: celebration of American-Japanese trade, with sumo wrestling and kite flying.
South County Hot Air Balloon Festival, Kingston.

August
Charlestown Chamber Seafood Festival.
Newport Folk Festival: the best and biggest in the country.
JVC Jazz Festival, Newport.
WaterFire, Providence.

September
Cajun & Bluegrass Music and Dance Festival, West Greenwich: non-stop Louisiana Cajun music extravaganza.
Annual Tuna Tournament, Galilee.
International Boat Show, Newport.
Heritage Festival, Providence.
Providence Waterfront Festival.
Annual Taste of Rhode Island, Newport.
Waterfront Festival, Providence.

October
Newport Harvest-by-the-Sea Festival: month-long celebration.
Octoberfest, Pawtucket.
Annual Autumnfest, Woonsocket.
Columbus Day Festival, Federal Hill, Providence

November
Montgolfier Day Balloon Regatta, Providence.

December
Christmas in Newport: much of the town and several mansions lavishly decorated, candlelight tours and concerts.
Festival of Lights, Wickford Village.
First Night, Providence: family orientated city-wide arts and entertainment celebration.

Fishing boats on their moorings in Galilee

▶▶ Block Island   210B1

Block Island is something of an under-rated getaway destination. Formed of rock debris dumped by two glaciers in the Ice Age, the island has 200-foot clay cliffs, 365 glacial ponds and an open terrain. Known by Indians as Manisses ('Island of the little God') and mentioned by the Italian explorer Giovanni da Verrazano in 1524, the island was explored by and named after the Dutchman Adriaen Block before being settled by the English in 1661.

In the 19th century Block Island became a weekend pleasure resort, but by the 1960s much of the town was boarded up and its Victorian charm lay crumbling and forgotten. Today it has been spruced up, but not overdone; the Victorian character is jealously preserved and nightlife can be described as distinctly sleepy. There are more bicycles than cars outside the main town, and its attractions are deliberately low key. In fact, the island is nowhere near as busy as Martha's Vineyard or Nantucket. The authorities are promoting the island for 'green' tourism as it has appeal for naturalists and for walkers, with both coastal and inland trails; but beware of the deer ticks, for Lyme Disease (see page 263) is prevalent.

The island is 7 miles by 3 miles at its maximum dimensions, and is small enough to cycle round at leisure (bicycles can be hired at the port). Alternatively, taxi-drivers will give a tour for about $20 (the older drivers tend to have the best anecdotes), or you can see the island on horseback. **Black Rock Point**, at the island's southern tip, and **Clay Head** (with trails), at the north-eastern end, have fine cliffs. The Greenway Trails are recommended for flora and fauna and there are guided nature walks for visitors during the summer.

The main town is officially called **New Shoreham**, but is usually known as Block Island, and has a small beach. Beaches on the south coast have no undertow (unlike those on the mainland) and are ideal for families. **Corn Neck**, at the north end, has the longest beach. Surfers should head for the south coast, while **Chaqum Pond** is the place for windsurfing.

GETTING TO BLOCK ISLAND
The fastest ferry crossing is from Galilee (1 hour 10 minutes). Other ferries operate from Providence, New London (Connecticut) and Montauk (Long Island); for car reservations, tel: 401/783 4613. Flights can be taken from Westerly (New England Airlines, tel: 401/466 5881, or 1-800/243 2460).

BLOCK ISLAND WILDLIFE
In 1991 the Nature Conservancy listed Block Island among the 12 'Last Great Places' in the Americas, and 23 per cent of the island is now held for nature conservation. The island is the home of the rare northern harrier and is one of only two habitats in the US for burying beetles and regal fritillary butterflies. May brings out the snow-white flowers of the shad bush, while autumn sees a spectacular bird migration of some 150 over-wintering species.

A FREAK VIEW
West Side Baptist Church on Block Island is the only church in the US from where you can see the sun both rise and set over the Atlantic Ocean.

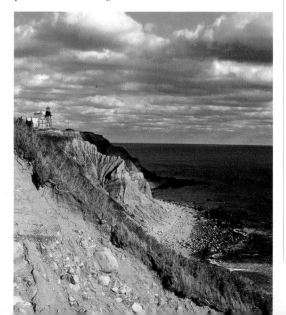

A view along the dramatic Mohegan Bluffs towards Southeast Lighthouse, at the southern end of Block Island

NEWPORT BRIDGE 138 · Providence · 114 · First, Second & Third Beaches · Easton's Pond · 138A

FARELWELL ST · AMERICAS CUP AVE · BROADWAY · Old Colony House · Wanton-Lyman-Hazard House · Touro Synagogue · Hunter House · Gateway Visitor Center · Brick Market · Newport Historical Society · Redwood Library · Newport Yacht Club · Bowen's Wharf · Trinity Church · Newport Casino (Tennis Hall of Fame) · Kingscote · Easton Beach · MEMORIAL BOULEVARD · Cliff Walk · Easton Bay

Rose Island · Goat Island · Newport Harbor · Ida Lewis Yacht Club · King Park · THAMES ST · SPRING ST · NARRAGANSETT AVE · The Elms · 40 Steps · Salve Regina College · POINT AVE · OCHRE

Narragansett Bay · WELLINGTON AVE · Morton Park · BELLEVUE · Chateau-sur-Mer · The Breakers · Ochre Point · Easton

Fort Wetherill State Park · Fort Adams State Park · Eisenhower House · HARRISON AVENUE · Murphy Field · RUGGLES AVE · Rosecliff · Beechwood Mansion · Sheep Point · COGGESHALL AVE

Hammersmith Farm · BRENTON ROAD · Lily Pond · Rovensky Park · Almy Pond · Marble House · Belcourt Castle

RIDGE ROAD · HARRISON AVENUE · Newport Country Club · OCEAN DRIVE · Goose Neck Cove · Seafair · Wildacre · Cherry Neck · Hazards Beach · Gooseberry Island · Baileys Beach · Cliff Walk · Midship Rock · Lands End

Castle Hill · OCEAN DRIVE · Brenton Point State Park · Prices Neck · Rhode Island Sound

Brenton Point · 0 ___ 1 ___ 2 km · 0 ___ 1 mile

Newport Bridge, leading over Narragansett Bay

▶▶▶ Newport   *210C2*

With the combined attractions of its historic summer mansions and colonial architecture, its jazz festival, its sailing and regattas, its golf, its beaches and its nightlife, Newport has a lot to offer visitors. Although the town gets busy at summer weekends, accommodation is plentiful with a large concentration of B&Bs.

Newport is an important lobster town; lobsters can be bought fresh off the boats at Aquidneck Lobster Co in Bowen's Wharf near the harbour, at the hub of the town's crafts and gift shops. The three main beaches are called, unsurprisingly, First Beach, Second Beach and Third Beach. Additionally, there are a couple of small beaches off Ocean Drive. Parking fees at the beaches are expensive, but it is only a mile or so to cycle out from the town centre. Good views of the ocean can be had from the 3½-mile **Cliff Walk▶▶**, which snakes above rocky shores and beaches, and offers fascinating glimpses of some mansion back gardens. Good shoes are needed to walk it in its entirety. Just outside town is a major naval base. Allied navies come to the Naval War College to carry out both war games and the real thing (much of the 1990 Gulf War was planned here).

Newport in its early days was a centre for religious tolerance, thanks to the liberal attitude of Roger Williams

Looking towards Trinity Church's white steeple

ENIGMA VARIATIONS
The provenance of the curious building in Newport's Touro Park is obscure. Various explanations claim that it has Viking origins, that it was built in conjunction with the solstice, that it was a beacon, that privateers stored their booty in it, that giants with green eyes and red hair erected it, or that it was a windmill. However, carbon-dating in 1993 indicated that the structure dates from either the 16th or early 17th centuries.

AMERICA'S OLDEST TAVERN
Threatened with demolition in the 1950s, Newport's White Horse Tavern, dating from the 17th century, was fortunately rescued and still survives as the oldest tavern in the US. Churches on either side had objected to the renewal of its liquor licence; to get round this, a state law was specially passed to the effect that only taverns built before 1700 with a church on either side can obtain a new licence!

A FORESIGHTED PLEA
'These old houses and old doorways are a stock-in-trade for Newport, and there is a decided question whether the so-called march of progress, which prompts the tearing down or extensive remodelling of old structures, will in the long run pay the owners as well as if they were put in repair and their features preserved, so that in years to come they may continue to attract strangers who are interested in the old and quaint.'
– *Newport Daily News*, 15 April 1910.

(see page 211), the founder of Rhode Island. In colonial times Jews and Quakers made it their home, and this cultural diversity was instrumental in the town's success.

COLONIAL NEWPORT Despite devastation in the Revolutionary War and a long period of neglect, colonial Newport still survives to a remarkable extent: there are 200 buildings over 200 years old (the biggest such concentration in the country). Until the late 1960s, the town looked drab and many houses were tar-covered. Although many buildings were torn down, 60 were saved by Operation Clapboard, a campaign to encourage people to buy and renovate a historic house, and Newport's dreamed-of face-lift became a reality. Pineapple motifs are found on many of Newport's older buildings, the fruit being a symbol of hospitality in the state (sailors returning from the tropics used to display a pineapple in their windows to show they had returned safely and were receiving visitors).

Today, **Town Green** looks a typically timeless New England green, dominated by **Trinity Church▶** (1726), which still has box pews and a galleried interior. In fact, the green was a 20th-century beautification scheme: houses were moved here after buildings were cleared.

In **Touro Park** is the town's most celebrated enigma, an open-sided stone structure in the centre of a green (see panel). Near by is the library, opened in 1748 and the oldest in the US. It is a classical, wooden building, designed to resemble stone.

The **Touro Synagogue▶▶** is the oldest Jewish place of worship in the country, and dates from 1763. A century earlier, Portuguese and Spanish Jews, fleeing religious persecution, found sanctuary in Newport. The elegant interior is a real surprise and contains the famous letter from George Washington to warden Moses Seixas extolling religious tolerance.

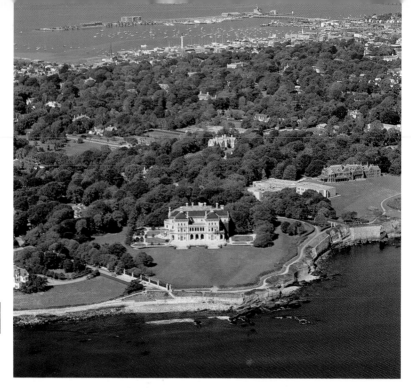

Aerial view of The Breakers, showing the cliff walk that skirts its grounds

NEWPORT CASINO
This American Renaissance period-piece began in 1880 as a social and residential club, gaining popularity with old-money families as lawn tennis boomed. The Newport Casino hosted the US National Tennis Championships (later to become the US Open) from 1881 to 1914, and is still the venue for major competitions as well as court tennis (real tennis) and bowls tournaments. The 13 grass courts are the only ones in the nation available for public use. Tournaments held today include tennis, sumo, bowls and croquet. For more information, tel: 401/849 3990.

At 54 Washington Street is **Hunter House** (1748) a colonial-era house open to the public. It has period furniture made locally and a charming old-world garden.

At 17 Broadway, the restored **Wanton-Lyman-Hazard House** (1675) is Newport's oldest colonial house (open Thu–Sat in summer). In Thames Street is the **Museum of Newport History▶**, a treasure-house commemorating Newport's remarkable past, with exhibits on fishing, crafts, religion and social history. The **Doll Museum**, at 520 Thames Street, has over 600 antique and modern dolls (*open* Wed–Mon).

The **Newport Casino▶▶** has never had anything to do with gambling, taking its name from the Italian for 'little house' (see panel). Inside the Casino is the **Tennis Hall of Fame▶▶**, the world's largest tennis museum and a shrine to the tennis greats, where new additions undergo an induction ceremony. In addition to the displays of vintage tennis equipment, there are entertaining interactive videos featuring quizzes and comparisons of the game techniques of the stars.

THE MANSIONS In the 19th century Newport became a summer playground for the élite. Mansions modelled on Italian palazzi, French châteaux and English stately homes appeared along **Bellevue Avenue▶▶▶** and **Ocean Drive▶▶▶**. No expense was spared as European crafts-men were employed and the rooms packed with costly *objets d'art*. First came the old-money families; later, the new-guard Vanderbilts and others added flamboyance and entertained in their fabulous 'summer cottages'.

Today, numerous mansions are open to the public. It is best to select a few contrasting types, then drive or cycle along Bellevue Avenue and along the 9½-mile Ocean Drive to enjoy the scenery. The Preservation Society of Newport County maintains eight properties (*open* daily in summer, with several also open on weekends in winter; reduced admission if visiting more than one property, including the five mansions on Bellevue Avenue). For further details, tel: 401/847 1000.

Kingscote▶, a grey clapboard Victorian Gothic house of 1839, is notable as being Newport's first 'cottage', and is more modest than its successors. The house contains family pieces of William Henry King, a China trade merchant. McKim, Mead and White, architects of the Newport Casino, added the dining room.

The Elms▶▶ (1901), a French Renaissance château built by Horace Trumbauer for a Pennsylvania coal magnate, was modelled on the Château d'Asnières near Paris.

Château-sur-Mer▶▶ (1852) was the first truly grand cottage, with its French-style mansard roof. Inside, a wall-painting of the Tree of Life accompanies the staircase, with overhead paintings of sky, birds and foliage. This was a year-round rather than a summer residence and was enlarged by Richard Morris Hunt in the 1870s, his first commission in the High Victorian grand manner although he later reverted to French and Italian styles.

The Breakers▶▶▶, on Ochre Point Avenue, was designed by Richard Morris Hunt for Cornelius Vanderbilt and took 2,500 workers two years to complete in 1895. It was modelled on a 16th-century Italian *palazzo*, with French additions, and no expense was spared. The music room was constructed in Paris and shipped over, and there is a huge hall of Caen marble. The grandest gesture in an architectural medley of styles is the formal dining room, festooned with gilded garlands of fruit and cherubs, decorated with wall-paintings and alabaster pillars, and lit by chandeliers. It is perhaps testament to the Vanderbilts' wealth that the house was only seen as the 'summer cottage', used for about ten weeks each year, and that, accordingly, the youngest daughter inherited it.

Rosecliff▶▶, a graceful building of 1902, was modelled by Stanford White on the Grand Trianon palace at Versailles and features a Court of Love and a heart-shaped staircase. *The Great Gatsby* was filmed here.

217

The Ballroom at Rosecliff, the grandest of all ballrooms in Newport, where leading socialites were entertained and many dazzling soirées were held

THE COAL MAN'S RETREAT
In 1894 Pennsylvania coal magnate Augustus van Wickle gave his wife Bessie a steam yacht for her birthday. They cruised into Narragansett Bay and set their hearts on owning a summer retreat at Bristol, north of Newport. Their first house burned down in 1906, but their new 45-room 'cottage', Blithewold, survives and is open to the public. It is a delightful amalgam of English manor, colonial and Dutch styles. Bessie filled the grounds with exotic trees and flora.

The Astors' **Beechwood Mansion▶** (1856) is presented by costumed guides, who treat visitors as if attending a dinner party with the Astors in the 1890s, and who play the part of servants and debutantes. Special events include tea-dance tours, coming-out parties and murder mystery tours. The house lacks the physical glamour of many of the others, but many visitors prefer this livened-up approach.

Marble House▶▶▶ (1892) was the first of the 'gilded era' houses and was modelled on the Grand and Petit Trianons at Versailles. Although smaller than The Breakers it is even more ornate. It was built for William Vanderbilt by Richard Morris Hunt, who was also involved in designing the pedestal of the Statue of Liberty and New York Public Library. A whimsical Chinese Tea House stands close to the Cliff Walk.

Belcourt Castle▶▶ (1891), modelled on the Louis XIII hunting lodge at Versailles, has an intimate half-timbered courtyard, and 60 rooms filled with European treasures, including 13th-century stained glass and a 13,000-piece crystal chandelier from Imperial Russia.

Hammersmith Farm, a 'mansion' of interest for its links with JFK

Hammersmith Farm▶, on Ocean Drive, can be reached by taking a Viking Cruises tour (see panel on page 217), or by a short drive or cycle ride. Built in 1887–9, it gained worldwide prominence in the 1950s when Jacqueline Bouvier and John F Kennedy had their wedding reception here. It later functioned as the Summer White House, and Kennedy's presidential desk can be seen. Compared to the other mansions it is somewhat a return to normality, its décor having a luxurious 1940s and 1950s look. It is still a working farm, the only one in Newport, and is rated the top wedding venue in the whole of the US.

Along **Ocean Drive▶▶▶** are the America's Cup Museum and the summer home of the New York Yacht Club, where hundreds of regattas are held each year. Apart from Hammersmith Farm, the mansions here are private; look for 'Normandy', designed in the style of a Normandy farmhouse.

North of town, at Portsmouth, **Green Animals▶▶** is a bewitching topiary garden featuring 21 animal creations ingeniously formed from privet and yew, and numerous other geometrical boxwood figures, as well as a toy museum. For **Blithewold▶▶** see top panel.

NEWPORT FIRSTS
● In 1803 Newport was the first town in the US to have its streets installed with gas lighting.
● A Newport man was the first person brave enough to eat a tomato (the fruit was previously thought to be poisonous).
● The town's synagogue was America's first (1763), as was its ferry (1657), open golf tournament (1895) and free public school (1640).

SMITH STREET
FRANCIS STREET
GASPEE STREET
State Capitol
Cathedral of St John
Roger Williams National Memorial
NORTH MAIN STREET
CANAL STREET
Brown University
THAYER STREET
HOPE STREET
95 HIGHWAY
New Union Station
FRANCIS STREET
Providence Art Club
First Baptist Church of America
ANGELL STREET
WATERMAN STREET
Gov Henry Lippitt House
INTERSTATE
MEMORIAL BOULEVARD
Old Union Station
Chamber of Commerce
KENNEDY PLAZA
Post Office
Old Market Building
Rhode Island School of Design & Art Museum
The Athenaeum
Brown University
Civic Center
SABIN STREET
City Hall
Fleet Bank
Court House
Gov Stephen Hopkins House
First Unitarian Church
FOUNTAIN STREET
The Arcade
SOUTH MAIN STREET
Hafenreffer Museum
John Brown House
Rhode Island Historical Society Library
ATWELLS AVE
Federal Hill
BROADWAY
EMPIRE STREET
WEYBOSSET STREET
DORRANCE STREET
New Federal Court House
DYER STREET
WATER STREET
BENEFIT STREET
THAYER STREET
219
Public Library
Beneficent Congregational Church
Ocean State Theater
Providence River
Cathedral Square
Johnson and Wales College
INTERSTATE HIGHWAY 195
WICKENDEN STREET
Cathedral of Sts Peter and Paul
Heritage Harbor Museum
River
BROAD STREET
EDDY STREET
Davol Square Market Place
PONT STREET BRIDGE
Fox Point
Roger Williams Park
0   250   500 m
0   250   500 yards

▶▶ Providence

210B3

Easily reached by commuter train or bus from Boston, Providence is well worth a visit as an example of a city renaissance. Founded by Roger Williams in 1636, it prospered as a China Trade and Triangle Trade seaport. Its downtown is still compact enough to explore on foot and has a skyline graced by church spires, the State House and the art deco Fleet Bank – a mini-skyscraper known locally as the Superman Building. The presence of both **Brown University**, founded in 1764 and centred on College Green, and the **Rhode Island School of Design (RISD)** lend the area a college-life air, with plenty of cafés, funky boutiques, nightclubs and bookshops along Thayer, Hope and Wickenden streets. At the fore of the recent climate of change has been the ongoing rejuvenation of the river, with the creation of walkways and a park; in summer gondolas operate and outdoor concerts take place. In an attempt to rejuvenate the whole downtown shopping area, artists have been enticed with tax-free incentives; however, many stores stand empty still. At 65 Weybosset Street, **The Arcade**, the nation's oldest covered shopping mall (1828), is a three-tier Greek Revival structure which houses food stalls and shops.

Marble marvel: the smallest state boasts a State House as imposing as any

The Carrie Tower, a landmark of Brown University's campus

The State House▶▶ (free tours Mon–Fri, 9.30–3.30), built of Georgia marble, was modelled on the Capitol at Washington DC, and boasts the world's fourth largest self-supporting marble dome. Gilbert Stuart's portrait of George Washington hangs in the Executive Chamber, while the 1663 Charter granted by Charles II is displayed at the entrance to the Senate.

Set on College Hill close to downtown, historic East Side displays fine examples of colonial, Federal, Greek Revival and Victorian domestic architecture, 19th-century industrialists' mansions and steep cobbled streets. Its pride and joy is **Benefit Street▶▶▶**, the city's 'mile of history'. Restoration began back in the 1950s with the founding of the Providence Preservation Society, which bought up houses and pushed for conservation laws. A magnificent view extends from **Prospect Terrace**, a park where Roger Williams is buried on Congdon Street. Elsewhere along Benefit Street peep inside the **Old State House**, with its tiny general assembly room, and the **Athenaeum▶**, a Greek Revival building of 1838 where Edgar Allen Poe met Sarah Helen Whitman in the bookstacks (she is thought to have inspired his poem *Annabel Lee*). **The First Baptist Church▶** (1775) has a magnificent 185-foot steeple, a galleried interior and a Waterford crystal chandelier. The Browns, who endowed Brown University, were Baptists and intended it to be a Baptist ministry school; it has become an eminent and ultra-liberal Ivy League university, but some commencement ceremonies are still held in the church.

At 224 Benefit Street, the **RISD Art Museum▶▶** has an outstanding collection which includes paintings by US masters, French Impressionists and modern artists. Highlights among artefacts of the ancient world are a wooden Buddha (*c*1150) from Japan and a 4th-century Roman mosaic (*Open* Wed–Sun 12–5, Fri 10–8). Foremost among the historic houses open to view is the **John Brown House▶▶**, built at 52 Power Street in 1786 for a wealthy China trade merchant, and later extended. It contains John Brown's chariot of 1782 (the earliest American-made vehicle in existence) and a spectacular turn-of-the-century bathroom with tiled murals of water nymphs. Other museum attractions include the **Haffenreffer Museum of Anthropology** in South Main Street, with numerous Native American artefacts, and the **Heritage Harbor Museum** opening by 2000 – to feature a museum of immigration and an exhibition on diners (see panel on page 221).

Federal Hill is the Italian quarter, with lively festivals and good restaurants, at its most animated around Atwells Avenue. South of downtown, **Roger Williams Park** is a Victorian creation with bandstand concerts and lakes. It contains a natural history museum and

TOURS OF PROVIDENCE
Guided walking tours start from the old schoolhouse at 21 Meeting Street, while trolley tours start from Kennedy Plaza. Cruises on the *Bay Queen* start from Warren and take in Narragansett Bay (tel: 410/245 1350).

BIRTH OF A BOOM
North of Providence the Blackstone River Valley was once a hive of textile mills and the cradle of the American Industrial Revolution – the catalyst for huge social change later in the 19th century. The nation's first mass-production of cotton yarn using water-powered machines took place in 1793 at Slater Mill in Pawtucket. Samuel Slater had been a manager at Arkwright Mills in Derbyshire, England, and brought technical know-how with him. The mill now functions as a museum, and gives demonstrations.

planetarium, as well as a zoo with over 600 animals, including a wetlands area inhabited by native New England species.

▶ South County

210A2

South County makes up Rhode Island's south-western corner. Bathing and beaches are the main draw of the coast itself, although wildlife reserves here and in numerous inland wetlands attract naturalists.

Sedate **Watch Hill** is both a fishing port and resort town, with long beaches. Its Flying Horse Carousel, built in 1867, is the oldest in America. Lively family entertainment is provided at Misquamicut, where **Water Wizz** offers amusements, miniature golf, a giant water-slide and a roller rink.

There are several beaches between the resort towns of **Charlestown** and **Narragansett**. Near the latter, the **South County Museum▶** displays a range of reconstructed New England buildings, including an old-time store and a cobbler's shop (*Open* May–Oct, Wed–Sun).

The quaint community of **Wickford▶**, off scenic Route 1A, has a pretty view of the harbour and abounds in antique, craft and speciality shops. John Updike set his novel *The Witches of Eastwick* here. Signposted off Route 1A, the **Gilbert Stuart Birthplace**, near Saunderstown (*Open* Apr–Oct, Thu–Mon), was the home of the artist who created the portrait of George Washington seen on dollar bills. At Wakefield, the **Washington County Jail** (1792) has changing local history exhibits and original jail cells and rooms (*Open* May–Oct, Tue, Thu and Sat 1–4. *Admission* free).

Native American monument, Narragansett

221

THE BIRTHPLACE OF THE DINER
Rhode Island can claim to be the true birthplace of that uniquely American institution, the diner. The semi-mobile cabins that can still be seen throughout the US (there is a fine surviving example in the centre of Providence, just off Kennedy Plaza) had its origins during the early Industrial Revolution in the Blackstone Valley, when workers were fed by horse-drawn food carts.

A MARINE FEAST
Bargain-priced fresh lobsters can be bought at Galilee, near Point Judith, when the boats come in at around 4–5pm. Take a plastic bag.

Galilee: fishing is important all along Rhode Island's coastline

Map labels:

5

CDN

Lake Memphremagog

Alburg
Swanton
Lake Carmi
1177m
Jay Peak
Newport
Derby
Norton
1015m
Gore Mt

Enosburg Falls
Hazens Notch
Brownington
Island Pond

St Albans
Bakersfield
Lowell
Barton
Orleans
Lake Willoughby
Bloomfield

4

Hyde Log Cabin
Grand Isle
Fairfax
Jeffersonville
Craftsbury Common
Glover
Bread and Puppet Museum
East Burke
996m

Lake Champlain
Milton
Smugglers Notch
1339m
Mt Mansfield
Morrisville
Greensboro
Lyndonville
Burke Mt

Winooski
Essex Junction
Stowe
Hardwick

Burlington
Ben and Jerry's Ice Cream Factory
Cabot
Danville
St Johnsbury

Shelburne
Winooski
1244m
Camels Hump
Waterbury
Peacham
Lower Waterford

Shelburne Museum
MONTPELIER
Groton

Ferrisburgh
Rokeby
1260m
Mt Ellen
Northfield
Barre
Wells River

Vergennes
Bristol
Granite Quarries
Williamstown Gulf

3

Chimney Point
Morgan Horse Farm
Lincoln
1165m
Brookfield Gulf
Brookfield
Chelsea
Bradford

Middlebury
Bread Loaf Mt
Moss Glen
Randolph Gap

Texas Falls
Hancock
Bethel
Justin Smith Morrill Homestead

Shoreham
Leicester
Goshen
Green Mountain National Forest
Sharon

NEW YORK

NEW HAMPSHIRE

Sudbury
Brandon
Pittsford
Norwich

Orwell
Marble Exhibit
Proctor
Killington
White River Junction

Benson
Wilson Castle
Woodstock
Quechee Gorge

Rutland
1293m
Killington Peak
Bridgewater

2

Fair Haven
Poultney
Plymouth Notch
958m
Mt Ascutney
Windsor

Wallingford
Felchville

Danby
Ludlow
Perkinsville

Pawlet
Weston
Springfield

Dorset
965m
Bromley Mt
Londonderry
Chester

Manchester
1163m
Big Equinox
Hildene
Magic Mt
Grafton
Bellows Falls

Arlington
Green Mountain Nat Forest
1200m
Stratton Mt
Jamaica
Townshend

1

1055m
Haystack Mt
Newfane
Putney

Park McCullough House
Wilmington
West Dover
Brattleboro

Bennington
Marlboro

Green Mountain Park
Harriman Res
Brigham Young's Birthplace

0   20   40   60 km
0 10   20   30 miles

See drive pages 240–1

MASSACHUSETTS

A   B   C

Vermont retains the character of a retreat from the busier outside world

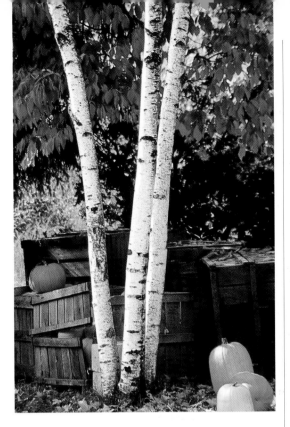

The Northeast Kingdom in the autumn

VERMONT Vermont is a survivor, a rural state of mountains and forests, much of it quite unspoilt. The landscape is folded; its very name, derived from the French words for green mountain, is descriptive enough for much of the year (although the forests you see today have taken over after cleared farmland was abandoned a century or so ago). Towns are distinctly on the small side; even Burlington is far from being a buzzing metropolis, and Montpelier, the state capital, has a village-like quietness at night. A few days' driving around the state will leave memories of quiet, winding roads and huge red barns, of hand-painted signs pointing out automatic bank cash machines and home-made maple syrup outlets, of smart designer shops and country stores. Vermonters thrive on crafts, music and literature, and are strongly involved in the visual arts of painting and sculpture. The events calendar always looks busy.

THE RURAL HERITAGE In the second quarter of the 19th century, Vermont was the wool capital of the world. Spain had been forced to sell off a large part of its herds of sheep in 1811 to pay off Napoleonic War debts, and many of the sheep came here. Wool production only declined in Vermont after the Civil War, when the railroads in the West allowed sheep from Wyoming and Montana to dominate the wool trade. Foreign competition from Australia accompanied this downturn.

▶▶▶ REGION HIGHLIGHTS

Vermont

Right: red barns and silos are a common sight

'They hewed this state out of the wilderness, they held it against a foreign foe, they laid deep and stable the foundation of our state life because they sought not the life of ease but the life of effort for a worthy end.'
– President Theodore Roosevelt, 1902.

FIRSTS IN THE NATION
Vermont was the first state in the USA:
● to manufacture a postage stamp (at Brattleboro, 1846).
● to offer troops in the Civil War.
● to found a Boy Scout Club (at Barre, 1909).
● to install a chair-lift (at Mount Mansfield 1940).
● to abolish slavery.

Today, cows and sheep no longer outnumber the inhabitants, however dairy farming is by far the largest agricultural industry. Fruit and vegetable farming, producing hardy crops which can survive the harsh winters, also takes place. Other industries include granite and marble extraction.

The fragile character of 'Vermontness' has been preserved, but only just. Proximity to the Big Apple and to Boston might change all that, although large advertising signs are banned in this last bastion of rural perfection. A state law lays down ten tough environmental conditions to be met by all new large developments, including a requirement that new structures should not adversely affect the 'aesthetics, scenic beauty, historic sites or natural areas' of the vicinity.

VERMONT FOR VISITORS The southern part of Vermont, with its relatively affluent communities of Bennington, Manchester and Woodstock, is seductive vacation territory. Northern Vermont is appreciably quieter and emptier, except for the area around Burlington and Shelburne. The Northeast Kingdom (the north-east corner of the state) is less sophisticated, ideal for those who like to make their own discoveries.

For hikers, the 260-mile Long Trail crosses the state from the Massachusetts line to the Canadian border, via the Green Mountains and Mount Mansfield (4,393 feet), the highest peak in Vermont. Vermont's towns are distinctly on the small side; even Burlington is far from being a buzzing metropolis and Montpelier, the state capital, has a village-like quietness at night. A few days' driving around the state will leave memories of quiet, winding roads, huge red barns where the cattle herds winter, of hand-painted signs advertising home-made maple syrup outlets, of smart designer shops contrasting with country stores and hippy survivals. Vermonters thrive on crafts, music and literature.

The first pumpkins of the season: they must be picked before the frosts arrive

Events

For further information contact the state tourist office (see page 266) or alternatively the local chambers of commerce.

January
Ice Harvest, Brookfield.
Winter Carnival, Stowe: top winter event.

February
Stratton Winter Carnival, Stratton.
Fisk Trophy Race, Woodstock: oldest continually run ski race in the US.

March
Maple Festival, Woodstock.
US Open Snowboarding Championships, Stratton.

April
Vermont Maple Festival, St Albans.

May
Champlain Valley Quilt Show, Shelburne.
Spring Farm Festival, Woodstock.
Lilac Weekend, Shelburne: 400 lilacs in full bloom.

June
Balloon Festival and Crafts Fair, Quechee and Essex.
Discover Jazz Festival, Burlington.
Lake Champlain Balloon and Craft Festival, Champlain Valley/Essex Junction.

July
Bennington Museum Antiques Show.
Fiddlers' Contest, Hardwick.
Marlboro Music Festival, Marlboro College (ends Aug).
Old Time Farm Day and Grand Old Fourth Celebration, Shelburne.
Vermont Mozart Festival, various locations (ends Aug).
Vermont Quilt Festival, Northfield: largest quilt event in New England.

August
Antique and Classic Car Rally, Stowe.
Bennington Battle Day Celebration.
Vermont Antique Dealers' Association Antiques Show, Stratton.
Vermont Craft Fair, Manchester.
Vermont Craft Fair, Rutland (ends September).

Autumn colour comes to the Northeast Kingdom

September
Antique and Classic Car Show, Bennington.
Champlain Valley Exposition, Burlington: dairy days and funfair.
Harvest Festival, Shelburne.
National Traditional Old-Time Fiddlers' Contest, Barre.
Northeast Kingdom Fall Foliage Festival, various locations (ends October).
Stratton Arts Festival, Stratton Mountain (ends Oct).
Apple Days, Brattleboro: hay rides, cider pressing and apple pie contest.

October
Apples and Crafts Fair, Woodstock.
Northeast Kingdom Foliage Festival, various locations.
Foliage Craft Fair, Stowe.
Mount Snow Craft Fair, West Dover.

November
Thanksgiving Weekend Craft Show, Killington.
Vermont Hand Crafters Craft Show, Burlington.

December
Wassail Christmas Festival, Woodstock.
Prelude to Christmas, Manchester.

Vermont

The archetypal New England clapboard church, Bennington's Old First Church

THE BATTLE OF BENNINGTON
On 16 August 1777, British General Burgoyne sent Hessian and Indian troops to capture military supplies stored in Bennington as part of his attempt to split the colonies in two in an advance down the Hudson river. Brigadier-General John Stark countered by sending two detachments to head off the British. The battle actually took place at Walloomsac Heights (now in New York State) 5 miles from Bennington; it began at 3pm, and two hours later the British were forced on the retreat. The British failure to procure supplies resulted in defeat at Saratoga two months later, and in surrender on 7 October.

GRANDMA MOSES (1860–1961)
Born in New York State, Grandma Moses lived in Virginia and later in Bennington. As an artist she was self-taught, and her primitive, even child-like style, which captured the public imagination, is immediately identifiable. Typically her work shows village scenes or hill landscapes with tiny figures. She was perhaps more significant for recording a particular time and region in America's past than for her gifts as an artist.

▶ Barre   222B3

Pronounced 'Barry', this is a blue-collar town adjacent to the **Rock of Ages▶**, the world's largest granite quarry, which covers a 50-acre site. Self-guided tours from the visitors' centre (Mon–Fri) give a view of the quarry, where huge blocks are lifted by derricks, and of the manufacturing division and the finished products. **Hope Cemetery**, established in 1895, has choice examples of memorials crafted from Barre granite.

▶▶ Bennington   222A1

Tucked into Vermont's south-west corner, Bennington is doubly famous for its college and for the Battle of Bennington, a turning point in the Revolution (see panel). A bronze panther marks the site of the Catamount Tavern where Ethan Allen and the Green Mountain Boys plotted against the British for the capture of Fort Ticonderoga. Allen's house was beside the **Old First Church** (1805), whose magnificent steeple dominates the old village, up the hill from the modern town. The beautifully sited churchyard has a good number of fine carved tombstones. Among these are the graves of Revolutionary War soldiers from both sides, as well as the resting place (follow the arrows) of the poet Robert Frost (see page 209), whose epitaph records 'I had a lover's quarrel with the world'.

The entire district of Old Bennington is worth taking in for its crisp examples of Federal-style homes. At the far end, the **Bennington Battle Monument**, a 306-foot memorial tower, rises close to the site of the storehouse that sparked the battle. An elevator whisks you up Vermont's tallest structure for a view over three states.

Bennington Museum► (*Open* daily) has a collection of Grandma Moses paintings (see panel), as well as numerous examples of Bennington glassware and pottery, plus musical instruments, Revolutionary War exhibits and the oldest Stars and Stripes flag in existence.

Route 67 passes the **Park McCullough House►** (*Open* May–Oct), in West Street, North Bennington, a cheerful yellow 35-room Second Empire Victorian mansion. Built as a summer cottage in 1875, and occupied by four generations of one family up to 1965, it retains original furnishings and even the owners' clothing, diaries and 37,000 documents. It hosts regular music recitals.

Also on Route 67A, **Bennington Center for the Arts** is an exclusive, liberal and progressive institution where plays, readings and an August music festival are presented. South of town, **Southern Vermont College** is the home, from May to October, of the professional Oldcastle Theatre Company (tel: 802/447 1267).

Joseph Cerniglia Winery, New England's largest, is on scenic Route 103 and offers free tastings.

► Burlington 222A4

Set beside Lake Champlain on the state's western border, Burlington is a university town whose population increases drastically in the autumn, and which hosts numerous arts and music events. Apart from the considerable attractions of Lake Champlain, the largest city in Vermont is a place worth stopping at for its shops. It has a range of 'environmental' stores, sidewalk cafés and the pedestrianised area of Church Street Marketplace. Of the town's four beaches, North Beach is the best.

Lake Champlain►►, 128 miles long and up to 12 miles wide, and the largest body of fresh water in the US outside the Great Lakes, lies between the Hudson river and New York to the south, and the Richelieu river and Montreal to the north. Lake views can be enjoyed from a number of points on the shore, notably Red Rocks Park in South Burlington and Sand Bar State Park at Milton (where there are windsurf and boat rentals). To appreciate the lake's shoreline and sunsets, try a cruise on the *Spirit of Ethan Allen* from Burlington (tel: 802/862 8300).

The **Lake Champlain Maritime Museum►**, near Vergennes (Open May–Oct) has historical and maritime displays, boat-building demonstrations and a working forge. On Grand Isle, **Hyde Log Cabin** dates from 1783 and is one of the country's oldest log cabins. Built by surveyor Jedediah Hyde Jr, whose family stayed here for 150 years, the interior houses maps and bygones.

CHAMP
Lake Champlain has its own version of Scotland's Loch Ness Monster, known as Champ. This creature gets occasional 'sightings'. In 1982 the Vermont House of Representatives passed a resolution to protect the beast from 'any wilful act resulting in death, injury or harassment'.

ACROSS THE LAKE
The ferry from Burlington to Port Kent, NY, is handy for visits to Ausable Chasm (*Open* mid-May–early Oct). This sandstone gorge with its rapids and whirlpools surging beneath 200-foot cliffs, can be seen from a boat ride and a 3⁄4-mile walkway. Further south, on Route 74, a ferry gives access to the New York side at Fort Ticonderoga, begun in 1755 by the French to block the British, and now mostly reconstructed and marketed for the heritage industry. Between mid-May and mid-October costumed guides explain the history, and cannon firing and period music supply the background atmosphere.

227

The lively Church Street Marketplace, Burlington

New England's long, cold winters bring plenty of snow, and New Englanders certainly know how to make the most of it. Resorts, though generally small, offer great variety; locals flock to them at weekends. To make the most of a full week you may wish to sample a range of places or activities.

FURTHER INFORMATION

● The brochure *Skiing in New England* is available from Discover New England (see page 266).

● Maine Handicapped Skiing assists those with disabilities, including the blind, with programmes at Sunday River; tel: 207/824 2440, 1-800/639 7770; fax: 207/824 0453.

● The American Skiiing Company's Magnificent Seven Pass covers Killington VT, Mount Snow VT, Sugarbush VT, Sugarloaf ME, Sunday River ME, Attitash Bear Peak NH and the Canyons in the Rockies.

ICE CLIMBING

Frozen waterfalls are targets for ice climbers. Novices are taught how to use an axe and might typically try a 30° climb. Contact the International Mountain Climbing School, PO Box 1666, North Conway, NH 03860 (tel: 603/356 7064; e-mail: guides@ime-usa.com).

Many gondolas are open to non-skiers

Downhill (Alpine) skiing and cross-country skiing You can ski in all six New England states, but Vermont, New Hampshire and Maine are the prime downhill destinations. Snowboarding has gained massive popularity with teenagers in particular; beginners will find themselves falling a lot, but learning is rapid. Some areas have dedicated snowboard parks, with jumps and half-pipes. You can hire skis, boots and snowboards at all resorts, and childcare is available; the standard of instruction is high.

Weekends, Christmas and President's Week in February are peak times. Snowmaking guarantees good conditions from November to April in many areas. After dark, some slopes stay open for night skiing, or you can try out tubing – hurtling down a run on a rubber tyre – or take a guided snowshoe walk. During the day you may like to try a horse-drawn sleigh ride.

From Stowe, you can take the high-speed gondola up Mount Mansfield – which has steeper top-to-bottom runs plus easier terrain on Spruce Peak nearby, or ski over to Smuggler's Notch, the premier family winter resort. Killington (now linked to Pico) is New England's biggest resort and ranks top for nightlife. Its season runs from October to June, and there are more than 100 miles of trails, the highest from 4,241 feet. Stratton, the birthplace of snowboarding, is a single mountain with a full range of runs, and an attractive resort at its base. Wachusett is the closest ski area to Boston and is excellent for children, beginners and intermediates. Massachusetts' main skiing is in the Berkshires, including Jiminy Peak.

The White Mountains ski areas each have enough skiing for three days or so (if you plan to stay longer the Ski New

Hampshire Pass is useful). Of these, Bretton Woods is best for families and beginners, while Waterville Valley, Attitash Bear Peak and Loon are all-rounders – Loon having plenty for non-skiers including an animal park and a skating rink – and Cannon appeals to intermediates and experts.

Maine's resorts, out of range for day trips from Boston or New York, avoid the weekend crowds. Sunday River encompasses eight mountains, and has the largest snow-making system in New England; it includes long easier runs with views all the way. A few days here can be com-bined with Sugarloaf, where the treeless summit offers the highest skiing in New England (2,820 feet vertical drop from the 4,237-foot summit), and superb views over three states and Canada.

Cross-country (Nordic) skiing Much of this sport's appeal lies in its sense of freedom: you can take prepared trails at your own pace and stop where you like. Cross-country on flat trails is easily mastered, but even experienced downhill skiers should have some instruction in the technique for steeper descents. Passes and equip-ment are less expensive than for downhill skiing.

Stowe is the birthplace of American cross-country, and includes four interlinked areas con-stituting New England's premier network. The original one, Von Trapp, has glorious views toward Mount Mansfield as well as wooded trails leading up through conifers and birches to a tiny log cabin where skiers are greeted with an open fire and bowls of soup. In addition to the many cross-country centres, the Catamount Trail gives scope for long-distance skiing through the length of Vermont (for information: Catamount Trail Association, PO Box 1235, Burlington, VT 05401; tel: 802/864 5794).

In the White Mountains there are fine views of the Presidential Range from Bretton Woods and Great Glen – both good for beginners – as well as from the more challenging trails at Jackson, New Hampshire's main cross-country area.

In Maine, Sunday River and Sugarloaf both lie below the downhill resorts of the same name; Sugarloaf has especially fine views and some rewarding trails for beginners. Acadia National Park offers coastal skiing on its carriage roads.

SNOWMOBILING
Dedicated snowmobile routes exist all over north-ern New England, with large networks in the White Mountains and in the Rangeley Lakes areas of Maine (from where you can ride into Canada), as well as Vermont. Equipped with chains and skis, these exciting machines have impressive traction and are easy to drive; youngsters aged 12–18 must have instruction. Some snowmobiles are two-seaters.

Several resorts have ded-icated snowboard parks but most ski slopes are also open to snowboards

Vermont

► **Manchester** 222A1

Pristine-looking old Manchester Village, with its white houses and marble sidewalks, has been a pleasure resort and spa since the 1850s. Nowadays the village merges into Manchester Center, often something of a traffic jam owing to the popularity of its outlet shopping and crafts and country stores.

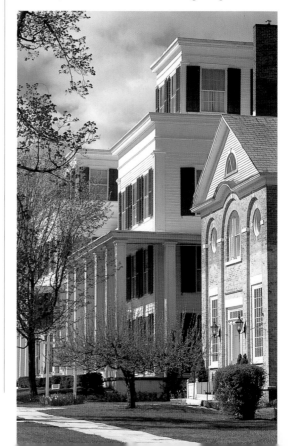

On the southern fringes of the village is **Hildene►►** (*Open* mid-May–Oct), a 24-room Georgian Revival mansion, the home of Robert Todd Lincoln, son of Abraham and Mary Lincoln. Mary discovered this élite mountain village retreat and the Lincolns spent the summer here in 1863 to recuperate in the midst of the Civil War. Robert made Hildene his home, and his descendants lived here until 1975. Today, the house, with its family furnishings and memorabilia, offers an informative insight into the lives and times of the Lincolns. Highlights include landscaped grounds and a self-playing Aeolian organ. Also in Manchester is the **American Museum of Fly Fishing** (*Open* year round), with rods and reels of President Eisenhower, Bing Crosby and other celebrities.

Manchester lies beneath the commanding peak of **Mount Equinox►►** at 3,835 feet the highest point in the

COVERED BRIDGES
Spanning rivers and streams all over the region, wooden covered bridges, built from the 1830s onwards, are now recognised as historic landmarks. Pretty structures, often painted in reds, greens and blues, and by the nature of their setting almost inevitably highly picturesque, they are collected by photographers (particularly in the fall foliage season). Their *raison d'être* seems to be to protect the wooden bridge from the weather, particularly snow – though some say they prevented horses from taking fright. They are usually named after their builder or the river they cross.

230

Manchester, with its upmarket shops, is popular as a base for fishing and other outdoor sports

Taconic Mountains, it is reached by the Skyline Drive toll road and has a mountain-top inn. On the way up the views unfold spectacularly; you pass Little Equinox Mountain and a Carthusian monastery, built in 1960.

At Arlington, south of Manchester, the **Norman Rockwell Exhibition** comprises reproductions of the famous illustrator's work (see page 150). A 15-minute film show is included. North-west on Route 30, **Dorset▶** is a showcase village in a conspicuously attractive setting and with a summer playhouse (tel: 802/867 5777).

▶ Middlebury and the Green Mountains   222A3

Middlebury is a small but bustling college town, picturesque and unfussy, dominated by the four-tiered wedding-cake steeple of its Congregational Church. Crafts are thick on the ground here, with the non-profit-making Vermont State Craft Center based with other craft outlets in the old mill complex in Frog Hollow. On Park Street, the Sheldon Museum (displaying furniture and decorative arts) has been open since 1882.

Out of town on Route 23, past a rare two-way covered bridge, the **Morgan Horse Farm** (*Open* May–Oct) still breeds the famous Morgan horses and gives tours of its stables (see panel). Further north, **Vergennes** has over 100 craft and other shops in its Factory Marketplace. At Ferrisburgh is **Rokeby▶** (*Open* May–Oct, Thu–Sat), a fascinating 11-room Quaker family home that was once a focus of abolitionist activity, and a stop on the Underground Railroad.

West of **Orwell** is a relic of the Revolutionary War: Mount Independence, a peninsula jutting into Lake Champlain which was fortified to defend against a British attack from Canada. The visitors' centre fleshes out the historical background, and trails lead past blockhouses, a stockade and the remains of batteries.

The **Green Mountain National Forest** describes an area of densely wooded, rounded hills covering much of western Vermont. Much of it is unspoilt and offers countless opportunities for walking. On Route 125, the 1-mile **Robert Frost Trail** begins close to the site of his summer cabin: Frost's verses are placed along the route, which crosses bilberry bogs and passes through scrub and woodland. **Silver Lake**, east of Leicester, has a 2½-mile shoreline interpretive nature trail, and there is a shorter circuit around the nearby **Falls of Llana** (both in Branbury State Park). More dramatic hikes include the hour-long walk to **Sunset Ledge** from Lincoln Gap, east of Lincoln. **Bristol Ledges** (1,825 feet) is the highlight of a 1-mile trail above the pleasant town of Bristol, and provides excellent views of the village and of Lake Champlain. More ambitious is the 3–4 hour walk on the Long Trail to **Mount Abraham** from Lincoln Gap, with its rocky 4,006-foot summit rising above the timberline.

Kingsland Bay, on Lake Champlain north-west of Vergennes, and **Lake Dunmore** in Branbury State Park are good for swimming.

MORGAN HORSES
In the 18th century, a Massachusetts school-teacher named Justin Morgan came to Vermont and created the country's first horse breed. He was second owner of a rough-coated, hardy colt born in 1793 called Figure, which had attributes of both draught and riding horse, and was muscular and compact with plenty of stamina but a gentle disposition. Figure, renamed Justin Morgan, was first used as a working horse, then for breeding in Woodstock. From 1878 Colonel Joseph Battell Hardy continued the stock line. Morgans seen at the Morgan Horse Farm and elsewhere look much now as they did then, and they commonly live to 30 years.

231

Visitors to Morgan Horse Farm can see where these sturdy working horses are trained

Vermont

The golden dome of the State House, Montpelier, seen against the early autumn sky

MOUNTAIN GREENERY
As you ascend Mount Mansfield, notice the changes in vegetation as the climate gets harsher. The typical New England trees are found lower down (sugar maple, yellow birch and beech). Further up the slope are pine, white birch, red spruce and balsam fir, and finally tundra. At the summit is the largest community of arctic-alpine flora in Vermont.

'Vermont's Finest' is a Ben & Jerry's ice-cream

▶ Montpelier   222B3

Vermont's state capital is scarcely more than a country town graced by the golden dome of the State House. A good local view of the town can be obtained by climbing from Elm Street to Winter Street and up into Hubbard Park, where a stone tower in the woods affords an all-round panorama. Life continues at an amiable pace in a town small enough to make a relaxing base. Alongside the alternative lifestyle of the Horn of the Moon Café, on Langdon Street, Montpelier has the New England Culinary Institute, a large insurance industry and a high proportion of lawyers.

The **State House▶** (*Open* weekdays. Admission free) has been restored to its original 1859 appearance internally and is the third building on its site. The first State House became too cramped, while its 1838 successor was the victim of an exploding stove. Brochures for self-guided tours are available. Next door, the **Vermont Museum** (*Open* Tue–Sun), run by the Vermont Historical Society, has well-displayed, changing exhibitions about various aspects of state life.

Ben & Jerry's Ice-Cream Factory▶▶ (see also page 234), near Waterbury on Route 100 north of I-89, has become Vermont's biggest visitor attraction. The free samples are the lure; although the tour omits the factory on Sundays, the samples are larger. The tours are very popular: you may have to wait hours, but there are kids' activities (face-painting and the like) and ice-cream to be eaten. Cow souvenirs of the wackiest kind proliferate in the gift shop. There is also a Hall of Fame, featuring the biro-scrawled napkin used by former school-friends, Ben Cohen and Jerry Greenfield, to plan their ice-cream pick-ups on their marathon promotion journey ('Scoopathon') across the US, giving free samples of their super-premium ice-cream as they went. It proved a hugely successful public relations venture. From humble beginnings in an abandoned filling station in Burlington in 1978 on an $8,000 investment, their ice-cream business has soared.

Other Vermont specialities are produced at the Morse Farm maple sugar plant, outside Montpelier, and the Cold Hollow Cider Mill, on Route 100.

▶▶ Mount Mansfield and Stowe   222B4

Vermont's highest peak, **Mount Mansfield** (4,393 feet) rises amid some of the state's grandest scenery. At the Stowe Mountain Resort, on Route 108 some 6 miles north of Stowe, are the toll road and gondola up the mountain. The toll road winds up the slopes for 4½ miles (bicycles are not allowed) and is open from May to October. Further north along Route 108, at Spruce Peak on the right, a chair-lift gives access to the Alpine Slide, a summer sled ride. At **Smugglers Notch**, the road rises to 2,162 feet, with 1,000-foot cliffs on either side. During the War of 1812, when trade with Canada was forbidden, much cattle smuggling took place here.

Stowe, the main skiing and recreation centre for the area, has a wide choice of high-class dining and lodging. Many of its hotels have an Austrian appearance, including the Trapp Family Lodge, still owned by the Trapps of *The Sound of Music* fame. The Stowe Recreation Path gains charming riverside views, and leads to a covered bridge.

▶ Plymouth Notch
222B2

This tiny and remote hamlet was the birthplace and home of 'silent Cal', Calvin Coolidge (1872–1933), the president of the United States between 1923 and 1929 (see page 42). Today the hamlet is part museum, and one ticket covers all the sites. The modest homestead that was the **Coolidge Birthplace** is much as it was, with a quilt and a miniature chest of drawers he created himself; the **Coolidge Homestead** is the family's later home. The visitors' centre tells of the president's life, while the (still-functioning) store displays a 'Drink Moxie' sign – a memento of his favourite drink. Upstairs in the latter building, the **Coolidge Hall** served as the Summer White House: the nation's affairs were conducted with a staff of two from this humble place. The huge barn next to the visitors' centre houses a collection of family carriages.

The village **cheese factory**, built in 1892, offers handmade cheddar-like products, including an extra-sharp cheese matured for two years. Cheese-making takes place from Monday to Wednesday, when visitors are welcome to watch the process.

MOUNT MANSFIELD
The remarkable resemblance the mountain has to an upwards-facing head has meant that each protuberance is named accordingly on the map: the Forehead, the Adam's Apple, the Chin and the Nose. Native American folklore speaks of the mountain as a sleeping giant. The Chin, reached by a 1¼-mile trail, is the true summit.

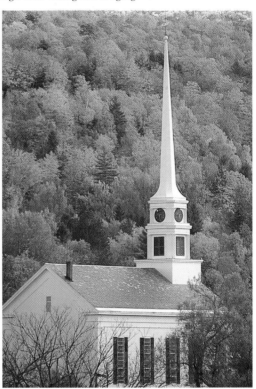

Stowe's church marks the start of the 5-mile Recreation Path

SILENT CAL
A dinner party guest once jested, 'Mr President, I have made a bet with my friends that I can get more than two words out of you this evening.' Coolidge replied 'You lose.'

Out of Vermont's rolling hills and lush valleys come a range of distinctive products. There are the famous traditional cheeses (including cheddar, colby and Monterey jack); there are McIntosh apples and there is cider; there is honey, chocolates and hams. And then there is maple syrup, and Ben & Jerry's.

LIQUID GOLD
Maple syrup is sold in a variety of grades: Fancy, or Grade A Light Amber (delicate flavour, light colour); Grade A Medium Amber (the most popular); Grade A Dark Amber (stronger flavour, dark colour); and Grade B (robust colour and flavour, good for cooking). You can sample them all at the New England Maple Museum in Pittsford (see page 235) or the Maple Grove Maple Museum and Factory in St Johnsbury (see page 236). During the maple-sugaring season (March and April) visitors are welcome at farms listed in the brochure *Maple Sugarhouses Open to Visitors*, available from Vermont Department of Agriculture, 116 State Street, Montpelier, VT 05620-2901 (tel: 802/828 2416).

Vermont farm produce includes maple syrup (below) and cider (right)

Vermont's finest All over Vermont there are black-and-white cows. A good many are the Holstein (Holstein-Friesian) cows grazing in the fields; others are Woody Jackson's Holy Cows. Woody Jackson is an artist and his famous symbols of Vermont appear on anything from mugs and boxer shorts to the T-shirts produced for Ben & Jerry's.

Ben & Jerry's makes Vermont's Finest All Natural Ice-Cream, in over 30 'euphoric flavors'. But making great ice-cream (and frozen yoghurt) is only part of the Ben & Jerry's story that has so captured the public imagination. For Ben Cohen and Jerry Greenfield, serving the community is just as important as making a profit: 7.5 per cent of pre-tax profits go to non-profit organisations working for progressive social change, and half the proceeds of the Waterbury factory tours (see page 232) go to Vermont charities. So popular have Ben and Jerry found their ice-creams to be, that they have now taken them abroad, notably to Britain.

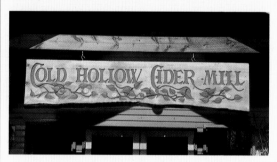

Maple syrup See steam billowing up from the sugar houses that dot the Vermont landscape and you know spring has arrived. Ideally the temperature will be about 40°F in the daytime but there will still be a light frost at night. Under these conditions sap rises up the sugar maple tree (*Acer saccharum*) and the sugar farmer gets 'a good run' – any warmer and the tree bursts into bud and the sap stops rising.

The farmer drills holes in the trunk, into which he fits spouts through which the sap drains, either into galvanised buckets or into long plastic pipes that feed directly into a holding tank in the sugar house. The buckets (up to three per tree) take several hours to fill and about 40 gallons of sap will have to be boiled down to make one gallon of syrup.

▶ Proctor   222A2

Proctor and its larger neighbour Rutland are at the heart of Vermont's marble-producing district (see panel). **Rutland** has plenty of budget accommodation serving the huge **Killington** ski area (see pages 229 and 243). Massive blocks of rock are cut and dressed at the Vermont Marble Company, whose **Marble Exhibit** (*Open* daily, May–Oct) displays the virtues of marble here in the form of a marble chapel (complete with Leonardo da Vinci's Last Supper, also in marble) and a series of bas-reliefs depicting every US president.

Wilson Castle▶, south of Proctor, was built in 1874 by Dr Robert Johnson for his wife Sarah, who had set her heart on living in a castle in the Green Mountains. Unfortunately, the marriage broke up just as the 32-room castle was being completed. It is still lived in and feels like it, with a welcome lack of roping off. Despite being an architectural hotchpotch, with Dutch gables and French Renaissance-style mansards and turrets, it is a good example of an opulent Victorian status symbol, designed to impress, with stained glass and painted ceilings. Far Eastern and European antiques adorn an interior dramatically bathed in golden light. (*Open* daily late May–mid-Oct, 9–6.)

North of Pittsford on the Route 7, the **New England Maple Museum** is at the back of a huge gift shop selling syrups by the gallon, maple candy and of other Vermont specialities. The exhibition shows the many ways of making maple sugar that have been used in past centuries, with murals, utensils and the most complete collection of old sugar-making equipment in existence; there is also a short film and free samples of the various grades of maple syrup.

235

One of dozens of Victorian stained-glass windows in Wilson Castle

VERMONT MARBLE
This material is extracted from Dorset Mountain near Danby, the largest underground marble quarry in the world. The qualities of the 400-million- year-old rock are advertised in an extravagant marble bridge in Proctor. More famous examples of its use are at the Beinecke Rare Book and Manuscript Library at Yale University in New Haven, the US Supreme Court in Washington, DC, and the UN Building in New York City.

A sculptor works in Vermont marble

▶▶ St Johnsbury and the Northeast Kingdom

222C4

The modestly sized town of **St Johnsbury▶**, known locally as St Jay, harbours a few surprises. One is its main street itself, a fetching Victorian survival, with its brick mansions and granite churches. Another is the room at the back of town library housing the celebrated **Athenaeum▶▶** art museum (*Open* during library hours; *admission* free; see panel). Also on the main street, the **Fairbanks Museum and Planetarium** is yet another Victorian period piece; the museum houses natural history exhibits, tribal artefacts and dolls in its old-fashioned barrel-vaulted hall. The tiny **Maple Grove Maple Museum and Factory** is a sweet-smelling, sticky place where you can watch the sugar-making process and see maple candies being packed – and find your shoes sticking to the floor.

St Johnsbury is well placed for excursions into the three north-eastern counties that comprise the remote-feeling **Northeast Kingdom▶▶**. North of the town **Burke Mountain** (3,267 feet) is accessible by toll road and affords 120-mile panoramic views. **Lake Willoughby▶**, beside Route 5A, is popular for windsurfing, boating and fishing, and swimming for those hardy enough. Hikers can take the 7-mile circular route up adjacent **Mount Pisgah** (2,751 feet). Adventurous naturalists might care to seek out **Victory Bog**, a huge wetland preserve harbouring rare plants, as well as moose and black bears. The rural character of the area is exemplified by the **Bread and Puppet Museum▶**, south of Glover on Route 122 (see panel). There is also the farmers' **Co-operative Creamery** (*Open* Mon–Sat; closed Jan) at Cabot, which makes a renowned sharp cheddar cheese.

Craftsbury Common▶, conspicuously attractive and high up on a ridge road (part of a planned military route to Canada built in the 1780s), was painted white for the filming of Alfred Hitchcock's 1955 movie *The Trouble with Harry* and has stayed that way ever since. Route 14 north of here and the unclassified road south-west to Route 15 give a good idea of the quiet beauty of the Northeast Kingdom. Willey's General Store at nearby **Greensboro** is one of the best stocked in Vermont; its outside wall serves as the local notice-board.

St Johnsbury and the forests, hills and valleys of the Northeast Kingdom that surround it

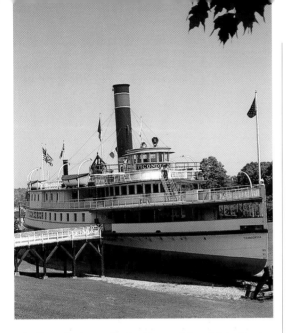

The SS Ticonderoga is preserved at the Shelburne Museum

BREAD AND PUPPET
Glover is the home of the Bread and Puppet Theater troupe, founded in New York in 1974. Its rickety looking barn, a free 'museum', displays the giant Expressionist-style puppets, masks and props used in previous shows and pageants. Sourdough bread is given to audiences, symbolising that theatre is as much a necessity as bread. Performances in the field across the road attract 20,000-strong audiences.

At **Brownington**, a back-of-beyond hamlet in the far north where the paved road turns to a dirt one, is the **Old Stone House**, the former county grammar school built by Reverend Alexander Twilight, a black minister, in the 1830s. The building now houses a local history museum (*Open* daily, Jul and Aug; mid-May–mid-Oct, Fri–Tue), which is run on a shoestring with everything donated by locals. Across the road, a path to the right of the church leads to an excellent viewpoint.

A NEW CONCEPT
'I did not want to create a village...I was anxious to create something in arrangement and conception that had not been tried.'
– Electra Havemeyer Webb, founder of the Shelburne Museum.

▶▶▶ Shelburne   222A4

At Shelburne is the remarkable **Shelburne Museum▶▶▶** (*Open* late May–mid-Oct; limited winter schedule), an astonishing collection of buildings, re-assembled and packed with Americana and American folk art, which was the creation of Mrs Electra Havemeyer Webb. Her love of everyday objects started as a hobby, the collection being housed in a public museum when the first building, a schoolhouse, was moved here in 1947. Other structures then followed, including a general store, jail, inn and covered bridge. The wide-ranging collection of objects – over 80,000 items in nearly 40 buildings – means there is something for most tastes. Allow a full day to see it properly (tickets are valid for two consecutive days). Do not miss the comprehensive quilt collection, the 1890 private rail car, the *Ticonderoga* (America's last-surviving vertical beam side-wheel steamboat, once in service on Lake Champlain) and the Electra Havemeyer Webb Building (a stylish New York apartment adorned with Impressionist paintings).

To the north, **Shelburne Farms▶** was an agricultural experiment set up with Vanderbilt money (see panel). Today it plays a semi-educational role in demonstrating stewardship and farm animals, with a family-oriented hands-on activity area, cheese-making, a farm trail, 90-minute tours and farm animals.

Also of interest are the **Vermont Teddy Bear Co**, on Route 7, and **Vermont Wildflower Farm**, in Charlotte.

A FARM OF THE FUTURE
Shelburne Farms was founded in the late 19th century by Dr William Seward Webb and Lila Vanderbilt Webb as a grand agricultural experiment. Dr Webb purchased 32 farms and hired the services of landscape architect Frederick Law Olmsted, designer of Central Park in New York City, and forester Gifford Pinchot, known in the US today as the father of forestry. Architect Robert H Robertson designed the three main buildings on the property. The Shelburne House, once the Webbs' family residence, is now a comfortable inn and restaurant (*Open* mid-May–mid-Oct).

Quilts and rugs, weather-vanes and whirligigs, trade signs and decoy ducks, baskets, boxes and wooden toys – New England's myriad antique shops, its dozens of crafts shops and many of its museums are stuffed with examples, old and new, of these folk crafts.

STENCILLING

Kitchen utensils, containers, walls and pieces of furniture were commonly painted and decorated with motifs. Some of these patterns were applied with stencils, and itinerant stencillers would work from pattern books, using milk-based paints in dusky shades.

238

DO-IT-YOURSELF

Visitors interested in patchwork and quilting will enjoy a browse in the many shops that sell everything needed. Keepsake Quilting (Senter's Marketplace, Center Harbor, New Hampshire; catalogue available) claims to be America's largest quilt shop, with thousands of small prints as well as plains. Paints for stencilling may be found in crafts supply shops but are also readily available in many hardware shops.

Right: a spinner practises an ancient craft
Top: crazy quilting

SPRUCE GUM BOXES

Lumbermen whiling away the evenings in the logging camps of Maine, New Hampshire and Vermont used to carve little wooden boxes for a wife or sweetheart to hold a gift of spruce gum. These were often in the shape of books and fitted with a slide at one end, and typically carved with hearts and a cross.

Quilts and coverlets Winters have always been hard in New England and the early colonials certainly needed the quilted bed coverings that had long been traditional in Europe. Fabric was in short supply, so the tradition of piecing scraps of left-over fabric together was an economic necessity. Some patchwork designs crossed the Atlantic with the early settlers: 'Log Wood,' used in the north of England, for instance, became known as 'Log Cabin'; and some Pennsylvania quilts, made by settlers from Germany, used designs known in Europe since the Renaissance. Other patterns, such as 'Bear's Paw', were clearly inspired by new experiences. As material became

more available, small pieces were appliquéd on to larger areas, often representing the farmhouse, its occupants and animals, so that the quilt was a personal journal of its creator's life. Old quilts are collectors' items, while modern ones are sold widely across New England.

The colonial coverlet, woven in cotton in overshot patterns, traditionally in blue and cream, is another craft that dates back hundreds of years. Popular as throw-overs, modern versions of these cotton rugs in various, usually pastel colours may be found in numerous crafts outlets.

Baskets and boxes Market baskets, half-bushel and bushel baskets, fish baskets, berry baskets, clothes baskets, sewing baskets, feather baskets (in which to collect feathers until you had enough to stuff a pillow) – in the days before containers were made of mass-produced material, the Native Americans made baskets in dozens of shapes and sizes, traditionally using the brown ash (*Fraxinus nigra*). The Native Americans are still noted for their basketry, though now it is made for the tourist trade. Glass beads may have been replaced by plastic, and coloured strips are no longer dyed with berries, but basketry is an unbroken tradition, passed from generation to generation. The Shakers, who made a unique contribution

Scrimshaw jagging wheels or pie-crimpers

SCRIMSHAW
Dating from the whaling boom of the early 19th century is the type of carving called scrimshaw. Using a sail needle or jack-knife, sailors out at sea carved exquisitely detailed designs on whalebone or teeth, which they then etched in black. There are many examples of scrimshaw in maritime museums and the old captains' houses.

239

CIGAR STORE FIGURES
The Shelburne Museum in Vermont (see page 237) has a room full of these carved figures. Anything up to 6 feet high, they normally depicted Native Americans, wearing or carrying the tobacco leaves that they introduced to the colonials.

to American crafts, were also famed for their baskets as well as their oval boxes and furniture (see pages 148–9).

Carving Native Americans introduced the early colonials to the use of duck decoys in hunting. Made at first of skin and feathers, they were later made from wood carved and painted more and more realistically until the decoy became a traditional art form. The Shelburne Museum in Vermont has the largest decoy collection in the world.

New England's was a seafaring and a farming community, dependent on the weather, and many buildings would have a weather-vane on the roof, cut from metal or carved in wood in a variety of shapes. Along the coast, fish, mermaids or ships were popular designs, while a farm building would often be topped by a cow or sheep. A variant, the 'whirligig', had paddles that kept it turning in a wind; the noise it made, they say, kept the moles at bay. So sought after are these traditional pieces of folk art now that thieves have been known to go to the extent of dropping a line from a helicopter to grab an antique off a roof. Reproductions are popular, decorative items.

Boat-builders turned their skills to woodcarving too, and some made magnificent figure-heads for the ships they built. Woodcarvers produced signs to hang outside shops, painted to advertise their speciality. They also made little models of subjects dear to them: a maple-sugaring scene, a team of working horses, or farmers chain-sawing.

Weather-vanes are now more decorative than functional

Southern Vermont is prime territory for crafts, from the fancifully ornate to such simple items as these turned dishes at the Weston Bowl Mill

Drive

Southern Vermont

See map on page 222 (yellow route).

This is a tour of southern Vermont's choicest rural retreats. Allow a full day to sample the crafts shops and village atmosphere, and maybe to take in a walk in Townshend State Park.

Start from **Manchester▶** (page 230). A few miles east, **Bromley Ski Area** stays open all year round and operates an alpine slide and a chair-lift up to a 360-degree lookout with views stretching over five states. There are a number of hiking trails from the summit.

Then stop off at **Weston▶**, home to the Vermont Country Store, to browse in its quintessentially Vermont-style crafts shops, of the homespun rather than the designer variety. Clustered around the green and village bandstand are the old sawmill, now housing a tinsmith's workshop and a display of antique tools, and the Weston Playhouse, Vermont's oldest professional summer theatre (tel: 802/824 5288). Just to the north, in an appealingly ramshackle old sawmill which began life in 1902, the Weston Bowl Mill carries inexpensive wooden products, while southwards the Toy Works stocks wooden toys, marionettes and more. The Farrar-Mansur House (*Open* Memorial Day–Columbus Day) is a former colonial tavern.

Chester▶ is quiet and prosperous looking, with some classic old-fashioned shops, including a drugstore with an enamel sign and the famously offbeat Inn at Long Last along its main street. The National Survey Charthouse ('Clear, correct, complete' boasts its motto) has a stock of world maps and excellent local hiking maps, as well as art supplies. A rare group of stone houses are found a mile out of Chester by turning off the main street by the Jiffy Mart.

Rising from a bridge, immaculate **Grafton▶▶**, a former woollen and

Covered bridge at Brattleboro

soapstone-quarrying village, was rescued from part dereliction and is now one of Vermont's best-looking villages. It makes a point of having plenty of nothing to do, though there are a historical society and natural history museums. Crafts-watchers can observe a smithy at work and watch cheddar cheese being made at the Grafton Village Cheese Company. A covered bridge can be seen in Townshend Road.

On Route 35 to Townshend, the road is briefly unpaved. Continue 2 miles

rural centre. The Museum and Art Center in Union Railroad Station opens May to October. Connecticut River Tours offer cruises on the *Belle of Brattleboro* (Wed–Sun in summer and foliage time).

Maple-syrup stalls accompany Route 9 west. **Marlboro College**, a liberal arts establishment that is one of America's smallest colleges with just 260 students, hosts a major summer chamber music festival, founded in 1951 by the legendary Rudolf Serkin, which attracts big

The Old Tavern Inn, in the pristine village of Grafton

west of Townshend on Route 30, past the **Scott Covered Bridge▶** on the left, then turn left across the dam to **Townshend State Park▶** (fee payable). Here you can walk 1,100 feet up Bald Mountain, which rises above the treeline and affords fine views of Mount Monadnock and West River Valley. The 1.8-mile trail has both steep and gentler routes. Near by, Townshend Dam (free entry) offers swimming and canoeing from a man-made sand beach.

Newfane offers a touch of grandeur around its green, with its county courthouse, Congregational Church and old inns. **Brattleboro**, a red-brick administrative and manufacturing town, is more of a cultural than a

names. Its Tyler Gallery is a showcase of regional artistic talent (*Open* Mon–Fri during the school year; free).

Westward, the road climbs to **Hogback Mountain▶**, giving an extensive view south, with the prominently pointed Haystack Mountain (3,420 feet) visible to the northwest. Close by, the slopes of Mount Olga offer pleasant walks in Molly Stark State Park. **Wilmington** is a small resort town on the main road; but there are quieter accommodation options near by in the Mount Snow resort area to the north. Go west to **Bennington▶▶** (see page 226) before turning north to explore **Arlington** and enjoy the spectacular scenic drive up **Mount Equinox▶▶** (see page 230) on the way back to Manchester.

*A fisherman faces the
challenges of the
Quechee Gorge*

▶▶▶ Windsor   222B2

Windsor has the longest covered bridge in New England,
spanning 460 feet over the Connecticut River and the border with New Hampshire. On Main Street are the
Vermont State Craft Center and the former Elijah West
tavern, known as the **Old Constitution House** (*Open
May–Oct, Wed–Sun*). Vermont's constitution was signed
here in 1777, and a historical display relating to this
accompanies period furnishings, toys and artefacts. From
June to September and at all foliage time a train runs
from Bellows Falls to the Chester area. On South Main
Street, the American Precision Museum, housed in an
1846 armoury and machine shop, is a tribute to historic
technical innovations.

North of Windsor, **White River Junction**, once a busy
railroad junction with 50 passenger trains daily and an
eight-track crossing, has tours of Catamount Brewery.
South-west of Windsor, **Mount Ascutney▶** (3,144 feet)
can be ascended by following hiking trails from Routes
44, 44A and 131, or by taking the 3.8-mile toll road. Its
summit, a 1⁄2-mile walk from the car park, looks over the
Green and White Mountains, as well as Mount
Monadnock and Lake Sunapee in New Hampshire.

You get a good idea of the rural feel of Windsor County
by taking Route 106 through Felchville, with its minia-
ture-looking buildings, then along the flat valley bottom,
past cornfields and maple-syrup outlets. Stoughton Pond

lies just off the main road, and offers swimming, a picnic
site and a nature trail in very pretty surroundings.
Perkinsville is grander but quite unspoilt, with white
chainlink fencing around its green.

▶▶ Woodstock   222B2

A self-consciously pretty village at the heart of Vermont,
with its own covered bridge and numerous handsome
Federal-style homes, Woodstock has captured the public
imagination as epitomising that elusive quality called
'Vermontness'. However, the crowds of visitors and the
concentration of boutiques, galleries and designer shops
have also given it the veneer of a sophisticated all-year
resort. Money was poured into Woodstock and the overhead wires buried by the Rockefellers, who had family

ties with the Billings Farm and Woodstock Inn. The Dana House Museum in Elm Street offers a glimpse inside one of Woodstock's many well-preserved Federal-style architectural gems.

To get to the **Billings Farm and Museum▶** (*Open* 1 May–31 Oct) follow Elm Street out of the village and turn right past the bridge on River Road. This premier local attraction provides a rare chance to look around a working farm, with butter-making, crafts and milking demonstrations. Established in 1871, the farm has had an outstanding Jersey herd since the 1880s, and in the pristine milking parlour each cow's name, birthday, pedigree and honours are recorded above its stall. The museum offers preserved bygones and a film show, while a renovated 1890s farmhouse gives a glimpse of a well-to-do farming household. The **Vermont Raptor Center**, 1½ miles from town on Church Hill Road, displays around 26 species of owls, hawks and eagles which, owing to their injuries, cannot survive in the wild.

Route 4 east of Woodstock crosses the **Quechee Gorge▶▶**, dubbed the 'Little Grand Canyon' of the Ottauquechee river. The 165-foot chasm can be looked into from the road bridge itself or from the half-mile trail to the bottom. An old riverside mill in the former textile village of Quechee is home to Simon Pearce Glass, where you can watch glass-blowers and potters at work. The Theron Boyd House, very much a survival of the pre-electric era, is open to the public and worth a visit as it is the state's oldest unaltered dwelling.

West of Woodstock lie **Bridgewater**, offering tours of the Mountain Brewery, makers of Long Trail Ale, and **Killington**, the largest ski area in Vermont. Summer attractions at the latter include tennis, golf, a playhouse (tel: 802/422 9795) and a music festival. Easily accessible by chair-lift, 4,241-foot Killington Peak has a nature trail, enabling study of its mountain plants, and views extending to the Adirondacks and White Mountains.

243

Woodstock offers chic shopping (below) and a look at 19th-century agriculture (above)

EUREKA: A SCHOOL
At Springfield, Eureka Schoolhouse stands next to an 1870 covered bridge and is Vermont's oldest one-room schoolhouse. Completed in 1790, it was abandoned in 1900 and underwent wholesale restoration in 1968. It is now open to public view (Open Memorial Day–Columbus Day).

New England

244

CHILDREN'S MUSEUMS
- **Connecticut** Manchester, Mystic Seaport, New Haven and Niantic.
- **Rhode Island** Pawtucket.
- **Maine** Portland.
- **New Hampshire** Portsmouth, Londonderry, Keene; Science Center at Manchester.
- **Massachusetts** Boston; Dennis and Falmouth on Cape Cod; Acton, Dartmouth, Easton, Foxboro and Holyoke.

AMUSEMENT PARKS
- **Connecticut** Quassy Amusement Park, by Lake Quassapaug, Middlebury.
- **Maine** Funtown, Saco, biggest children's park in southern Maine; Aquaboggan Water Park, Saco.
- **Massachusetts** Riverside Park, Agawam, near Springfield, largest amusement park in New England; Water Slide and Family Fun Center, Westport, near Fall River; on Cape Cod, Cartland, Wareham (buddy and indy-style carts, bumper boats); Water Wizz (wet and wild thrills and spills).
- **New Hampshire** Plenty around Weirs Beach, Lake Winnipesaukee (see panel, page 197), and at Hampton Beach on the coast. In the White Mountains, Santa's Village, Six Gun City, Whale's Tail water-slide, Attitash Alpine Slide, StoryLand.

One way of getting supper: an improvised fishing expedition

New England for children

The great outdoors In summer, take a whale-watching cruise or lobster-trapping outing (see pages 164 and 116); join an organised moose search or a sunrise beaver-spotting canoe trip (see pages 200–1); go for a swim, a sail in a lake, or take a picnic on a walk in a forest park. There are hire facilities on many rivers for canoeing and rafting.

In the mountains and forests of the northern states there is excellent mountain-biking (ski-lifts carry the bikes to the mountain top), and there are miles of cycle trails on Cape Cod National Seashore (see page 132). At many ski resorts you can take a cable-car to the top of the mountain for a spectacular view (especially in the autumn). In some places (such as Attitash Bear Peak in New Hampshire and Jiminy Peak in Massachusetts) you can take a chair-lift up and a slide down. In the winter, there is the whole gamut of snow sports (see pages 228–9), and as for spectator sports, there are baseball and basketball matches galore to watch.

Museums and attractions 'Hands-on' is the buzz word. Children's museums can be found throughout the region (see panel) and many others have special rooms, exhibits or events for children. Listed below are just some of the dozens of attractions featured in official state guides. Aquaria and a selection of amusement parks are listed separately in the side panels.

CONNECTICUT
Mystic Seaport and **Norwalk Maritime Aquarium** are popular with older children who like ships, history and the sea. The **Denison Pequotsepos Nature Center** near Mystic has non-releasable birds of prey and seven miles of trails. In the Connecticut River Valley, the **Steam Train and Riverboat** combines a train ride with a riverboat cruise. The **Science Center of Connecticut**, West Hartford, has hands-on exhibits and a planetarium. You can see inside a lighthouse by visiting the **Old Lighthouse Museum** in

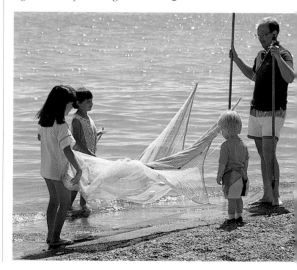

Stonington, handle a live python in the discovery room of the **Peabody Museum**, New Haven—where you can also visit the **Connecticut Children's Museum**—and take a model human body to pieces at the **Children's Museum of South Eastern Connecticut** in Niantic (see page 107).

MAINE

The **Children's Museum** in Portland is one of the best of its kind in New England—meet Mr Bones, the cycling skeleton, and read the news on television. The **Maritime Museum at Bath** has a variety of exhibitions in its restored shipyard buildings. The **Seashore Trolley Museum** at Kennebunkport has the world's largest street and railway car collection, while at **Boothbay Railway Village** (see page 121) you can take a train ride through gnome-inhabited woods. **York's Wild Kingdom**, on Route 1, is a zoo and amusement park. Try to visit a lighthouse.

MASSACHUSETTS

In and around Boston The city is so visually exciting that most children will get a thrill out of just being there: take them up one of the skyscrapers (**Prudential Skywalk** or **John Hancock Observatory**), enjoy the free entertainment of **Faneuil Hall Marketplace**, ride the swan boats in the Public Garden, take in Harvard Square, visit the **Mapparium** and USS *Constitution* in Charlestown Navy Yard. Older children will find **Filene's Basement** fun for bargain shopping. The comprehensive **Computer Museum** has superb hands-on displays, while the **Children's Museum**, the **New England Aquarium** and the **Museum of Science** are all big crowd-pullers. Sports fans can take tours of Fenway Park and the FleetCenter (see pages 68 and 81). On a hot summer's day, take a boat trip from Long Wharf to Georges, the largest of the Boston Harbour Islands, for a picnic. Water-taxis go from there to other islands, where you can explore old forts.

At **Salem** on the North Shore (see page 184) you can go into a jail cell, attend a mock trial and do some gravestone rubbing at the **Salem Wax Museum**. At Plymouth (see pages 177–9), **Plimoth Plantation** and the *Mayflower II* make an expensive but unforgettable outing. The **New Bedford Whaling Museum** is one of the best.

The Springfield area and the Pioneer Village History really comes alive at **Old Sturbridge Village**, a re-creation of life in the 1830s (see page 173). Young dinosaur experts will insist on seeing the quarry of dinosaur tracks at **Dinosaur Land** in South Hadley and on meeting Tyrannosaurus rex in the **Springfield Science Museum**. See page 175 for the **Words and Pictures Museum** in Northampton, in the Pioneer Valley, and see the panel for the **Basketball Hall of Fame**.

History comes alive at Old Sturbridge Village

FOR THE SPORTS ENTHUSIAST
Young basketball fans will want to try their skill at the Basketball Hall of Fame in Springfield, Massachusetts (see page 187); tennis players should visit the Tennis Hall of Fame in Newport (see page 216); the action-packed Sports Museum of New England in Lowell gives a hands-on taste of everything sporty (see page 171).

AQUARIUMS
● New England Aquarium, Boston.
● Marinelife Aquarium, Mystic, CT.
● Maine Aquarium, Saco, ME.
● Aqua Circus Aquarium and Zoo, West Yarmouth, Cape Cod, MA.
● Maritime Aquarium, Norwalk, CT.

Boston Common's very famous ducklings

HOLIDAY READING
Small children will love Robert McCloskey's 1940s classic *Make Way for Ducklings* (available in several languages), the endearing story of a mother duck looking for a home for her family by Boston's Charles river. Bring the book to life by taking a guided walk from Boston Common along the route described in the book, with readings and stops to feed the ducklings' descendants. Children leapfrog the bronze duck sculptures in the Public Garden.

Cape Cod and the islands Here are miles of sandy white beaches for windsurfing, swimming and sailing. At Brewster is the excellent **Cape Cod Natural History Museum** (see page 155), while the Wellfleet Bay Sanctuary has programmes for the under-sixes and canoe trips for the over 12s (who must be accompanied by an adult).

NEW HAMPSHIRE
At the **Ruggles Mine**, near Grafton, you can tap away with a hammer and explore the old mine. **Christa McAuliffe Planetarium**, Concord, is one of the world's most advanced, while **New Hampshire International Speedway**, near Canterbury, is the biggest venue of its kind in New England. **Clark's Trading Post** is a museum, railroad and bear show. **StoryLand** at Glen is a good theme park for younger children. Not to be missed is the cog railway up Mount Washington (see page 205). In Portsmouth, on the coast, children can join in workshops in some of the **Strawbery Banke** buildings (see page 202).

RHODE ISLAND
Roger Williams Park in Providence hosts a zoo, natural history museum and planetarium, and there's boating in the park. Older children will learn about the factory age at the **Slater Mill Historic Site**, birthplace of the American Industrial Revolution (see pages 36–7), at Pawtucket, while younger ones will enjoy a trip on the canal. Many of the **Newport Mansions** will impress young and old alike. For Newport's **Tennis Hall of Fame**, see panel on page 216.

Vermont
Fun is the word too at **Ben & Jerry's** ice-cream factory (see pages 232 and 234). Take in a visit to a maple syrup museum and sample the sugar candy at **New England Maple Museum**, Pittsford, or **Maple Grove Maple Factory**, St Johnsbury. The **Shelburne Museum** (see page 237) is certainly one for all ages. Birds of prey are rescued and sheltered at the **Vermont Raptor Center**, near Woodstock, while at Norwich the Montshire Museum of Science is an excellent hands-on museum (see panel, page 242).

A Ben & Jerry's could well be the highlight of the day

Arriving

Visa formalities

Visitors to the US must have a full passport. UK citizens may arrive without a visa providing they have a return ticket and intend to stay for a period less than 90 days.

Citizens of Ireland, Australia, New Zealand and Canada, and those intending to stay longer than 90 days must obtain a visa from a US embassy before departure.

Visa extensions can be obtained in the US from the United States Immigration and Naturalisation Service offices (see the telephone book under Federal Government Offices).

Before arrival UK citizens will be given an I-94W Non-immigrant Visa Waiver form (asking you, among other things, if you are seeking entry to engage in criminal or immoral activities and if you are engaged in terrorist activities or genocide).

People arriving without a return ticket or sufficient funds to cover their stay might not be admitted, as they might be considered to be planning to work illegally in the US. In order to show the immigration officer that you have adequate funds it is sensible to take one or two credit cards, and plenty of US-dollar traveller's cheques. Give an address where you intend to stay on your first night.

Airports

Boston's Logan Airport is the international terminal for New England, and has the usual complement of car-rental desks and currency exchange facilities (*Open* Mon–Fri 8am– 9:30pm; weekends 11am–9:30pm) as well as a hotel reservation desk covering the whole of New England (no commission charged to customers; *Open* daily 8:30am–11:30pm).

Another possibility is to fly to New York, which has good access to southern New England, and bus and train links to Boston (reached in four to five hours). Montreal is a useful port of entry for northern New England. Check with your airline whether you need to re-confirm your international return flight home.

There are also airports at Windsor Locks, LT (Bradley International) and Providence (Theodore Francis Green State).

Getting into Boston

Excellent public transport gets you into downtown Boston. From Logan Airport's terminal building, leave the main exit and cross to the courtesy bus

stand, where buses marked with a circled T provide a free shuttle service to Airport subway station, on the Blue Line (see pages 52–3). Alternatively, the Airport Water Shuttle carries passengers to Rowes Wharf in the Financial District (last service 8pm; no service Saturdays or Sunday morning). On weekdays a non-stop Logan Express shuttle van operates from the airport to South Station in the Financial District (tel: 1-800/23 LOGAN); in 1998 taxi fares to downtown Boston and Cambridge were about US$10–18 compared to 85¢ on the subway, US$10 on the water shuttle. There are also buses to South Station (tickets $6). Worcester Airport Limo (tel: 508/756 4834) offers a good-value service from Logan Airport to hotels in Massachusetts.

The Connecticut Valley Railroad is one of only two steam railways in New England

Customs regulations
On entering the US, visitors over 21 years of age may bring in duty-free items that include: 200 cigarettes or 50 cigars or 2kg of tobacco; 1 US litre of alcohol; US$100 worth of gifts.

Forbidden imports include meat, seeds, plants and fruit.

Time
There are four time zones within continental, or mainland USA. Boston falls within the Eastern Standard Time zone, as do New York, Washington DC, Miami and Cleveland.

When it is 12 noon in Boston, it is 9am in San Francisco, 3am the next day in Sydney, 12 noon in Montreal, 5am the next day in Auckland and 5pm in London.

Daylight Saving Time alters the time by one hour from Mar/Apr to Oct/Nov.

What to take
From spring to autumn take a range of clothes for all temperatures, including waterproof clothing for whale-watching and hiking, and comfortable, sturdy shoes for walking around cities and along rural trails. Winters can be very cold so bring a top coat, scarf and/or hat, gloves and waterproof shoes or boots.

Take a first-aid box, your driving licence, a photocopy of your passport (if you lose your passport, this will make replacement much easier), a photocopy of your travel insurance (leave the original at home in case of loss), credit cards, any medicines prescribed to you, sun lotion (in summer) and an umbrella – just in case!

249

A ride round Faneuil Hall Marketplace provides an easy introduction to Boston

Essentials

Climate and seasonal considerations

New England has warm summers, pleasant if somewhat unreliable spring and autumn seasons, and extremely cold winters. In summer, Maine has plenty of sun but few really hot days.

Spring can bring glorious weather, with warm days and cool nights; there are fewer tourists than in summer and autumn, so room rates are lower. Maple sugaring takes place in northern New England. Inland, April is 'mud season', while blackflies (whose bites are not so much painful as annoying) proliferate in late May and early June in parts of the north.

Memorial Day is the start of the migration to the beaches, and summer begins in earnest on July 4.

More museums and houses open in summer than at any other time of year. July and August see the coastal and lake resorts crowded and the roads clogged with traffic, as the temperatures soar. The events calendar is similarly packed with festivals.

Fall foliage attracts visitors from all over the world, making autumn the busiest season; hotel rates are high and the famous leaf-peeping areas, such as the Berkshires, White Mountains and Green Mountains, become very busy. Conversely, the coast sees fewer crowds after Labor Day (the first Monday in September). The days are mild, the nights cool.

Winter invariably brings snow to many parts of New England

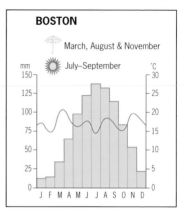

BOSTON

March, August & November

July–September

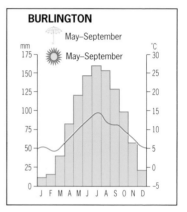

BURLINGTON

May–September

May–September

There are also plenty of events, such as country fairs and crafts markets, happening at this time, and the roadside stall is a common sight.

A marked lull occurs after the leaves fall in late October, but much happens at Christmas and First Night (see page194). Winter brings enough snow to many areas to make New England a major winter sports destination (see pages 228–9), and when natural snow is lacking, the region has the greatest snow-making capacity in the US.

There are regular TV and radio weather forecasts, one TV channel has non-stop weather reports.

> ❏ 'There is a sumptuous variety about the New England weather that compels the stranger's imagination – and regret...in the spring I have counted one hundred and thirty-six different kinds of weather inside four-and-twenty hours.'
> – Mark Twain, speech given in New York City, 22 December 1876. ❏

Your credit card enables you to get cash from an Automatic Teller Machine

Money matters

Currency There are 100 cents (¢) in a dollar ($). Coins in general circulation are 1¢, 5¢, 10¢ and 25¢; dollar notes (always called dollar bills) come in denominations of $1, $5, $10, $20, $50 and $100. Curiously, 50¢ and $1 coins do exist but are rare. Note the terminology: a cent is also known as a penny; a 5¢ coin is a nickel; 10¢ a dime; 25¢ a quarter; 100¢ a dollar, nicknamed a buck. An amount such as $3.60 is described as 'three-sixty' or 'three dollars and sixty cents', but never 'three dollars sixty'. Always carry plenty of change.

Credit cards These are widely accepted and essential if you want to rent a car. It is wise to take two cards, as the car-rental company may take one as a deposit in case the car is damaged or not returned.

Traveller's cheques Take US-dollar traveller's cheques, which are accepted almost everywhere as cash, and no extra commission is charged. Get $10, $20 and $50 denominations; $100 cheques may be difficult to change in shops. Keep the counterfoils separate from the cheques, in case they are lost, and make a record of those you have spent. If they go astray, contact any bank and new cheques should be issued promptly. Traveller's cheques in denominations other than US dollars are less easy to exchange and should be avoided if possible.

Banks Many banks have only one branch in each town, and often open 10–4 Monday to Thursday and 10–6 on Friday; bank cheques are rare. Nearly all banks have Automatic Teller Machines (ATMs) to dispense cash; most major credit cards can be used in these, providing you have a Personal Identity Number.

Sending money from abroad The easiest ways to get cash sent to the US are by Western Union, Thomas Cook and International Money Order.

Sales tax Except in New Hampshire, sales tax is added to certain items, including meals and lodging.

Tipping Tipping is universal. You are expected to tip 15 per cent for a meal, haircut, massage or taxi, and a few dollars to the bell hop who carries your bags to your room. Leave small change at a bar.

Opening times

Many museums close on Monday and on public holidays (although some actually make a point of being open on holidays). Smaller museums, many houses and other attractions open in summer between Memorial Day (the last Monday of May) and Labor Day (the first Monday of September) or mid-October. Visitor attractions often open 10am–5pm (or 4pm if guided tours are given); few places open before noon on Sunday.

Offices mostly open Monday to Friday, 9–5; some open at 8am.

Most shops are open on Sunday.

Evening meals are generally taken fairly early in the evening and restaurants stop serving earlier than in Europe.

In this book, information on the opening times of places to visit has been provided for guidance only. Things do change: check locally before planning visits.

Public holidays

Remember that roads and visitor attractions are often busy, and accommodation gets heavily booked up at public holiday weekends.

- **New Year's Day** 1 January.
- **Martin Luther King Day** 15 January.
- **Lincoln's Birthday** 12 February (Vermont only).
- **George Washington's Birthday** Third Monday in February. Also known as President's Day.
- **Patriot's Day** Monday nearest 19 April (Massachusetts only).
- **Fast Day** Last Monday in April (New Hampshire only).
- **Memorial Day** Last Monday in May; commemorates Americans who died in wars. This signals the start of the summer season.
- **Independence Day** 4 July; anniversary of independence from Great Britain in 1776.
- **Battle of Bennington Day** 14 August (Vermont only).
- **Labor Day** First Monday in September; celebration in honour of the American worker, which also marks the end of summer.
- **Columbus Day** Second Monday in October.
- **Election Day** First Tuesday after the first Monday in November (New Hampshire, Rhode Island, Vermont).
- **Thanksgiving** Fourth Thursday in November; a roast turkey dinner is traditionally cooked in tribute to the

Independence Day is celebrated with fireworks, pageants and parades

first harvest by the Pilgrim Fathers.
● **Christmas Day** 25 December.

Travel insurance

Medical costs are high in the US, and
travel insurance is essential and will
pay directly in case of emergency. Shop
around for the best value and cover,
and take a copy of the policy with you
(leave the original at home). Your
insurance should cover the following:

● Delayed departure and baggage.
● All reasonable medical, hospital and
emergency dental treatment. Expenses
and flight home by air ambulance,
if necessary.
● Personal liability.
● Cancelling or curtailment in the
event of the illness or death of yourself, your travelling companion or a
close relative; or in the event of
redundancy; or in the event of being
called as a witness; or in the event of
your home being damaged by fire,
flood or storm or being burgled; the
policy should compensate the cost of
the holiday.
● Belongings and money, including
sufficient cover for your camera.
● Items left in a car in daytime or
overnight.
● Any special risks in such activities as
motorcycling, waterskiing, winter
sports and rock-climbing.
    Ensure too that the policy carries a
24-hour emergency telephone number.

If you should fall ill, keep receipts of
all medical expenses and drugs.
    Points to note:
● Contact lenses and dentures usually
require special insurance cover.
● Delays under 12 hours are not
normally covered.
● You usually have to pay the first
given amount of any claim, and there
is normally a maximum amount that
can be claimed for each item.
● Cover is not normally provided for
pre-existing illnesses.

*Wherever you are staying in the summer
months, there's usually a festival going
on near by: (above) jazz in Burlington,
and (below) the Maple Festival in St
Albans, Vermont*

Getting around

The most flexible way of exploring New England is undoubtedly by car. Rental rates are low and driving standards good. While the public transport network is better than in much of the rest of the US, it will generally only convey you to the main centres. However, using Boston as a base, it is feasible to have a car-free holiday: Cape Cod, Newport, Providence, Cape Ann, Old Sturbridge Village, New Haven, Concord, MA, and Portsmouth, for instance, have good bus and/or rail connections. With the wide availability of bicycle hire it is possible for people with sufficient stamina to explore rural areas.

Roads

Traffic in the US drives on the right. Apart from the congested roads of downtown Boston, driving in New England is a pleasurable experience. On the whole, traffic cruises along with reasonable distance between vehicles.

The speed limit is generally 55mph on country roads. On the turnpikes (toll roads) and Interstate highways (the equivalent of European motorways) the speed limits are 55mph or 65mph, although traffic tends to go 10mph faster; some roads have minimum speed limits. Overtaking on the inside is allowed; many drivers prefer to keep in the middle lane all the way as this avoids getting sucked into 'traffic must exit' lanes.

Even on highways, traffic moves at a slower speed than in Europe

Country roads are obviously more interesting for touring, but can be slow going, with speed limits down to 25mph at some bends and police radar checks enforcing the law at the most unlikely spots. Signposting is not especially good in New England, with turnings appearing without prior warning. Also note that interstate roads may have a local number.

Car rental

Car rental is easy to find and, on the whole, cheaper than in Europe; discounts can often be negotiated. British travellers may, paradoxically, save money by booking in Britain. Drivers must be at least 25 years old to rent a car.

Virgin Holidays (tel: 01293/617181 in the UK) offer a comprehensive fly-drive package tour that includes flight to Boston, car rental from the airport and pre-booked accommodation. Typically, the 14-night itinerary would include Boston, Maine (Freeport or Acadia), the White Mountains, Vermont, Newport, Mystic and Cape Cod.

All airports have car-rental desks. Some car-rental companies offer free shuttle services to nearby airports, stations and towns. It is possible to pick up and leave the car at different places; it is usually much cheaper when these places are within the same state. Choosing one of the smaller compact/sub-compact/class A cars in the range will save on fuel bills. It is possible to rent camper-vans (known in the US as RVs), some of which are large enough to accommodate a family.

Take a credit card for booking and payment (it doubles as an identity document if the car goes missing or gets damaged). Collision Damage Waiver (CDW), a strongly recommended optional extra, covers you if someone else causes damage to the car. Drivers who are not covered can return home to find huge repair bills debited to their credit card. Check if taxes and mileage are included (US$10 or so per week). Deals on longer-term rental are available and competition is cut-throat: shop around.

Mopeds for hire on Martha's Vineyard – a good way to get around

255

It pays to shop around the rental companies. Dollar (tel: 1-800/800 4000) and Thrifty (tel: 1-800/367 2277) often offer competitive rates. Another option is to book from Britain through Hire for Lower (0171/491 1111) which gets cut-price deals through Alamo.

Driving licences (permits)

Holders of licences from most countries, including Australia, Canada, Ireland, New Zealand and the United Kingdom, can drive in the US without having to obtain an International Driving Licence. Always carry your driving licence when you drive – you may be asked to show it at any time.

Car breakdown

On Interstate highways, stay in the car (raising the bonnet will alert attention) and await police help; there are no emergency phones. Sometimes someone with a CB radio may help you. If a rental car breaks down, call the number the company has given you. It may be possible to hire a mobile phone from the car-rental company.

Driving tips

Fuel Petrol (or 'gas') is lead-free; check the recommended octane level when you hire your car. Gas pumps are activated by raising a small lever (not always obvious) on which the piston rests. Sometimes you have to pay before filling up. Gas is not expensive (but remember that the US gallon is about 17 per cent smaller than its British counterpart).

Hazards Winter conditions cause frost heaves on the road, and snow and ice hardly make things easier. However, snow ploughs clear the roads very efficiently, making driving in deep winter quite feasible. Rental cars in New England should come with all-season tyres; snow chains are not needed. Cat litter can be put down to ease the car out if stuck in the snow! Beware of moose, which like the salt that runs off the road; colliding with one can cause a fatal accident. Moose are particularly prevalent in the White Mountains and inland. Also keep an eye out for deer.

Driving in Downtown Boston can be hair-raising for visitors and is best avoided if at all possible

Automatic cars Hire cars tend to be automatic, with cruise control enabling you to set a maximum speed (which cancels itself when you hit the brake; press 'reset' to return to your previous speed).
Accordingly, you can drive along with both feet off the pedals, just steering a straight course.

If you have not driven an automatic car before, ask the car-rental office to explain the controls. These are quickly mastered, providing you keep your left foot on the floor at all times (it does not activate the pedals) and start and park the car in 'park' mode. For treacherous conditions and steep downhill sections first and second gears can be used. Hire cars usually come with air-conditioning. When parked, cars tend to drizzle a pool of water out of the air-conditioning system.

Drink-driving Avoid at all costs. Police can stop you on the slightest pretext and, if you fail a breath test, they will take away your licence on the spot. Keep any alcohol unopened and in the boot.

Parking You must park in the direction of the traffic. Parking is not usually allowed where traffic would have to go on to the left side of the road to get round the parked vehicles, but the roads are usually wide enough anyway. Never park by a fire hydrant. Meter-feeding is prohibited.

Red traffic lights Unless a sign says 'No turn on red' (or similar) you can turn right at a red traffic light if the road you are turning into is clear and after you have come to a stop; i.e., treat the light like a 'give way' sign.

Stop You must stop when a school bus stops to unload or let on children. This rule applies even if the bus has stopped on the other side of the road.

In towns give way to pedestrians on crosswalks (thick white lines painted across the road). Many intersections do not have priority markings: look around for octagonal stop signs. First arrivals at intersections have priority unless markings on signs indicate otherwise. To be safe, stop and wait for the other cars to make the first move. At intersections, cars from opposite directions turning left pass in front of each other. Single flashing lights are sometimes used to indicate priority: flashing orange means go with care (you have priority), while flashing red means stop and then go if it is safe.

U-turns In town centres, do not attempt U-turns unless it is indicated that you can do so.

Cycling

New England has plenty of opportunities for the cyclist, with ready-made cycle trails on Cape Cod and in the Pioneer Valley, for example, and scenic country roads in the Berkshires and northern Vermont; cycling is also a feasible option in and around Newport Mountain biking is very popular, particularly in the White Mountains, and ski resorts often offer this facility when the snows have gone. The loop road in Acadia National Park is scenic (although traffic gets busy in summer) and there is not a lot of distance to cover. Nantucket and Block Island are excellent for exploring by bike; Martha's Vineyard has dangerous roads (too narrow to accommodate traffic safely) but some bike paths. There is no shortage of hire outlets in the region.

Hiking

Country walking for pleasure is mainly confined to state and forest parks, where ready-made trails are well signposted. There is usually an indication of the time needed, and the length and difficulty of the walk, and free maps are generally on offer. The finest areas in New England for walking are the White Mountains and Acadia National Park, although there are many smaller parks with one or two outstanding trails. Naturalists particularly enjoy the trails in the wilds of Baxter State Park in Maine.

Many of the best routes are mentioned in this book. Because of the prevalence of tree cover, good views can be hard to find; you often see nothing except trees until you

Left: the circled road number (11) indicates a local road, while the number enclosed in a shield (7) indicates a federal road

reach the summit of the hill. Ask locally which routes go above the tree-line.

Long-distance walks include the **Appalachian Trail**, which stretches for 2,035 miles between Georgia and Maine, and Vermont's 260-mile **Long Trail** over the Green Mountains and Mount Mansfield.

A range of practical walking guidebooks covers the New England states. For further information contact the **Appalachian Mountain Club (AMC)**, Box 298 Gorham, NH 03581 (tel: 603/466 2721) or the **White Mountain National Forest**, US Forest Service, 719 North Main Street, Laconia, NH 03246 (tel: 603/528 8721), or the **Green Mountain National Forest**, 231 North Main Street, Rutland, VT 05701 (tel: 802/747 6700).

A coastal trail gives the freedom to look around as you travel

257

Public transport

Selected train trips Commuter rail services from Boston and New Haven are inexpensive, and tickets can be bought immediately prior to travel. Long-distance Amtrak services can fill up and should be booked in advance. Some basic trips are suggested here.

● **Amtrak** (tel: 1-800 USA-RAIL). Northeast Corridor: Boston South Station, Providence, Mystic, New London, Old Saybrook, New Haven, New York, Philadelphia.

● **Metro-North** (tel: 1-800/METRO INFO; in New York, tel: 212/532 4900). New York (Grand Central), Rowayton, South Norwalk, New Haven, with connections to New Canaan, Danbury and Waterbury.

● **MBTA Commuter Rail** (tel: 617/374 1234). Boston North Station to Fitchburg via Concord (MA); Rockport via Salem (for bus to Marblehead), Manchester (MA), Gloucester; Ipswich. Boston South Station to Providence.

The 'T' is useful for travelling between Boston and the North and South Shores

Selected bus trips Boston services leave from South Station and/or Logan Airport. Bus companies tend to be organised regionally.

● **Concord Trailways** (tel: 1-800/639 3317) covers much of New Hampshire and parts of Maine, including Concord NH, and Maine to Bangor via Camden.

● **Plymouth and Brockton** (tel: 508/746 0378) serves Cape Cod (including Provincetown).

● **Bonanza Buses** (tel: 1-800/556

Trolleybus tours operate in Boston

3815): Connecticut, Rhode Island; the Maine coast, the Berkshires (from New York), Cape Cod for ferries to the islands. Includes Providence, Fall River, Portsmouth, Portland and Bangor.
● **C&J Trailways** (tel: 1-800/258 7111: the coastal towns of New Hampshire and Maine, including Newburyport and Portsmouth.
● **Peter Pan Trailways** (tel: 1-800/343 9999): western Massachusetts and Connecticut, covering Amherst, Hartford, Foxwoods, Old Sturbridge, Lowell, New Haven and New York.
● **Greyhound International** (tel: 1-800/231 2222): Hartford, Springfield; long-distance routes across the USA.
● **Vermont Transit Lines** (tel: 617/ 526 1801 or 802/864 6811): numerous towns in Vermont, New Hampshire and Maine, notably Lowell, Montpelier, Burlington, Brattleboro, Portland, Portsmouth, Augusta and Bangor.

Selected ferry trips See gazetteer entries for Block Island (page 213), Martha's Vineyard (page 160), Nantucket (page 162) and Provincetown (page 159). One option is to tour Rhode Island by ferry from Providence, calling at Newport and continuing to Block Island (Interstate Navigation, tel: 401/783 4613).

Domestic airlines Taking internal flights is an expensive means of getting about.
   In addition to flights from and to Logan Airport at Boston, domestic airlines serve Bangor, Bradley International Airport near Hartford, Bridgeport, Burlington (VT), Groton, Hyannis, Lebanon-Hanover (NH), Manchester (NH), Martha's Vineyard, Nantucket, New Bedford, New Haven, Portland, Providence and Worcester (MA).
   Major carriers include:
● **Cape Air** (tel: 1-800/352 0714).
● **Delta** (tel: 1-800/221 1212).
● **Northwest Airlines** (tel: 1-800/225 2525).
● **US Airways** (tel: 1-800/428 4322).
   In addition, short-hop charter flights and scenic aerial tours can be arranged at a number of the small rural airports.

The only trains in much of the north of the region will be those on tourist railways

259

Canny planning
Public transport can help you get round the busy times of year. For example, when the whole of the world seems to be at one giant convention in downtown Boston, getting a hotel room there can seem impossible. Consider instead a commute from an outlying town such as Concord MA, Salem or Quincy, all highly pleasant bases with good standards of accommodation, and with excellent transport links enabling you to be into Boston in a short time.
   Bus, train and air services also take the hassle out of trying to plan a circular car tour of New England, since it is possible to drive from one place, leave the car at another and travel back by public transport; beware, however, of heavy one-way drop-off charges.
   You could further dodge the crowds by visiting New England in spring, by visiting the coast in autumn or even winter, by venturing into the mountains in the summer, or by going to the busier resorts during the week and saving money on hotel bills by staying in Boston at the weekend.
   See the inside front cover of this book for some suggested itineraries.

Communications

Language

Exposure to American films and TV has ironed out some of the differences between English and American as spoken on either side of the Atlantic, but there are numerous linguistic pitfalls awaiting the unwary traveller. Common speech features about 4,000 words used differently in the two countries. When you 'make a call' you never dial 'double-eight', it's always 'eight, eight'; when the connection is made, you are not 'through' (to Americans it means 'finished'). 'A quarter past ten' and 'quarter to ten' become 'quarter after ten' and 'quarter of ten'. A 'fortnight' makes no sense to an American. 'Cheap' denotes something of poor quality to an American; use 'inexpensive' to refer to the good-value hotel you have found!

British	American
banknote	bill
bill (for payment)	check
bonnet (of car)	hood
boot (of car)	trunk
ground-floor	first-floor
lift	elevator
nappy	diaper
pavement	sidewalk
petrol	gas
post (letter)	mail (letter)
puncture	flat
queue	line
road surface	pavement
tights	panty hose
toilet	bathroom or restroom
trousers	pants
underground (train)	subway

Newspapers Apart from the national *USA Today*, the tabloid *National Enquirer* and the financial *Wall Street Journal*, newspapers are local. The *Boston Globe* and *Boston Herald* are both dailies, with listings on Thursday and Friday respectively. The *Boston Phoenix* comes out on Saturday and has listings and comments on the city's entertainments. The *Christian Science Monitor*, highly regarded for its unbiased reporting, is published on weekdays and has items of international news. International newspapers and journals are sold at the kiosk in Harvard Square, Cambridge.

Television There is a huge choice of channels, frequently boosted by the installation in many hotels and homes of cable TV. ABC, CBS and NBC are the major three national networks, with hundreds of affiliated local stations. The Public Broadcasting System

Hot off the press: this news-stand does brisk business in Harvard Square, Cambridge

(PBS) has some good imported programmes. Many hotels have pay channels, with a range of recently released movies; a free preview channel allows you to sample them.

Radio Local radio is part of the holiday experience. Flick through the channels and you will find evangelistic preaching, pop, country and western, and classical music. Public and college stations are found on FM.

Postal services

Post offices generally open Monday to Friday, 9–5. Vending machines outside dispense stamps. Stamps are also available from vending machines in hotels, supermarkets and other places for a little extra cost. Air mail takes about seven days to Europe.

It is cheaper to send postcards and aerogrammes than letters. Mail within the US can take a week to cross the country. Parcels can only be sent in containers bought from post offices; sea mail is appreciably cheaper than air mail and takes around six weeks. Faxes are widely used in the US and are available in numerous street bureaux and hotels.

Telephones

Telephones are privately operated by various companies. Hotel telephones tend to be the most expensive (although local calls may be free). Pay telephones are found everywhere and are reliable but much more costly to use than private appliances. Pay telephones take 5¢, 10¢ and 25¢ coins, and if telephoning long-distance or non-local (anywhere in the local call area considered far enough away) you will need fistfuls of change. Pre-paid cards will make life simpler and are obtainable by quoting your credit card number over the phone; companies offering them include AT&T (tel: 1-800/876 3128) and MCI (tel: 1-800/390 2164). Some public telephones have a slot for credit cards. It is cheapest to telephone between 6pm and 8am.

The dialling tone is a continuous hum; long beeps denote the ringing signal, short ones mean the number is engaged, and a high-pitched noise means that the number is unobtainable. Numbers beginning with 1-800 or 1-888 are toll-free; they are sometimes followed by a group of letters (which appear on the dial, and double up with the numbers). Local calls are either free or very cheap (10¢). For the operator dial 0. Begin direct-dial long-distance calls by dialling 1 first.

State codes Dial the following codes when phoning from a different code area (they are usually preceded by 1):
● **Boston** 617.
● **Connecticut** (south-western) 203.
● **Connecticut** (rest of state) 860.
● **Maine** 207.
● **Massachusetts (western)** 413.
● **Massachusetts (southern and eastern)** 508.
● **Massachusetts (northern)** 978.
● **Massachusetts (Greater Boston, outer areas)** 781
● **New Hampshire** 603.
● **Rhode Island** 401.
● **Vermont** 802.

Overseas call codes International calls can be made from any telephone. For the international operator, tel: 1-800/874 4000. Omit the first 0 if applicable from area code:
● **Australia** 01161.
● **Canada** no extra code needed.
● **Ireland** 011353.
● **New Zealand** 01164.
● **United Kingdom** 01144.

Public telephone box in Boston's Chinatown

Emergencies

Crime
The endless production of movie and TV thrillers in the US can give the impression of a country rife with street crime. This is, of course, a far-fetched notion; most of New England is charmingly relaxed. However, it is wise to be on guard in quiet city areas, particularly at night, to lock car doors if you are driving, and to be careful about where you park. Central Boston is generally very safe in daytime. Dorchester in Boston is crime-ridden, but few visitors have reason to go there. There are other notable no-go areas in larger towns such as Hartford and Bridgeport.

If confronted by a mugger, do not resist him. A wise precaution is to carry a $20 bill separately from other valuables, in the hope that this will satisfy the attacker.

Embassies and consulates
Embassies
● **Australia** 1601 Massachusetts Avenue NW, Washington, DC 20036-2273 (tel: 202/797 3000).
● **Canada** 501 Pennsylvania Avenue NW, Washington, DC 20001 (tel: 202/682 1740).
● **Ireland** 2234 Massachusetts Avenue

Boston is a safe city but you should take normal precautions at night

NW, Washington, DC 20008 (tel: 202/462 3939).
● **New Zealand** 37 Observatory Circle NW, Washington, DC 20008 (tel: 202/328 4800).
● **United Kingdom** 3100 Massachusetts Avenue NW, Washington, DC 20008 (tel: 202/462 1340).

Consulates All of these are in Boston:
● **Canada** Copley Place (tel: 617/262 3760).
● **Ireland** 535 Boylston Street (tel: 617/267 9330).
● **United Kingdom** Federal Reserve Plaza, 25th Floor, 600 Atlantic Avenue (tel: 617/248 9555).

Emergency telephone numbers
Police There is no general New England emergency number. For police in Boston and Cambridge, tel: 911). For other assistance call the operator on 0.

Police
Police are armed. If they stop your car, give straight and polite answers and stay seated.

Health and insurance
Basic precautions and remedies
Travellers without health insurance should take out travel insurance (see page 253).

No special vaccinations are required

In rural areas, watch out for poison ivy and ticks

263

to enter the US. Tap water is safe to drink. Pharmacies stock an adequate range to cover minor ailments, although many painkillers that are normally available over the counter will require a prescription in the US.

Natural hazards Deer ticks are tiny insects that can fall on you unawares and burrow into the skin, causing **Lyme Disease**, an unpleasant condition that normally starts with a circular rash. It is followed by flu-like symptoms and lethargy, leading in some instances to numbness, tingling, arthritis, meningitis or heart failure. It is important to get treatment as soon as symptoms occur, as the condition can worsen rapidly. The highest risk areas are Connecticut, Rhode Island and Massachusetts. To reduce the chance of contracting the disease, wear light-coloured clothing (so that the dark ticks can be spotted and brushed off), tuck your trouser legs into your socks when walking in the countryside, get a companion to inspect your back and head, and wear repellents. If bitten by a tick, remove it with tweezers, and seek medical attention if the mouthpart has been lodged in the skin. Blood tests can determine whether you have been exposed to Lyme Disease.

Stream water may carry **giardia**, a bacteria causing serious intestinal problems; only drink stream water if it has been purified (iodine tablets are best), filtered or thoroughly boiled (for at least five minutes). **Poison ivy** can cause a painful rash if the skin rubs against it (see panel, page 200).

Bears frequent the northern woods of New England. Although generally timid, they can turn aggressive if you get between a mother and cub, or if they are otherwise surprised. Loud noises usually frighten them off. See also panel, page 201.

Lost property
If you lose your bags on a flight, make a report before leaving the airport building. Compensation by the airline will not amount to a great deal, so a good travel insurance policy (see page 253) should be taken out. For items lost or stolen during your travels, get a receipt from the police: this is needed for an insurance claim. Lost traveller's cheques will be replaced providing you still have the counterfoils.

Lost credit cards
● **American Express** (tel: 1-800/528 2121).
● **Diners Club/Carte Blanche** (tel: 1-800/234 6377).
l MasterCard/Access (tel: 1-800/826 2181).
● **Visa** (tel: 1-800/336 8472).

Lost traveller's cheques
● **American Express** (tel: 1-800/221 7282).
● **Thomas Cook** (tel: 1-800/223 7373).

Other information

Camping

New England has hundreds of campsites, both privately and state owned. Each state tourist office publishes lists of campsites at state parks, which are public recreation areas usually set up with hiking trails and picnic facilities. Prices are reasonable but grounds in the more frequented areas, such as Acadia National Park, tend to fill up rapidly in summer. See also Natural Hazards on page 263.

Dates

Dates are written with the month first. Hence 6/12/1950 denotes 12 June 1950.

Visitors with disabilities

Car parks all have parking spaces for the disabled; Boston's subway stations have lifts as an alternative to stairs; and public buildings are accessible to wheelchairs. Cars with hand controls can be rented from Avis, Dollar and Hertz. Certain hotel chains such as Holiday Inn have rooms or suites designed for guests with disabilities.

Freewheeling Made Easy: United States Eastern Seaboard has information for wheelchair users and covers hotels, visitor attractions, support services and transport. It is available from FT Publishing, Duck Street Barns, Furneux Pelham, Herts SG9 0LA, UK (tel: 01279/777 966).

Mobility International USA (PO Box 10767, Eugene, Oregon; tel: 541/343 1284; fax: 541/343 6812) promotes opportunities for the disabled in educational exchanges, training and travel. The Society for the Advancement of Travel for the Handicapped (347 Fifth Avenue, Suite 610, New York, NY 10016; tel: 212/447 7284; fax: 212/725 8253) offers advice and assistance on aspects of travel, while the Travel Information Service (MossRehab Hospital, 1200 West Tabor Road, Philadelphia; tel: 215/456 9602) collects and disseminates information about accessibility.

Electricity

The US electricity supply is 110 volts AC. Appliances come fitted with

CONVERSION CHARTS

FROM	TO	MULTIPLY BY
Inches	Centimetres	2.54
Centimetres	Inches	0.3937
Feet	Metres	0.3048
Metres	Feet	3.2810
Yards	Metres	0.9144
Metres	Yards	1.0940
Miles	Kilometres	1.6090
Kilometres	Miles	0.6214
Acres	Hectares	0.4047
Hectares	Acres	2.4710
Gallons	Litres	4.5460
Litres	Gallons	0.2200
Ounces	Grams	28.35
Grams	Ounces	0.0353
Pounds	Grams	453.6
Grams	Pounds	0.0022
Pounds	Kilograms	0.4536
Kilograms	Pounds	2.205
Tons	Tonnes	1.0160
Tonnes	Tons	0.9842

MEN'S SUITS

UK	36	38	40	42	44	46	48
Rest of Europe	46	48	50	52	54	56	58
US	36	38	40	42	44	46	48

DRESS SIZES

UK	8	10	12	14	16	18
France	36	38	40	42	44	46
Italy	38	40	42	44	46	48
Rest of Europe	34	36	38	40	42	44
US	6	8	10	12	14	16

MEN'S SHIRTS

UK	14	14.5	15	15.5	16	16.5	17
Rest of Europe	36	37	38	39/40	41	42	43
US	14	14.5	15	15.5	16	16.5	17

MEN'S SHOES

UK	7	7.5	8.5	9.5	10.5	11
Rest of Europe	41	42	43	44	45	46
US	8	8.5	9.5	10.5	11.5	12

WOMEN'S SHOES

UK	4.5	5	5.5	6	6.5	7
Rest of Europe	38	38	39	39	40	41
US	6	6.5	7	7.5	8	8.5

Acadia National Park in Maine has several campsites – for more information contact the park headquarters in Bar Harbor (see page 113)

two-pin plugs. Visitors with European appliances should bring an adaptor.

Photography
Many museums ban flash photo-graphy; a tripod may be useful. All

types of film are available but it can be hard to find film for colour slides (rather than prints) in smaller places. Film should be kept cool. A skylight filter helps to reduce haze and protect the lens on an SLR camera.

Places of worship
The Boston Yellow Pages lists churches in the Greater Boston area under 'Churches'; these include Baptist, Catholic, Greek Orthodox, Congregational and Evangelical.
● **Jewish Religious Information Services** 177 Tremont Street, Boston (tel: 617/426 2139).
● **The Islamic Center of New England** 470 South Street, Quincy (tel: 617/479 8341).

Smoking
Tobacco is inexpensive, but smoking is discouraged in many public places, such as restaurants and inns. It is banned on public transport.

Toilets
Known as restrooms, bathrooms or comfort stations, toilets can be diffi-cult to find in city centres, as public facilities are scarce. Restaurants and bars may allow only customers to use the facilities. Petrol stations are a good bet. Many restrooms, even men's, have baby-changing facilities.

Many towns and villages have several places of worship
Left: Cohasset in Massachusetts

Tourist Offices

Gathering free information on an area is no problem in New England, where each state issues a free road map, as well as brochures describing its visitor attractions. In addition to the state-run tourist offices, nearly every important town has a chamber of commerce, stocked with tourist information.

Discover New England, Unit C–3A, Heritage Place, 205 Worcester Court, Falmouth, MA 02540 (tel: 508/540 8169; fax: 508/540 8195; e-mail DiscoverNE@aol.com) is the international marketing arm of the six states. It produces a free colour brochure (in UK, tel: 01732 742777) and provides a wide range of information for visitors.

DestINNations (represented in the UK by North America Travel Service, tel: 0113 243 0000; fax: 0113 243 0919) specialises in arranging tour itineraries, with accommodation, round New England.

State tourist offices
• **Greater Boston Convention and Visitors Bureau** 2 Copley Place, Suite 105, Boston, MA 02116-6501 (tel: 617/536 4100, or 1-800/ SEE BOSTON; fax: 617/424 7664; website: www.bostonusa.com).
• **Connecticut Office of Travel and Tourism** 505 Hudson Street, Hartford, CT 06106 (tel: 860/270 8080; fax: 860/270 8077; website: www.state.ct.us/tourism/).
• **Maine Office of Tourism State House**, Station 59, Augusta, ME 04333 (tel: 207/287 5711, or 1-800/533 9595; fax: 207/287 8070; website: www.visitmaine.com).
• **Massachusetts Office of Travel and Tourism** 13th floor, 110 Cambridge Street, Boston, MA 02202 (tel: 617/727 3201, or 1-800 447 MASS; fax: 617/727 6525).
• **New Hampshire Office of Travel and Tourism** 172 Pembroke Road, PO Box 18567, Concord, NH 03301 (tel: 603/271 2666, or 1-800 FUN INNH; website: www.visitnh.gov).
• **Rhode Island Tourism Division** 1 West Exchange Street, Providence, RI 02903 (tel: 401/222 2601, or 1-800 556 2484; fax: 401/222 2102; website: www.visitrhodeisland.com).
• **Vermont Department of Tourism and Marketing** 134 State Street, Monpelier, VT 05602 (tel: 802/828 3237; fax: 802/828 3233).

The Tourist Information Centre in Chatham, MA, is one of several on Cape Cod

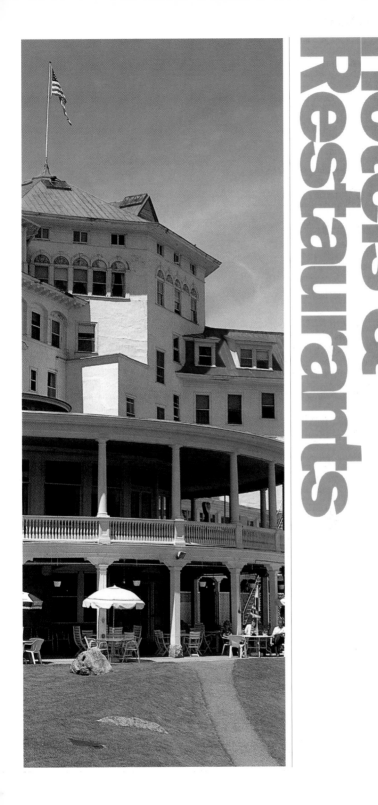

Hotels & Restaurants

ACCOMMODATION

The following recommended hotels and restaurants have been divided into three price categories:
- **budget** (£)
- **moderate** (££)
- **expensive** (£££)

Some establishments straddle two categories. New England inns can range from genuine old-world hostelries filled with antiques and collected bits and pieces to large de luxe modern buildings. Bed and breakfasts (B&Bs) are often up-market; you pay extra for the privilege of staying in someone's home, but breakfast is included. Some hotels and inns include self-catering town houses and cottages. The cheapest accommodation is generally provided by motels, which are usually adequate in facilities but not generally strong on character (although there are some in fine scenic settings). It is often possible to negotiate cheap deals by telephone. Some motels will give you a discount over the phone if it seems that you might go elsewhere, but not if you turn up on the spot. Always check to see if sales and state tax are included. Some make an additional charge for service. Many hotels and inns have packages including Full American Plan (accommodation with breakfast, lunch and dinner) and/or Modified American Plan (accommodation with breakfast and dinner).

Mid-range chain hotels are of a consistent standard and are easy to book. Any of the following should prove to be reliable:
Best Western (tel: 1-800/528 1234: in UK 0800 393130)
Holiday Inns (tel: 1-800/ HOLIDAY; in UK 0800 897121)
Ramada (tel: 1-800/2RAMADA; in UK 0800 181 737)
Westin Hotels (tel: 1-800/228 3000; in UK 0800 282 565)
A good upmarket chain is the Sheraton (tel: 1-800/325 3535; in UK 0800 353535).

Useful state-wide organisations include:
Connecticut
● Lodging reservations can be made in Connecticut by calling 1-800/CT BOUND. Accommodation lists can be obtained from state tourist offices (see page 266).
Massachusetts
● Telephone 0171-978 5233 (in UK) or 1-800/447 MASS (in USA and eastern Canada) for a copy of the *Massachusetts Vacation Guide*.
Rhode Island
● Bed and Breakfast of Rhode Island (Box 3291, Newport, RI 02840; tel: 401/849 1298).
Vermont
● Vermont Department of Tourism and Marketing, distributes *Four Seasons Vacation Rentals*, a guide to the range of cottage rentals in the state; available from 134 State Street, Montpelier, VT 05602 (tel: 802/828 3237).

Useful British organisations include:
● New England Country Homes Ltd, Manor Courtyard, Bignor, Pulborough, West Sussex, RH20 1QD (tel: 01798 869020; fax: 01798 869013), a UK-based firm that arranges packages in self-catering accommodation throughout New England.
● US Welcome Ltd, 33A High Street, Ruislip, Middlesex HA4 7AU (tel: 01895 622233; fax: 01895 622244) has a free advisory and booking service, and describes distinctive and individually owned places to stay in its book *Selected Hotels and Inns*.
● House Exchange is organised by the Vacation Exchange Club, Box 820 Haleiwa, HI 96712 (tel: 1-800/638 3841).

BOSTON AND CAMBRIDGE (MASSACHUSETTS)

Agencies
B&B Agency of Boston (tel: 617/720 3540 or 1-800/248 9262; fax: 617/523 5761; from UK 0800 895128). The biggest B&B apartment agency in the city, with some excellent locations, such as the Waterfront, Beacon Hill, Back Bay and the North End. Also self-catering apartments from studio size upwards.
Host Homes of Boston Box 117, Waban Branch, Boston, MA 02168 (tel: 617/244 5156). B&B, some in the centre and many in the suburbs. Some self-catering, too.
Bed and Breakfast Associates Bay Colony Box 57166, Babson Park Branch, Boston, MA 02157 (tel: 617/449 5302, or 1-800/347 5088). Covers a range of locations and costs.
Bed and Breakfast Cambridge & Greater Boston Box 665, Cambridge, MA 02140 (tel: 617/720 1492, or 1-800/888 0178). Has information on accommodation in private homes, apartments and short-term apartment rentals, with locations in Cambridge, Greater Boston and outlying towns such as Lexington and Concord.

Accommodation
Boston Harbor (£££) 70 Rowes Wharf, Boston, MA 02110 (tel: 617/439 7000, or 1-800/752 7077, fax: 617/330 9450). Fine site beside the harbour and aquarium, with traditional furnishings. Water shuttle to airport.
Boston International AYH Hostel (£) 12 Hemenway Street, Boston, MA 02115 (tel: 617/536 9455). Dormitory accommodation, self-service kitchens, daily activity programmes. Non-members welcome.
Boston Park Plaza (£££) 50 Park Plaza, Arlington Street, Boston, MA 02117 (tel: 617/426 2000; in Massachusetts 1-800/462 2022; continental US 1-800/225 2008; fax: 617/426 5545). Stylish, grand hotel built in 1927; 1,000 rooms; 82 luxurious rooms in the Towers. Adopts an 'Environmental Action Program' (through recycling and other means).
Cambridge House (££) 2218 Massachusetts Avenue, Cambridge, MA 02140 (tel: 617/491

268

6300, or 1-800/232 9989; fax: 617/868 2848). Convenient location; old-world furnishings in 1892 house and carriage house. B&B only. 12 rooms.

Charles (£££) 1 Bennett Street, Boston, MA 02138 (tel: 617/864 1200, or 1-800/882 1818). Modern hotel in Charles Square development.

Copley Square (££–£££) 47 Huntington Avenue, Boston, MA 02116 (tel: 617/536 9000, or 1-800/225 7062; fax: 617/267 0351). Victorian hotel offering acceptable comfort at a reasonable price. Café Budapest for formal dining and an informal bar.

Eliot (£££) 370 Commonwealth Avenue, Boston, MA 02215 (tel: 617/267 1607; fax: 617/536 9114). Renovated with period décor; quieter rooms are at the back.

Fairmont Copley Plaza (£££) 138 St James Avenue, Boston, MA 02116 (tel: 617/267 5300, or 1-800/527 4727; fax: 617/247 6681). Built in 1912, one of the grand old hotels of Boston. Worth visting for the décor alone!

Four Seasons (£££) 200 Boylston Street, Boston, MA 02116 (tel: 617/338 4400, or 1-800/332 3442; fax: 617/423 0154). Looks on to the Public Garden; traditional elegance and comfort.

Inn at Harvard (££) 1201 Massachusetts Avenue, Cambridge, MA 02138 (tel: 617/491 2222, or 1-800/458 5886; fax: 617/492 4896). Near Harvard Square, and although run by Doubletree Hotels, it is owned by Harvard University. Pleasantly appointed with art on loan from the Fogg Museum.

Le Meridien (£££) 250 Franklin Street, Boston, MA 02110 (tel: 617/451 1900, or 1-800/543 4300; fax: 617/423 2844). In the old Federal Reserve Building; 326 rooms; out-standing Julien restaurant.

Lenox (££–£££) 710 Boylston Street, Boston, MA 02116 (tel: 617/536 5300, or 1-800/225 7676; fax: 617/267 1237). Turn-of-the-century building in a good location by Copley Square.

Omni Parker House (£££) 60 School Street, Boston, MA 02108 (tel: 617/227 8600, or 1-800/843 6664; fax: 617/742 5729). Fine 1920s hotel with excellent central location.

Regal Bostonian (£££) Faneuil Hall Marketplace, Boston, MA 02109 (tel: 617/523 3600, or 1-800/343 0922; fax: 617/523 2454). Excellent comfort and service; European-style hotel in building dating from 1824.

Ritz-Carlton (£££) 15 Arlington Street, Boston, MA 02117 (tel: 617/ 536 5700, or 1-800/ 241 3333; fax: 617/536 1335). Considered by many to be Boston's top hotel; overlooks Newbury Street and the Public Garden; traditional décor.

Susse Chalet Inn (£) 211 Concord Turnpike, Boston, MA 02130 (tel: 617/661 7800, or 1-800/258 1980; fax: 617/265 9287). Feasible budget option with access to city centre by Red Line.

CONNECTICUT

Connecticut River Valley

Bishopsgate Inn (££–£££) 7 Norwich Road, Goodspeed Landing, East Haddam, CT 06423 (tel: 860/873 1677). Close to the Goodspeed Opera House. Furnished with antique and reproduction furniture.

Copper Beech Inn (£££) 46 Main Street, Ivoryton, CT 06442 (tel: 860/767 0330). Named after the tree that shades the 19th-century main building. Period furnishings; a variety of rooms, some in the carriage house, some with cathedral ceilings. Excellent dining.

Griswold Inn (££) 36 Main Street, Essex, CT 06246 (tel: 860/767 1776). The earliest three-storey building in Connecticut, its structure largely unaltered over two centuries. Compact rooms, lots of character and antiques.

Inn at Chester (££–£££) Route 148, 318 West Main Street, Chester, CT 06412 (tel: 860/526 9541 or 1-800/949 STAY). 41 rooms, one suite; comfortable country inn with a noted dining room.

Saybrook Point Inn (£££) 2 Bridge Street, Old Saybrook, CT 06475 (tel: 860/395 2000). Furnished with flair, more a hotel than an inn; health club. Highly recommended.

Simsbury Inn (££–£££) 397 Hopemeadow Street, Simsbury, CT 06070 (tel: 860/651 5700, or 1-800/634 2719). Modern 100-room hotel north-west of Hartford. Roomy foyer and French country styled rooms with reproduction furniture; caters to business and leisure travellers. Golf nearby.

Susse Chalet Inn (£) Rocky Hill, CT 06067 (tel: 860/563 7877) (I-91 exit 24.) Good-value motor lodge.

Hartford

Holiday Inn Downtown (£££) 50 Morgan Street, Hartford, CT 06120 (tel: 860/549 2400 or 1-800/HOLIDAY). Convenient and central.

Litchfield Hills

Boulders Inn (£££) 387 Lake Road, New Preston, CT 06777 (tel: 203/868 0541; fax: 860/868 0541). Small inn built in 1895, with superb view of Lake Waramaug. Eclectic décor; games, waterfront, boating.

Cornwall Inn (££) Route 7, Cornwall Bridge, Cornwall, CT 06754 (tel: 860/672 6884). A group of buildings, dating from 1810 and including a motel; restaurant; 17 rooms.

Ragamount Inn (££) 8 Main Street, Salisbury, CT 06068 (tel: 860/435 2372). Welcoming 160-year-old country inn furnished in colonial style; good restaurant. Nine rooms.

Toll Gate Hill Inn (£££) Route 202, Litchfield, CT 06759 (tel: 860/567 4545; fax: 860/567 8397). Out of town on the road to Torrington. Charming colonial building.

Tucker Hill Inn (£–££) 96 Tucker Hill Road, Middlebury, CT 06762 (tel: 203/758-8334). Not a historic Inn, but a 1923 clapboard house with B&B; makes a pleasant and welcoming base, strategically located.

269

Hotels & Restaurants

Mystic

Antiques and Accommodations (££–£££) 32 Main Street, North Stonington, CT 06359 (tel: 860/535 1736, or 1-800/554 7829). Primrose yellow Victorian house with cottage annexe, furnished with an eye for detail and graced with choice antiques, some of which are for sale. Nature tours available.
Inn at Mystic (£££) Junction Routes 1 and 27, Mystic, CT 06355 (tel: 860/536 9604, or 1-800/237 2415; fax: 860/572 1635). Colonial style, 68 rooms, harbour views; hot spa; boating.
Old Mystic Inn (££) 52 Main Street, PO Box 634, Old Mystic, CT 06372-0634. Charming, 1784 house with carriage house annexe and gazebo on the lawn. Eight bedrooms, including family rooms. Quiet location.
Sea Breeze Motel (£) Route 1, Stonington, CT 06378 (tel: 860/535 2843). Modern décor; handy for Mystic's attractions; 25 rooms.

New Haven

Regal Inn (£) 1605 Whalley Avenue, New Haven, 06515 (tel: 203/389 9504). On northern side of town; good value.
Three Chimneys Inn (£££) 1201 Chapel Street, New Haven, CT 06511 (tel: 203/789 1201; fax: 203/776 7363). Victorian mansion with antiques, four-poster beds and tapestries.

New London

Queene Anne Inne (££) 265 Williams Street, New London, CT 06320 (tel: 860/447 2600). Characterful 1903 mansion with antiques and stained-glass windows; 10 rooms.

Norwalk

Silvermine Tavern (££–£££) 194 Perry Avenue, New Haven, CT 06850 (tel: 203/847 4558). From Merritt Parkway, exit 39. Ten rooms, - dating from 1642; lots of character.

MAINE

Acadia and Bar Harbor

Bayview (£££) 111 Eden Street, Bar Harbor, ME 04609 (tel: 207/288 5861 or 1-800/356 3585). Prime position by the ocean, on the edge of town. Three contrasting accommodation categories: three-storey townhouses, modern main hotel and old-world-style inn.
Cleftstone Manor (£££) 92 Eden Street, Bar Harbor, ME 04609 (tel: 207/288 4951, or 1-888/288 4951). Victorian extravaganza, ideal for a romantic retreat.

Bath

Fairhaven Inn (£–££) North Bath Road, North Bath, ME 04530 (tel: 207/443 4391 or 1-888/443 4391). Cedar-shingle house of 1790; handmade quilts and mahogany four-posters in the six rooms.

Baxter State Park

Chesuncook Lake House (££) Route 76, Box 656, Chesuncook Village, Greenville, ME

04441 (tel: 207/745 5330 or 207/695 2821 for Folsom's Air Service). Idyllic hideaway since 1864, accessible only by boat or floatplane and listed as a historic site in the National Register. French-influenced New England cuisine. Boating available.
Pamola Motor Lodge (£) 973 Central Street, Millinocket, ME 04462 (tel: 207/723 9746). Nearest motel to Baxter State Park; restaurant.

Bethel, Rangeley and The Western Lakes

Bethel Inn and Country Club (££–£££), Village Common (Box 49), Bethel, ME 04217 (tel: 207/824 2175, or 1-800/654 0125; fax: 207/824 2233). The main hotel for Bethel, expanded into a sport and health resort with conference facilities; condos available.
Herbert (£–££) PO Box 67, Kingfield, ME 04947 (tel: 207/265 2000, or 1-800/THE HERB). Atmospheric 40-room beaux arts inn of 1918 with many original features. Moose and deer heads adorn the walls of the lobby, where there is a grand piano and open fire. No TVs. Packages available for skiing at nearby Sugarloaf.
Hunter Cove on Rangeley Lake (££–£££) Mingo Loop Road, Rangeley, ME 04970 (tel: 207/864 3383). Lakeside cabins sleeping 4–8, with kitchens, baths and living rooms; sand beach, swimming, boat rental, golf.
Rangeley Inn and Motor Lodge (£) Box 160, Rangeley, ME 04970 (tel: 207/864 3341 or 1-800/MOMENTS; fax: 207/864 3634). Turn-of-the-century inn beneath Saddleback Mountain, close to the lake.
Sunday River Inn (£) RR3, Box 1688, Bethel, Maine 04217 (tel: 207/824 2410; fax: 207/824 3181). Winter-only inn with its own cross-country skiing area, and near Sunday River downhill ski area. Casual, atmosphere rather than luxury; private and family rooms with shared bathrooms, plus dormitories.

Boothbay Harbor

Pines (£) Sunset Road (Box 693), Boothbay Harbor, ME 04538 (tel: 207/633 4555). Quiet motel just out of town.

Eastport

Motel East (£) 23-A Water Street Eastport, ME 04631 (tel: 207/853 4747). Well-equipped rooms with kitchenette areas; views across the bay towards Canada.

Freeport

Freeport Inn (££) 335 US Route 1 South, Freeport, ME 04032 (tel: 207/865 3106, or 1-800-99-VALUE; fax: 207/865 6364). Modern building set back from main road, a short drive from the factory outlet shops at Freeport. Also owns the nearby café where you have breakfast, and the Muddy Rudder restaurant.
Harraseeket Inn (£££) 162 Main Street, Freeport, ME 04032 (tel: 207/865 9377, or 1-800/342 6423; fax: 207/865 1684). A modern re-creation of a traditional inn: Federal-style beds, fireplaces and a formal dining room.

Moosehead Lake
Birches Resort (££) The Birches Road, Rockwood, ME 04478 (tel: 207/534 7305, or 1-800/825 9453). Fifteen cottages, sleeping 2–15; boating.
Chalet Moosehead (£) Birch Street, Greenville Junction, ME 04442 (tel: 207/695 2950). Motel and cottages with private beach on Moosehead Lake.
Rockwood Cottages (£) Box 176, Rockwood, ME 04478 (tel: 207/534 7725). Eight cottages, sleeping 2–7, on Moosehead Lake; craft to rent; one week minimum stay in July and August.

Penobscot Bay
Castine Inn (££–£££) Main Street, Castine, ME 04421 (tel: 207/326 4365; fax: 207/326 4570). Attractive location by the harbour, with good views from the top floor. Paintings and four-poster beds in the 20 bedrooms.
Craignair Inn (£–££) Clark's Island, Sprucehead, ME 04859 (tel: 207/594 7644). A remote backwater ideal for a quiet escape: this cosy inn has creaky floors, antiques and pretty rooms; there is a more modern feel to the Vestry, a former chapel. Fresh fish is served in the dining room.
East Wind Inn and Meeting House (£–££) Box 149, Tenants Harbor, ME 04860 (tel: 207/372 6366). Simple, pleasing rooms.
Keeper's House (£££) Lighthouse Road, Isle au Haut, ME 04645 (tel: 207/ 367 2261). Former lighthouse keeper's house: no road leads to it and no electricity; lit by lanterns and candles.
Norumbega (£££) 61 High Street, Camden, ME 04843 (tel: 207/236 4646; fax: 207/236 0824). Spectacular 1886 castle within sight of Route 1 with lavish interiors and Empire furnishings. Garden and bay views.
Pentagoet (£££) Main Street, Castine, ME 04421 (tel: 207/326 8616 or 1-800/845 1701). Country-style Victorian bedrooms.
Samoset Resort (£££) Rockport, ME 04856 (tel: 207/594 2511; outside Maine, 1-800/341 1650). Large modern luxury hotel and timeshare complex with its own golf course, right by the ocean near Rockland. Formal restaurant and informal bar. Town houses available.
Whitehall Inn (£££) 52 High Street, Camden, ME 04843 (tel: 207/236 3391; fax: 207/236 4427). Former captain's house of 1843 with a later wing. American cuisine is served.

Portland
Pomegranate Inn (£££) 49 Neal Street, Portland, ME 04102 (tel: 207/772 1006 or 1-800/356 0408). Quiet, back-street B&B with tasteful, crisp interior.

York and Kennebunkport
Black Point Inn (£££) 510 Black Point Road, Prout's Neck, Scarborough, ME 04074 (tel: 207/883 4126, or 1-800/258 0003; fax: 207/883 9976). Charming inn sited at the end of a peninsula. Cottages in the grounds will appeal to families.

Captain Jefferds Inn (££–£££) Pearl Street, Box 691, Kennebunkport, ME 04046 (tel: 207/967 2311 or 1-800/839 6844). Clapboard sea-captain's house, built in 1804. Rooms have old dressers and chests; books, painting, ceramics and glass.
Cliff House (£££) Box 2274, Bald Head Cliff, Ogunquit, ME 03907 (tel: 207/361 1000; fax: 207/361 2122; e-mail: Cliffhouse@Maine.com). Modern complex, a low-rise but densely developed site on low cliffs outside the village of Ogunquit. Compact rooms, but the view is superb.

MASSACHUSETTS

The Berkshires
Blantyre (£££) 16 Blantyre Road, Lenox, MA 01240 (tel: 413/ 637 3556; fax: 413/637 4282). A Tudor-style castle in fine grounds, with superb guest rooms. Slightly less grand rooms in the carriage house and cottages.
Orchards (£££) 222 Adams Road, Williamstown, MA 01267 (tel: 413/458 9611 or 1-800/225 1517; fax: 413/458 3273). Supremely luxurious. English antiques adorn the 49 rooms.
Red Lion Inn (££–£££) 30 Main Street, Stockbridge, MA 02162 (tel: 413/298 5545; fax: 413/298 5130). Antique-laden interior befitting this celebrated old inn, sited in a village centre immortalised by artist Norman Rockwell.
River Bend Farm (££) 643 Simonds Road, Williamstown, MA 01267 (tel: 413/458 3121). On the National Register of Historic Places; four-poster beds, washstands and spinning wheels.
Wheatleigh (£££) Hawthorne Road, Lenox, MA 02140 (tel: 413/637 0610; fax: 413/637 4507). Built in 1893 in the style of a Florentine palace; high ceilings and some modern furnishings. Rooms vary in style and size.
Williams Inn (£££) On the Green, Williamstown, MA 01267 (tel: 413/458 9371 or 1-800/828 0133; fax: 413/458 2767). Large, comfortable; in prime position at the top of the village green.
Williamsville Inn (££) Route 41, West Stockbridge, MA 01266 (tel: 413/274 6118). Old inn by itself on a lonely country road; pretty rooms with antiques; storytelling on Sunday nights in winter.

Cape Ann
Inn on Cove Hill (££) 37 Mount Pleasant Street, Rockport, MA 01966 (tel: 978/546 2701). Dating from 1792 and furnished with period pieces.
Old Corner Inn (££) 2 Harbor Street, Manchester, MA 01944 (tel: 978/526 4966 or 1-800/830 4996). Built in 1865; later a Dutch summer embassy.
Sally Webster Inn (££) 34 Mount Pleasant Street, Rockport, MA 01966 (tel: 978/546 9251). Prettily furnished with rocking-chairs and candle lanterns.

271

Cape Cod

Captain Freeman Inn (££–£££) 15 Breakwater Road, Brewster, MA 02631, (tel: 508/896 7481 or 1-800/843 4664; fax: 508/896 5618). Victorian sea-captain's home with pretty rooms, in village centre but a short walk from the beach; pool; B&B only; restaurant located across the road.

Captain's House Inn (£££) 369 Old Harbor Road, Chatham, MA 02633 (tel: 508/945 0127 or 1-800/315 0728; fax: 508/945 0866). Charming inn, with 19 good-sized rooms in four buildings.

Chatham Bars Inn (£££) 297 Shore Road, Chatham, MA 02633 (tel: 508/945 0096, or 1-800/527 4884; fax: 508/945 5491). Ocean views; main building plus cottages comprising 152 rooms.

Dan'l Webster Inn (££) 149 Main Street, Sandwich, MA 02563 (tel: 508/888 3623 or 1-800/444 3566; fax: 508/888 5156). Historic inn in old-world village street, built in 1692 as a parsonage. Good-size, well-appointed rooms and public areas.

Inn at Fernbrook (££) 481 Main Street, Centerville, MA 02632 (tel: 508/775 4334). Fascinating Queen Anne style house with turrets and sloping cathedral ceilings.

Mostly Hall (£££) 27 Main Street, Falmouth, MA 02540 (tel: 508/548 3786). Fine 1849 house with cupola and wrap-around veranda; stylishly furnished and in parkland setting. Bed and breakfast only.

Penny House Inn (££) Box 238, Route 6, North Eastham, MA 02651 (tel: 508/255 6632, or 1-800/554 1751; fax: 508/255 4893; e-mail: pennyhouse@aol. com). Set back from main road; variety of rooms; B&B only.

Marblehead

Harbor Light Inn (£–£££) 58 Washington Street, Marblehead, MA 01945 (tel: 781/631 2186; fax: 781/631 2216). Old-fashioned inn with creature comforts and excellent continental breakfasts.

Martha's Vineyard

Charlotte Inn (£££) 27 South Summer Street, Edgartown, Martha's Vineyard, MA 02539 (tel: 508/627 4751; fax: 508/627 4652). Highly commendable inn comprising five buildings in landscaped grounds.

Daggett House (££–£££) 59 North Water Street, Box 1333, Edgartown, Martha's Vineyard, MA 02539 (tel: 508/627 4600 or 1-800/946 3400; fax: 508/627 4611). A 17th-century tavern with a secret staircase and period interiors. Fine views.

Harbor View Hotel (£££) 131 North Water Street, Edgartown, Martha's Vineyard, MA 02539 (tel: 508/627 7000, or 1-800/225 6005; fax: 508/627 8417). Refurbished Victorian hotel in period style, in quiet neighbourhood. Ocean views.

Oak House (£££) Sea View Avenue, Box 299, Oak Bluffs, Martha's Vineyard, MA 02557 (tel: 508/693 4187 or 1-800/245 5979; fax: 508/696 7293). Victorian house with pretty rooms, near beach; quieter rooms are at the back.

Outermost Inn (£££) Off Lighthouse Road, RR1, Box 171, Gay Head, Martha's Vineyard, MA 02535 (tel: 508/ 645 3511; fax: 508/645 3514). Civilised hideaway, with restrained décor and views of Gay Head lighthouse. Sailboat available for charter.

Nantucket

Hosteling International Nantucket (£) 31 Western Avenue, Nantucket, MA 02554 (tel: 617/731 6692). Cheapest accommodation on the island, reached by a three-mile ride on a cycle path from the town. On Surfside Beach. Closed mid-October to mid-April.

Jared Coffin House (££–£££) 29 Broad Street, Nantucket, MA 02554 (tel: 508/228 2405). Located in the historic heart of Nantucket town: six buildings centred on a brick mansion. Oriental carpets and antiques set the tone; other rooms have reproduction furniture.

Wauwinet Inn (£££) 120 Wauwinet Road, Box 2580, Nantucket, MA 02584 (tel: 508/228 0145, or 1-800/426 8718; fax: 508/325 0657). Out of town, amid fine beaches. Comfortable retreat with 25 well-appointed rooms and five cottages.

White Elephant Inn (£££) 50 Easton Street, Box 1139, Nantucket, MA 02554 (tel: 508/228 2500, or 1-800/475 2637; fax: 508/228 7639). Right on the harbour, with plenty of boats and boating activity. English country style in main inn; luxurious comfort in The Breakers.

Newburyport

Clark Currier Inn (££–£££) 45 Green Street, Newburyport, MA 01950 (tel: 978/465 8363 or 1-800/360 6582). Stylishly restored Federal-period mansion with eight rooms.

Old Sturbridge

Old Sturbridge Village Lodges and Oliver Wight House (££–£££) Route 20 West, Sturbridge, MA 01566 (tel: 508/347 3327 or 1-800/733 1830; fax: 508/347 3018). Owned by Old Sturbridge Museum. The house dates from 1789 and has Federal-style furnishings in the 10 rooms. There are also 47 single-storey village units and two suites.

Pioneer Valley

Deerfield Inn (££) 81 Old Main Street, Deerfield, MA 01342 (tel: 413/774 5587 or 1-800/926 3865; fax: 413/773 8712; e-mail: innkeeper@deerfieldinn.com). In the heart of the historic village; 23 rooms, with antique and reproduction furnishings; country breakfasts and candlelit dinners.

Inn at Northampton (£–££) 1 Atwood Drive, northampton, MA 01060 (tel: 413/586 1211, or 1-800/582 2929; e-mail: INNNOHO@ avanet.com). Good-value modern 124-room hotel with covered and outdoor pools and steak room. On the edge of college town renowned for its cultural events.

272

Lord Jeffery Inn (£££) 30 Boltwood Avenue, Amherst, MA 01002 (tel: 413/253 2576 or 1-800/742 0358; fax: 413/256 6152). A 48-room inn facing the green in the town centre, a minute's walk from the college.

Whately Inn (££) Chestnut Plain Road, Whately Center, MA 01093 (tel: 413/665 3044, or 1-800/942 8359; fax: 413/665 4969). Has four rooms with antiques and four-poster beds.

Plymouth

Blue Spruce Motel (£) 710 State Road, Plymouth, MA 02360 (tel: 508/224 3990 or 1-800/370 7080; fax: 508/224 2279). Modern hotel on Route 3A 6 miles south of town.

Pilgrim Sands Motel (££) 150 Warren Avenue, Plymouth MA 02360 (tel: 508/747 0900 or 1-800/729 7263; fax: 508/746 8066). South of town near Plimoth Plantation; it has a private beach and sea views.

NEW HAMPSHIRE

Cornish

Chase House (££) RR2, Box 909, Route 124, Cornish, NH 03745 (tel: 603/675 5391 or 1-800/401 9455; fax: 603/675 5010). Near Cornish–Windsor covered bridge and Saint-Gaudens National Historic Site. Elegantly restored home of the chief justice of America under President Lincoln. Meadow and river views.

Hanover

Hanover Inn (£££) Main and Wheelock Streets, Hanover, NH 03755 (tel: 603/ 643 4300, or 1-800/ 443 7024; fax: 603/646 3744). Georgian inn, fronting the green at the hub of Dartmouth campus and adjacent to Hopkins Center for the Performing Arts.

Lake Sunapee

Dexter's Inn and Tennis Club (££) Stagecoach Road, Sunapee, NH 03782 (tel: 603/763 5571, or 1-800/232 5571; e-mail: dexters@kear.tds.net). Small, idyllically set inn above Lake Sunapee; tennis facilities.

New London Inn (££) Main Street, New London, NH 03257 (tel: 603/526 2791, or 1-800/526 2791; fax: 603/526 2749; e-mail: nlinn@srn.com). A 1792 inn on the village street.

Lake Winnipesaukee

Manor on Golden Pond (£££) Route 3, Holderness, NH 03245 (tel: 603 968 3348, or 1-800/545 2161; fax: 603/968 2116). English-style manor house by Squam Lake.

Nutmeg Inn (££) 80 Pease Road, Meredith, NH 03253 (tel: 603/279-8811). Made from old ship's timbers, this 18th-century black-shuttered house has rare, wide 'king boards' that were reserved for the Royal Navy. Quiet position between Route 104 and the lake.

Red Hill Inn (££–£££) Route 25B, Box 99M, Center Harbor, NH 03226 (tel: 603/ 279 7001; fax: 603/279 7003). Nicely situated country inn overlooking Squam Lake.

Tamworth Inn (££–£££) 15 Cleveland Hill Road, Tamworth, NH 03886 (tel: 603/323 7721, or 1-800/933 3902; fax: 603/323 2026; e-mail: inn@tamworth.com). Full of personal touches, with each room different.

Wakefield Inn (££) 2723 Wakefield Road, Wakefield, NH 03872 (tel: 603/522 8272 or 1-800/245 0841). Restored house and coaching inn of 1815.

Wolfeboro Inn (££–£££) 90 North Main Street, Wolfeboro, NH 03894 (tel: 603/569 3016, or 1-800/451 2389; fax: 603/569 5375). An expanded inn with 43 rooms by shore of Lake Winnipesaukee; old-world tavern with good-value food and a remarkable beer selection.

Mount Monadnock Region

Amos Parker House (£–££) Route 119, Box 202, Fitzwilliam, NH 03447 (tel: 603/585 6540). Attractive house jnear a village green.

Benjamin Prescott Inn (£) Route 124, East Jaffrey, NH 03452 (tel: 603/532 6637). Small historic inn by itself in rolling countryside; house full of artefacts and knick-knacks. 10 rooms.

Inn at East Hill Farm (££) Mountain Road, Troy, NH 03465 (tel: 603/242 6495, or 1-800/242 6495; fax: 603/242 7709). Year-round farm vacation resort, good for outdoor activities.

Portsmouth and Coast

Exeter Inn (££) 90 Front Street, Exeter, NH 03833 (tel: 603/772 5901, or 1-800/782 8444; fax: 603/778 8757). Georgian-style inn with 50 guest-rooms.

Martin Hill Inn (££) 404 Islington Street, Portsmouth, NH 03801(tel: 603/436 2287). Within a short walk of the historic district; antique furnishings.

Sise Inn (££–£££) 40 Court Street, Portsmouth, NH 03801 (tel and fax: 603/433 1200, or 1-800/267 0525). Former merchant's house of 1881; comfortable, Victorian character.

White Mountains Region

Balsams Grand Resort Hotel (£££) Dixville Notch, NH 03576 (tel: 603/255 3400, or 1-800/255 0600; fax: 603/255 4221; e-mail: TheBalsams@aol.com). The last word in luxury, this hotel ranks among the finest hotels in the state. Resort facilities and fine views.

Bretton Woods Motor Inn (£–££) Route 302, Bretton Woods, NH 03575 (tel: 603/278 1500, or 1-800/258 0330; fax: 603/278 3457). Part of the Mount Washington Hotel chain; excellent location for exploring the Presidential Range (which is short on accommodation).

Christmas Farm Inn (££–£££) Box CC, Route 16B, Jackson, NH 03846 (tel: 603/383 4313 or 1-800/HI-ELVES; fax: 603/383 6495). An 18th-century inn with cottages, dairy barn suites, log cabin and 'salt box' building.

Cranmore Inn (££) Kearsarge Street, North Conway, NH 03860 (tel: 603/ 356 5502, or 1-800/ 526 5502; fax: 603/356 6052). A welcoming guest house.

Darby Field Inn (£££) Bald Hill, Conway, NH 03818 (tel: 603/447 2181 or 1-800/426 4147; fax: 603/ 447 5726). Memorable mountain views from each of the 16 rooms.

Franconia Inn (££–£££) Route 116, Easton Road, Franconia, NH 03580 (tel: 603/823 5542, or 1-800/473 5299; fax: 603/823 8078). Overlooks Mount Lafayette and Franconia Notch; 35 rooms.

Mill House Inn (££) Main Street, PO Box 696, Lincoln, NH 03251 (tel: 603/745 6261, or 1-800/654 6183). Modern complex adjoining shopping and restaurant centre in former paper mill. Close to sports facilities and performing arts centre.

Mountain Club on Loon (££–£££) Loon Mountain, Kancamagus Highway, Lincoln, NH 03251 (tel: 603/745 2244, or 1-800/229 STAY; fax: 603/745 2317). Resort hotel; golf, skiing, fitness centre.

The Mount Washington Hotel and Resort, Bretton Arms Country Inn and Bretton Woods Motor Inn (£–£££) Route 302, Bretton Woods, NH 03575 (tel: 603/278 1500, or 1-800/258 0330; fax: 603/278 8838). A range of styles and prices, at the foot of Mount Washington; owns the railway up the mountain, as well as cross-country and downhill ski areas, tennis courts and a golf course. Mount Washington Hotel itself is an astonishing 1902 survival, a grand hotel, complete with ballroom. Bretton Arms has classic inn rooms and a fine restaurant; the Motor Inn is a good budget family option.

Woodstock Inn (£–££) Main Street, Route 3, North Woodstock, NH 03262 (tel: 603/745 3951; fax: 603/745 3701; e-mail: relax@ WoodstockInnNH.com). Inexpensive but pretty Victorian-style rooms in main inn, with shared bathrooms; private bathrooms in the two nearby houses that serve as annexes, where one bedroom has a ladder up to a tiny room in a turret. Pub with own microbrewery is partly within an old (re-erected) railroad station.

RHODE ISLAND

Block Island
Manisses (£££) Spring Street, Block Island, RI 02807, (tel: 401/466 2063; fax: 401/466 2858). Elegantly furnished Victorian hotel on the National Register of Historic Places.

Surf (£–££) Dodge Street, Block Island, RI 02807 (tel: 401/466 2241). Victorian hotel overlooking the harbour.

1661 Inn and Guesthouse (£££) Spring Street, Block Island, RI 02807 (tel: 401/466 2421; fax: 401/466 2858). Some of the 29 rooms have ocean views; lavish breakfasts.

Newport
Cliffside Inn (££–£££) 2 Seaview Avenue, Newport, RI 02840 (tel: 401/847 1811 or 1-800/845 1811). Grand 1880s house filled with Victorian pieces; close to Cliff Walk.

Francis Malbone House (££–£££) 392 Thames Street, Newport, RI 02840 (tel: 401/846 0392). Harbour views from this grand historic inn. Polished floorboards, reproduction furniture and fireplaces.

Ivy Lodge (££–£££) 12 Clay Street, Newport, RI 02840 (tel: 401/849 6865). Victorian house offering the only B&B accommodation in the mansions district. Good-sized rooms.

Providence
Day's Hotel on the Harbor (££) 220 India Street, Providence, RI 02903 (tel and fax: 401/272 5577). Modern hotel overlooking harbour and I-95.

Old Court (££) 144 Benefit Street, Providence, RI 02903 (tel: 401/751 2002; fax: 401/272 4830). A B&B in the city's prettiest quarter; Victorian décor.

Providence Biltmore (£££) 11 Dorrance Street, Providence, RI 02903 (tel: 401/421 0700, or 1-800/294 7709; fax: 401/455 3050). A 1920s art deco building; good service and handy downtown location.

South County
Richards (£–££) 144 Gibson Avenue, Narragansett, RI 02832 (tel: 401/789 7746). Victorian house with high ceilings and antiques, and set in a quiet street. B&B only, but the breakfasts are inspired.

Shelter Harbor Inn (££–£££) 10 Wagner Road, Westerly, RI 02892 (tel: 401/322 8883). A secluded retreat with creature comforts: a cluster of buildings around a renovated 19th-century country inn.

VERMONT

Bennington
Molly Stark Inn (£–££) 1067 Main Street, VT 05201 (tel: 802/442 9631 or 1-800/356 3076; fax: 802/442 5224). An 1860 inn on road to Brattleboro; quieter rooms are at the rear.

South Shire Inn (£££) 124 Elm Street, Bennington, VT 05201 (tel: 802/447 3839; fax: 802/442 3547). Prettily decorated and furnished; near town centre.

Burlington
Inn at Essex (££–£££) 70 Essex Way, off Route 15, Essex Junction, VT 05452 (tel: 802/878 1100, or 1-800/288 7613; fax: 802/878 0063; e-mail: innessex@ together.net). Modern hotel and conference centre styled on a country inn. The New England Culinary Institute operates the restaurants and room service.

Radisson Hotel (££) 60 Battery Street, Burlington, VT 05401 (tel: 802/658 6500, or 1-800/333 3333; fax: 802/658 4659). Great views of the lake and easy access to the water, parks and downtown area.

Chester
Chester Inn (£££) Box 589, On the Green, Chester, VT 05143 (tel: 802/875 2444 or 1-888/CHESINN). Wonderfully idiosyncratic, all rooms in different styles; local produce; tennis and fishing.

274

Grafton

Old Tavern at Grafton (££–£££) Route 35, Grafton, VT 05146 (tel: 802/843 2231, or 1-800/843 1801; fax: 802/843 2245). Painstakingly restored inn of 1788 with antiques, four-posters and canopied beds in its 14 rooms. Across the street are 21 more rooms.

Killington

Inn at Long Trail (££) Route 4 (Box 267), Killington, VT 05751 (tel: 802/775 7181 or 1-800/325 2540; fax 802/747 7034). Welcoming rustic lodge near Pico ski slopes and Appalachian trail. Dinner served at weekends only.

Manchester

Aspen Motel (£–££) Route 7AN, Box 548, Manchester, VT 05255 (tel: 802/362 2450).Reasonable and comfortable.
Cornucopia of Dorset (£££) Route 30, Dorset, VT 05251 (tel: 802/867 5715 or 1-800/769 4903). Ten rooms, wrap-around veranda; pampers guests.
Equinox (£££) Route 7A, Manchester Village, VT 05254 (tel: 802/362 4700, or 1-800/362 4747; fax: 802/362 4861). Celebrated inn, much expanded; rooms at rear look towards Mount Equinox.
Hill Farm Inn (££) RR2, Box 2015, Arlington, VT 05250 (tel: 802/375 2269, or 1-800/882 2545; fax: 802/375 9918). Long-established inn with unspoilt river setting.
Marble West Inn (£–££) Dorset West Road, Dorset, VT (tel: 802/867 4155). Gracious and personal house with stencilled hallway, open gas fires in the library and breakfast room, and a grand piano in the sitting room. The eight bedrooms enjoy tranquil rural views and have polished wood furniture; there are no TVs.
Reluctant Panther (£££) West Road, Box 678, Manchester Village, VT 05254 (tel: 802/362 2568, or 1-800/822 2331; fax: 802/362 2586; e-mail: panther@sover. com). Spacious and elegantly appointed rooms, most with fireplaces; jacuzzis.
West Mountain Inn (£££) West Mountain Inn Road (Route 313), Arlington, VT 05250 (tel: 802/375 6516; fax: 802/375 6553; e-mail: info@westmountaininn.com). Former farmhouse, in secluded mountainside location. Hiking and ski trails within the grounds; llama ranch.

Marlboro

Whetstone Inn (£–££) South Road, Marlboro, VT 05344 (tel: 802/254 2500). Reasonably priced inn, convenient for the Marlboro - summer music festival.

Middlebury

Middlebury Inn (££–£££) 14 Court House Square, Middlebury, VT 05753-0798 (tel: 802/388 4961, or 1-800/842 4666; fax: 802/388 4563; e-mail: midinnvt@sover. net). Large village inn dating from 1827.

Special programmes include hiking and nature packages.
Swift House Inn (££–£££) 25 Stewart Lane, Middlebury, VT 05753 (tel: 802/388 9925; fax: 802/388 9927). Former home of a Vermont governor comprised of three buildings, the main house dating from 1815.

Montpelier

Inn at Montpelier (££–£££) 147 Main Street, Montpelier, VT 05602 (tel: 802/223 2727; fax: 802/223 0722). Variety of rooms in comfortable inn within walking distance of the town; you can eat out on the porch on fine evenings. Two Greek Revival and colonial-style buildings (early 1800s).

Rutland

Mountain Top Inn (££–£££) 195 Mountain Top Road, Chittenden, VT 05737 (tel: 802/483 2311, or 1-800/445 2100; fax: 802/483 6373). Remotely situated north of Rutland, on a hillside overlooking the Chittenden Reservoir and the Green Mountains; games and sports activities included in room price. Sleigh rides, skating, golf, cross-country skiing trails.

St Johnsbury and The Northeast Kingdom

Inn on the Common (£££) North Main Street, Craftsbury Common, VT 05827 (tel: 802/586 9619, or 1-800/521 2233). Occupies three small buildings in a pretty village; guests eat together; croquet lawn, tennis and swimming pool.

Shelburne

Shelburne House (££–£££) 103 Harbor Road, Shelburne Farms, Shelburne, VT 05482 (tel: 802/985 8498; fax: 802/985 8123). Built by Lake Champlain in 1899 by Lila Vanderbilt Webb and William Seward; Queen Anne Revival style, with original furnishings, similar to the mansions of Newport RI. Romantic setting by lake Champlain.

Stowe

Gables Inn (£–£££) 1457 Mountain Road, Stowe, VT 05672 (tel: 802/253 7730, or 1-800/GABLES-1; e-mail: inngables@aol. com). Former 1850s farmhouse furnished in early American style; more expensive rooms in Carriage House and in the two Riverview Suites. Imaginative, breakfasts.
Grey Fox Inn and Resort (£–££) 990 Mountain Road, Stowe, VT 05672 (tel: 802/253 8921, or 1-800/544 8454). Run by the Diender family from the Netherlands, hence its authentic Dutch Pancake Café. Rooms in the inn have fireplaces, and there is a motel annexe and more luxurious rooms and suites in the Mountain View building. Apartments available.
Inn at the Brass Lantern (££) 717 Maple Street (Route 100), Stowe, VT 05672 (tel: 802/253 2229, or 1-800/729 2980; fax: 802/253 7425). Fine views of Mount Mansfield. Rooms are attractively decorated with quilts and period antiques.

Stoweflake (££) Box 369, Mountain Road, Stowe, Vermont 05672 (tel: 802/253 7355, or 1/800 253 2232; fax: 802/253 4419; e-mail stoweflk@server.net). Larger hotel, family run; fine facilities, including restaurants, pub, conference room, tennis and golf.

Stowehof Inn and Resort (££–£££) Box 1139, 434 Edson Hill Road, Stowe, VT 05672 (tel: 802/253 9722, or 1–800/932 7136; fax: 802/253 7513). Austrian-style chalet completed in 1950 using entire tree trunks and timber from old barns in its construction, and set in tranquil grounds outside Stowe. Folksy, rustic lounge with views of Mount Mansfield; 50 rooms all in different styles. Winter sleigh rides.

Trapp Family Lodge (£££) 42 Trapp Hill Road, Stowe, VT 05672 (tel: 802/253 8511, or 1–800/826 7000; fax: 802/253 5740). Still owned by the von Trapps of *The Sound of Music* fame – the family grave is here too – the Austrian-style lodge is a rebuilding after the original structure was destroyed by fire in 1980. Rooms have floral stencilling and Austrian print fabrics, and enjoy beautiful mountain views; most have balconies. Fresh flowers were important to Maria von Trapp, and the Lodge employs two florists to present spectacular greenery in the public areas.

Ye Olde England Inne (£–££) 433 Mountain Road, Stowe, VT 05672 (tel: 802/253 7558, or 1–800/477 3771 (from UK 0800 962 684). English owners have given the inn a distinctively old English tone, with scones set out for fireside afternoon tea. Modern suites in the Bluff House annexe, in addition to traditional rooms in the inn; two-bedroom cottages available. The Pickwick pub features some 150 ales; across the road, the Partridge Inn is an excellent fish restaurant.

West Dover

Four Seasons Inn (£) West Dover, VT 05356 (tel: 802/464 8303). Pretty Victorian décor with sloping ceilings.

Weston

Darling Family Inn (££) 815 Route 100, Weston VT 05161-5404 (tel: 802/824 3223). Former farmhouse with hand-crafted quilts and American and English antiques; five guest rooms plus two cottages (good for families).

Woodstock and Quechee

Quechee Bed and Breakfast (££–£££) Box 80, Route 4, Quechee, VT 05059 (tel: 802/295 1776). Fine cliff setting overlooking scenic Ottauquechee River, close to village. Spacious rooms.

Woodstock Inn (£££) 14 The Green, Woodstock, VT 05091-1298 (tel: 802/457 1100, or 1–800/448 7900; fax: 802/457 6699). Owned by the Rockefeller family offering good comfort, golf, antique hunting, and biking packages.

276

RESTAURANTS

Quantities are usually generous in New England's restaurants and diners. The obvious attractions are the seafood, often served with drawn (melted) butter. Prices often include a salad with a choice of dressing. For more general information about New England cuisine see pages 20–1.

New Englanders have dinner earlier than Europeans: always check opening times. Reservations are recommended in popular places, especially at the peak of the season. Casual dress is generally acceptable, although some restaurants require a jacket and tie. Many places have a no-smoking policy.

You can also eat very adequately and inexpensively at diners, pizza parlours and other places. There is no problem in asking for a 'doggie bag' at most of these places. Vegetarian food is becoming more widely available, but many establishments have a very limited choice for those who exclude fish as well as meat from their diet. State tax is normally added to the cost of a meal, and tips of 15 per cent are expected.

It is advisable to telephone ahead before arriving as many restaurants close one day or more a week, and it may be necessary to book in advance.

BOSTON AND CAMBRIDGE

Ambrosia on Huntington (££–£££) 116 Huntington Ave., Boston (tel: 617/247-2400). The presentations are breathtakingly handsome, and the fusion cuisine is exquisite at this spacious restaurant. Save room for dessert because they actually taste as good as they look.

Anthony's Pier 4 (££) 140 Northern Avenue, Boston (tel: 617/423 6363). Favourite Waterfront restaurant offering traditional New England fare.

Aujourd'hui (£££) The Four Seasons, 200 Boylston St., Boston (tel: 617/338-4400). Overlooking the Boston Public Garden, this top dining destination provides the perfect setting for the exquisite regional dishes and scrumptious desserts. A wonderful special occasion restaurant.

Barking Crab (££) 88 Sleeper Street at Northern Avenue, Boston (tel: 617/426 2722). Good food, served in this wooden shack by water's edge; eat outside in summer or snuggle beside a wood-burning stove in winter.

Bartley's Burger Cottage (£) 1246 Massachusetts Avenue, Cambridge (tel: 617/354 6559). Daily specials, plus over 40 hamburger varieties.

La Bettola (££–£££) 480 Columbus Ave., Boston (tel: 617/ 236-5252). A rustic trattoria-like atmosphere belies the serious Italian cooking at this restaurant that opened in 1997. Look for the unusual, but delicious, specials.

Biba (££–£££) 272 Boylston St., Boston (tel: 617/426-7878). One of the most celebrated restaurants in Boston, check out the funky art on the walls, the chic clientele, and most importantly, the eclectic American fare that features interesting dishes such as lobster pizza.

Blue Diner (££) 150 Kneeland Street, Boston (tel: 617/338 4639). Celebrated Boston institution near South Station open 24 hours a day, except for the small hours of Monday morning. Hearty meat dishes, barbecue items, and classic diner fare. No reservations.

Boston Sail Loft (£) 80 Atlantic Avenue, Boston (tel: 617/227 7280). The best budget seafood on the Waterfront, as well as a Sunday brunch 12–3pm.

Casablanca (££) 40 Brattle St., Cambridge (tel: 617/876-0999). This landmark bar/restaurant, filled with the ghosts of famous Bostonians, was overhauled in the early 1990s. Since its renovation it has become a dining destination for its innovative Mediterranean cuisine and not just a place to linger over a drink.

Chez Henri (££) 1 Shepherd St., Cambridge (617/354-8980). Classic French bistro fare with a Cuban accent may be an unusual idea but it seems to work at this lively, relaxed spot. The prix fix dinner is also excellent value.

Chilis Grill and Bar (£) 114 Mount Auburn Street, Cambridge (tel: 617/876 8990). The inexpensive Mexican food makes this a popular student haunt. Also in Copley Plaza hotel.

Clio (£££) The Eliot Suites Hotel, 370 Commonwealth Ave., Boston (tel: 617/267-1607). Understated elegance defines this hushed, supper-club style restaurant that opened in 1997. The wonderful food, French with Asian accents, is the star and the staff adds to the experience by being attentive and knowledgeable.

Daily Catch (£–££) 323 Hanover Street, Boston (tel: 617/523 8567); additional branches at 261 Northern Avenue and 215 Elm Street. Informal, cramped North End oyster bar with good seafood at low prices.

Dakota's (££) 34 Summer Street, Lobby Level, Boston (tel: 617/ 737 1777). Seafood specialities; classy and patronised by a well-heeled clientele. Next to Filene's department store.

Durgin Park (£–££) 30 North Market Street, Faneuil Hall Marketplace, Boston (tel: 617/ 227 2038). This crowded historic spot, opened in the 1830s, specialises in generous portions of chowder, baked beans, pot roast, chunky prime ribs and more.

East Coast Grill (££) 1271 Cambridge Street, Cambridge (tel: 617/491 6568). Spicy American and equatorial cuisine; expect to wait at peak times.

Elephant Walk (£–££) 900 Beacon St., Boston (tel: 617/247-1500). The concept behind this restaurant is a menu that includes both Cambodian and French dishes, as was common in the era of Cambodian colonialism. The only caution: it may be hard to decide what to eat in that everything is delicious.

L'Espalier (£££) 30 Gloucester Street, Boston (tel: 617/262 3023). Sublime French and American cuisine and a long and well-chosen wine list make this one of Boston's most celebrated and popular restaurants. Reservations recommended.

Figs (£) 42 Charles St., Boston (tel: 617/742 3447). Choose from a wide array of excellent and creative pastas and pizzas at reasonable prices. Also available are fresh, interesting antipasti and salads.

Galleria Italiana (££)177 Tremont St., Boston (tel: 617/423 2092). Feel transported to Italy at this small, intimate trattoria-style eatery Fans rave about the homemade pastas, seafood, and simple desserts. Also enjoyable is a snack of antipasti at the wine bar located in the front room of the restaurant.

Gardner Museum Café (££) 280 The Fenway, Isabella Stewart Gardner Museum, Boston (tel: 617/566 1088). A popular place to stop for lunch while taking in the sights of the museum.

Grendel's Den (£–££) 89 Winthrop Street, Cambridge (tel: 617/491 1160). Wide-ranging menu, from European to Middle Eastern to Indian in an informal studenty atmosphere.

Hamersley's Bistro (££) 553 Tremont St., Boston (tel: 617/423-2700). The superb country French food is the draw at this spare, yet cozy bistro. The food is hearty and the pleasant staff exudes an inviting warmth.

Henrietta's Table (££) The Charles Hotel, 1 Bennet St., Cambridge (tel: 617/661-5005). Set up like a farmer's market, the entry to this restaurant sets the tone for the fresh, regional American cuisine. Enjoy the fresh baked bread, and the specialty items smoked to order in the open kitchen.

Ho Yuen Ting (£–££) 13a Hudson Street, Boston (tel: 617/426 2316). Well worth venturing into Chinatown to sample the excellent seafood.

Icarus (££–£££) 3 Appleton St., Boston (tel: 617/426-1790). The understated sophistication, the creative American food, the well selected wine list, and the attentive staff keep regulars coming back to this South End favourite.

Il Panino (££) 11 Parmenter Street, Boston (tel: 617/720 1336). Plain setting, but accomplished Italian cooking. Located in the North End its often very busy.

Iruna (££) 56 John F Kennedy Street, Cambridge (tel: 617/868 5633). Spanish food; salads, paella and more.

Jae's Cafe & Grill (£) 520 Columbus Ave., Boston (tel: 617/421-9405). This funky pan-Asian restaurant has a menu that includes Korean, Japanese, and Thai specialties. Expect a wait, as it is often crowded.

Jimmy's Harborside (££– £££) 242 Northern Avenue, Boston (tel: 617/423 1000). A favourite seafood restaurant in the Waterfront district, complete with harbour views; chowder, bouillabaisse, scampi and daily specials. Jacket and tie after 6pm.

Joe's American Bar and Grill (££) 279

Dartmouth Street, Boston (tel: 617/536 4200). Grills and seafood are the popular choices at this trendy hotspot in Back Bay.

Joyce Chen (££) 115 Stuart Street, Boston (tel: 617/720 1331). Mandarin, Shanghai and Szechuan cuisine. Good-value lunch buffets on weekdays. In Back Bay.

Julien (£££) Hotel Meridien, 250 Franklin St., Boston (tel: 617/451-1900). One of the most beautiful restaurants in the city; fans also rave about the exciting and well-prepared French-inspired menu. The perfect place to celebrate a special occasion.

Lala Rokh (££) 97 Mount Vernon St., Boston (tel: 617/720-5511). Excellent Persian food is served, interesting artwork adorns the walls, and candlelight and Persian music complete the experience. The flavourful and interesting food is worth experiencing for those with an adventurous palate.

Legal Sea Foods (££) 35 Columbus Ave, Park Square, in the Boston Park Plaza Hotel, Boston (tel: 617/426 4444). Also at 5 Cambridge Center, Cambridge (tel: 617/ 864 3400), Prudential Center (tel: 617/266 4800) and Copley Plaza (tel: 617/266 7775). Chain offering top-quality seafood: simply presented with very fresh ingredients.

Lucia Ristorante (££–£££) 415 Hanover Street, Boston (tel: 617/523 9148). Top-class North End Italian restaurant with specialities from the Abruzzi region.

Maison Robert (£££) 45 School St., Boston (617/227-3370). Located in the Old City Hall, and opened in 1971, Maison Robert is something of a Boston institution. The classic French cuisine has been somewhat updated in recent years but the whole experience is still timeless and special.

Mistral (££–£££) 223 Columbus Ave., Boston (tel: 617/ 867-9300). A great place to people watch, this hip and friendly spot boasts creative pizzas and an eclectic menu.

Pignoli, 79 Park Plaza, Boston (tel: 617/338-7500). Superb New Italian cuisine in an unusual setting. The atmosphere is casually charged, a favourite in the city.

Rialto (£££) The Charles Hotel, Cambridge (tel: 617/ 661-5050). Awarded four stars by the Boston Globe in 1994, Rialto is a top choice for a special occasion. The food is excellent, drawing inspiration from France, Italy, and the Mediterranean. The dining room is comfortable and sophisticated, the wine list extensive, and the staff knowledgeable.

Salamander Restaurant (££–£££) Carter Ink Bldg., 1 Athenaeum St., Cambridge (tel: 617/225-2121). New American food is presented in a high-styled space with an open kitchen complete with a high-tech barbecue. The portions are as generous as the food is ambitious.

Sonsie (££) 327 Newbury St., Boston (tel: 617/351-2500). Opening on to fashionable Newbury Street, Sonsie has the feel of a chic Parisian café. Diners come as much to be seen as to enjoy the eclectic international menu that features brick-oven pizzas, as well as Asian

and Moroccan accented entrees.

Sultan's Kitchen (£) 72 Broad St., Boston (tel: 617/728-2828). Open only for lunch, this simple restaurant serves fresh and delicious Turkish cuisine at very budget prices. The tara-masalata scores raves as do the pitta sandwiches and shish kebabs.

Tremont 647 (££–£££) 647 Tremont St., Boston (tel: 617/266-4600). Located on the ground floor of a refurbished townhouse, the bustling open kitchen is the focus of this small and stylish American restaurant. The food is American bistro with international accents.

Union Oyster House (££–£££) 41 Union Street, Boston (tel: 617/227 2750). Boston's oldest restaurant; an oyster house since 1826. On the Freedom Trail and near Faneuil Hall. The seafood specialities are best but there is also meat, poultry, salads and sandwiches.

Zinc (£££) 35 Stanhope St., Boston (tel: 617/ 262-2323). A favourite of stylish Bostonians, Zinc has the feel of a French brasserie. Don't miss the selections from the raw bar. There is also an interesting wine list with some hard-to-find French selections.

CONNECTICUT

Connecticut River Valley

Chart House (£–£££) 129 West Main Street at Route 9, Chester (tel: 860/526 9898). Converted Victorian brush factory overlooking a waterfall. You can also sample the well-prepared New England cuisine.

Copper Beech Inn (£££) 46 Main Street, Ivoryton (tel: 860/767 0330). Elegant French cuisine with a menu that changes daily; reservations essential at weekends.

Griswold Inn (££) 36 Main Street, Essex (tel: 860/767 1776). Old-fashioned character, with 1738 bar-room, cosy Gun Room, riverboat-style Steamboat Room, and a dining room constructed from a covered bridge. Traditional New England and classic American dishes.

Inn at Chester (£££) 318 West Main Street, Chester, (tel: 860/526 9541). The Post and Beam dining room at the inn serves renowned New England cuisine.

Greenwich

Baang Café and Bar (££) 191 E. Putnam Ave., Greenwich (tel: 203/637-2114). This exciting restaurant is colorful and fun, creating a scintillating air. The menu—mostly Chinese with other Asian and Western influences thrown in—has deliciously exotic combinations like sizzling whole red snapper in a red chili black bean sweet sauce.

Le Figaro Bistro de Paris (££) 372 Greenwich Ave., Greenwich (tel: 203/622-0018). The dining room is decorated in a lovely belle epoch mode and the food is classic French bistro fare. The combination works very well and is complemented by a well-chosen wine list and a heavenly crème brulée for dessert.

La Grange (££) The Homestead Inn, 420 Field

Point Rd., Greenwich (tel: 203/869-7500). Classic French cuisine is served in an inviting and cozy country inn setting. The dining room has a colonial atmosphere, complete with a big stone fireplace, and the staff is always attentive.

The Ivy (££) 554 Old Post Rd., #3, Greenwich (tel: 203/661-3200). Located in an ivy-covered Victorian house in a residential neighbourhood, the updated Italian fare makes The Ivy worth a visit. The pastas and appetizers offer many unusual combinations.

Pasta Vera (£–££) 48 Greenwich Ave (tel: 203/661 9705). Somewhat cramped and with no frills but exemplary Italian cuisine.

Restaurant Jean-Louis (£££) 61 Lewis St., Greenwich (tel: 203/622-8450). You will be in for a wonderful treat at this tiny nouvelle French restaurant where the service is formal and solicitous and the food is executed in the flawless French tradition. Especially noted are the excellent seafood preparations.

Hartford
Carbone's (£££) 558 Franklin Avenue, Hartford (tel: 860/296 9646). Intimate and romantic; Italian-American food.

Kashmir (£–££) 481 Wethersfield Avenue, Hartford (tel: 860/296 9685). Northern Indian cuisine.

Max Downtown (££–£££) 205 Main Street, Hartford (tel: 860/522 2530). Serves excellent contemporary American cuisine, with an imaginative blend of ingredients.

Litchfield Hills
Boulders Inn (£££) Route 45, New Preston (tel: 860/868 0541). The view of Lake Waramaug is the backdrop for well-presented fare such as filet mignon, duck with raspberry sauce or sea scallops provençal.

Chaiwalla (£) 16 Main Street, Salisbury (tel: 860/435 9758). Tea-shop with a tempting array of cakes, and several varieties of leaf teas are available.

Hopkins Inn (£££) 22 Hopkins Road, New Preston (tel: 860/868 7295). Celebrated restaurant in a Victorian summer house.

Jessie's (£–££) 142 Main Street, Winsted (tel: 860/379 0109). Bastion of Italian cooking, known for their own spicy clam soup.

The Pub (£–££) 1 Station Place, Route 44, Norfolk (tel: 860/542 5716). Atmospheric pub, with pizzas and burgers jostling among more unusual and expensive options.

Toll Gate Hill Inn (£££) Route 202, Litchfield (tel: 860/567 4545). Traditional New England cuisine served in a pleasant and relaxed 18th-century setting.

West Street Grill (££) 43 West Street (Route 202), Litchfield (tel: 860/567 3885). A view of the village green complements the imaginative menu.

Mystic
Randall's Ordinary (£££) Route 2, North Stonington (tel: 860/599 4540). Everything is

colonial: the menu, the building (dating 1685) and even the waiters' attire.

New Haven
Frank Pepe's (£) 157 Wooster Street, New Haven (tel: 203/865 5762). Deservedly popular pizza-only establishment. The famous white clam pizza is not to be missed.

Norwalk
Avery's Little Kitchen (£) 49 South Main Street, South Norwalk (tel: 203/855 8515). Jamaican specialities, including curried goat and coconut pastry.

Silvermine Tavern (££–£££) 194 Perry Avenue, Norwalk (tel: 203/847 4558). From Merritt, Parkway exit 39. A romantic setting for traditional New England fare.

MAINE

Acadia and Bar Harbor
Asticou Inn (£££) Route 3, Northeast Harbor (tel: 207/276 3344). Formal fixed-price dinners in a stately setting; reservation in advance is essential.

George's (££–£££) 7 Stephen's Lane, Bar Harbor (tel: 207/288 4505). Romantic, candlelit restaurant; the dinner-only menu has a distinct Mediterranean flavour.

Bath
Kristina's Restaurant and Bakery (£–££) 160 Centre Street (tel: 207/442 8577). The bakery's pies and cakes are renowned. Also exemplary is the new American cuisine, seafood and grills.

Bethel
Mother's Restaurant (££) Upper Main Street, Bethel (tel: 207/824 2589). Cosy Victorian-style house; eat on the porch in summer for a special treat.

Sudbury Inn (£–££) Lower Main Street, Bethel (tel: 207/824 2174, or 1-800/395 7837). Imaginative menu and excellent cooking; also inexpensive sandwiches and pizza. Accommodation available.

Sunday River Brewing Company (£) Sunday River Road, Bethel (tel: 207/824 3541). Popular hostelry near ski resort serving its own brewed beers and light meals.

Boothbay Harbor
Andrew's Harborside (££) 8 Bridge Street, Boothbay Harbor (tel: 207/633 4074). Typical New England seafood restaurant with a fine harbour view.

Black Orchid (££–£££) 5 By-Way, Boothbay Harbor (tel: 207/633 6659). Fine Italian cooking in a *trattoria*.

Freeport
Harraseeket Inn (£££) 162 Main Street, Freeport (tel: 207/865 9377). Airy and spacious upstairs; hunting-lodge style downstairs. They serve formal dinners and less formal lunches.

 279

Harraseeket Lunch and Lobster Co. (£)
Main Street, South Freeport (tel: 207/ 865
4888). Excellent value, no-frills eatery serving
fried seafood and lobster dinners.

Penobscot Bay
Cappy's Chowderhouse (£–££) 1 Main Street,
Camden (tel: 207/236 2254). Popular seafood
diner with quieter area upstairs overlooking
harbour. The food runs to chowder, seafood,
sandwiches and burgers. There is also a bakery downstairs. No reservations.
Castine Inn (££–£££) Main Street, Castine
(tel: 207/326 4365). New England cuisine.
East Wind Inn (£–££) Tenants Harbor (tel:
207/372 6366). Rustic décor and a menu that
features poultry and seafood.
Fisherman's Friend (£) School Street,
Stonington (tel: 207/367 2442). Seafood,
meat and poultry; and the speciality is fried
fish on Fridays.
Pentagoet (£££) Main Street, Castine (tel:
207/326 8616). Formal dinners available to
the public; booking advised.
Village Restaurant (£–££) 7 Main Street,
Camden (tel: 207/236 3232). The unpretentious fare and surroundings belie the lovely
view overlooking the water.
Waterfront Restaurant (££) Bayview Street,
Camden (tel: 207/236 3747). Serving
excellent seafood; there are also great views,
especially from the outdoor deck.

Portland
Back Bay Grill (£££) 65 Portland Street,
Portland (tel: 207/772 8833). Serves wide-
ranging menu with jazz supplying the
background mood; jacket advised.
Café Always (£–££) 47 Middle Street, Portland
(tel: 207/774 9399). Creative cuisine served
in an art-deco setting.
J's Oyster Bar (£) 5 Portland Pier, Portland (tel:
207/772 4828). No-frills shellfish and beer
haunt, as popular with locals as with visitors.
Street & Co (£–££) 33 Wharf Street, Portland
(tel: 207/ 775 0887). Among Maine's finest
seafood establishments.

York and Kennebunkport
Arrows (£££) Berwick Road, Ogunquit
(tel: 207/361 1100). Subtly flavoured and
well-presented offerings on a seasonally chang-
ing menu.
Cape Arundel Inn (£££) Ocean Avenue,
Kennebunkport (tel: 207/967 2125).
Sophisticated dinner-only menu and a view that
overlooks the shore.
Dockside Guest Quarers and Restaurant (££)
York Harbor off Route 103 (tel: 207/363
2722). On its own island, and unbeatable
place for views and seclusion. Varied menu.
Hurricane (££–£££) Perkins Cove Ogunquit
(tel: 207/646 6348). Good seafood entrées
and desserts.
The Impastable Dream (££) 17 Main Street,
Kennebunk (tel: 207/985 6039). Cheerful, no-
frills pasta place in an old Cape Cod cottage.
No reservations; closed Sundays.

Mabel's Lobster Claw (££) 425 Ocean Avenue,
Kennebunkport (tel: 207/967 2562). This
family-style eatery is a favourite haunt of
George and Barbara Bush.
Warren's Lobster House (££) 11 Water St.,
Kittery (tel: 207/ 439 1630). On the
waterfront, this popular seafood venue also
boasts a large salad bar.

MASSACHUSETTS

The Berkshires
Church St Café (££) 65 Church Street, Lenox
(tel: 413/637 2745). Carefully considered
style: classical music, art, greenery and
varied fare.
20 Railroad Street (£) 20 Railroad Street,
Great Barrington (tel: 413/528 9345). Popular
brisk-service bar/restaurant.
Red Lion Inn (££–£££) 30 Main Street,
Stockbridge (tel: 413/ 298 5545). Oyster pie
and scallops are among the New England
specialities served in this charming old-world
dining room.
Sophia's Restaurant and Pizza (£) Routes
7/20, Lenox (tel: 413/499 1101). Nothing
fancy about this eating place; good, honest
fare, including Greek salads, pasta, pizzas and
grinders (filled rolls).
Williams Inn (£££) On the Green,
Williamstown, (tel: 413/458 9371).
Stylish, formal dining-room in one of the area's
finest hotels.

Cape Ann
Brackett's Ocean View (££) Main Street,
Rockport (tel: 978/546 2797). On the harbour.

Cape Cod
Captain Linnell House (££–£££) 137 Skaket
Beach Road, Orleans (tel: 508/255 3400). A
classical Revival house with stylish interior and
accomplished cooking.
Chillingsworth (£££) 2449 Main Street, Route
6A, Brewster (tel: 508/896 3640). This is the
finest French and nouvelle cuisine served on
the Cape, priced accordingly.
Ciro and Sal's (££–£££) 4 Kiley Court,
Provincetown (tel: 508/487 0049). Authentic
Italian restaurant. Highly recommended, it is a
favourite of the locals.
Coonamessett Inn (££–£££) 311 Gifford St.,
Falmouth (tel: 508/548 2300). Old-world
inn with regional fare. Accommodation also
available.
Dan'l Webster Inn (£–££) 149 Main Street,
Sandwich (tel: 508/888 3623). Lighter
luncheons include inexpensive sandwiches,
salads, soups; Sunday brunches, seafood and
meats for more expensive meals.
The Flume (££) Lake Avenue, off Route 130,
Mashpee (tel: 508/477 1456). Run by a Wampanoag chief who serves unpretentious
seafood, including superb chowder.
High Brewster (£££) 964 Satucket Road,
Brewster (tel: 508/896 3636). Charming
former farmhouse with exposed beams

and panelling making a memorable setting for fixed four-course menus.
Land Ho! (£) Route 6A and Cove Rd, Orleans (tel: 508/255 5165). Informal eating-place offering grilled fish, chowder, sandwiches and burgers.
The Paddock (££–£££) West End Rotary (next to Melody Tent), Hyannis (tel: 508/775 7677). Formal sophistication sets off the Continental-American cuisine.
Stir Crazy (£–££) 626 MacArthur Boulevard, Pocasset (tel: 508/564 6464). Cambodian restaurateur offers Southeast Asian dishes with a spicy character, featuring coconut milk, beansprouts, peanut sauce and lots of chilli. Closed Mondays; no Sunday lunch.
Up the Creek (££) 36 Old Colony Road, Hyannis (tel: 508/771 7866). Informal, friendly and lively.

Fall River
T.A. Restaurant (££) 408 South Main Street, Fall River (tel: 508/673 5890). Portuguese-American fare.

Martha's Vineyard
Andrea's (£££) Upper Main Street, Edgartown, Martha's Vineyard (tel: 508/627 5850). Continental and north Italian cuisine served in a range of dining rooms, plus lighter meals served in the bistro, which hosts live music.
Home Port (££) North Road, Menemsha, Martha's Vineyard (tel: 508/645 2679). Unpretentious and wholesome fare such as seafood and home-baked bread. Dinner only.
Lambert's Cove Country Inn (£££) Off Lambert's Cove Road, West Tisbury, Martha's Vineyard (tel: 508/693 2298). Good for a romantic dinner. Accommodation available.
L'Etoile (£££) 27 South Summer Street, Edgartown, Martha's Vineyard (tel: 508/627 5187). French and New England specialities in an elegant setting.
Oyster Bar (£££) 162 Circuit Avenue, Oak Bluffs, Martha's Vineyard (tel: 508/693 3300). American bistro in an art deco setting. They are especially noted for fish, but pasta, pizza and specials are also featured. Open for dinner only.
Zapotec (££) 10 Kennebec Avenue, Oak Bluffs, Martha's Vineyard (tel: 508/693 6800). Innovative Mexican cooking.

Nantucket
Brotherhood of Thieves (£) 23 Broad Street, Nantucket (no reservations). Like an old English pub with long tables, beamed ceiling and fireplace and live entertainment. Typical fare is sandwiches, chowder, fish, seafood and burgers.
Company of the Cauldron (£££) 7 India Street, Nantucket (tel: 508/228 4016). Whitewashed interior, occasional harp playing and a fixed-price menu. Two seatings for dinner only.
Espresso Café (£) 40 Main Street, Nantucket (tel: 508/ 228 6930). Serves good value lunches and light snacks.

Jared Coffin House (£££) 26 Broad Street, Nantucket (tel: 508/228 2400). Formal dining: federal-period furnishings; American cuisine.
Topper's (£££) Wauwinet Road, Nantucket (tel: 508/ 228 8768). Elegant dining; new American cuisine.

New Bedford
Freestones (££) 41 William Street, New Bedford (tel: 508/993 7477). Interesting place to eat in the historic area. A former bank with mahogany panels and marble floors. The menu features light meals as well as more ambitious entrées.

Newburyport
Ciro's (£–££) 1 Market Square, Newburyport (tel: 978/463 3335). Situated beside the park and river. Serves excellent Italian food, with generous salads and tempting desserts; good value.
Scandia (£££) 25 State Street, Newburyport (tel: 978/462 6271). Seafood and meats, well presented in a lovely candlelit dining room.

Pioneer Valley
Deerfield Inn (£££) 81 Old Main St, Deerfield (tel: 413/774 5587). The dining room is full of antiques and, suitably for this historic village, the menu often features recipes from the Historic Deerfield museum's cookery books.
Lord Jeffery Inn (£££) 30 Boltwood Avenue, Amherst (tel: 413/253 2576). The menu features poultry, fish and game and the atmosphere is one of casual sophistication.
Whately Inn (££) 193 Chestnut Plain Road, **Whately Center** (tel: 413/665 3044, or 1-800/942 8359). The large dining room hosts dinners and Sunday lunches; book early to avoid disappointment.

Plymouth
Inn for All Seasons (££–£££) 97 Warren Avenue, Plymouth (tel: 508/746 8823). Former summer mansion, now with three small dining rooms, that features seafood specialities. Closed Monday.
Lobster Hut (£) Town Wharf, Plymouth (tel: 508/746 2270). Excellent value seafood, best eaten outside on the deck overlooking the harbour.

Salem
Chase House (££) Pickering Wharf, Salem (tel: 978/744 0000). Restaurant with lots of character like the low ceilings and exposed brick walls. Grills and seafood are the favoured meals.
Ravi's Fine Indian Cuisine (£) 6 Hawthorne Boulevard (Route 1A), Salem (tel: 978/744 6570). Serves meat, fish, and vegetarian food.

NEW HAMPSHIRE

Canterbury
Creamery Restaurant (££–£££) Canterbury Shaker Village (tel: 603/783 9511).

Hotels & Restaurants

Shaker-inspired cuisine with four-course dinners on Fridays and Saturdays, Sunday brunches and lunches.

Concord
Hermanos Cocina Mexicana (£–££) 8 Hills Ave, Concord (tel: 603/224 5669). Ably concocted Mexican dishes; leave room for the desserts.

Hanover
Hanover Inn (£££) Main and East Wheelock streets, Hanover (tel: 603/643 4300, or 1-800/443 7024). The Daniel Webster Room is one of the top restaurants in the state; if you want a lighter meal, these are available in the Ivy Grill.

Lake Winnipesaukee
Corner House Inn £–££) Route 113, Center Sandwich (tel: 603/284 6219). Cosy, old-fashioned inn with traditional dishes such as crab cakes and veal Oscar.
Hickory Stick Farm (£–££) 60 Bean Hill Road, Belmont (tel: 603/524 3333). Dinner only, the menu has duck specialities; red meat, vegetarian cuisine and seafood too.
Le Chalet Rouge (££–£££) 385 West Main Street, Tilton (tel: 603/286 4035). Good French cooking.
Tamworth Inn (££–£££) 15 Cleveland Hill Rd, Tamworth (tel: 603/323 7721, or 1-800/933 3902). New American cuisine.
Wolfeboro Inn: Tavern (£) 44 North Main Street, Wolfeboro (tel: 603/569 3016, or 1-800/451 2389). Old-world tavern room, no frills but lots of history and often crowded. Serves good-value food and a variety of worldwide beers.

Mount Monadnock Region
The Boilerhouse at Noone Falls (££–£££) Route 202, Peterborough (tel: 603/924 9486). Set by illuminated waterfalls, the ambitious menu and the well-chosen wine list make this a great choice for a special occasion.
Latacarta (£–££) 101 Noone Falls, Peterborough (tel: 603/924 9486). Nutritious and tasty eating is the essence of this New Age establishment, which is housed in a former cinema. Menu changes daily; closed Monday.

Portsmouth
B.G.'s Boathouse Restaurant (£–££) 191 Wentworth Rd (tel: 603/431 1074). Popular seafood venue, accessible by boat. No reservations.
The Brewery (£–££) 56 Market Street (tel: 603/431 1115). Ales brewed on the premises and an appetising range of food including stir-fries and spicy shrimp. Live entertainment Wednesday to Saturday.
Molly Malone's (£) 177 State Street, Portsmouth (tel: 603/433 7233) Steaks, seafood and more are served in generous helpings.

White Mountains
The Balsams Grand Resort Hotel (£££) Route 26, Dixville Notch (tel: 603/255 3400, or 1-800/255 0600). One of the finest restaurants in the state; jacket and tie.
Christmas Farm Inn (£££) Route 16B, Jackson Village (tel: 603/383 4313). The mixed menu includes 'heart healthy' dishes as well as other specialities.
The Darby Field Inn (£££) Bald Hill, Conway (tel: 603/447 2181). Commendable specials as well as regular items in a pine-panelled dining room.
Margaritaville (£) Route 302, Glen (tel: 603/383 6556). Family-run establishment which offers genuine Mexican food.
Polly's Pancake Parlour (£) Hildex Farm (I-93, exit 38), Route 117, Sugar Hill (tel: 603/ 823 5575). Home-made pancakes, waffles, French toast and quiches all made using home-ground flour.
Scottish Lion (££) Route 16, North Conway (tel: 603/356 6381). Fine views of the mountains from the dining room make this a popular spot for Sunday brunch and American-Scottish evening fare. There is also a fine selection of Scotch whiskies.
Snowvillage Inn (££–£££) Snowville (tel: 603/447 2818). A distinctive Austrian flavour to the cooking. Accommodation available.
The Timber Mill (£) Millfront Marketplace, Main Street, Lincoln (tel: 603/745 3603). On former sawmill property. Reasonably priced Mexican, American and European cuisine.

RHODE ISLAND

Block Island
Finn's Seafood Bar (££) Water Street, Block Island (tel: 401/466 5391). Eat inside or outside.
Manisses (£££) Spring Street, Block Island (tel: 401/466 2063). Elegant surroundings for dinner.

Bristol
Lobster Pot (££) 119 Hope Street, Bristol (tel: 401/ 253 9100). Noted seafood haunt on the waterfront.

Newport
Brick Alley Pub (£–££) 140 Thames Street, Newport (tel: 401/849 6334). Cheerful, low-ceilinged restaurant that serves American cuisine and pasta. An added bonus is that it is open late.
Christie's (££) Off 351 Thames Street, Newport (tel: 401/847 5400). Prime position with a terrace right on the harbour; an apt setting for sampling seafood and Rhode Island wines.
Gary's Handy Lunch (£) 462 Thames Street, Newport (tel: 401/847 9480). Good stop-off for a sandwich and coffee (closed evenings).
Salas' (££) 354 Thames Street (tel: 401/846 8772). Bustling, and popular with families tucking into corn-on-the-cob, lobster and clams. No reservations.

Star Clipper Dinner Train (£££) 102 Connell Highway, Newport (tel: 401/849 7550, or 1-800/462 7452). Three-hour rail trip along Narragansett Bay with four-course meals and a murder mystery themed dinner on Fridays.

Wave Café (££) 580 Thames Street, Newport (tel: 401/846 6060). Not roomy, but serving good Italian food.

White Horse Tavern (£–££) Marlborough Street, Newport (tel: 401/849 3600). America's oldest tavern (1673), complete with age-darkened beamed ceilings, white-washed walls and small rooms. Champagne Sunday brunches, lunches, dinners.

Providence

Al Forno (£££) 577 South Main Street, Providence (tel: 401/273 9760). Leading Continental/Italian restaurant. Reservations not taken.

Casa Christine (££) 145 Spruce Street (tel: 401/453 6255). Expertly created Italian pastas and entrées in this family-run eatery on Federal Hill.

Cecilia's West African Restaurant (£) 486 Friendship Street, Providence (tel: 401/621 8031). Worth seeking out for Liberian food, and reggae on the weekends.

Hemenway's (£££) 1 Old Stone Square, Providence (tel: 401/351 8570). Top-notch seafood venue with a lively atmosphere. Reserve a table in advance

Ocean Express (£–££) 1-800/Allens Avenue, Providence (tel: 401/461 3434). Fresh seafood; ideal for family dining.

South County

Champlin's Seafood (££) Port of Galilee, Narragansett (tel: 401/783 3152). Scallops are the speciality here; also oysters and lobsters. Sit outside on warm days.

Shelter Harbor Inn (££–£££) Route 1, Westerly (tel: 401/322 8883). Changing menu and a wine list as long as your arm.

South Shore Grille (£££) 210 Salt Pond Road, Wakefield (tel: 401/782 4780). Fine waterfront restaurant with a regularly changing menu.

Tiverton

Evelyn's Nannaquaket Drive-In (££) 2335 Main Road, Tiverton (tel: 401/624 3100). Just outside Fall River; diners can eat generous portions of fried seafood, looking on to Nannaquaket Pond.

VERMONT

Bennington

Alldays and Onions (££) 519 Main Street, Bennington (tel: 802/447 0043). This well-stocked deli, which opens as a restaurant in the evening, will surprise you with its innovative menu.

Blue Benn Diner (£) Route 7, Bennington (tel: 802/442 8977). Typical diner with

excellent breakfasts served all day, plus tortillas and burritos.

Bristol

Mary's (££) 11 Main Street, Bristol (tel: 802/ 453 2432). Hung with Vermont paintings and an unpretentious atmosphere. Beautifully cooked food such as lamb and eggplant curry.

Grafton

The Old Tavern at Grafton (£££) Route 35, Grafton (tel: 802/843 2231). Two dining rooms, one with Georgian furniture, the other with a low ceiling, panelling and exposed beams. Sample New England specialities and local cheeses.

Manchester

Arlington Inn (£££) Route 7A, Arlington, (tel: 802/375 6532, or 1-800/443 9442). The dining room draws admirers from afar for its American cuisine. Accommodation available.

Garlic John's (£–££) Route 11 and Route 30, Manchester (tel: 802/362 9843). Italian trattoria open for dinner only.

Quality Restaurant (£–££) 735 Main Street, Manchester (tel: 802/362 9839). Unpretentious, situated right in the heart of town.

Middlebury

Middlebury Inn (££–£££) 14 Court House Square, Middlebury (tel: 802/388 4961). Village inn dating from 1827.

Newfane

The Four Columns (£££) West Street, Newfane (tel: 802/365 7713). An elegant setting for modern American cuisine.

Proctor

Vermont Marble Inn (££–£££) 12 West Park Place, Fair Haven (tel: 802/265 8383). An intimate dining room offering eclectic fare. Accommodation available.

Stowe

Villa Tragara (££–£££) Route 100 south of Stowe (tel: 802/244 5288). A former farmhouse graced with an intimate atmosphere for commendable fixed-price five-course dinners.

Woodstock and Quechee

Bentleys (££) 3 Elm Street, Woodstock (tel: 802/457 3232). Graced with Victorian décor; the menu ranges from the standard to the ambitious; the desserts are especially recommended.

Firestone's (£–££) Waterman Place, Route 4, Quechee (tel: 802/295 1600). Serving interesting Mediterranean-inspired fare in an upbeat setting.

Prince and the Pauper (£££) 24 Elm Street, Woodstock (tel: 802/457 1818). Nouvelle French, served in a colonial building.

Index

A

Index

285

Index